PENGUIN BOOKS

DYNASTIES

David S. Landes is Professor Emeritus of History and Economics at Harvard University. He is the author of the bestselling *The Wealth and Poverty of Nations*, which was shortlisted for the Samuel Johnson Prize.

Dynasties

FORTUNE AND MISFORTUNE
IN THE
WORLD'S GREAT FAMILY BUSINESSES

DAVID S. LANDES

PENGUIN BOOKS

PENGUIN BOOKS

Published by the Penguin Group
Penguin Books Ltd, 80 Strand, London WC2R ORL, England
Penguin Group (USA) Inc., 375 Hudson Street, New York, New York 10014, USA
Penguin Group (Canada), 90 Eglinton Avenue East, Suite 700, Toronto, Ontario, Canada M4P 2Y3
(a division of Pearson Penguin Canada Inc.)
Penguin Ireland, 25 St Stephen's Green, Dublin 2, Ireland (a division of Penguin Books Ltd)
Penguin Group (Australia), 250 Camberwell Road, Camberwell, Victoria 3124, Australia
(a division of Pearson Australia Group Pty Ltd)
Penguin Books India Pvt Ltd, 11 Community Centre, Panchsheel Park, New Delhi – 110 017, India
Penguin Group (NZ), 67 Apollo Drive, Rosedale, North Shore 0632, New Zealand
(a division of Pearson New Zealand Ltd)
Penguin Books (South Africa) (Pty) Ltd, 24 Sturdee Avenue, Rosebank, Johannesburg 2196, South Africa

Penguin Books Ltd, Registered Offices: 80 Strand, London WC2R ORL, England

www.penguin.com

First published in the United States of America by Viking Penguin,
a member of Penguin Group (USA) Inc. 2006
First published in Great Britain by Viking 2007
Published in Penguin Books 2008

1

Illustration credits: pp. 13, 37 Hulton Getty Archive/Getty Images; p. 75 Mansell/Time & Life Pictures/
Getty Images; pp. 117, 168 Keystone Features/Hulton Archive/Getty Images; p. 153 Francis Apesteguy/
Time & Life Pictures/Getty Images; p. 194 Kazuhiro Nogi/AFP/Getty Images; p. 217 General Photographic
Agency/Hulton Archive/Getty Images; p. 246 Time & Life Pictures/Getty Images; p. 261 Shel Hershorn/
Time & Life Pictures/Getty Images; p. 274 François de Wendel

Printed in England by Clays Ltd, St Ives plc

ISBN: 978-0-140-28188-0

To Sonia and the whole family

Contents

PART THREE

TREASURES OF THE EARTH

PREFACE AND ACKNOWLEDGMENTS

*T*his is a book about family and business, success and disappointment, love and discord. At its heart is the dynasty, the succession and interaction of family members over generations; and the firm, the business unit that embodies and expresses this interaction.

Why "dynasty"? Say the word, and many images come to mind, exotic and dramatic, from the silken lineages of Chinese emperors to the soap-opera oil magnates of the 1980s television series of the same name. My interest in dynasties began with economic history— the review and analysis of economic trends and the deeds and achievements of economic actors. As a historian, I was quickly drawn into the drama of these stories and the larger-than-life quality of many of these competitors for wealth. These tales trace the tangled histories of legendary lineages such as the Fords, the Rockefellers, and the Guggenheims. But one need not be a Rothschild or a Toyoda[1] to have use for the lessons in this book; our own families play central roles in most of our lives, and the successes, failures, and cautionary notes of these narratives can inform and inspire us all. We can learn a great deal about business from these dynasties; moreover, these are extraordinary men and women, full of eccentricities and genius, and they provide a wealth of entertaining tales.

Consider, by way of example, the legendary patriarch, the bold enterpriser who sets out to do well for himself and ends up founding an empire. Nathan Mayer Rothschild fits the bill. A child of the mid-eighteenth century, he was the third son of a German Jewish trader in "miscellany"—that is, whatever people were ready to sell or buy. He was not a handsome or imposing man. But this counted little next to a super-keen mind, a sharp tongue, and a sense of dignity and authority that some families need many generations to acquire. When a haughty English merchant threatened not to sell to him simply because the merchant disliked Rothschild's attitude, Nathan responded that there were plenty of Englishmen he could buy from, and decided to leave for England the next day. Once there, he quickly moved from merchandise into banking, and outdid the best of his competitors. The Brits were not always ready or able to understand the force of this outsider, who ignored or repudiated the rules of proper behavior. One day a powerful, wealthy English dignitary pushed his way into Nathan's office and interrupted the busy banker at his task. Nathan summarily told him to take a chair; he'd be with him in a minute. The man was offended: "Do you know who I am?" he said, pointing to the royal crest on the lining of his top hat. Nathan's reply: "Take two chairs." And back to work he went. Another time, some nosy type asked him how he had made his fortune. Answer: "Minding my own business." It is from such brash, keen, dedicated material that great dynasties are founded.

Tales of money, power, and kinship inevitably entail drama and passion, especially with the passage of generations: as wealth grows, so do the opportunities for disagreement. Consider here the Gucci clan. The patriarch, Guccio Gucci (1881–1953), was the son of an Italian leather craftsman. As a young man, he traveled to Paris and then London, where he kept his eyes open and caught on to the commercial advantages of fine workmanship and fashionable elegance. In particular, he noted the customers' hunger for the kind of luggage that announced its owner's taste and status. So when he went back home in 1920, he borrowed money and opened a shop to sell such leather goods, meeting with tremendous success. In subsequent decades, his sons continued his work, opening branches in Italy and then abroad.

Guccio held the enterprise together, but after his death, his children and grandchildren engaged in protracted and costly disputes that made the fortunes of some of Italy's busiest lawyers. The virulence and vindictiveness that characterized these quarrels are an embarrassment to the Gucci family and to Italian culture. Acrimony peaked when the divorced wife of Guccio's grandchild Maurizio got angry enough to contemplate murder. She mentioned offhandedly to her housekeeper that she would love to be rid of her ex-husband. To the right person, that kind of careless remark was a business opportunity waiting for action—and the housekeeper was the right person. Soon thereafter, some hit men gunned Maurizio down on the steps of his office and then tried to blackmail his former wife. So much for the Maurizio branch of the family. The Gucci firm and name ended up in alien corporate hands, and the wife ended up behind bars, on the bad end of a twenty-six-year sentence.

THESE ARE JUST BRIEF EXAMPLES from an enormous body of case studies of family business achievement, from mom-and-pop shops and local gas stations to monuments of market renown. As compelling and informative as such studies are, today's prevalent economic thinking has chosen to ignore the family firm as a subject of serious study and has all but written it off as obsolete and inconsequential. I believe that this view is both wrong and dangerously misleading.

Wrong because statistics show us that the great majority of the world's enterprises today are family firms. In the European Union, family firms make up 60–90 percent of businesses, depending on the country, and they account for two thirds of GNP and jobs.[2] In the United States in the mid-1990s, more than 90 percent of firms were family units, accounting for more than half the country's goods and services; further, one third of the Fortune 500 (the country's five hundred largest firms) were said to be family controlled or to have founding families involved in management. What's more, these family firms tended to be the best performers, far outpacing on average their managerial (non-family) competitors.[3]

Dangerously misleading, because the nations of the developing world, particularly those most desperate for economic development, urgently need family enterprise. Their cultural, political, and economic circumstances are not mature enough for managerial business structures. In these places—Africa, the Arab Middle East, much of South Asia, much of South America—family firms are the best hope for successful development. Businesses in these regions need the trust and training that family makes possible, and the resources that family can mobilize. Failure to understand the nature and dynamics of family-based private capitalism would severely handicap economists and policy makers alike.

Still, the current economic orthodoxy sees family enterprise as inappropriate, ineffective, and essentially finished as a major economic engine, favoring instead corporate or joint-stock managerial models. Alfred D. Chandler, Jr., who stresses several factors in today's business world that argue for managerial structures, has best expounded these views. First, he says, as companies grow, the increases in both production and distribution create problems that can be solved only by employees with functional specialization. The knowledge and skills required, he argues, go far beyond what any given family, however prolific, can muster. This compels firms to seek out appropriately trained outside personnel. (As we shall see in the pages that follow, even families with exceptional gene pools and numerous progeny have trouble keeping up with the demands of diversification, particularly in technology-intensive industries such as automobile manufacturing.) Second, over time, even family members who remain interested in the business generally prefer to leave the less exciting jobs to salaried execs and managers.

The world changes with the increase of knowledge. New discoveries prompt new ways of doing business that call for new personnel. The evolution of the chemical industry during the last two centuries offers a particularly good case study in the managerial revolution. The early examples of the chemical industry were found in the manufacture of acids and alkalis for use in textile and metals manufacture. Factories were located near the raw materials or near the users, and family-based firms held up well to competition. But research in the manufacture of synthetics, which were often superior to natural substances, opened the way to a whole range of new activities and technologies—dyes, drugs, and photographic aids (photography itself being a new technology), to begin with, then nitrogen, rubber, fuels, fibers, and light metals. These were to some extent outgrowths of science courses in institutions of higher education, which acted as magnets to candidates for careers in these new fields.

The new chemical firms thrived, especially in those societies where good instruction was available, such as Germany and France. Mostly the firms began as family enterprises, but the complexity and cost of the work called for heavy investment and early on led to mergers that took the form of joint-stock, limited-liability managerial corporations. The German company IG Farben ("Colors, Inc.") is an excellent example of this kind of enterprise, having been built on trained personnel, research laboratories, and a progression of patents for ever-newer products.[4] When shareholders complained of stingy dividends, Carl Bosch, first chairman of IG Farben, reminded them of higher duties: "IG is not here to give big profits to its stockholders. Our pride and our duty is to work for those who come after us, to establish the processes on which they will work."[5]

Then, as the technology shifted, an industry that was once well suited to family enterprise became the perfect candidate for managerial capitalism. From there, it was a small step to join together family firms to form the conglomerates and trusts of turn-of-the-century America, which provided a big boost for the economy. The old style of growth called for building companies, at which the family firm excels. The new style called for buying and combining companies. Robert Sobel tells by way of illustration the story of a party of well-lubricated business types celebrating their mergers and acquisitions. One of them recalls that there is a steel mill nearby:

"Let's buy it!"

"But it's midnight."

"So what?"

They get the owner out of bed, and he responds, "My plant is worth two hundred thousand dollars, and it's not for sale."

"Really? We'll give you five."

How could the owner say no?[6]

Or take the recent Hollywood version, as shown by this exchange between Julia Roberts and Richard Gere in *Pretty Woman* (1990):

"What do you do for a living?"

"I buy companies."

"And what do you do with the companies?"

"I sell them, and if they don't sell, I break them up into little pieces and sell the pieces."

For the purposes of this study, I shall define a dynasty as three successive generations of family control. No small achievement. Growth, diversification, and technological advance can all work against the continuity of the family firm. To these factors I shall add another: success. Simply put, as the firm develops power and prestige, the heirs find many interesting and amusing thing to do rather than run the business. Many of the families profiled here persist in business despite these temptations. Others have largely handed over the reins and moved on to other pursuits. Typically, rather than wear the shirtsleeves of their forefathers, they finish in silks and velvets, and focus on politics, culture, or the unabashed pursuit of the good life.

AS A RESULT OF THESE PATTERNS, family firms are seen by economists and government planners as transitional and therefore obsolete—dinosaurs on the edge of extinction. Any seriously ambitious business, it is assumed, must take managerial form, even from the start. And yet, with all the arguments stacked against them, family firms continue to succeed. According to a recent *BusinessWeek* report, "One of the biggest strategic advantages a company can have, it turns out, is bloodlines. Companies in which the founders or their families have maintained a strong presence—in management, on the board, or as significant shareholders—do distinctly better than their managerial competitors. Such concerns averaged 15.6 percent return, as against 11.2 percent for non-family firms, with annual revenue growth at 23.4 percent against 10.8 percent."[7]

Clearly, then, the family firm is not about to disappear. To ignore it would be foolish, if not irresponsible. Even where the absence or the desertion of suitable heirs leads to a firm's sale, liquidation, dissolution, or conversion to a managerial unit, the fact remains that that family firm found and built a place in the world of trade and industry, and thereby played a role in the larger process of economic development. The vast majority of new businesses throughout the world remain family enterprises, and I believe this will remain the case for the foreseeable future.

The experience of Egypt under Mohammed Ali in the 1800s is a poignant historical illustration of the dangers of ignoring the family firm in favor of centralized and managerial models in economic planning. Ali was an Albanian lieutenant in the Ottoman army who followed the British into Egypt in the early nineteenth century. He took power, and later consolidated it by inviting to dinner 470 of the Mamelukes (the foreign occupiers who had ruled the land for several centuries), then closing the palace gates and shooting them down like dogs.

Once he was in charge, Ali set about modernizing his country based on top-down Western models. Egypt had many things going for it including rich soil, and Ali chose to use farming to raise the necessary funds for the industrial revolution he sought to launch. To do so, he shifted Egypt to cash-crop agriculture, with special emphasis on high-quality cotton. The crops flourished in the fertile Nile delta, and the state-controlled earnings were effectively reinvested in a massive educational and industrial effort, which included the building of schools to train technicians, and a wide variety of mills and shops for making textiles, metals and metal products, chemicals, and the like. Ali even moved to gain autonomy from European suppliers by buying models of machines and making copies of them in Egypt. His vision, in other words, was very much like the reaction of continental European countries to news of technological advance across the Channel: once Britain industrialized, they felt compelled to do the same.

In many ways this modernization plan was promising. The funds were available, and the final picture of a modern industrial economy seemed plausible. In Egypt, however, one critical factor was lacking: people. No native entrepreneurs, no potential managers, no volunteers. Ali brought in foreigners to run his plants and appointed Egyptians to watch over them—essentially to get in their way. As for workers, he began with slaves from the south (an old African tradition), but they died so fast in the brutal working and living conditions that he soon turned to corvée labor (temporary, generally seasonal, forced labor). Again the working conditions were so brutal that some peasants mutilated themselves to avoid conscription. Most others mutilated the machines instead. Before long there were more machines idle than in use, and standard repair took the form of cannibalizing one machine to fix another, until few machines remained working.

Egypt would have done a lot better had it focused on generating family enterprises to lay the foundation for a healthy economy, rather than attempting to leap directly into state-controlled top-down production models. So while it may be true that as most corporations, and indeed industries, grow, the appeal of managerial structures increases, nothing beats family enterprise for nurturing entrepreneurs and developing new business ventures.

Today, as the world economy progresses, our most underdeveloped countries in Africa, the Arab Middle East, and Latin America are falling even farther behind, and the current approach to growth and entrepreneurship is not helping. An influx of successful managerial corporations would certainly be a boon, but these societies are all characterized by ill-educated populations, marked sexual inequalities, and deep-seated attitudes of machismo. Why should rational enterprise move there? Generally, it does so for one reason only: to exploit cheap labor for manufacturing. These are the worst jobs, and they provide no real opportunity for advancement, or even hope. Ultimately the small influx of capital these wages bring does little to better the general economic foundation of these countries. The way I see it, these people need family capitalism.

Looking at the role of families in business, French historian Michel Hau feels that "the dynastic phenomenon has thus been neglected, more or less by accident."[8] His countryman Louis Bergeron thinks otherwise, believing that people have been too enthusiastic, pushing "the myth of the enterprise seen as an enlarged family."[9] I disagree with both, and see neither neglect nor myth. Rather, I see opportunity.

THIS BOOK TAKES UP the story of family enterprise in modern times, from the seventeenth and eighteenth centuries to the present. One can certainly point to examples of families with great business acumen and legacies in earlier periods (the mere mention of the name Medici effectively summarizes both the role of private dynasties in trade and the links between wealth, status, and political power in late medieval Europe), but the more modern period follows a broad shift in the world economy that is of particular interest to the present-day reader. These modern dynasties transcend local and even national contexts, and have been instrumental in creating a global business environment.

Most of the examples treated here come from the West, specifically Western Europe and the United States. Why? These countries have in fact been the leaders of economic development and innovation, the makers of modernity—and much of this development, innovation, and modernity has been the work of family enterprise. One can certainly find important examples of transgenerational achievement in other parts of the world, but more often than not these are linked to Western operations and techniques. This explicit statement of Western leadership will undoubtedly arouse objections from those who feel that the West has gained its edge by domination and exploitation, and is smug enough in its wealth and good fortune without further compliments. To this age-old anti-imperialist lament I can only say that this is world history as it has played out, that this is what we are examining here, without any moral assessment of "good" or "bad," "just" or "unjust."

The topic of dynasty is broad, which presents the immediate problem of organization: how to choose, arrange, and approach these diverse and varied stories? What is the basis for selection? The longevity of a particular dynasty? The most compelling and instructive anecdotes? The economic importance of a given family? On the whole, I have been guided by the principle that dynastic performance is determined by two dominant factors, and I've tried to select examples that show the influence of these factors. The first is the nature of the business activity in question—let me briefly contrast, by way of illustration, the banking industry, which builds on personal connections (whom do you know? whom can you trust?), and the high-tech industry, which requires a constant influx of knowledge that no one family, however prolific, can keep up with. The second factor is how the particular society views the business activity. Is the pursuit of money and power lauded, or viewed as crass?

This book is divided into a number of broad categories based on the dynasties' primary business activity: banking, automobiles, and the mining and working of raw materials. Within these sections, I have chosen families from different places and, where feasible, different eras, the better to illustrate the relevance of environment and habit: Europe is not America, and within Europe, England is not France, France is not Holland, Holland is not Germany.

For each case treated, I have indicated the preferred sources. In some instances, I have come to know personally the family in question, even children and grandchildren. But these are the exception. My chief reliance is on printed material, usually published, also on private papers and conversations, and these are noted in the specific chapters. These sources do not always agree, nor will they or my interpretation thereof always satisfy, much less please, the persons and families concerned. But that is in the nature of history and historiography.

At this point, I should like to acknowledge the help received in the course of writing and editing. First, I am indebted to colleagues and friends who have shown interest in this book and enriched it with comments and advice. Among these: Franco and Maggie Amatori, Elizabeth Antébi, Steven and Joyce Antler, Daniel Bell, Maxine Berg, Elise Brezis, Caroline Bloomfield, Alfred Chandler, Pierre Chaunu, François Crouzet, Jean-Claude Daumas, Charles Davidson, David and Aida Donald, Suzanne Dworsky, Stanley Engerman, Leila Fawaz, Niall Ferguson, Wolfram Fischer, Robert Fogel, Claude Fohlen, Ben Friedman, J. K. Galbraith, Gil Garbor, Geneviève Gille, Claudia Goldin, Merle and Marshall Goldman, Véronique de Wendel Goupy, Victor Gray, Leah Greenfield, Diane Griliches, André Grjébine, Patrick Gros, Michel Hau, Patrice and Margaret Higonnet, Gerald Holton, Lee and Barbara Huebner, François Jéquier, Dale Jorgenson, Virginia Kahn, Riva Kastoryano, Morton and Phyllis Keller, Henry and Nancy Kissinger, John Komlos, Irwin Landes, Richard Landes, Jacques Le Goff, Maurice Lévy-Leboyer, André Leynaud, Jonathan Liebowitz, Peter Mathias, Bob Mnookin, Joel Mokyr, Berthilde de Montremy, Randall Morck, Clara Nuñez, Ann Parson, Martin Peretz, Richard and Irene Pipes, Rémy Prudhomme, Michael and Ruth Rabin, Ellen Reeves, Henry and Nitza Rosovsky, Emma Rothschild and Amartya Sen, Eytan Shishinsky, André Shleifer, Robert and Barbara Solow, Fritz Stern, Anita and Robert Summers, Larry Summers, Barry Supple, Charlotte Temin, Peter Temin, Gabriel Tortella, Hermann and Monique Van der Wee, Judith Vichniac, Henriette de Vitry, Robert and Denise Wise, Leah Zell, and Geraldine Zetzel.

Second, I owe thanks to those who helped me find photograph illustrations: Emil Steiner, Andrew Fishkopf, Eric Whitten, François de Wendel, and Lori Levine of Getty Images. Finally, I owe a special debt of gratitude to those who read and corrected the various versions of the manuscript, the more so as I was ill during part of the writing and could not have completed the work without their help. I am thinking here especially of Jane Isay and Ben Yalom. The latter particularly was tireless in reading and rereading and did a yeoman editorial job. I am also indebted to Wendy Wolf, chief editor for my publisher, wise and selective in her critiques, and to Sandra Dijkstra, my devoted agent, loyal friend, and caretaker. And above all, to my loving spouse and partner, Sonia, who has never failed to set me right when I needed her, especially when I didn't know I needed her. Thank you, all.

Part One

BANKING

PROLOGUE

*B*anking is uniquely rich ground for the family firm for two essential reasons. First, success in banking historically draws on personal connections—whom do you know, whom do you trust, and who trusts you? Second, unlike many of the industries we will look at later in this book, banking relies primarily on a single, homogeneous commodity: legal tender. In contrast to, say, the automobile industry, banking does not require the development of ever-more-efficient technologies, so there is less need to go outside of the family in constant search of the most skilled scientists to deal with that decade's, or year's, most important innovations.

To be sure, the world has a multitude of currencies, and one has to know and work with rates of exchange in order to know the value of debts and assets. But these rates are public, and eyeglasses and calculators will usually suffice to deal with questions of value. It is the human component, the character and intelligence of the people one works and deals with, that calls for art and judgment. Other fields of commercial and industrial activity, with their diversity of goods and services, call for a subtle and discriminating range of response to business opportunity, built around fundamental questions: Is the price right? Is the product good? The answer to those questions in banking is usually evident. The crucial question concerns risk: Can we count on these people to deliver? This, as we shall see, makes personal connections, handed down from generation to generation, paramount.

Banking is a natural outgrowth of trade. Some merchants find opportunities to help others by lending them money at interest or other form of profit, and other merchants in need of cash learn of and gain from such possibilities. Sometimes things do not work out as planned or hoped, and the lender loses, unless he holds some security to cover his risk. And sometimes one person's loss is another's fortune. Ultimately for some, these formal or informal lending relationships become more interesting or more profitable than trade, and the banker is born.

Banking, it has been said, is other people's money. People who have command of liquid assets, generally not their own, make them available to others who need them, and charge those others for use and risk. Historically, the earliest such bankers began as merchants and eventually went from pursuing their own commercial ventures to financing those of others. Rich merchants, turned "merchant bankers," found other kinds of clients as well: from simple landlords to the highest lords and rulers of the land where they operated. One could hardly say no to clients such as these, but lending to rulers had inherent risks, and the richest bankers, those with the most powerful clients, soon found themselves caught in the grip of their debtors. In the Middle Ages, for example, Italian merchants operating in such foreign lands as England became the ultimate resource of king and court. They certainly could not refuse to lend to the authority whose consent they needed to continue living and working in that country, could they? So Edward I (reigned 1272–1307) had his Ricciardi and Frescobaldi, and Edward III (1327–1377) his Bardi and Peruzzi. Some of these bankers became rich and famous for a time, but all of them ended insolvent, for they had no power to enforce repayment of their loans. Loans to kings were intrinsically risky. Sovereigns can delay, equivocate, repudiate, while business people are held to punctuality. Their reputation is everything, and the essence of reputation is exactitude. When Edward III defaulted in the 1350s—wars are expensive—it killed his bankers. *Tant pis.*

Nonetheless, the pattern continued for centuries. Individual creditors would inevitably go under, but royalty could always find other creditors. The shrewder bankers knew how to turn the connections they made in court to advantage elsewhere, and each one felt that he would not repeat the mistakes of his predecessors.[1]

At the extreme, the ruler could not only seize but imprison, even kill. The best-known example in European history, perhaps, is the sorry fate of Nicolas Fouquet, financial counselor to the king of France. The young Louis XIV did not trust this man he had inherited from his predecessors. In the king's eyes, Fouquet was a commoner by origin, excessively wealthy—how had he gotten so rich without stealing?—and, with his private army, potentially seditious. And then Fouquet exaggerated his implicit impertinence by inviting the king to a banquet in his honor, a banquet that surpassed the quality and elegance of the royal court itself. Big mistake. The lavishness of Fouquet's hospitality simply infuriated Louis, and Fouquet found himself in jail for his efforts.

The comparable Chinese case was a minister named Heshen, favorite of the Qianlong emperor (reigned 1735–1795), who was executed and had his fortune confiscated on the death of his master. In these autocracies, death was an alarm bell, because it reopened all contracts and understandings. A rich man died and his family had to come to new terms with the ruler or his henchmen. A ruler died and every deal was renegotiable. The safest precaution was to hide wealth, which meant sterilization. Immobilization by concealment was the curse of Asian economies.[2]

The biggest threat to continuity, remember, was enrichment and success. We will see this story repeated across industries, but it is most pronounced in banking. Once the bankers, or their children, had the wherewithal to indulge their inflated ambitions, they tended to copy their "betters"—that is, to buy landed estates, purchase honors and titles, live the life of idleness and self-indulgence that was the salient mark of gentility. Or they converted merchant wealth into political power, put their descendants into the highest places, and married them to rank. The most prominent example is the Medici, medical doctors or apothecaries to start with (hence the name), then makers of woolens, then merchants, moneylenders, and competitors for power in Florence, then rulers in Florence, then members of the French royal family on the distaff side, with kings in the belly. By the time we get to know them, they are no longer in trade; they are lenders. The earliest representatives are shrewd, keen, appropriately ruthless and vindictive. But genetics has its ups and downs: the later Medici were vain, bigoted and/or pleasure loving, fundamentally incapable; after some two hundred years (1737), the Florentine line discreetly died out with nary a whimper. In the words of Pasquale Villari: "Such was the end of the younger branch of the Medici, which had found Tuscany a prosperous country, where art, letters, commerce, industry and agriculture flourished, and left her poor and decayed in all ways, drained by taxation, and oppressed by laws contrary to every principle of sound economy, downtrodden by the clergy, and burdened by a weak and vicious aristocracy."[3]

The Medici were not alone. Consider the example of the great German merchant dynasty the Fuggers of Augsburg in Bavaria. We first hear of them in the fourteenth century. They began as weavers, perhaps as putters-out, then moved into international trade (silk, wool, linen, spices), then into moneylending. They lent money at rates often above 20 percent. (What ever had happened to the prohibition of interest [usury]?) They also worked mining concessions in the Tyrol (silver) and Hungary (copper).[4] The Fuggers helped finance the election of Charles V to the throne of the Holy Roman Empire, receiving in return for these and other services leases of the quicksilver mines at Almaden (crucial to the separation of silver from dross) and the silver mines at Guadalcanal—both in Spain. The links to Spain via Charles opened the door to commercial and mining interests in the New World; by the second quarter of the sixteenth century the Fuggers had become the closest thing to a worldwide multinational. Meanwhile the family established close ties to the Roman Church—what else in Bavaria?—which paid off in honors and a highly lucrative trade in indulgences. (Can salvation ever be too dear?) No wonder Jacob Fugger, when urged to retire and enjoy his wealth, said he had no intention of quitting. For many businessmen *l'appétit vient en mangeant.*

The commercial and financial fortune of the Fuggers was closely linked, first, to a burgeoning central European trading world comprising the Rhenish and Danubian basins, the transalpine industrial centers, and the Slavic borderlands; and second, and increasingly, to the prosperity of Antwerp and its central role as pivot/ link between transatlantic, Spanish, and central and northern European trade.[5] Antwerp's role anticipated and warned of the shift of the center of European economic and cultural-intellectual gravity from south to north, from Mediterranean to transalpine, from Catholic orthodoxy to Protestant sectarianism. The city itself was predominantly Catholic but put trade before faith—until, that is, religious troubles and nationalist agitation in the Low Countries led the Spanish rulers to crack down on what the Catholic Church defined as heresy. The city did not crash, but each setback, such as the Spanish bankruptcy of 1557, was aggravated by bad feelings. In the end, Protestant and Jewish businessmen left for Amsterdam or places north, while Catholics retreated to France and Italy. The glory days of the Fuggers, Welsers, and other south German business dynasties were over. Land and rank would offer consolation.

Wealth was not always favorable to reproduction; several of the most important Fugger lines died without issue. But in 1530 two of the Fuggers were elevated to the rank of count; in 1534 they were granted the right to coin money; and in 1541 they were awarded jurisdiction over their lands and their inhabitants. Given the values of the day and place, none of this was really compatible with trade. One or two of the descendants were drawn by what we may call intellectual or artistic activity: genealogy, a study of horse breeding, the collection of books and manuscripts, and of course art purchases and patronage. These were the practices of gentility, the signs of status, wealth, and taste, and, with growing interest and demand, could pay off. No one did these things better than these *nouvelles dynasties.*

In the centuries that followed, the landed Fuggers quietly multiplied on their estates, a living recollection of better times. Two of the Fugger branches, incidentally, still survive. One of the members is even engaged in preparing a doctoral thesis in economics. And some of them have returned to commerce and business in the twentieth century: idleness chafes and opportunity beckons. They are no different in this from other scions of fortune, trading name, education, and manners for good jobs. And the family holds periodic reunions in the public foundations of its ancestors by way of celebrating dynastic pride.

IN BANKING, connections count. That means family, continuity, good marriages, dynastic succession. This is well stated by Walter Bagehot, a well-known popular economist of the nineteenth century: "The banker's calling is hereditary; the credit of the bank descends from father to son; this inherited wealth brings inherited refinement." Or, as a chairman of the Hambros bank put it, "Our job is to breed wisely."[6]

Historically this has been a field, then, where name was the assurance of experience, honor, business acumen, and mutual confidence. The reigning assumptions were that the customer dealt with one bank and did not shop around for better terms. For the bank's part, it kept the customer's circumstances confidential and would not accept any new business that would create a conflict of interest with that client.

Character and connections foremost, then. Technical knowledge matters somewhat—increasingly so as banks have found themselves accepting paper from, or lending money to, industrial and commercial enterprises of a scientific bent. But banks can always hire expert appraisers and advisers when needed. They have continued to rely primarily on their sense of the borrower's reliability and intelligence, reinforced by the kind of security (land, buildings, stocks of raw materials and finished goods) that would cover the debt in the event of disaster. Even so, business has its ups and downs, and family-held banks have often let personal relations lure them into crisis—or worse, into a crisis involving *many* banks, as these firms are often linked by collective obligations. The irony is that these links were designed to divide and diminish risk; yet in time of a business crash they had the opposite effect.

Another irony is that while banking judgments and performance rest largely on character, it seems clear that banking is bad for bankers' character. It is one thing to have to go out into the marketplace and solicit customers, and quite another to let the customers come and solicit your help and favor. The first pattern encourages businessmen to be polite and considerate; the second promotes arrogance and condescension. If bankers do not go into electoral politics, it is because few if any people like them. They are just not likable. On the other hand, many of them have used their money to buy office, even nominally "elected" office. What's the point of being rich if you can't buy what you want?

This privilege of self-indulgence turns out to be the greatest threat to continuity in a profession that dotes and thrives on continuity. Most of the major dynastic banks have not wanted for potential heirs, even when inheritance is limited to males. Entrepreneur bankers, proud men that they are, have tended to wed obedient, prolific spouses who know and do their motherly "duty." But who says the male heirs will do theirs, especially when their wealth provides for so many distractions?

As stipulated above, this volume really begins in modern times with the story of European, particularly Western European, economic development—the preparation and completion of an industrial revolution and the transformation of the techniques and organization of trade. This was the process that made us and the rest of the world what we are. So we find our banking dynasties sometime after the Medici and Fuggers, beginning in the eighteenth century.

The British story is the most important, given Britain's priority in this process. Great Britain was a country ruled by a monarchy of feudal antecedents and by an elite composed of landowners and gentlemen similarly drawn from seigneurial or faux-seigneurial ancestry. It was also a nation successful in trade and precocious in invention and industrial technology. Under the circumstances, one might reasonably have expected British businessmen to enjoy high status and general admiration. They had made Britain what it was: the richest country in Europe, indeed the world, and implicitly the most powerful. And yet the older elite looked down on these saucy, greedy chasers after money and social status and made it a point of pride and decency to put them down. And the tradesmen and manufacturers in their turn sought to use their wealth to buy land, make pompous marriages, and leave business to lesser beings. Rather than assert themselves as a new and higher breed, they sold out, accommodating themselves "to an elite culture blended of preindustrial aristocratic and religious values and more recent professional and bureaucratic values that inhibited their quest for expansion, productivity, and profit."[7]

Within this business world, banking held top rank, and international and large-scale commerce generally enjoyed greater respect than industrial endeavors. Merchants and shippers after all could do their business while staying clean: orders and receipts, bills and remittances, paper and more paper. But manufacturers had to soil their clothes, get down on their backs and bellies and knees, callus their palms and work their muscles. Their very handshake announced their grubby calling. That was the hierarchy.

So families like the Barings, the Barclays, and the Rothschilds stayed on in banking, "becoming indistinguishable [but not quite] from the old aristocracy." They sent their children to the best private schools, Eton and Harrow, then on to Oxford or Cambridge if these heirs were interested and willing. They, the money dealers, strove to put money down, to put it in its "right subsidiary place in the scale of values," to transcend it in the pursuit of elegance and good marital alliances, in the maintenance of tradition and higher civilization. And if some go-getter made a success by violating these tacit rules of proper behavior, just turn away and let him take the money. In the view of these self-appointed cultural arbiters, the higher, tacit purpose of these rogues was to make a world where they themselves would be out of place.

The dominant model was the gentlemen's club, the kind of place that turned potential into actual. This was where hard talent was appropriately softened, where scientists could escape the vulgarity of plastic zippers, where oilmen could avoid talking about dirty liquid, money, and profit. This was where one learned the gestures and tones of haughty superiority and humble deference; where one put manners before achievement. Hasty acceptance of improvement was deprecated; quick scrapping of old equipment showed want of respect for one's forebears, want of discretion. Competition could drive the laggards out of business, whereas they should be cherished. The British had once seen the free market as a guarantee of performance; genteel continuity now made it socially undesirable.

Between 1880 and 1914, some three dozen families with important merchant banking interests succeeded in getting accepted into the upper reaches of British society.[8] Social histories give the impression that these crass newcomers brought with them bad habits—the gross self-indulgence of a new plutocracy. But study of these dynasties shows them to be ever concerned to make the right impression. As they acquired the means, they spent large sums to buy country estates and luxury town houses, and to play the well-defined role of gentry—to do those things that were seen as a contribution to order and decency. If anything, they were stricter in governance and etiquette than the older aristocratic families. They felt more comfortable that way.

One
THE BARINGS
The Rise of Modern Banking

Alexander Baring, 1st Baron Ashburton (1774–1848)

*T*he Baring Bank was the first of its kind: a modern all-around merchant bank that traded in commodities and lent money to other traders. This family of British bankers rose quickly to wealth and prominence, exerted remarkable financial and social power for some generations, and then ultimately suffocated on its own success, as the few offspring who might have proved worthy successors were drawn off to more appealing pursuits made possible by their wealth and station. This is a model that is repeated time and time again throughout the history of family dynasties, and it is one we will encounter in other parts of this study.

The issue of continuity is a constant problem for family firms. Failure will, of course, kill the business. But so will success, with all the diversions and temptations of fortune. How did the Barings avoid this fate? Answer: they were philoprogenitive, meaning they had lots of children, enough that there were usually some eager and talented offspring who wanted a chance at fortune in business. If they turned out inept, they could be exiled to lesser jobs. The family was strict in these matters and, if necessary, would bring in outsiders as needed, until some good Baring would turn up.

The Barings can be traced back to the late fifteenth century in Groningen, in what is today the Netherlands. They first rose in status as Protestant clergy in the now-German city of Bremen. Then, through marriage and inheritance, they became partial owners of one of the area's leading wool mills. At a young age, Johann Baring found himself destined for business rather than a pastoral career; in 1717 he was apprenticed to a major wool-exporting house in Exeter, in England's West Country, selling Bremen linen in England and English woolens in Germany. He did so well that one of the leading merchants of Exeter, a dealer in tea, coffee, spices, sugar, and similar groceries, allowed this bright young foreigner to marry his daughter and sealed the union with a substantial dowry. When this grocer father-in-law died, the dowry became a small fortune, some five million dollars in today's money.

Johann, who eventually changed his name to John, set the wheels of dynasty in motion. He did well with his money, and developed both a name and many material assets. When he died of consumption in 1748 at the young age of fifty-one, he left behind his widow, four sons, a daughter, a large house, a carriage, an estate of some 40,000 pounds (ten million in today's dollars), and a prosperous, reputable business. His eldest son got fifteen thousand pounds; the other children, two thousand pounds each. His widow took over the business and promoted their wool manufacture and export so assiduously that by the time of her death in 1766, the family fortune had increased to seventy thousand pounds. She also kept a close eye on the children, sent them off for schooling and apprenticeship without sentiment, and never let herself be deceived as to their talents and prospects. As the youngest son put it, she was a mother "excellent in many respects, but very severe."[1]

The family firm had been established, and in the process of being passed down to the next generation began to show signs of being what we can call a dynasty. That generation, however, was quite uneven in both its business acumen and ambition. John, the eldest, upon whom the greatest sum of money had been bestowed (and perhaps *because* of this great sum), was the least interested in trade. An easygoing gentleman, he bought himself a country estate and nursed political ambitions. Though nominally a partner in the business, he left his younger brothers, Francis in London and Charles in Exeter, to their own devices. It was the new London branch that made the best going. Francis was smart and sharp, and he leapt at the burgeoning opportunities of international commerce. He knew wools and cloths best, but he made many connections that led him into other commodities: dyes, cochineal, copper, diamonds—whatever could be bought and sold at a profit. Some of this he did for others; some of it he bought and shipped on his own account.

Trade entailed finance—especially long-distance trade, where bills of exchange could not be realized until commodities were sold and delivered. Here an intermediary, ready to accept (endorse and guarantee) commercial paper, made all the difference in a trader's ability and readiness to ship and receive. Francis quickly recognized the fortune to be made here; he began to trade less and facilitate more. The liabilities he thus incurred frightened his mother, but they could be handled so long as the paper acceptances rested on real transactions and were not simply cover for a loan—what the bankers called accommodation paper. After all, goods were goods, and English buyers wanted and had use for these exotic commodities.

Francis's mother gave him sharp warnings against the temptation of quick profit, and tried to keep him focused on manufacturing. After all, the family had a constant and profitable stream of business: the workers in the factory at Exeter toiled from five in the morning to nine at night and still could not keep up with the overwhelming demand. So she counseled patience, and she had a point. But Francis could smell the fortune that awaited the well-informed merchant banker. What he needed was knowledge—about commodities, people, politics, even weather. And as he gathered it, he made both mistakes and *coups de fortune*.

While Francis honed his own skills, he still had family to work with and think about. John, remember, had given up trade for gentility. Brother Charles, the youngest, was put in charge of the Exeter operation, and no one could have been more poorly suited to the monotony of industry. Charles was a dreamer and an avid shopper for opportunities. His ability to discern golden propositions from trash, however, was poor. Every time he traveled and left the prudent presence of mother and brothers, he fell victim to charlatans and schemers.

It may be, however, that Charles was not always wrong. A case in point: in 1776 he arrived in London accompanied by, in Francis's words, "three low persons, projectors, who had offered a plan for spinning Wool by Machinery."[2] Francis, who was under the weather, pressed for money, and skeptical as always of Charles's projects, gave the visitors a cool welcome, especially when he learned that they wanted to build spinning mills in Devon. What a strange notion! Might as well build castles in Spain. The eager promoters then went off to Lancashire, which was certainly the right place. On learning that Charles was ready to put twenty thousand pounds into this venture, Francis told him that he was on his own. The London-Exeter partnership was then dissolved. Barings would start over.

Students of the British industrial revolution will recognize here the kind of ambition that made the fortune of Arkwright and other pioneers of the factory system. True, these heroes of industrial history made their fortunes in cotton, as the techniques for machine spinning of wool were not yet ready. But who is to say that Charles Baring and associates would not quickly have realized this and moved over to cotton, exactly as the spinning industry had already done?

In the end, Francis helped Charles out of this financial mire, but he did it with petulance and resentment. He made his brother a loan, but never expected to be repaid and took the occasion to patronize and scold. Charles felt aggrieved: "Your letter," he wrote, "is a cruel one. I have never deserved from you such expressions."[3] Francis was in no mood to back off. You've made a mess of things, he wrote back, and you want to blame your want of success on bad luck. Luck, my eye, he seemed to respond, writing that he had never known a bad outcome "in which ultimate miscarriage was not to be discovered in the outset."[4]

Some people grow kinder with age. Francis Baring grew grumpier, to the degree it seems that he must have worked at it. Writing in 1803, when he was getting ready to retire, he reflected on the uncertainty of continuity in business. Money yielded no assurance, he stated, pointing out that one generation makes it but cannot count on the wisdom of the next. The younger offspring tend toward spending—otherwise they are seen as mean, which no one wants. The achievements of one prudent man could not last more than some sixty years. The posterity of merchants, he wrote, see the pursuits of their predecessor as beneath them, or they turn the business over to agents, "which is only a more rapid road to ruin."[5] (Clearly Francis was not a fan of managerial capitalism!)[6]

In his latter years, Francis was not pleased with his replacements. He could stand frivolity in the young, he said, but when they turn it into habit, "I must withdraw that indulgence, for it—merits none."[7] He was hard. His oldest, Thomas, was certainly not cut out for business. He liked the country life, politics, the gentility of a knighthood. You couldn't really blame him. In the England of those days, rich people could buy office, even elected office—hence the term "pocket borough." The second son, Alexander, however, was made for the counting house. In Philip Ziegler's well-chosen phrase, he "was born middle-aged." Nonetheless, his father found him disappointing. Francis wanted him to take up a partnership with the Hopes of Amsterdam, which would have made a powerful international combination. But Alexander wanted to live and work at home, preferring the pleasures of the moment to "the most brilliant prospects." In Francis's view, this made Alexander a fool and an ingrate.

His brother Henry is said to have been an inveterate, obsessive gambler. Ziegler calls him a successful one, who several times broke the bank in Paris. I have my doubts; the cardinal rule of rational gambling is, once you break the bank, never go back. In any event, the family kept Henry, though nominally a partner, far away from management.

The two younger brothers were sent east for seasoning. William looked promising, but his health and temper were fragile, and he died in 1820 aged forty. George, the youngest, married for love, against the family's will (thus breaking another cardinal rule of family management: marry for money), lost a fortune in opium speculation, and went bankrupt. His older brothers saved him, albeit reluctantly, and packed him off to a villa in Tuscany, where he smoked cigars, drank too much, and sank into do-nothing euphoria.

Meanwhile, with all his grumpy complaints, Francis Baring took leave of the business. In 1796 he bought at auction for some twenty thousand pounds a reversionary interest in an estate and manor house whose pedigree ran back to Saxon times. When the occupant with life interest, Mrs. Angerstein, died unexpectedly four years later, Francis Baring found that he had picked up this major property at a bargain price (some three to five million in our money) and therefore insisted on paying an additional seven thousand pounds to the owner, who was a friend of his. He said this additional payment was "absolutely necessary for his peace of mind," and stipulated that the money should not be returned, not even in his friend's will. I call that uncommon decency and generosity. The old grump, it seems, had a generous side, and could not always live up (or down) to his reputation.

As he aged, he continued to acquire. In 1801 he spent the enormous sum of £150,000 on another estate, hired a leading architect to redo the house for some £25,000, and spent another £40,000 to plant and landscape the grounds, all the while picking up adjoining properties as they became available. Ever more the lord, he kept a large flock of prizewinning sheep and bought fine specimens of Dutch and Flemish art—Rembrandt, Rubens, van Dyck, Cuyp. He liked his Rembrandts not too dark and his Rubens ladies modest. Francis was one smart investor.

Historians suggest that Francis would have liked a peerage, but he settled instead for indirect social promotion by marrying his children into aristocratic families. (There lay the path of social promotion and commercial demotion in a society that confused rank with merit and sacrificed achievement to eminence. The story has it that when Francis's son Alexander got elected to a snooty, fastidious Whig dining club, it was on condition that he lend fifty pounds to any member who asked. That's what bankers were good for.)

BY THE TIME of his death in 1810, Francis himself was "the first merchant in Europe; first in knowledge and talents, and first in character and opulence."[9] How did he climb so high? By financing war.

Bankers, Ziegler tells us, do not like war. Too much risk of accident, violence, miscalculation, political stupidity, and military idiocy. But risk works both ways, and the potential for big profits accompanies the risk of big losses. The best opportunities for Barings and other bankers during the years of French Revolution (1789–1799) and Empire (1804–1814) lay in lending to the British government, which needed funds for its own military activities and for subsidies and loans to continental allies. With the war machine revving at high speed, there was no end to demand for the Barings' money. The hard part was collecting coins and paper acceptable in the receiving country. Francis Baring pointed out correctly that constraints on trade made it hard for Britain to mobilize the necessary instruments. Even so, Barings made a yeoman's effort to gather the necessary currencies and deliver, using Hamburg as exchange bridge and pivot.[10] In such transactions, however, Barings was no match for a firm then rising on the Continent and uncommonly resourceful and energetic in matters of exchange. This was the Rothschilds of Frankfurt, with whom the Barings were destined to clash repeatedly. Still, at the time, Barings had the upper hand, and as the saying goes, they made hay while the sun was shining. Yes, there was great risk involved in financing war. But state borrowers were the best kind: they might be short one day, but in the long run they could pay with interest. And no nation was a better bet from this point of view than the United Kingdom. No country had a richer, more active economy; no country was better placed to protect its maritime commerce.

It should be no surprise that bankers were also the ideal intermediaries when remitting funds to other countries, including one's enemies. None were so resourceful. The issue came up, for example, in regard to the Louisiana Purchase. France was ready to sell the enormous swath of land to the United States, by way of building up the new republic as an adversary to the British. And Britain was happier to see the land in American than in French hands. The bank best suited to finance the deal was Barings, with its especially close American connections. At the time of the agreement Britain and France were momentarily at peace, so there appeared to be no conflict between the business and national interests. But the terms of payment provided for monthly remittances over a period of years, so an ethical and political question was raised: Was it right for a loyal British firm to send funds to its country's hereditary enemy in a time of unrest and, eventually, war? Barings got an informal governmental go-ahead, but this permission still left them exposed to hostile criticism by political dissenters, ever-angry William Cobbett, for example. So Barings deftly handled this loan through Hopes in Amsterdam, with the same result for the bank. Similar devices made it possible to bypass restraints of trade, which Barings opposed in principle. How sweet it is to make money while adhering to principle!

Fortunately for the bankers, the end of the war and the restoration of the French monarchy were not the end of the story. France had to indemnify its enemies and victims for the damages of battle and Napoleonic occupation. But how could France raise the money? The French banker Gabriel-Julien Ouvrard put forward the suggestion that Hope and Baring might supply the funds. The duke of Wellington liked the idea; so did the duc de Richelieu. Barings were ready to lend the money, but they were again concerned that the British government would look askance at them for lending to their enemy, the French.[11] Yet British foreign secretary Viscount Castlereagh, initially opposed to France's paying its obligations with other people's money, had now changed his mind and approved the idea. By the end of 1816, British-Dutch financial intervention was seen as the answer to everyone's problems: pay up, get the allied troops out, return to the normalcy of a restored French monarchy. Ironically the only opponent seems to have been France's Prince Talleyrand, who found it beneath French dignity to rely on a British banker.

Barings handled the operation with passionate prudence. They tried to get the allied governments to guarantee the bonds but were told that this was out of the question. The very symbolism was unacceptable: Why should the creditors guarantee the debt? Barings quickly yielded; it had been worth a try. But they stipulated that they would not be contractors and thus liable for the operation. They would be intermediaries and take a commission—no more, no less. The allies agreed, but in fact Barings expected to hold the bonds against a rise as international peace took hold and the French regime stabilized. Their expectations were confirmed, and they made a large capital gain. It is not hard to guess what they would have said had things gone the other way: "Remember, we told you we were not contractors." That is banking at its best: heads, I win; tails, you lose.

It was in this connection, though, that Barings made a grave error in judgment. They helped raise some 315 million francs for the French government in 1817, with the value of bonds rising with each issue. Even the bonds marketed in London and Paris ended up in Paris. Nothing testified so well to the recovery of French credit. Even so, Alexander Baring lamented to Wellington that sales were getting harder, that credit was overstretched. Wellington shrugged him off, thinking that once again Barings were trying to subscribe at a cut-rate price. They were near the end, and the upcoming bond issue was to be the last: pay up and get those troops out. Sensitive to criticism that they were exporting capital at a time when British industry and agriculture were caught in a depression, Barings said they would like to yield the leadership to French bankers—to anyone, that is, except the Paris Rothschilds. Alexander Baring told the French banker Laffitte that he had no objection to working with Rothschilds, in spite of these newcomers' presumptuous intrusion into Barings' spheres of influence. But then he reversed himself and said his associates would not allow him to do business with Jews. Hopes, he said, felt that their honor would suffer if they had to work as equals with a bunch of Frankfurter Yidden.

Rothschilds learned of the exclusion and shared their bitterness with David Parish, Anglo-German banker from Hamburg. It is always hard to keep secrets in banking; and besides, other bankers wanted Rothschilds to know; and besides, Rothschilds wanted to shout their rage. Parish told them not to blame it all on Hopes. Barings had also told him (Parish) that Jews were different, that you couldn't work with them. Jews were greedy, Barings said, worked on twenty transactions at a time like a bunch of stock jobbers. All they wanted to do was churn and make money.[12] As though Barings were above that kind of thing.

What's more, the Barings almost had reason to regret the operation. They had been too optimistic. The market was tired; sales were poor; and they might well have found themselves in default. Fortunately the great statesmen of Europe had themselves bought into the loan and had good personal reasons for altering the terms to their advantage. They comforted themselves with the feeling that they had done their duty to their country and the world at large. How much better to do it while benefiting personally!

The end of this particular venture was an enormous financial payday, as Barings made a spectacular £720,000 ($150 million today), perhaps the greatest profit ever from a single banking operation. But they also had made themselves an unforgiving enemy in the Rothschilds.

It was here that success began to catch up with the Barings. They were now seen by many as a world power—indeed in Europe they had earned the nickname "The Sixth Great Power"—and could influence, or even control, the fate of nations. But now the primary partners of the bank began to retire to lives of gentility and ease. At the time, although England was the great capitalist industrial nation of the world, business was seen in Britain as a crude, second-class activity, beneath the dignity of the aristocracy. Francis Baring, son of Sir Thomas, never felt that his own firstborn son, Thomas,[13] should go into the bank. This young man, heir to a great fortune, could aspire to a baronetcy or better. Ideally, then, Thomas should go into public life and lead the larger community. Shy of that, even a quiet existence as country gentleman was preferable to money grubbing in London.

Needless to say, such self-indulgent sentiments were not conducive to banking success. And while Francis saw Thomas as fit for a different life, he also hoped his other sons would continue to lead the bank. Just as Francis himself had done, his children began buying estates, hiring small armies of gardeners and domestics, lavishing hospitality on friends and connections. Knighthoods, which they had earned, were not enough. The Barings "owned" seats in the House of Commons and spent an uncommon share of their time there. Some would say that such activity brought them influence and information, which then helped the bank. Others would say that maybe the bank would have been better off without these opinionated amateurs.

In any event, the bank became increasingly dependent during the post-Napoleonic years on non-Baring partners, such as Swinton Holland, Humphrey St. John–Mildmay (son-in-law to Alexander Baring and a petulant, fearful milquetoast), and particularly Joshua Bates. Ziegler describes Bates as "the most imaginative" of Alexander Baring's appointments. But Baring's imagination lay in appreciating Bates's lack thereof. Born in the United States, Bates spent much of his early business life in the counting house of a Boston merchant who traded with Russia and India. Bates had an intimate knowledge of American business and businessmen. Dour, dry, and dull, he was a tireless workhorse who earned the respect, if not the love, of business friends and rivals. He was the ideal specialist in commercial credit and paper. Cautious by nature, he was not a man to put Barings in debt in order to make money. When the great panic of 1837, brought about by overspeculation in the American markets, shook British and French banking to the core, Bates could congratulate himself on never having discounted a bill with the Bank of England.[14]

Bates himself pinched pennies. He fired his gardener because the man could not keep up with his own personal expenses: "He has too many children, which is the great difficulty with all labouring men. I must discharge him." He fired two servants who conceived a child (even though they were ready to marry), feeling perhaps that it was better to set a cautionary example for the rest of the help. And he held his own wife to an allowance figured down to buttons, thread, and charity. He himself was seduced by rank, and finding high-status Britons economical of gesture and speech, he tried to regulate his own behavior accordingly. Thrift, always and everywhere. Or maybe his taciturnity simply reflected prudence: words could cost.

Even so, his progress in society moved slowly, especially with his Baring partners, who did not want to confuse business with friendship. Mrs. Bates in particular was not deemed adequately presentable to society. When Bates asked his senior partner Alexander Baring (Baron Ashburton) if Lady Ashburton would present his wife and daughter at court, Ashburton contrived a lame excuse not to comply. "This is the first favor I have asked of this family," wrote Bates, "and it will be the last."[15]

The decades after 1820 were a much quieter period for Barings, which saw world financial eminence and leadership pass to the Rothschilds. While Joshua Bates was a competent and steady leader, he and the other non-family partners lacked the temperament and nerve to take advantage of an age of railways and industry. Sulking in their London fortress, the Barings—family and partners—were inclined to blame their discomfiture and frustration on the cunning and unethical behavior of their Jewish competitors. Such prejudices partly reflected the cultivated stupidity of British high society, which used anti-Jewish sentiment as an expression of casual, but not indifferent, exclusion and superiority. Membership, after all, is defined as much by what one rejects as what one accepts. In business the Jews were condemned as volatile and facile, nimble rather than steady, wanting those Christian virtues that were the great asset of such firms as Barings. As late as the end of the century, a Barings partner named Gaspard Farrer could write an American correspondent to ask whether the New York partners of the Lazard bank were "of the usual repulsive Jewish type." (Ziegler, writing of this Farrer fellow, describes him as "tainted by the fashionable anti-Semitism of his time but in most respects humane and liberal."[16] Indeed. Whence this nonsense: "in most respects"? Such bigotry is simply incompatible with humaneness and liberalism.)

Edward Baring (1828–1897), senior partner during the last quarter of the century, was the most notable of the Barings, of his day, both for his personal excesses and for his management of the bank. Edward was of the best British banking tradition: self-confident, stuffily distinguished in manner and appearance, impatient with boredom but somewhat boring himself. He was a person of most generous disposition to those he liked, and he was for many years extremely successful, to the point where some thought him the first banker of London, and hence the world. In 1885 he was offered a peerage, along with Nathan Rothschild. The government, as Gladstone's private secretary clumsily put it, "thought desirable at this moment to give an addition of commercial strength to the House of Lords." Ziegler remarks ironically: "Neither the reason nor the company could have been particularly appealing to Baring."[17] Still, one does not look such an honorific gift horse in the mouth. Edward Baring thanked the government and prepared to play a new, more active role in politics as the first Baron Revelstoke.

To go with the title, he also undertook a massive campaign of enlargement and refurbishing of his town house in Mayfair. Tens of thousands of pounds went toward decoration: marble staircase, rococo ornament, paneling from some of the best houses in France, sculpture, paintings, and objets d'art. Entertainment there was as lavish as the furnishings, though sometimes unconventional and vulgar: one visitor remembered seeing the three sons stand on the main staircase and compete to see who could pee farthest. Meanwhile, the Baron also bought land near Plymouth, near his wife's relations. Here, away from the city, he could comfortably berth his 150-ton yacht, a new-style symbol of money and status.[18]

All this elegance came crashing down in 1890. Revelstoke had lent great sums to the Argentine government, an investment that turned disastrous as Argentina dealt with revolutionary fervor and unrest. This, coupled with major withdrawals by the Russian government, brought Barings, for all its glorious history, to the edge of bankruptcy. Remember, unlimited liability is unlimited, and the partners were liable, as the legal formula puts it, to their last shilling and acre—plus houses and animals and paintings and furniture. One can imagine the family turmoil that erupted!

Ultimately, others rallied round Barings, with the Bank of England especially returning the favors of yesteryear by putting together a rescue syndicate. The Bank acted because it was in the public interest to act; nonetheless, its governor, William Lidderdale, vehemently reproached Barings for incompetence: "The business was entirely managed by Revelstoke, and he did not seem the least to know how he stood; it was haphazard management, certain to bring any firm to grief."[19] These criticisms found an echo in the highest government circles. Thus George Goschen, Chancellor of the Exchequer, expressed goodwill and regrets, but said that the British government could not and would not help. W. H. Smith, Leader of the Commons and First Lord of the Treasury, responded similarly.

This left the crisis squarely in the hands of high finance—the Bank of England and whomever else they could rally. The most powerful bankers, of course, were the Rothschilds, who had both personal and professional reasons to resist aiding the Barings. Roth-schilds felt strongly that the very effort would draw attention to un-secured paper, precipitate a *crise de confiance,* and bring down many other houses as well. On a personal level, the Rothschilds had, as we have seen, a long-standing grudge against the Barings for their having kept the Rothschilds out of the war reparations effort, not to mention for the Barings' vulgar anti-Semitism. Lord Salis-bury, the British prime minister, sent for Nathan Lord Rothschild, whom he knew well, and found him ill disposed toward offering any assistance. Nathan felt that Barings had to go, that the partners would do well to retire to the country on small pensions. Everyone agreed, however, that a failure to support Barings would have the direst consequences for all. Nathan's own bank, he said, stood rea-sonably well, and was ready to support, not Barings directly, but the Bank of England in such measures as it saw fit to undertake.

The Baring family members themselves tightened their belts and circled their wagons around the central banking business—but not without some resentment that their wealth and name had been harmed by Baron Revelstoke's immoderate behavior. Still, they all pitched in, beginning with T.C. (Thomas Charles), who had left the firm only two years before because of disagreements with Revel-stoke over his decisions regarding Argentina. Legally he could eas-ily have limited his own liability and distanced himself from the family crisis. Instead he chose to stand firm with family. Ziegler tells us that T.C. went to the Bank of England, withdrew several bagsful of banknotes, gold coins, and securities, then drove back to Barings with the load. On arrival, he got into a quarrel with the driver over an alleged overcharge of sixpence. In the midst of this ironic argu-ment, one of the bags fell, burst open, and spread its load over the London street. In less starchy cities, such a mishap would have triggered a riot!

From New York, younger brother Tom lamented Revelstoke's vanity and extravagance. Still, he cabled his total support, offering the huge sum of £250,000 (say, sixty million of our dollars) as his contribution to a security fund for Barings' debts. Cousin Ashburton offered fifty thousand pounds. Friends and professional representatives offered smaller amounts. The largest guarantee, though, in the initial amount of four million pounds (a billion of today's dollars) and eventually climbing to seventeen million, came from the syndicate led by the Bank of England, which included the biggest merchant and joint-stock banks in England. Under pressure from the Bank of England leadership, Rothschilds eventually contributed, despite great reluctance on Nathan's part. His cousin Alphonse, in Paris, approved: "By saving Barings from this catastrophe, [N. M. Rothschild] are serving their own interests, for at this moment the House of Baring is the keystone of English commercial credit and its collapse would provoke terrible consequences for English trade in all parts of the world. You must feel very proud about the contribution you have made, by your personal efforts, towards avoiding the worst misfortune."[20]

So Barings were rescued, but at enormous cost. The prestige of private banking would never be the same.

AFTER THE CRISIS, the bank had to be completely reorganized, and the old management had to go. Nothing less would do, if only to reassure clients. Some rejoiced: if the Barings had friends, they also had enemies, who would never forgive their arrogance and high-handedness. But even the enemies had to salute the family's sense of honor and responsibility. This reputation for probity would be the most precious asset of the newly reorganized firm, which would be called Baring Brothers and Company, Limited. Liability would now be limited, and there would be some official outside influence, as the company would now have public shareholders.

Nominally T.C. would be the bank's head, and he put the entirety of his own capital into the business. The effective leader, however, would be John, son of the retired Baron Revelstoke. John was disheartened at first; he feared that T.C., old and curmudgeonly, would drive away business. But a rush to help by other relatives lifted his spirits. And as his spirits rose, he gave vent to the cheap anti-Semitic rubbish that seems characteristic of Barings and many aggrieved losers in the banking world at that time. In a letter to his uncle Evelyn of January 1891:

> Things have turned out more satisfactorily than we dared hope. . . . My own feeling is that we ought to finish the crying and all buckle to and make a fight for it, so as to circumvent if possible the machinations of these blasted Jews. I would like to see them all crucified upside down, but in the meantime they are reaping a huge advantage from what the newspapers delight in calling the "Baring smash."[21]

Like his father, John (who took over the title Baron of Revelstoke) was an autocrat by temperament, but he had better business judgment and was more prudent, more risk averse. During the years that followed the disaster, he watched his spending, and his attitude. Gradually, however, improving circumstances encouraged a return to hauteur and condescension.

Elitist in the extreme, John had a taste for the company of beautiful women, less for the women themselves than for the prestige these beauties reflected upon him. He was the very stereotype of the uptight British banker, and when considering this type, sexual prowess is not the first thing that comes to mind. If ever he managed to get between the legs of his longtime mistress Lady Desborough, their sex, in Ziegler's words, "must have been suffused by snobbery and etiolated almost beyond recognition."[22] Revelstoke was also taken by Nancy Langhorne, a beauty of modest origins and immodest aspirations. He wanted to marry her, but treated her like a risky speculation. "Do you really think that you could fill the position that would be required of my wife? You would have to meet kings and queens and entertain ambassadors. Do you think you can do it?" No wonder she ended by marrying Waldorf Astor. One biographer of the Astors feels that Revelstoke had a lucky escape. Nancy would have made mincemeat of him, chewed him up and spit him out. For one thing, rich as he was, he may not have been rich enough. "What I like about rich people," she said, "is their money."[23]

By the turn of the century, the bank's finances had somewhat recovered. In 1905 Revelstoke went on a purchasing spree: a Bechstein grand piano, twelve dozen bottles of expensive Margaux wine, and two jade dogs from Cartier. He began hunting regularly and bought several motorcars—the newest luxury item. He leased a fine house in Carleton House Terrace, filled it with art, hired the best cook money could buy, offered dinners that included intimate entertainment by the finest artists or even companies of artists, often brought over from the Continent. If asked to defend these extravagances, he would have argued that wealth and highborn company were evidence of the bank's rehabilitation. The Barings, after all, were heirs to almost two centuries of financial eminence and power. Revelstoke's parties showed it, and the shine of luxury living reflected glamorously on the bank.

In the new century, Revelstoke called the tune. He had a horror of all industrial companies, an attitude that set him at variance with the economy of his day.[24] The few Baring relatives still involved in running the bank deferred to his presence and tone. The non-Baring employees suffered from the usual insecurity: Could they ever be sure of their place in the clan? Meanwhile, most family members were engaged in life outside the bank. Honors and titles were theirs by right and precedent; why slog away in the counting house?

Over time, the bank relied more and more heavily on outside managerial types, the more so as activities diversified and specialists became indispensable. Even so, central management lay with the family, to the point where the outsiders thought of themselves as Barings by adoption and emulation. Likewise, the firm continued to think of itself as a family business, despite the technicality of public shareholding. Gaspard Farrer, an outside partner, proudly made both points: "You will notice that I include ourselves among the private houses, for such we still consider ourselves. . . . [T]he control of the firm is absolutely in the directors' hands. You would perhaps be amused to hear that during my sixteen years here, we have only once had a shareholder at our Annual Meeting, and he came at our special request."[25]

John, Baron Revelstoke, died without issue in 1929. His younger brother and successor to the title, Cecil Baring, took the occasion to reiterate the continuity of family and enterprise. In a letter to the King's secretary:

> You will see that the concern remains, as a whole, a family affair, although it has always been laid down here, and we of the family constantly recognize, that there can be no place for one of our members unless he shews the requisite character and brains. . . . In spite of the loss which we have suffered . . . we are going to do our best to meet the responsibilities which are entrusted to us, and to conduct our business with the same impersonal ends which have guided our predecessors.[26]

"No place for one of our members unless he shews the requisite character and brains." That was more than one could say for a royal dynasty: a fool could rule, and often did.

In the decades that followed the death of Cecil Baring, third baron Revelstoke, outsiders and insiders alternated in the seat of power: Edward Peacock, hand-selected by Revelstoke, until 1954; Evelyn Baring to 1963; Rowland, alias Rowley, third earl of Cromer and a distant cousin, from 1967 to 1971 (when he was appointed British ambassador to Washington); John Baring, eldest son of Lord Ashburton, chairman of the Executive Committee from 1971 and then first chairman of the newly named Baring Brothers from 1974 to 1989. His successor as chairman was distant cousin Peter Baring; his deputy chairman, Nicholas Baring; head of Treasury and Trading, Michael Baring.

But through much of this, the head of the bank in all but title was a man named Andrew Tuckey, who was made chairman of Baring Brothers and Co., the merchant bank proper. The son of a tobacco farmer in Rhodesia, Tuckey was a fortunate escapee from a doomed white colonialism. He assimilated smoothly into the high society of London, became director of the Royal Opera House, purchased a manor house in Wiltshire, and generally proved very successful. It was he who revived the corporate finance department in the 1980s by winning for Barings the hundred-million-pound World Bank issue of 1981. In so doing he revived Barings' historic role as financier-elect to governments.[27] He led Baring Brothers into Japan and the emerging Asian markets. This was a good bet on the future of world economic growth; but as we shall see, big gains come with high risk.

During the years after World War II, the Barings group was split into a number of different firms. The organization became more complex, the assignment of power more fragmented. In the mid-1960s, the threat of a confiscatory wealth tax by the Labour government led the family to transfer the majority of the equity to a charitable entity, the Baring Foundation. In 1985, a new entity, Barings plc, was created to run the show. Baring Brothers remained the merchant banking unit, while the growing business of investment management went to another subsidiary, the Baring Investment Bank. Meanwhile, the firm went into stock market brokerage and jobbing in a big way, buying into outside enterprises and creating Baring Securities to pull these new pieces together.

Among the acquisitions: a piece of a British brokerage house operating in East Asia. The aim was to gain the services of one of the partners, a veteran broker named Christopher Heath, son of an army general who had spent the war as a Japanese prisoner. Heath would set up and manage a new subsidiary, Baring Far East Ltd., which would in turn own a new sub-subsidiary to be called Baring Far East Securities Ltd. (later rebaptized Baring Securities). It was getting harder and harder to keep track of the players, but Barings took the precaution of keeping the new enterprise separate from Baring Brothers, thereby avoiding a daily battle between two business and cultural worlds. More harmony, but less awareness and control.

The merchant bank itself continued to run on experience, selective memory, and instinct: essentially by the seat of its well-worn pants. A new partner of the post–World War II years put it this way:

> There are no written rules for doing good business. In the old days, when a client came to see his banker, the skill of the merchant banker was based on good information and good judgment. Today, the merchant banker more often goes out to see his client; and with the diversity and speed of modern communications there are no longer many exclusive sources of information. Judgment, therefore, becomes more important all the time. You must be a judge of people—if you make a mistake about a man, you lose. And when you lose, you can lose heavily.[28]

Much in the tradition of the great Barings themselves, Christopher Heath now had money beyond his wildest dreams, and he spent it accordingly. Like thousands of successful businessmen before him, he set about joining the country "squirearchy." He bought a manor house in Hampshire, conveniently near the Newbury racetrack. He bought Thoroughbred horses, started a stable, and raced his animals. He filled country and city houses with oil paintings and antique furniture, and garages with vintage Bentleys. His bill for cut flowers alone ran to seven thousand pounds a year!

These new tastes were anything but idiosyncratic. Luxury had become the fashion. At Barings, the modest furnishings of yore gave way to large, pretentious desks, and while the old-style bankers still wore jackets at work, the traders modernized—a room of young jokers in shirtsleeves getting too rich too fast. Every minute spent on ceremony or tradition was time lost from making money. New opportunities brought new men, and Heath made sure money was no object in hiring the skilled, the bright, and the bold. When one potential hire complained in 1986 that he had just bought a new house and that a move to New York would cost him eighty thousand dollars, Heath wrote him out a check on the spot for thirty thousand dollars. If we have a good year, he said, I'll reimburse the rest.[29]

Did all this high living and fast working bring in more or less money? The bank did not always know. They simply ran as fast as they could and paid today's distributions with tomorrow's expectations. What is certain is that it was a situation ripe for disaster. And in 1995, as in 1890, disaster hit. All it took was one "rogue trader"— in this case, a certain Nick Leeson—to topple the cart. Leeson was a brilliant and irresponsible kid who figured out how to use the bank's resources, and then the bank's reputation, to speculate on his own account. He bet heavily on Japan, which at first glance seemed reasonable enough. But he did it by investing enormous sums in the riskiest paper, derivatives. To legitimate his trades, he invented a customer, and when the market turned—he had entered just before the peak—he had this "customer" continue to invest, continually raising the ante in the hope of a change in fortune.

What happened was a case study in greed and tenacious denial, both by Leeson and by the partners themselves. They were so pleased by Leeson's paper profits that they could not bear to ask the prudent question: How could one trader make so much money so consistently? Thanks to Leeson, the 1994 bonus pool, due to be paid to partners in February 1995, was over one hundred million pounds. Four of the top directors would share £4.5 million, and Leeson alone would get £450,000.[30] No wonder no one wanted to face reality. So Leeson continued to invest enormous and highly leveraged sums, and by the time he was through, he had committed Barings for an amount far in excess of the firm's assets—so that when his depredations were exposed by the beginnings of inquiry and he suddenly disappeared, little could be done to redress the situation.[31]

Once the circumstances were brought to light, Barings reported the disaster to the Bank of England in the hope that, as in 1890, something might be done to save the firm; indeed, the Bank did make some exploratory moves in that direction. But nothing proved feasible, and a final, desperate, last-minute search for a savior in the person of the sultan of Brunei was aborted.

Why the difference from a century earlier?

First of all, the disparity between assets and liabilities was far greater. Second, the potential repercussions were substantially smaller. In 1890, it had been reasonably feared that a Barings failure would trigger a general collapse of merchant banks. In 1994, only a few merchant banks had survived; the joint-stock institutions were far bigger and stronger, and the disappearance of Barings would leave only traces of disturbance. Any effort at rescue would be motivated more by nostalgia and regret than by objective concerns. Third, the banking community was so appalled by the neglect and misfeasance that had brought down the firm—how could it have allowed such a monstrous deficit to arise without their knowing it?—that many preferred to maintain the failure as an object lesson for all. Failing on this level once was a tragedy, and it could be forgiven. But a second time, even one hundred years later, was just too much.

The structure of the company provided two more key differences, as far as the family itself was concerned. In 1890, the members of the Baring family who held shares in the firm faced unlimited liability for losses. Even their competitors shuddered at the thought of such personal devastation. In contrast, in 1994 the company had limited liability; the collapse of the bank would not swallow the family whole. Second, in 1890, the entire family rallied to save the firm. At the time, almost all of them felt that the failure of the bank would reflect on their collective and individual reputations, tarnish their name, and besmirch even those Barings unconnected with the house. Not so in 1994. The bank had served as a place of employment and promotion for a few of them, but the vast majority of the family had since moved out of the banking world and on to other places of comfort and gentility, along with the occasional career in public service. The bank had done well by them while it prospered, but who among them could identify with the strange crew of self-indulgent pirates currently running the business?

When Peter Baring retired in 1995, Andrew Tuckey replaced him as chairman of the group, only the second non-family man to gain the honor. It proved an empty one, for the bank was finished.

Why would any Baring want it? The firm and name were sold for a symbolic one pound to ING, a Dutch insurance company that was seeking to diversify into banking. Meanwhile, in 1999, Michael Baring, who had worked in the bank until its collapse in 1995, died of a heart attack while hunting in the Scottish highlands. (The game are not the only ones at risk!) The following year it was announced that the name Baring would be dropped; it was a disadvantage. The bank itself was closed; it could not catch up with debts received. So ended 250 years of wealth, power, and dynastic continuity.[32]

Two
THE ROTHSCHILDS

PERSISTENCE, TENACITY, AND CONTINUITY

NATHAN MAYER ROTHSCHILD (1777–1836)

*I*n 1966, Joseph Wechsberg, descendant of a central European family of Jewish businessmen, wrote a book called *The Merchant Bankers* and devoted the last chapter to the Rothschilds. One passage is relevant to our concerns:

> The Rothschild legend has long ago outrun the facts. This is the Rothschilds' own fault. They are even more reticent and aloof than other merchant bankers when family matters are concerned. They developed the technique of absolute discretion to perfection. . . . Significantly, no Rothschild-approved history of the family has yet

appeared. A whole library of books exists about the Rothschilds. All were written without their blessing, often against their wishes, mostly without their cooperation, and sometimes they have protested in court against them.

No one has ever gone through all the family archives. Perhaps once a Rothschild will be permitted but certainly not an outsider. The family has produced many diversified talents in the past two hundred years. Someday there will be a historian named Rothschild and he will write *the* book.[1]

Fortunately for us an outsider, Niall Ferguson, was granted access to records of the London branch of the family in the late 1990s, and wrote an excellent, indeed invaluable, history, *World's Banker*, at the family's request. Throughout the centuries, moreover, the strong sense of family identity and allegiance noted above has remained a critical feature of the Rothschilds.

More than anything, the Rothschilds are a case study in tenacity, a dynasty in which the traits of persistence and intense focus have been passed down from one extraordinary generation to the next. They go back as an identifiable family business to the mid-eighteenth century, starting from the most humble beginnings and working their way into a true multinational empire. And in spite of their huge success in everything from banking to winemaking, the Rothschilds have stayed focused and, unlike the Barings, have not allowed themselves to be diverted from the family's business concerns by the spoils of wealth. Few families have demonstrated such a long-standing sense of duty and commitment, and the rewards they've reaped through the generations are clear to see.

In our chapter on the Barings we saw the vast anti-Semitism in the upper echelons of British banking. The broader world of merchant banking, however, is dominated largely by Jews, so the Barings' success is remarkable in that "the Barings were not Jews,"[2] as Ziegler puts it. Well, the Rothschilds *were* and are Jews, and this religious and cultural identity has shaped the growth of their banking business and their lives on both the individual and family levels.

Through the centuries, their Judaism dictated their choice of spouses, friends, collaborators, and associates. It also did much to shape the attitudes of others toward them—those who knew them and those who did not; those who liked them and those who did not. To understand their success, then, we need to understand the world from which they came.

Frankfurt am Main, the ancestral home of the Rothschilds, was neither a pleasant nor an auspicious place to start a global empire. On the one hand, it was a major center of finance and trade. On the other, it was home to the first Jewish ghetto in Europe, the Judengasse, created in 1460 when the city council resolved to separate the city's Jews from the Christian population.[3] The council chose a narrow enclave for Jewish residence—a walled street barely twelve feet wide, with a small strip behind it for garbage and graves. The windows that faced toward Christian residences had to be boarded up, lest the Jews see the wrong things.[4] At first this enclosure was adequate for the small number of Jews permitted to live in Frankfurt; an average of fourteen or so households, with a limit set at two hundred individuals. But over the years, the real number of the ghetto's inhabitants grew, while its boundaries remained the same. By the time the Rothschilds began to make a place for themselves, in the mid-eighteenth century, some three thousand Jews were packed into that small enclosure, fifteen times the number it originally housed.

The gentile residents of Frankfurt—mostly Lutheran, with a minority of Dutch Calvinists and French Huguenots—had the pleasure of space and views: open places, parks, riverbanks, and ramparts converted to promenades. No such luck for the "accursed race," as the municipal regulations labeled the Jews. They were locked in their barren, stinking cage every evening, with not a tree or bush or blade of grass in sight. In the morning they were allowed outside the ghetto walls, but their business activities were strictly limited: mostly pawnbroking, money changing, and buying and selling secondhand goods. They were made to wear clothing that identified them as Jews (for men, two yellow concentric rings; for women, a striped veil), markers that singled them out for harassment and humiliation, beginning with little Christian children, who took these nasty, bullying habits with them into adulthood. The idea was to keep these Jews as poor, dirty, contemptible witnesses to the deicide allegedly perpetrated by their ancestors almost two thousand years earlier. That the Jews persisted in their infamous faith under these conditions was seen as further proof of their wickedness, justifying any and all mistreatment.

The Judengasse was a terrible environment in which to live. But the adversity and oppression the Jews suffered in Frankfurt bred traits that would be central to the rise of the Rothschilds. First, a network of Jewish traders and financiers developed who offered one another what support they could in a world that banned them from trading relationships with much of gentile society. Second, the Rothschilds learned that family was their greatest resource, the one place where they could place absolute trust. As we will see again and again throughout this book, the societal attitudes toward money and industry, and toward particular segments of the population, exert great influence on the success or failure of family firms. Nowhere is this more evident than these first roots of the Rothschilds, who fought to overcome oppressive conditions, and became stronger, more savvy, and better connected as a result.

The early Rothschilds were pious observant Jews, money changers, and dealers in wool and silk (even though silk was technically forbidden to Jewish traders, being too noble a fabric). Mayer Amschel Rothschild (1743–1812), founder of the banking dynasty, was the fourth of five children to survive the pestiferous conditions of the Judengasse. (If so many Jews did survive, it was largely because of personal cleanliness, the result of rules that required washing before eating, for example.) As soon as he was old enough to walk, the boy accompanied his father to the synagogue in the mornings and evenings, and at the age of three he joined the other children in religion classes, where he learned to read and write Hebrew. This may sound difficult, but in fact the Hebrew alphabet is singularly phonetic; one learns to read quickly. The language of instruction was

Judendeutsch, a German form of Yiddish, without the Slavic accretions that marked the Yiddish of Eastern Europe. *Judendeutsch* was an early form of German, with numerous Hebrew increments. Indeed it has been argued that the primary purpose of all forms of Yiddish was to preserve an admittedly imperfect knowledge of Hebrew.

The *heder*, or Hebrew school, had no time for secular learning, and so it was outside of the classroom, somehow, that the children learned arithmetic and geography and the other skills they would need later in life. Mayer Amschel stood out from the start as exceptional. He was seen as holding much promise for a successful rabbinical career, so in 1755 his father sent him to a rabbinical school in Fürth, a suburb of Nuremberg that was open to Jewish residence. The boy had hardly arrived when an epidemic of smallpox killed his father; his mother died nine months later. And so it was time for him to stop studying and earn a living.[5]

Mayer Amschel had a good head for figures, which was a great advantage in a world with multiple moneys. In 1757 he got an apprenticeship in Hanover, a far more tolerant city than Frankfurt. The job, with the Jewish firm Wolf Jakob Oppenheim, brought him invaluable experience. Oppenheim had strong relationships with noble clients, an area in which Jews excelled. Why? There were great risks associated with court banking, as sovereigns often defaulted on their loans, fearing little reprisal. Christian bankers, with relative freedom to select their clientele, often avoided these risks. The Jews learned to live with them, as a connection to the royalty was one of the few ways to escape the humiliations of Jewish status. Sometimes they guessed wrong, but the best of them were shrewdly prudent, and rulers found them relatively accommodating. The greatest danger lay in too much and too rapid success: by definition, quick enrichment hinted at fraud and dishonesty.

One specialty of money changers was a knowledge of the rare coins and medals that were bound to turn up in the sea of pieces that passed through their hands. There was a significant market among collectors for these items, and the savvy dealers would begin systematic hunting of rarities, which they then resold to specialists or, better yet, to noble and princely collectors. Oppenheim did a lot of this, and Mayer Amschel got an intensive course in coinship and courtship. He liked these pieces and he was a go-getter, traveling about in response to every hint of treasure, circulating lists to potential clients, shaving his margin or even selling at a loss to important people. That readiness to prefer connections to immediate profit testified to a long time horizon; most petty traders could not abide the thought of a loss.

As in all businesses, luck played a role. But luck is not random. Some people are better prepared than others to spot and seize happy chance, and Mayer was one of these. Among the princelings Mayer Amschel dealt with was Wilhelm, Crown Prince of Hesse and Count of Hanau, a two-bit legacy of centuries of seigneurial maneuver, marriage, and inheritance. Hesse was small and politically feeble, but well connected and exceptionally rich. Why rich? Because of a special kind of slave trade: the landgrave of Hesse and his son rented their subjects to other rulers to serve as soldiers. Among their best customers: the British Crown, which hired some twenty-two thousand Hessian troops during the Seven Years War.

Such wealth made princes such as Hesse ideal clients for a busy banker. First, they were constantly remitting commercial and promissory paper, to be discounted and collected. Then there were funds to be invested, by lending to other princes or by purchasing a variety of state bonds and other paper. Each contract held the possibility of further transactions—enough to make the fledgling financier dizzy.[6]

In the course of these maneuvers, Mayer Amschel learned a technique that was to prove extraordinarily productive over the long run: if you want access to a proud and indifferent prince, find a functionary who cannot afford to be proud and indifferent. In Hesse, Mayer Amschel found this friend in a certain Carl Friedrich Buderus, son of a gentleman's valet, young, bright, ambitious, and a member of the prince of Hesse's treasury. Over the years Buderus came to hold the highest post in the prince-become-landgrave's service, and was effectively a silent partner of Rothschild's, as we shall see.

Meanwhile Rothschild also continued his business as a merchant, dealing in fabrics, yarn, and goods from tropical and semitropical lands overseas, including spices, tea, coffee, chocolate—all the precious goodies that gave life zest. His crowded house in the Judengasse was jammed with crates, barrels, and stacks of merchandise, and he hired space outside the ghetto—a way of bypassing the anti-Jewish constraints. The family occupied what little space was left: a bedroom for Mayer Amschel and his wife, Gütel, who were busy making children. (Gütel had twenty pregnancies, ten successful.) In the other bedroom the children, boys and girls of all ages, piled together atop one another. As they grew old enough, they were enrolled in the business. Mayer needed their hands and minds, and besides, whom could he trust more than his own flesh and blood? The girls did the paperwork while the boys moved the goods and both took and made deliveries. As the older children married, their spouses joined the enterprise as workers and employees, but never as partners. The sons-in-law did the dirty work. The daughters-in-law brought substantial dowries, reflecting Mayer Amschel's rising status and wealth. In this world, the rich got richer but also had children, and the children made them richer still.

As business grew, Mayer Amschel found himself joining with others in loan consortia, becoming in effect a court financier. Still nominally a prisoner of the ghetto, he obtained permission to leave on Sundays and travel to places where Jews and pigs were customarily banned, save through payment of special fees. But he had to fight and petition for every concession, and even with Buderus's help and a pristine record of timely payment and reasonable prices, he obtained only grudging increases in privilege and credit from the landgrave. But now the Rothschilds had a special advantage: they had become an international firm. Not international within the German hodgepodge of kingdoms, principalities, and independent cities, but truly international: German-British.

It was Mayer Amschel's third son, Nathan Mayer Rothschild (whom we met briefly in the preface), who gave the Rothschilds a special advantage when he immigrated to England. Nathan Mayer was bright and enterprising, and he had the kind of pride that exasperated those who expected Jews to be suitably meek and deferential. He started in business in Frankfurt, handling the family's trade in British fabrics. These were the days of incipient industrial revolution (1780s and 1790s), and the British were far in advance of everyone else.[7] As a result, machine-made British goods cost substantially less than handwoven local manufactures and were in great demand. But trouble arose when one of the family's principal suppliers quarreled with Nathan Mayer and let him know that he would do him no favors: I don't have to sell to you. Nathan's bold and brusque response was the last thing the Englishman expected: and I don't have to buy from you.

Nathan Mayer told his father that he would leave for England the next day. And leave he did, taking with him capital that some have put at twenty thousand pounds—say, five million dollars of our money. That estimate seems quite high, but Nathan Mayer had custody of great resources, including Prince William's English government securities, which the Hessian ruler was eager to realize, and his father's seemingly endless credit with British Jewish London, so perhaps the figure is accurate. In any case, Nathan seems never to have run out of funds in England. With this capital, one English-speaking companion, a few addresses, and unlimited chutzpah, Nathan Mayer was ready to compete in Manchester.[8]

He quickly made a fortune in cottons and in 1806 married the daughter of one of the richest Jews in England, whose dowry was a delicious £3,248. When his prospective father-in-law asked for proof of his prospects, Nathan told him that if he was concerned about having his daughters provided for, he might just as well give them all to Nathan, and be done with it.

After some time in textiles, Nathan moved on to bigger things, first to trade in other goods and then to banking. After four years in Manchester, he moved to London and began competing with other bankers for a share of government issues. Like his father before him, Nathan was nervier than all of them. While his father remained head of the family, Nathan gained in power and, tacitly the "commanding general" of the clan, ran his office under strict rules of privacy and discipline. No one could enter unless summoned. One day an English dignitary pushed his way in. Nathan recognized the haughty eminence of his visitor. "Take a seat," he said. "I'll be with you in a minute." The visitor was offended by such offhand disrespect. "Do you know who I am?" he said, showing Nathan the royal crest on the inside of his hatband. Nathan was in no way disconcerted. "Take two seats."

It was a great time to work and earn in London. British businessmen were far ahead of anyone else in industrial enterprise and commercial technique, and they needed a constant flow of funds. The British Crown, fighting Napoleon's aspirations and paying the costs of war and imperialism, needed capital as well. The situation offered unprecedented opportunities for financial invention and manipulation, but only for those who had the required understanding, imagination, and daring. Nathan Mayer had come along at just the right time. Further, while British society has traditionally tended to look down on the ostentatious display of new wealth and on the toils of industry, banking has always been highly regarded—so once again we see societal reinforcement of the now multinational family firm.

The Rothschilds were singularly favored in this international context. For one, they had their own British-Continental axis, with family houses in both Germany and England. Further, they had access to the strong network of Jewish businesses and financiers that had developed through centuries of oppression in Eastern Europe. Most important, they had learned the importance of supporting one another in their restricted Judengasse life. The bonds forged in the ghetto served them now, as they would for generations to come. We shall never know how much the growing connections to the landgrave of Hesse meant to the wealth of the family, but in later years, Nathan Mayer and others bragged that it was the landgrave's money that had made all the difference. That may be, although the family's own resources, multiplied by skillful remittances and timely placements, also explain much. Nathan in particular was making a fortune in gold speculations, gambling successfully on the rise of the pound sterling, and continuing to export English goods through the thin barrier of the continental blockade, outdoing his competitors in clandestine transport across the Channel. He left nothing to chance, using surreptitious associates as required. French controls were loose and intermittent, the British looked the other way, and we shall never know the amount usefully or necessarily expended to bribe police and other functionaries.

But from 1810 on, Rothschild interest in commodities slackened as public seizures flourished, just in time to avoid heavy fines and confiscations. Their competitors and associates took a beating. More and more the family moved into money and banking. For one thing, the Elector of Hesse was looking for ways to hide and shelter his German and Danish income from Napoleon and his fiscal agents. For another, he needed help investing his payments from the British government and his interest on British bonds. The Elector would have preferred to deal with his old Calvinist bankers, Rüppell and Harnier and Gebrüder Bethmann, for example. They struck him as the very symbols of mercantile honor and long-established respectability. Whence these pushy Jewish intruders?[9]

Buderus, the Rothschilds' silent partner in Hesse, argued from performance. Rothschilds did better, charged less, worked faster. Mayer Amschel and sons scrambled around, using special carriages, prearranged relays of horses, hidden compartments. And Rothschild's florins, Buderus noted, were worth every bit as much as anyone else's. What's more, all this complaining and second-guessing cost money. Exchange rates could fall (they could also rise), and the Elector's hesitations cost him. That did it. At this point, the Elector had to leave his exile in Denmark (Napoleon had seized Schleswig-Holstein) and move to a new refuge near Prague. There he vexed his visitors with whining and complaints, all the while feeding them inedible food by way of proving his suffering and deprivation. Mayer Amschel's son Nathan Mayer had no need of the Elector's grudging hospitality. Nathan ate kosher. And he had the use of the Elector's money.

That made all the difference. Nathan's biggest coup was lending the British government the money it needed to finance Wellington's peninsular campaign against Napoleon. Nathan had just bought eight hundred thousand pounds in gold from the East India Company. (How had the company ever assembled such a huge sum? And why was it ready to dispose of it in England rather than use it for purchases and expenses in the Indies? And where did Nathan Mayer ever get the credit to pay for such a sum of precious metal?) He now apparently made it available to the Crown, though we have no record of this operation in the Rothschild archive. There remained the task of getting this money to Wellington in Portugal and then in France, and this, too, with all it entailed in commissions and profits on exchange, promised to be exceedingly lucrative. J. C. Herries, a Rothschild ally in the British government, understood this full well, as did Nicholas Vansittart, Chancellor of the Exchequer. The British Treasury knew what it wanted and expected: Nathan Rothschild was to take upon himself all risks and losses and was to be held responsible for any shortfall in deliveries. But given the magnitude of the task and the need for secrecy, "it [was] not thought unreasonable to allow Mr Rothschild a commission of 2 per cent" over and above costs and charges.[10] That came to a lot of money. Old-style merchant bankers such as Barings might look down on money changing, but no one could better gather and ship currency than practiced money changers.

When the war ended and Napoleon failed in his attempted restoration, it was time to pay the piper. France would be required to refund the costs of aggression-expansion outside, and now Allied occupation within—a huge sum, which would need a team effort to raise and disburse. Given the Rothschild contribution to the British and allied causes, the brothers hastened to Paris to share in the settlement. They came in handsome carriages, dressed in the latest fashions, accompanied by a small army of domestics. They rented large spaces (no home yet in Paris) and invited and sought invitations—in vain. To their infinite embarrassment and outrage, they found themselves excluded from the social events and financial deliberations. Some of this was snobbery: in this francophone milieu, the Rothschilds were heard as ill-spoken *arrivistes*. Even the most potent interventions—by the British prime minister, the Austrian ambassador to Paris, and the French king himself (the Rothschilds had lent him five million francs to ensure him a dignified return from exile)—miscarried in the face of implacable condescension and indifference. So the Rothschilds couldn't speak proper French. So what? said the French foreign secretary, the duc de Richelieu. "I have seen and received them in a perfectly correct manner. They visit me all the time, and we babble away in German."[11]

Most of this exclusion was envy and anti-Semitism: the key loan planners were Peter Labouchère of Hopes, son-in-law of Sir Francis Baring; Alexander Baring; and the Paris banker Gabriel-Julien Ouvrard, long infuriated by the success of whippersnapper James (Jacob) Rothschild, youngest of the five sons of Mayer Amschel. In this collection of distinguished Jew-haters, the only one who had the sense to bend prejudice to practicality was Alexander Baring, but he found it impossible to talk reason to his associates—the more so as Richelieu, for all his linguistic talents, felt the same way. So this huge postwar international loan—350 million francs at 5 percent, issued at the bargain price of 53—was floated without Rothschild participation. It was a great success.

But it was also a big mistake on the part of the other bankers, because the Rothschilds had no intention of lying down to be stepped on. For one thing, the loan was just the beginning. There remained the question of remittance, and the Habsburgs and lesser German princes wanted the money before it was available. That was where the Rothschilds came in: they lent the money at high rates of interest, and the bankers' syndicate ended by paying Rothschilds instead of France's creditors. For another, this was a reminder of who was best prepared to handle transfers and exchange in central Europe.

Revenge came with the second loan, designed to settle accounts and make it possible for the allies to withdraw from French territory. This loan was for 265 million francs (rather than the planned 350), and the bankers subscribed at an optimistic 76, half again as much as for the earlier loan, which was doing very well. This time, however, investors balked, the more so as the Rothschilds were now quietly driving the price down. The banking syndicate had to go back to the allies and the French government to secure a revision of the terms. They were helped in this appeal by the fact that the great statesmen of the alliance (Metternich, Nesselrode, Hardenberg) had personally subscribed and stood to lose a fortune on the original terms. So these terms were revised in favor of the banking syndicate. Even so, Metternich and the others never forgave Barings and consorts, and in effect excluded them from the international capital market. It was the Rothschilds who picked up the pieces.

MAYER AMSCHEL DIED in 1812. Before he went, he drew up a partnership agreement and will that laid out the principles he felt should guide the family enterprise into the future. These clear rules for order, family behavior, and the succession of power very much distinguished the Rothschilds from other banking dynasties, Jewish or otherwise, and gave Amschel's descendants a code by which they could direct and protect their business and private lives.

The will began by distinguishing Mayer Amschel and his direct male descendants from any other Rothschild relations, as well as from female progeny and their non-Rothschild spouses and offspring. There would, the will made clear, be no room in the business for sons-in-law. To this end, Amschel declared that "My daughters, sons-in-law and their heirs [have] no part whatsoever in the existing firm *M. A. Rothschild und Söhne* . . . nor the right to examine the said business, its books, papers, inventory etc. . . . I shall never forgive my children if they should against my parental will take it upon themselves to disturb my sons in the peaceful possession of their business."[12] It was an exacting set of rules, and certainly unfair to the daughters of all Rothschilds, then and in the future. It may be hard to argue with success, but one can certainly argue with injustice.

There was one more unspoken theme: the family should remain

Jewish and marry Jewish. No room for gentiles. This may seem commonplace in a religious community. But the Rothschilds were ascending into the world of great wealth, a world in which such proscriptions contradicted the prevailing social temptations and practice. Many Jews in Germany, especially, saw assimilation, and often conversion to Christianity, as a kind of emancipation. The most prominent example was the Mendelssohn clan. The patriarch, Moses (1729–1786), was a religious Jew, Enlightenment philosopher, friend and correspondent of such open-minded gentiles as Gotthold Ephraim Lessing. His son Joseph founded the Mendelssohn banking house, which rose to great prominence. Moses's younger son, Abraham, also a banker, baptized his children as Lutherans in 1816 and had himself baptized in 1822. Most of the successive Mendelssohn generations were baptized as well, the best known of them being Felix, the immortal composer. It is worth noting that successive generations of Mendelssohns found their marriage partners among similar families of Jewish apostates. Initially the old-time gentiles mistrusted or scorned them.[13]

For a similar yet different pattern, look at the Stieglitz family, court Jews in the tiny principality of Arolsen. In their pursuit of wealth, one branch moved to St. Petersburg and became bankers to the Russian Crown and court. Already in Arolsen they had converted to Christianity, and in Russia they married their daughter to the son of a similar apostate family. They duly celebrated the wedding with their in-laws, then cut them off; for how could a family of such wealth and distinction mix with such ignominious ex-Jewish *arrivistes*? One more generation, and the Stieglitzes gave up banking for the manorial life of the landed nobility in the Baltic provinces.

Their successors, the Günzburgs, were Jews enriched by the manufacture of vodka in the Russian provinces and become merchant bankers. They grew even wealthier as ally and partner of Western-European banks in Russian state bond issues and industrial flotations. Toward the end of the nineteenth century, they moved to Paris, where, in spite of the Dreyfus affair and other evidences of anti-Semitism, Jews were much better treated than in tsarist Russia. There, after World War II, a Baron de Gunzburg met and married the daughter of a Bronfman of the Canadian liquor dynasty—a most suitable union of common ethnic and commercial origins. The Gunzburg-Bronfmans still remember that they are Jews, mainly for the Canadian output, and identify accordingly.

The Rothschilds would have no such assimilation or apostasy. They were Jews, and they married Jews, for the time being at least. The marriages of Mayer Amschel's children reflected at first the family's rising wealth and status. These wives were characteristically better educated and styled than their Rothschild husbands, devoted as the men were to the counting house, business trips, and wheeling-dealing. The constraints were very strict, however, and soon the pool of suitable Jewish spouses shrank to nearly nothing. The bride hunt of Carl (Kalman) Rothschild is a case study of these limits. Early in his search for a mate, he wrote, "I could marry the most beautiful and the richest girl in Berlin, which I would not do for all the treasures in the world, because here in Berlin, if she herself has not been converted, then a brother or a sister-in-law has. . . . We ourselves have made our fortune as Jews, and we want nothing to do with such people."[14]

March 7 of 1817 found Carl prospecting in Hamburg, which was both a possible site for an arm of the family bank and home to a marriageable young woman, daughter of the Heines (later of literary fame). But she had been baptized, and Carl knew he could never trust a family of apostates. Further, the Rothschilds decided against setting up a branch in Hamburg. After numerous other stops and disappointments, Carl set his sights on a Miss Adelheid Herz of Frankfurt—lively, pretty, socially acceptable—and offered his hand in marriage. But when his mother and older brother Amschel, the strictest of the children—in a sarcastic moment, Carl called him Rabbi Amschel—learned that Miss Herz "knew nothing about Yom Kippur, Passover rites and rules, or *kashrut*," they wanted to call the whole thing off. Her family was simply not sufficiently observant. Here Carl held firm:

troth is troth, and a deal is a deal. Besides, he would see to it that they had a Jewish household. "It's a good husband who makes a good wife." They married in 1818.[15] This did not persuade Amschel to drop his disapproval. In a letter of 20 April 1818 to brother Salomon, Carl vented his resentment of Amschel's interference. "You know my character. You know I hold myself responsible in all circumstances and do not go gladly against my family's wishes." And in a second letter of the same date: "I am a *Jew through and through*."

Eventually the Rothschilds found a way to avoid such challenging searches for mates. Jewish custom banned marriages between nephews and aunts. It did, however, permit unions of uncles and nieces. This became common in the family. Beginning with James Rothschild and his brother and Salomon's daughter Betty, in 1824, sixteen of the eighteen matches made by Mayer Amschel's grandchildren were between uncle and niece or first cousins. Marriage within the family had many social and cultural advantages: the dowry remained part of the family fortune; habits and secrets could be concealed from outsiders; and everyone understood Yiddish, along with French, English, and German. Besides, marrying within the family offered the assurance of getting a worthy partner. Only a Rothschild was good enough for a Rothschild.[16]

This *politique matrimoniale* had, of course, two serious potential disadvantages. The first was its long-run incompatibility with love and romance. Mixing in the highest social and political circles, the children were bound to find attachments outside the family. The second risk, not unsuspected even in those days, was that endogamy accentuated a family's genetic features—some good, some bad.[17]

The first instance of willful exogamy waited for the death of Nathan Mayer. Nathan died in 1836, when he was only fifty-nine. He may have been the richest man in the world, at least in terms of liquid assets, but he had the misfortune to live in an age that did not know about antisepsis, and he came down with an infected boil or abscess on his lower back—no possible cure by amputation. The infection developed just as he left London for Frankfurt to celebrate the marriage of his son Lionel to Lionel's cousin Charlotte, daughter of Carl, and also to negotiate places for his sons in the family firm. Tough as he was, Nathan managed to master his pain and take his place at the wedding, and even to continue dictating letters and documents until the day before he died. But the inevitable moment came. *"Il est mort,"* went the message back to London. The brilliant entrepreneur and innovator was gone, and his like would not be found again.

With Nathan gone, anything was possible in matters matrimonial. In 1839, his fifth child, Hannah Mayer, announced to the family that she had fallen in love with Henry Fitzroy, the younger son of the earl of Southampton, and wanted to marry him—in an Anglican church ceremony, no less.[18] Fitzroy's family was not happy and cut off his allowance, which was a hard slap on the wrist. But the Rothschilds were simply furious. Where the British saw this as a social promotion for Hannah, the Rothschilds saw it as an act of disobedience and a betrayal. The angriest of the lot was Hannah's uncle James in Paris, the least religiously observant of the five sons of Mayer Amschel. He wrote a stern letter to his nephew Nat, Hannah's older brother and the only family member ready to accompany his wayward sister into the church (her mother went as far as the curb, then said a tearful good-bye):

> The story about Hannah Mayer made me so ill that I did not have the courage to pick up a pen and write about this matter. She has unfortunately robbed our whole family of its pride and caused us such harm as can no longer be redressed. You say, my dear Nat, that she has found everything but religion. But I believe that [religion] means everything. Our good fortune and our blessings depend on it. Well, we shall have to forget her and wipe her from our memory and never again during my lifetime will I or any other member of our family see or receive her. We just wish her all the best and banish her from our memory as if she had never existed.[19]

Nat would not let himself be intimidated. He replied that all his sister had done was marry a Christian in a Christian country. James wrote again:

What sort of example for our children a girl who says, "I marry against the wish of my family"? . . . Why should my children or my children's children follow my wishes if there is no punishment? . . . In our family we have always brought our children up from their early years to confine their love to members of the family. In this way their attachment for one another would keep them from marrying outside the family. This way the fortune would stay inside the family. Who will give me any assurance that my own children will do what I tell them if they see that there is no punishment forthcoming?[20]

Most of the family continued to boycott Hannah. Those who kept in touch eventually learned that the son of her union with Fitzroy, Arthur, was thrown from a horse, suffered incurable disabilities, and died young in 1858.[21] Hannah's husband died a year later. Then she herself fell seriously ill in early 1864 and spent months in bent, painful deformity before dying later that year. Some Rothschilds saw this chain of misfortune as a form of divine retribution—in the words of James's daughter Charlotte, "a long martyrdom."[22] Hard.

This litany of disapproval may seem tiresome, but it expresses a sharp family attitude that not only separated the Rothschilds from other successful Jewish families but also gave force to their sense of dynastic eminence and continuity. One cannot understand the history of the family, or their dogged persistence, without taking into account their outspoken Jewishness and patriarchy.

Even so, the family's rigid adherence to Mayer Amschel's rules began to lose force as time marched forward and future generations came of age. Nat's empathy with his sister was symptomatic of the changes in attitude. These were inevitable: one cannot become enormously rich, drink and dine with high-status dignitaries, and play and flirt with their children without absorbing new values and habits. And so it was with the Rothschilds. They purchased large estates, bought or built lavish mansions, courted the local squirearchy, and chased after, collected, and displayed decorative objects and art treasures.[23]

They engaged in endless rounds of amusement and entertainment, and even took to riding horses, an un-Jewish animal if ever there was one.[24] They organized hunts, again a most un-Jewish activity, and these on a scale that put their Gentile competitors to shame.[25]

WITHIN THE FIRM, business interests varied from one country to another. Nathan Mayer, we know, had been the leader of the family, and under him the London branch became the family's most powerful. (Rothschild houses on the Continent often called on London for help with railways and industrial ventures.) The big money in British banking was in international flotations, in lending to governments. No one had a richer, more valuable clientele of states and princes than the Rothschilds, and by the mid-nineteenth century, they stood alone at the peak of banking power, favored by the post-Napoleonic herd of monarchist regimes. Habsburg Austria, Prussia, Naples, Portugal, the papal states—no one borrowed without Rothschild help.[26]

The one place where the London house came a cropper was the United States, where it extended too much credit to impecunious state legislatures and gave too much support to the Bank of the United States, which failed in 1841. It would have taken an especially astute person, domiciled on that side of the water, to follow the complexities and business implications of American federal and state politics. The Rothschilds might have deputized one of Nathan Mayer's children to this effect and established a sixth branch, but none of those who went over the water liked what they saw in the United States. Their reticence was encouraged by their protective mother, who did not want to lose their company.

To meet the need, the house sent out a precociously enterprising employee, August Belmont, on a scouting expedition. Belmont was supposed to make a quick assessment of prospects in America and then go on to Havana, where the London house had bigger business. But he arrived in New York in the midst of the financial crisis of 1837, found that Rothschilds' representatives had gone bust, and decided to stay. He took to New York and did well there, both commercially and socially. Born Jewish, he had himself baptized and in 1849 married a daughter of Commodore Matthew C. Perry, an American naval hero and the man who later opened Japan to foreign trade. Belmont's bank handled Rothschild affairs with appropriate care and zeal, though not, perhaps, with full transparency.

Still, the Rothschilds did not like him, partly because of his religious apostasy, partly because of his insubordination and tender sense of independence, and partly because he was not one of the family but nonetheless chose to act with their authority. They had sent him on an errand and had ended up with a self-appointed agent. He simply ignored repeated orders from James to go to Cuba. By Rothschild standards, how could he be trusted? James was dismissive of him: "He is a stupid young man. . . . Such an ass needs to be kept on a short leash."[27] But that was it: he was anything but stupid. Intentionally obtuse, perhaps, but never stupid.

When Alphonse, son of James, visited New York in 1848–1849, the trip undertaken in part to get him away from the physical dangers and military obligations of revolutionary Paris, he was unfavorably impressed by the success and pretensions of this onetime employee. "I have had a few difficulties with Belmont," he wrote, "but I hope to settle them in due course. This gentleman is drenched in self-esteem and vanity. That's how one has to take him: he is American in the fullest sense of the term. Too bad that he hasn't come to Europe more often and learned to know the people he has to deal with."

Alphonse went on in another letter: "Belmont is a regular *grand seigneur* [how did he get so rich? at whose expense?], with sumptuous house, carriages, and footmen, and I had to count myself lucky that he was willing to allow me inside his office. [Now where had he learned that?] On the other hand, he is the unhappiest person on earth, what with his broken leg, always morose, always coughing. . . . This gentleman is consumed by conceit and vanity. . . . He has cultivated an independent air, more particularly a style and a manner that are the result of his escape from all active control. . . . The problem with Belmont is that he has spent twelve years as absolute master, at 2,000 [*sic*] miles distance from his bosses."[28]

Perhaps this exposure to European political violence on the one hand and flagrant, exasperating Belmontian prosperity on the other shaped Alphonse's sense of the American opportunity. In a letter to Paris:

> I should like to convince you of the daily importance of the prodigious development of this country and of the leap that it is about to make. . . . Within a few years, America will have drawn to itself the greater part of the trade of China and the Indies and will throne between the two oceans. Do not think that I am allowing myself to be dazzled by American vanity. This country possesses the elements of prosperity such that one would have to be blind not to recognize them, and one cannot but admire the energy and intelligence with which the people know how to exploit them. In Europe there are many prejudices about America, but these must yield to facts. In the light of these facts, as I now see them, I have no hesitation in saying that a Rothschild house and not a mere agency should be established in America. All the people I see here, in the highest ranks of trade, call for this insistently.[29]

But Alphonse's arguments fell on deaf ears. His father, doting in his latter years (he is said to have insisted on choosing the names for all his grandchildren), could not bear to send his son so far from home. The same for mother and sisters: business was not worth it if it kept loved ones so far apart. So what if Belmont was presumptuous and intractable? At least they knew him. Better a familiar pain than a strange one.

This failure to make the United States an integral part of the family network was surely the Rothschilds' biggest strategic mistake—but ya can't win 'em all. From the European perspective, the United States looked to be a small partner in those days. A great deal depended on timing. Thus a visit by James's third son, Salomon de Rothschild, in 1859–1860, on the eve of the American Civil War, showed a much less attractive picture. It also seems to have misled the bank into assuming that the South would win the war. That was a loser, and it cost the Rothschilds dearly. Who would suspect that fifty years later the American economy would be pushing Britain's for first place?

The London house remained the richest unit of the Rothschild multinational. But the passage of time changed it gradually from an active promoter and investor to a custodian of family fortunes. Frank Harris, he of the erotic *Life and Loves,* tells of a dinner conversation with Nathaniel (1836–1905) where he, Harris, reports gleefully on the profits allegedly made by Barings on the conversion of Guinness Breweries to a limited-liability company: the neat sum of a million pounds. The implication: Don't you wish you'd had the deal? Rothschild returns a soft answer: "We did have it. Turned it down." Harris: "Aren't you sorry now?" Rothschild: "When I turn down deals, I go home at night carefree and easy. When I take on a project, I can't sleep."

The tacit rules of the three-brother triumvirate that then ran London Rothschilds aimed at preserving sleep and peace of mind: no undertaking without unanimous consent. Meanwhile, the Paris house was active and successful in coal mining and railway development, garnering some of the most profitable concessions, in Belgium and elsewhere as well as in France. The firm had a keen sense of the compatibility and mutual support of selected investments, remained alert to the link between political influence and profitable exploitation (concessions, concessions), and was much helped by the availability of support from across the Channel. For all that, it paid too little attention to fundamental changes in the economy. These gave rise to a new banking world that the Rothschilds initially despised but had to come to terms with: the world of joint-stock banking—that is, banking conducted by corporate enterprises owned by limited-liability shareholders.

Joint-stock banking in France went back to the early eighteenth century, to John Law and his Banque Royale, with right-of-note issue and Law's so-called Mississippi bubble. The collapse of this scheme put such public promotions under a cloud that dissipated only toward the end of the Old Regime, with the establishment, with royal permission, of a *comptoir d'escompte;* and later, under Bonaparte, of the Banque de France. At that point, the creation of joint-stock companies with limited liability required royal (or under Napoleon, imperial) permission. After the restoration of the monarchy in 1815, parliament could also grant permission. The first companies to avail themselves of limited liability were builders of canals and bridges. Such tasks far exceeded the resources of even a rich few; and few rich were prepared to risk their personal fortune at a throw. These works projects also linked public authorization to rights of eminent domain.

Banks were something else. The state did not recognize here the need or desirability of limited liability; quite the contrary. The Bank of France needed such a privilege because of its right-of-note issue, where investors would find collective unlimited responsibility unbearable. Even so, a small but growing number of banking entrepreneurs saw limited liability as indispensable to new areas of credit: loans to and placements in industrial ventures with necessarily slow payoffs and potentially high risk. The answer was found at first in share partnerships that combined active managing partners with unlimited liability and passive shareholders with limited. Such partnerships—called *caisses* because the Bank of France had succeeded in reserving the appellation *banque* to note-issuing houses—did not require state authorization, and a few appeared in the late 1830s and 1840s, along with the growing investment in railways and heavy construction.

The house of Rothschild paid these financial neophytes little mind. It was too rich, too powerful. Read this adulatory testimony by the novelist-playwright Ernest Feydeau to the incomparable order and hierarchy of the Rothschild bank of Paris around mid-century:

> It had to be seen to be believed how, in that enormous banking house, he [James] ruled with a rod of iron! What marvelous order everywhere! How docile the employees were! And how intelligent!

What submissive sons! What a sense of hierarchy! What respect . . . I can't imagine it would be possible to find another banking house where everything would bear the stamp of such regularity, order, fitness, or respectability. Everything there smelled of great affairs, of a hard-won fortune acquired and well secured. Every head of department was *comme il faut*. The offices had an immaculate air that was a joy to behold. Finally, with the exception of a few slightly eccentric outbursts on the part of the boss, I never, in the fifteen years that I frequented the house, saw anything that was not altogether honorable, correct, and suitable.[30]

By comparison, the newcomers were not worth bothering about, and their field of activity too limited. But the Paris Rothschilds should have caught the murmur of innovation, the more so as some of their own people were exploring new ways. In particular, they had hired a brilliant young man, Emile Pereire (1800–1875), to help with the railway and investment side of the business, and this neophyte, in association with his brother Isaac, had a vision of credit and finance that went far beyond traditional bounds. As with London and August Belmont, James Rothschild was not used to such implicit insubordination. Zeal, yes. Initiative, maybe. But equality, never. So Emile left the firm and set up on his own.

The break came with the revolution of 1848. Once again, someone was not paying attention, and the Paris Rothschilds found themselves threatened with not only business failure but personal bankruptcy. Stability did not return until Louis-Napoléon was made president of the Second Republic. Meanwhile the brothers Pereire mobilized support for a "Crédit Mobilier," a joint-stock, limited-liability investment bank with a substantial capital of sixty million francs, second only to that of the Bank of France. This was seen by James Rothschild as a personal challenge, and he did his best to turn the new government against the project. To no avail. The authorities liked the idea of competition for Rothschild. Within a year of Louis-Napoléon's coup d'état of December 1851, the new Pereire bank received official approval.

The discomfited Rothschilds decided that the only way to meet this threat was to mobilize friends, organize their own competitive joint-stock banks (thus the Société Générale), and use their political connections to obtain fatter concessions and better terms, whether in France, Switzerland, Spain, or Austria. Which they did. The battle has been seen by many scholars as one between old bank (merchant houses) and new (corporate banks). Not at all. The Rothschilds understood as well as anyone that risky finance is best confined to low-risk enterprises; that limited liability has its place. But James de Rothschild would not allow himself to be bested by the brothers Pereire, a pair of impertinent pretenders.[31] All the more because the Pereire were favored by the parvenu imperial regime, which could not forget or forgive the ties between the Rothschilds and the house of Orléans; and the Pereire were supported by the banking family of Fould, rivals to the Rothschilds.

The Fould, Jews like the Rothschilds, had come to France from the east, from Lorraine, but unlike the Rothschilds, their ascent was marked by intermarriage, apostasy, and seigneurial-political aspirations. The Rothschilds bought their estates near Paris, the better to stay close to the action. The Fould bought theirs in the far south, land of haughty lords and docile peasants. Christian land. The two families could never like each other. So the Rothschilds squeezed; the Pereire tried too hard and took too many chances; the Fould had other interests; and in 1867, the Crédit Mobilier, too venturesome, failed.[32]

In the meantime, the imperial regime made peace with the Rothschilds, for the simple reason that a series of foreign adventures were bleeding the regime dry in the face of growing parliamentary resistance. James de Rothschild did not approve of these costly enterprises, but he recognized that the emperor was sincere in his overtures. So in 1862, the Rothschilds received ruler and court at Ferrières: banquet, hunt (more than nine hundred pheasants that fairly flew to meet the bullets), concert by the Paris Opera under the baton of Rossini. Emperor and banker-king made peace on the banker's terms. Had Napoleon III been Louis XIV, he'd have simply confiscated his subject's wealth and seized the château. What a difference two centuries and a half-dozen revolutions and coups d'état can make!

We may pause a moment to consider the château of Ferrières as monument, residence, museum, display piece. The English Rothschilds had set the example with their post-Nathan fantasies, in particular with the Mentmore of the 1850s. Niall Ferguson expresses cogently this urge to display:

> The Rothschild bid for noble status in Britain was uncompromising and nothing expressed this more tangibly than the houses the family built for themselves. They were more than mere imitations of eighteenth-century country houses. They were advertisements for Rothschild power, five-star hotels for influential guests, private art galleries: in short, centres for corporate hospitality.[33]

So now James had to do better, and he, too, hired the great architect Joseph Paxton, designer of the Crystal Palace of the Great Exhibition, master of the latest technical wizardry. Paxton had built Mentmore with hot running water and central heating. (Say no more: I have stayed in bourgeois British homes after World War II that had neither.) So for Ferrières, not only the latest in plumbing, but a separate structure for the kitchens a hundred yards from the house—to spare family and guests the merest hint of culinary odors, to say nothing of garbage—and a small underground railway to connect kitchens discreetly to the basement beneath the dining room, so that the food might arrive piping hot.

Everything exuded power and space—interiors, exteriors. The château had more than eighty rooms; the halls were display galleries; the gardens, with their ponds, bridges, greenhouses, and crystal palaces, were an improvement on paradise. The forked-tongue Goncourt detested it, like just about everything else Rothschildian: "Trees and waterworks created by spending millions, round a chateau costing eighteen millions, an idiotic and ridiculous extravagance, a pudding of every style, the fruit of a stupid ambition to have all monuments in one!"[34] The trouble with the Goncourt was their arse-kissing hypocrisy. They couldn't say no to a Rothschild invitation. And the Rothschilds were foolish enough to invite them.

The Frankfurt ancestral branch could not play such a role, if only because other German cities were taking the economic lead—Hamburg, but even more Berlin. But the German Rothschilds found a worthy correspondent and business partner in the firm of S. (Samuel) Bleichröder, exchange dealers to start with, but quick in matters of credit and payment, and like the early Rothschilds, eager masters of the cut-rate and concessionary deal. Reading the early history of S. Bleichröder is like replaying the career of Mayer Amschel. One big difference: the Bleichröders came later and participated actively in the German railway boom of the 1840s and the mining and industrial developments of the mid-century decades. Another difference: the firm of Mayer Amschel Rothschild did not have to cater to other banking firms, whereas the Bleichröders, initially at least, had to curry favor.[35]

In the generation that followed the revolutions of 1848, Germany saw the founding of a number of major joint-stock investment banks—this in spite of manifest reluctance by some authorities, notably Prussia and Frankfurt, to grant the necessary authorization. That was how Germany's first private joint-stock investment bank, the Darmstädter Bank, found its way to small-town Darmstadt rather than Cologne.[36] But *where* was less important than *what*. Germany was building its industrial revolution on heavy industry, the kind that needed heavy capitalization, which called in turn for financial mobilization. Joint-stock investment banks made the difference. In particular, four so-called D-Banken—from the key letter in their names—set an example of industrial and commercial promotion for the rest of Europe. These were the above-mentioned Darmstädter Bank (1853), the Berlin Disconto-Gesellschaft (1856), the Dresdner Bank (1872), and the Deutsche Bank (1871). To which one would add the Berliner Handelsgesellschaft (a limited partnership, hence not requiring royal authorization); the Vereinsbank and the Norddeutsche Bank in Hamburg; and then, in Habsburg territory, the Vienna Creditanstalt, a fortress of Rothschild influence and initiative in central and eastern Europe (destined to a very different fate, then, from that of the Crédit Mobilier).

These became above all promoters and financiers of industrial enterprise. Traditional credit thinking looked upon such immobilizations as precarious, and indeed long-term corporate investment and instant bank liability were self-contradictory in principle. But in an expanding industrial economy, growth took care of risk, and for the longest time, these joint-stock banks prospered exceedingly. They suited Germany's business structures and possibilities and did much to lift the country to a position of industrial dominance in continental Europe.

They also gave geographical extension to the growing competition between the Rothschilds and the Pereire. Abraham Oppenheim had been one of the founding shareholders of the Crédit Mobilier, and now the Pereire and Fould returned the favor. Other countries beckoned, and the Pereire were looking for partners in Italy, Spain, Belgium, even Austria. The Rothschilds quite naturally saw these moves as a challenge to their multinational hegemony.

Vienna was like Berlin; both were capitals of major political and economic units. Given the interest of the Habsburg monarchy in economic development, the Rothschilds were called upon to finance not only railway construction but also mining and heavy industry. As in France, they had a nose for the best; in Austria, it was the Nordbahn, the railroad that would link the Habsburg domains to coal, iron, and the industries of the Zollverein. Baron Georg von Sina, banker of Greek extraction and longtime pillar of Austrian finance, joined them in this endeavor, while gaining the valuable concession for the southern line to Lombardy and the Adriatic. Good enough; but then Sina sought to embarrass the Rothschilds by accusing them of disparaging emperor and crown. Why? A desire to push them aside? Anti-Semitism? Austria-Hungary was favorable territory in that regard. Sina came to a shareholders' meeting of the Nordbahn and called on Salomon and friends to resign. That was a mistake: Salomon announced he was prepared to buy back the shares of anyone who lacked confidence in the road's future. So it was Sina and friends who lost all the votes and felt obliged to resign.

The most dramatic move of the Vienna Rothschild house was the purchase in 1842, with imperial permission, of the ironworks at Witkowitz (modern Vikovice), in Moravia, now in the Czech Republic, followed by the award of the concession for coal and iron ore in a large part of Silesia. The Witkowitz complex was Austria's reply, one generation late, to the revolution in metallurgy that Belgium and France had already accomplished: the first rolling mills came in the early 1830s; puddling and coke smelting in the 1840s; further improvements and installations in the 1850s.[37]

Salomon was following here an investment strategy that was to mark the Rothschilds throughout their history: mine, buy, and sell raw materials. Reason told them that such commodities could only get scarcer and more valuable with use and technological advance. In those early days, it was primarily coal, iron, and mercury they were after. Later on, it would be copper, rubber, oil. And gold and diamonds were always eligible: How could one go wrong? On the whole, this strategy yielded less than a more systematic and direct support of manufacturing industry might have done; but it also proved safer.

In such matters, one derived great tactical advantage from simply being Rothschild. Take oil. The bank had acquired two important concessions in the Caucasus, then found them languishing in a backwater of monumental inefficiency. Prospects were poor, the more so under an anti-Semitic tsarist regime. How to get out? Henri Deterding and Marcus Samuel, who saw a brighter future for the Caucasus field, were ready to buy them out, so long as they could pay Rothschilds with shares in two underrated European oil companies, Royal Dutch (begun in Indonesia) and Shell. Deterding and Samuel may have thought they were getting oil for paper; but in the years that followed, Royal Dutch Shell (merged 1907) became the second-largest oil conglomerate in the world; and then the Russian Revolution of 1917 effectively wiped out Western holdings in the Caucasus. Talk of luck.

In Vienna, meantime, the Habsburg emperor made an exception for Salomon Rothschild, allowing him to become a citizen of Vienna and thereby the only Jew with permission to own real property in the capital. Salomon immediately bought the Römischer Kaiser hotel, where he had worked and lived as tenant for twenty years, had it renovated completely, and had the adjoining building rebuilt as business premises. A year later he followed this with a request to buy properties in Moravia and elsewhere, promising to build schools, pay instructors, and provide low-cost housing for employees and workers. Request granted. Salomon then went on a spending spree, buying estates and castles, the better to gild his escutcheon. No use. The conservative, intolerant society of the Austrian court had no intention of admitting Jews, even Rothschilds—especially Rothschilds—to its polite circles. Whenever he could, Salomon ran off to Paris to be with his beloved daughter Betty and her husband, James, and to enjoy an openness impossible in Vienna or Moravia. Derek Wilson feels that Salomon's achievements in the face of hostility and arrogant ignorance were in many ways more impressive than those of his brothers. "Nathan and James had established their banks in the capitals of liberal and enlightened states [relatively speaking]. Salomon's successes, by contrast, had been gained only by steady, persistent pressure against the laws, customs and prejudices of an empire whose attitude toward the Jews was as antiquated as it was unyielding."[38]

Tenacity in the face of adversity is a recurring motif of dynastic enterprise. For the Rothschilds, each house was helped by support from the others. They all saw family at the heart of their interests.

Rothschilds' recognition of the usefulness of the new sector of investment banking and its success in promoting an international network of allied firms brought satisfaction and misgivings. On the one hand, the old family multinational could still see itself at the top of the financial pyramid. It was no accident that the French government turned to Rothschilds to handle the payment of the war indemnity—*les cinq milliards*—after the defeat by Germany in 1871. Who else could manage and coordinate international payments on so huge a scale? No accident that the rival firm of J[unius] S[pencer] Morgan, which had helped finance the young, post-Sedan successor regime, should find itself excluded from the really big game; or that such pushy new joint-stock banks as the Société Générale and Crédit Lyonnais should find themselves, even with French Treasury support, reduced to collecting crumbs from the banquet table.[39]

But if the indemnity loans signaled Rothschildian preeminence, they also marked a growing split within the family between the Anglo-French axis on the one hand, Prussian-Austrian on the other. This was a division not so much in business as in political interests: with the rise of Germany and the defeat of France, Europe was finding a new balance of power, one where Britain would realign its continental ties in favor of its traditional enemy, France; and this meant that Rothschilds had to share and adjust accordingly. The adjustments hurt both firm and family, but the pain was mitigated by a westward trend of family residence and personal interests. It was more fun to live in Paris than in Frankfurt or Vienna, where local branches were simply closed down.

This cooling between western and eastern branches also chilled relations with Bleichröder. As banker to Bismarck and financial representative of the triumphant Prussians in Paris indemnity negotiations, Gerson v. Bleichröder (note that "von") could not carry success lightly. The Rothschilds, used to obedience, found the new version hard to take. It is this more than anything that accounts for the otherwise surprising alliance of Rothschilds and Hansemann's Disconto-Gesellschaft: merchant bank with joint-stock bank. As Mayer Carl of the Frankfurt house put it in a letter to his cousins in London: "[Hansemann] is a *fine* and *great friend of the house,* much more so than Bleichröder who is merely a *vain* and *ambitious* fellow hunting after *personal advantages & distinctions* which may be of service to him but which cannot be of consequence *to our personal* interests."[40] That was it: banking is people.

Meanwhile the indemnity loans announced the transition to a new era. These joint-stock banks were proliferating and growing at an unmatchable rate. No help for it: economies were growing, capital was accumulating, new entries made room for themselves and took in depositors and associates far more freely than the fussy old merchant banks. In January 1871, Mayer Carl von Rothschild in Frankfurt complained about this free-and-easy approach: "All these banks are only too glad when they have an opportunity to invest money and show that they are the only parties who make loans and push us aside." And in November: "The mania for starting new banks and crédits mobiliers is becoming a regular nuisance and will no doubt end in a catastrophe, as nobody knows what all these establishments are to do with the money of subscribers."[41]

In the good old comfortable days, private bankers could sit back and let the customers come and plead. That was when Rothschilds could swing international deals by themselves and then share a little with outside houses. Now the individual Rothschild houses found they had to work things out with local or regional banks, and then maybe bring the other family houses into the action. As Frankfurt and Vienna grew relatively weaker, they found it harder to be happy with their cousins in London and Paris—in spite of all those endogamous marriages.

For the Rothschilds, the transition to more competitive banking could not have come at a worse time. The hazards of illness were cutting down the second generation of the sons of Mayer Amschel. After the death of James in 1868, the 1870s brought disaster. Among those taken: Nat, 1870; Anselm, 1874; Mayer, 1874; Anthony, 1876; Lionel, 1879. In Germany, Mayer Carl's health was declining, leaving the Frankfurt house in the hands of pious, unenterprising Wilhelm Carl. Small wonder that after the latter's death, the Rothschilds found no one to salvage a moribund ancestral post in a country whose emphasis on industrial enterprise made unlimited-liability family partnerships uncomfortably hazardous.

When it came time to renew the traditional family partnership agreement in 1905, the general feeling was that it no longer made sense. *Fini* the great achievement of Mayer Amschel and the five brothers.

But was it really over? How could this family empire close up shop? The Rothschilds owned too much, and had too many connections, to go quietly into the night. Instead, time and time again, from that point to the present day, opportunities seem to have presented themselves to the Rothschilds—and some savvy and entrepreneurial family member has always been there to capitalize.

NATHAN MAYER had given himself heart and soul to making money. His descendants, direct and collateral, worked rather to spend it—a theme we shall see repeat itself for many of the great dynasties. But unlike many of the great dynasties where the offspring begin to stray, many Rothschilds remained powerful in the business world. It is as if they possessed a secret genetic gift for making money.

Fortunately, because it was so easy now to sleep on the fruits of success. Founder Mayer Amschel would never have understood the unbusinesslike diversion of some of his descendants, the carefree cultivation of eccentricity and personal interests. The old devotion was gone. Partners kept odd hours, did not turn up at the office until near noon, ate lunch, napped, then went to club or home. In the office, technicians and money managers patiently awaited their pleasure. Listen to Batsheva de Rothschild, née Bethsabée, who described her father Edouard (1868–1949), son of Alphonse, as "one of the last gentlemen of the century, with a highly developed sense of honour"; and his son Guy, who said of him that he was a man caught between the old Europe and the new, a man happier watching his horses race than sitting at his desk in the rue Laffitte. Meanwhile those Rothschilds who had lost patience for office discipline and duty devoted themselves to hobbies and play, to love and dalliance, to good causes such as Jewish emancipation and Zionist Palestine, or to such other kinds of business as viticulture and oenology. Wines paid, especially good wines.

Take the Maurician line of the family. Maurice (1881–1957), black sheep of the Paris branch, bank dodger but not draft dodger, was eventually excluded from the family and participation in de

Rothschild Frères (he never wanted it anyway), perhaps because of persistent unlucky speculations, perhaps because of told and untold sexual escapades.[42] One cousin remembers his chasing her around a table; she was fifteen and he forty-two.[43] Remember, of course, that in the Rothschild family, cousins were fair marital game.

Maurice spent the Second World War in the United States. Vichy France was not healthy for Jews, let alone Rothschilds, but Maurice got out with a fortune in gems sewn into his satchel and, speculating on scarce commodities, did so well that he may have been the richest member of the family when he died.[44] That's the advantage of having piles of money: lose a fortune, win a fortune. But remember to quit when you're ahead.

Maurice's son Edmond outdid his father, perhaps because his mother was a Pereire (the family of James's old rivals), so that he had business genes plus money on both sides. He was a youth of twenty when World War II ended, and decided that the way to more wealth was to follow his likes. That's not banking; that's entrepreneurship. He liked travel and tourism, had a friend who had moved into a new kind of organized tourism, and with him and others developed the Club Méditerranée: *gentils membres, gentils moniteurs,* sun, sand, and sex. He invested in resort hotels and bungalows, housing complexes in Paris, chalets and ski lifts in the Alps, frozen food, trailers, toys—all the amusements and conveniences of rising incomes and economic growth. Any one of these ventures would have crowned a life of achievement. With all this, he needed business headquarters and banks in Geneva and Paris, plus holding and investment companies. The man was a winner.

Or take his cousin Henri (1872–1947), also French but of British descent (great-grandson of Nathan Mayer). Henri was brilliant, versatile, focused, and unfocused. He took a medical degree, specialized in pediatrics, started his own hospital (not so big as the one financed by James in 1852), built a private laboratory, published more than a hundred articles on pasteurization and infant nutrition, did work on radioactivity, helped found the Fondation Curie. At the same time, he became a passionate devotee of the new motor sports and built a factory to make vans and taxis, and ambulances during the Great War under the brand name Unic. He also invented a burns unit that could be brought into the battle zone. Also airtight tubes to keep soldiers' rations such as meat paste and jam fresh and clean. And he still found time to organize a free wartime distribution of pasteurized milk in Paris. He also brought out a new toilet soap called Monsavon and an excellent mustard, both of which are still around, both winners. And while he was at it, he wrote plays under the nom de plume André Pascal, and built the Pigalle theater to show them. And there and elsewhere he met beautiful actresses and starlets whom he sailed around the Mediterranean in his pointedly named yacht, the *Eros*. He also introduced Diaghilev's Ballets Russes to Paris and financed the brilliant performances of Nijinsky and Pavlova. He traveled much and comfortably: we have a photo of him posing triumphantly on the corpse (?) of a crocodile in the British Sudan.[45]

And while he was at it, he fathered a son, Philippe (1902–1988), who himself made history in film production (the media are the most rewarding and pleasurable diversion of rich heirs) and developed the Mouton claret as competitor to the Rothschild family's Château Lafite. Philippe, like his father, was a potent wencher. He writes that his "adventures" were curtailed by his wife's final illness: "a few lady journalists conveniently around, a willing Swede in the snow, this and that . . ."[46] Curtailed?

Remember Philippe? He wrote that he had never thought of himself as Jewish, or even as a Rothschild. Should we believe him? It is not clear that he even believed himself. "Is that true?" he wrote in his autobiography. Reading the page again, I wonder. We often deny the truths that deep down mean most to us. The French knew who he was. The banks that lent him money for the development of his vineyard knew who he was. The Germans who pursued the family, killed his wife in a concentration camp, and occupied the vineyard in World War II knew who he was. He fed his dog steak on a silver dish. He knew who he was.

But he had lost the sense of religious significance and identity.

His first wife was the Comtesse de Chambure, of an old French Catholic family, so confident of her status that she voluntarily returned to a Paris under German occupation. The countess did not like the idea of flight. How could she? Why should she? "I am a Frenchwoman. Why should I leave my country?" The Germans arrested her and shipped her along with hundreds of Jews to the death camp at Ravensbrück, where she was savagely beaten and thrown alive into the incinerator.

When Philippe married his second wife, he chose Pauline Potter of Baltimore, designer for Hattie Carnegie in Paris, self-made orphan of a disastrous union. Faith and ritual did not matter; as they did not in his numerous flirtations and *pirouettes d'amour*. This man, we saw, boasted of his sexual appetite, especially after his release from prison, where he had been held by order of Vichy as Jew and resistant: "I fell in love eight times a day."

Religion? Forget it. What has religion to do with love or sex? There was Marinetta, once a princess, now demoted to countess. She took him around to all the churches in Italy, prayed for his soul. "You must forget about being a Jew," she told him. [We call this tolerance, or maybe solicitude.] "Well," Philippe replies, "I can't forget being a Rothschild, or that it was my ancestor Kalman who saved the Pope's finances. He was allowed to kiss the Pope's hand."—"Not the hand. The ring. Nobody ever kisses the Pope's hand."—"Well," says Philippe, "seeing as Kalman rescued the kingdom of Naples, drained the Tuscan marshes, and repaired half the Roman roads in Italy, I guess the Pope didn't mind what he kissed."

Marinetta found the whole relationship frustrating. She thought she was saving him; instead, found him irretrievably Jewish. He was, she said, like the rest of his people: "stiff necked, cussed and proud. Why couldn't [they] eat pork chops and settle down?"

Philippe's differences with his larger family found expression in his campaign to get his own wine, Château Mouton Rothschild, reclassified as a *premier cru,* on a par with the preeminent Château Lafite-Rothschild, purchased by James and now managed by Elie and later Eric de Rothschild. The Lafite clan looked down on Philippe and

Mouton. To them, he was a wine merchant with a single vintage, a dealer, whereas they were cultivators, seigneurs who did wine along with other things, different qualities of wine, including the one unbeatable, incomparable, ineffable Lafite, *grand cru* going back to the eighteenth century. All of which made Philippe the more determined to affirm his right to stand on the topmost level, to assert his ability to market different qualities of a preeminent vintage. Of course, the list of *premiers crus* was normally given alphabetically, which put Mouton after Lafite; and while he could persuade state authorities to promote his wine, he could hardly get them to change the order of the alphabet.

Through all these diversions, the heart of the family has remained the bank, now reduced to the branches in London and Paris. The former is the more important, partly because its activity has never been interrupted, essentially because it operates in the bigger financial center, the most important in Europe. There is now a branch in the United States, in New York, which is managed by Gerald Rosenfeld, formerly with Lazard, a nonmember of the family. (In general, the Rothschilds have become so accustomed to European ways that American culture and manners rub them the wrong way.) And Edmond, who is an authentic Rothschild, has founded his own Swiss bank, which he runs apart from the family firm.

For the Rothschilds, banking is still a family business.[47] The family remains a dynasty. The name spells wealth, dignity, and the highest connections. The structure of the business has changed repeatedly over the past century, with new firms taking over selected assets and focusing each on its own line of activity. All of that means jobs for descendants and in-laws, who are tested and chosen for higher responsibilities as openings appear. The old Jewish ties have loosened considerably, at least in terms of observance; but the Jewish identification remains, and the Jewish community will not give up or release its princes. It needs them now, as much or more than it did more than 150 years ago.

The family ties are as strong as ever. When the London family found itself running out of interested and willing talent toward the end of the millennium—in particular when Evelyn and Jacob, alias Lord Rothschild, split over the desirability of an injection of outside capital (a sure formula for the end of a family firm)—London turned to Paris for reinforcement. Evelyn saw himself approaching retirement and asked David, head of the Paris branch, to succeed him. As Evelyn said to a London *Times* reporter in 1996, "The first important strength of the family is unity. As you sit here and you talk to me, you are talking to David, and if you talk to David, you are talking to me."

This is one talented and remarkably influential family, and banking and finance would be much the poorer without it. It can look back on 250 years of success, the work of half a dozen generations. The more recent descendants have been lured into all manner of entrepreneurial diversions and recreations, but a central core of bankers remains, persistent and tenacious. To be sure, Rothschilds can no longer keep up with the big joint-stock banks in capital and coverage. But for many people, an account with this spectacular family bank is in itself evidence of credit and distinction. Name matters. Family matters.

The Rothschild family is perhaps the most important and tenacious dynasty in modern business history. Only a few royal dynasties have shown as much persistence across centuries, and these have enjoyed far less power and opportunity to shape events. Now the English branch, in recognition of its historic role and the obligations that entails and implies, has created an archive to assemble and make available papers and records to scholars and researchers. The head of the archive for many years was Victor Gray, now replaced by Melanie Aspey. The family representative is Emma Rothschild (b. 1948), herself a professional historian, daughter of Victor Rothschild and his second wife, Teresa Mayor. When one recalls how reticent business firms have traditionally been, how reluctant to open their papers to outsiders, one can only admire and congratulate such enlightenment.

Three

THE MORGANS

FROM FAMILY DYNASTY TO THE
PARTNERSHIP OF STRANGERS

JOHN PIERPONT MORGAN, SR. (1837–1913)

*T*he Morgans offered a very different response to success and growth from that of the Rothschilds. The latter, we saw, insisted that their bank be an exclusively family enterprise—no outside partners—and have held to that. The Morgans, we shall see, were not numerous enough to do that; nor did they see outside partners as intruders. On the contrary, they needed them. The result was a family bank that moved on to a mix of family control and partnership management and from there to a Morgan-less managerial corporation.

The Barings began in England as middling cloth merchants.

The Rothschilds began in Frankfurt as omnibus traders and dealers. The Morgans went back in the New World to a young Welshman who came to Boston in 1636 and moved west to a place newly named Springfield, where he and descendants farmed land and raised cattle, but then went on to richer, urban activities in the early nineteenth century. The grandfather of John Pierpont, Joseph Morgan, left the land to turn hotelier in Hartford, with an array of business interests conceived and lubricated with divers liquids and liquors: thus a lucrative tavern (the Exchange Coffee House), a canal company, steamboats, and the railway from Hartford to Springfield, later a link in the line from New York to Boston. Joseph bought real estate and was one of the founders of the Aetna Fire Insurance Company. Active in politics and the Congregational Church, he made personal and business connections in every direction.[1] He gave up the coffeehouse for the larger City Hotel, bought another hostelry in New Haven, borrowed from banks—he was not afraid of debt—and lent to private parties.

Most important, he put his son Junius Spencer into trade. Junius began in Hartford with a firm called Howe and Mather, but a decade later, after his father's death in 1847—Joseph left an estate of over a million dollars, figure forty to fifty million of our money—Junius went after bigger game up Boston way. Some seven years later, in 1854, he would move to London and send son John Pierpont to school in France and Germany. This deviant, untypical breakout from local to regional to national to international over the course of generations was the building of a global family fortune.

Still, as we know, one can lose as well as win in trade, and the Morgans joined luck to judgment, nerve, and inherited wealth. The Hartford house of Howe and Mather traded in raw materials and dealt in dry goods, linking the regional economy of western New England and upper New York state to Boston at one end, and to New Orleans at the other. From the beginning, junior partner Junius had far-reaching aspirations, which he couched in familial terms: he would build a dynasty. His models were Barings and Rothschilds—family as performance and assurance. Junius had two sons; the three daughters didn't count for banking purposes, rather for well-calculated matrimony (another form of business). But Junius, Jr., died at age twelve, leaving only the younger boy, John Pierpont, as the focus of Junius, Sr.'s hope.

Junius sent the lad to elite private schools, the better to learn and meet. The youngster was big for his age and thin for his height, what the French call a *force de la nature*. He more than held his own with his classmates, but his health left much to be desired, and work had to be compensated by intervals of recovery and repose. Alternance was to become the pattern of his life: fierce spells of activity followed by long vacations and months of travel. J. Pierpont was no Weberian Calvinist. Banking does not require unremitting application, at least not at the level of negotiation. But associates must be available to help around the clock and calendar and take charge during absences. Some of these associates might be appointed partner, that is, might receive remuneration in the form of a percentile share of firm income. Very different, remember, from the Rothschildian structure, where partnership was reserved for members of the family.

Four years after grandfather Joseph's death in 1847, father Junius cashed in his share in Howe and Mather for $600,000 (no small sum) and took up partnership in Boston in a firm now to be called J. M. Beebe, Morgan and Company—the same trading business but bigger scale: import, export (cotton especially), endorsing and discounting of commercial paper. And it was there that he came to the attention of George Peabody, also American but a merchant banker of London.

This was a great opportunity, not only because Peabody's was a leading house in Anglo-American trade, but because Peabody himself was approaching retirement and wanted to devote himself to good deeds. He needed help: someone to run the office, supervise the accounts and collections. He ran into Junius Morgan in various transactions, liked what he saw, offered him a partnership in 1854. Very quickly, Junius found himself in charge, and when Peabody retired ten years later, in 1864, the firm became J. S. Morgan and

Company. We are told that Junius expected under the terms of the partnership to keep the name Peabody, and that Peabody's refusal was a bitter disappointment. But here Junius erred on the side of modesty, for the name of Morgan soon eclipsed in reputation and wealth that of the founding partner.

Histories of the house of Morgan tend to glide too quickly over the career of Junius. And yet it was he who won the family place and fame in international banking. Chance played a role here, too. In 1870, Otto von Bismarck, chancellor of Prussia and key figure in the emerging German federation, lured a proud and stupid emperor of France into war. The French lost. The emperor was captured. End of empire. A new, provisional government was formed, and it needed money. Driven from Paris to Tours, it could not get gold or cash from the vaults of the Bank of France.

Where to get it? The leading British bankers, including Barings and Rothschilds, had little faith in this opportunistic French political creation; even less in its readiness and ability to reimburse creditors. The Rothschilds, with branches in adversarial Frankfurt and Paris, were further torn between national loyalties, and thought better, especially in the face of Bismarck's hostility, than to help the French before the conclusion of some kind of peace treaty. It was at this point that J. S. Morgan and Company stepped forward and agreed to underwrite a loan. Junius and colleagues had done research and found that despite numerous changes in regime, France had never repudiated a debt. The loan was issued at a substantial discount of 15 percent below par, not unreasonable for a defeated nation and callow promoters. Yet the French were incensed and wounded: those were terms, they felt, better suited to perennial debtor nations. So much the better for the underwriters, who needed all the margin they could get.

Then the proclamation of the Paris Commune, with its disagreeable odor of radical extremism, sent the price down another 25 percent, and Junius found himself buying bonds madly to support the price. But then—such are the turns of fate—the French did him a huge favor. Furious to see their credit impugned, they brought out a liberation loan in 1873 and prepaid the older bonds at par. Junius made a fortune from this unanticipated windfall—some £1.5 million or 450 million dollars in today's money. Like the Rothschilds after the Napoleonic wars, he now felt himself a legitimately important player in international finance. And like the Rothschilds then, he found the old-timers, beginning now with the Rothschilds, unwilling to concede status to this brash and embarrassing newcomer. Morgan's, especially son Pierpont, was vexed and unforgiving. In the meantime, Morgan's intrusion was a salutary lesson to the older private merchant houses of the *haute banque internationale*. The latter understood now that they were not alone, that banking was getting crowded, especially now that joint-stock commercial banks such as the Société Générale and the Crédit Lyonnais were also entering the fray.

Junius S. Morgan continued to thrive by doing business with American exporters and importers. Much of this rise was the work of son John Pierpont, now graduating from apprenticeship to active management. The young man had from the start a keen head for business, to the point where Junius himself found his son's push and hustle hard to take, and was unsparing in his cautions and advice. How J.P. took all this is hard to say, because in 1911 he burned thirty years of intimate letters to his father. (When his father was alive, J.P. actually stayed in the office two evenings a week to catch—receive and send—the transatlantic post.) In the meantime, Junius did his best to provide his enterprising son with experienced guidance and working connections. No sooner had old man Peabody retired in 1864 than Junius helped arrange a business marriage for J.P. with Charles Dabney, thirty years J.P.'s senior. The new firm of Dabney, Morgan and Co. would serve as the dynasty's New York agents.

Junius was a tough act to follow. The father was determined to shape the son to the highest standards. His technique was to scold and chastise—and give no praise. (Not very different from N. M. Rothschild.) And J.P. exerted himself to meet these boundless demands, driving himself to fatigue, depression, even physical illness.

Needless to say, he relieved himself by transferring responsibilities to others. If he was going to meet these expectations, others would have to follow suit.

But not even his father could keep J.P. in line. A business report by R. C. Dun of later Dun and Bradstreet spoke of J.P.'s "peculiar brusqueness of manner" and of the unhappy effect of this haughty behavior. The word "brusque" appears in other documents, perhaps in imitation of the Dun report, perhaps because of its accuracy and appropriateness. Lots of people did not like Morgan's. J.P. would not haggle, and he dealt with others on a take-it-or-leave-it basis. Biographer Ron Chernow describes him as a "young moralist turned despot."

J.P. found it hard to find collaborators; no one was good enough. Only as the decades passed did the firm take its eventual form: a family bank administered by outside/inside managers—a mix of the traditional and new. Throughout, J.P. continued to call the tune. When he saw a man he wanted as partner and offered him the post, he would not take no for an answer. In one instance, he recruited a lawyer at the funeral of the lawyer's predecessor, making his presence at the ceremony serve two purposes. He terrified his associates, scared them to death. Lincoln Steffens, the investigative journalist, said that these partners did not dare go near J.P. unless summoned, and then dashed in and out like office boys. Hours at Morgan's exceeded normal endurance. The house was known as a partner killer, but it was worth it: Pierpont made them all wealthy beyond their dreams.

By the 1870s, it was J.P. in New York who was setting the tone for the Morgans' banking multinational. Junius in London was delighted to see himself accepted by Rothschilds and to join with them in business ventures. J.P. was less pleased. He thought his father too ready to accept favors and condescension. He wrote his brother-in-law Walter Burns, now Junius's partner in London, in January 1879: "I need scarcely tell you that having anything to with Rothschild's and Belmont in this matter is extremely unpalatable to us and I would give almost anything if they were out. The whole treatment of Rothschild's to all the party, from Father downwards, is such, as to my mind, no one should stand."[2] (J.P. almost surely thought of Belmont as still Jewish. So much for conversion.) In the meantime, J.P. learned to work with the Rothschilds in Anglo-American matters, as bank undertakings required. He could always blame such association on his father.

Rothschilds and Belmont, we may recall, were a reluctant, unhappy collaboration, and the Rothschilds, with their European snobbery, had missed the American boat. Junius Morgan, with his son's firm in New York, had not—could not—but then he found himself yielding priority to J.P. and American ventures. This frontier nation was a different world: large scale, full of business syndicates, monopolistic. And J.P. was just the man to find the funds and take these things in hand.

J.P. was physically big, aggressive, demanding, and he passed his own attitudes on to others. No point in playing the virtuous one with him; as he once put it, "A man always has two reasons for the things he does—a good one and the real one."[3] Charles Schwab, president of U.S. Steel, went to Monte Carlo with Baron Henri de Rothschild, to gamble and play around. Virtuous Andrew Carnegie was scandalized. George Perkins, J.P.'s right-hand man—the first of what would be a series of indispensable, managerial partners—told Schwab to ignore such sanctimony and to have a good time. He was speaking here for his boss. J.P. himself adored the ladies, made merry, gave generous gifts. One chorus girl bragged to another, "I got a pearl out of a fresh oyster at Shankley's." "That's nothing," said her friend, "I got a whole diamond necklace out of an old lobster."[4]

The old lobster had been born at a good time. The American economy took off after the Civil War, thriving on territorial expansion, renewed trade with Europe, and the technological beginnings of a second industrial revolution. At the heart of this growth were the railroads (seventy-five thousand new miles in the 1880s alone), which linked the two coasts and opened up an enormous frontier, and steam navigation, along with a new chemical industry and the merest beginnings of electricity.[5] The Morgan bank cultivated railway promotion in particular. It also saw oceanic transport as a field of opportunity, putting together in 1900–1902 a shipping combine, the International Mercantile Marine Company (IMM), whose most spectacular achievement was the construction a decade later of the legendary *Titanic*.

Linked to both transport sectors was iron and steel, and it was Morgan's that in 1901 put together U.S. Steel, a coalition of some fifteen integrated combines built around the Andrew Carnegie Homestead, Pennsylvania, plant and attached interests. This was then the largest combine in the world, capitalized at $1.4 billion. Morgan's did this because Carnegie was responding to moves by other steel works, some of them linked to Morgan's, by integrating backward and forward; and Carnegie could undersell those other mills. Morgan's wanted to allay this potential competition, and it just so happened that Carnegie was in the mood to listen: he had reached the point where he wanted to devote himself to spending rather than making money, for worthy causes of course.

This transaction left Carnegie feeling proud: "It takes a Yankee to beat a Jew and it takes a Scot to beat a Yankee." But it left J.P. disliking Andrew Carnegie, the more so as a prudish Carnegie vocally disapproved of J.P.'s free-and-easy lifestyle. Inevitably Carnegie came to feel that he'd sold too cheaply. The two men later met on shipboard, and Carnegie told Morgan he should have asked for a hundred million more; to which Morgan gave a put-down reply: "And you would have got it."[6]

J.P. had one great strength: he had a feel for new technologies and the business opportunities they created. It was not an accident that in 1892 he formed the General Electric Company, leader in the new industry along with Westinghouse. Henry Villard, president of Edison Electric, had come to him for help in taking over Edison's company. This was a mistake: Morgan was not by nature a helper; he was a driver. He arranged a counter-coup with the Thompson-Houston Electric Company to take over Edison, then asked Villard for his resignation. Thomas Edison himself made a few million by the deal, which made him happy enough. He wanted to go back to research anyway.

Whether these sectoral choices were the result of coincidence (right place, right time, or wrong place, wrong time) or careful analysis is hard to say. What is clear is that, so doing, Morgan's avoided unnecessary conflict with the London Rothschilds, with their strong preference for government loans and their distaste for what they deemed industrial speculation.

In general, this half-century between the American Civil War and World War I saw a revolution in finance and banking that pushed many of the old warhorses to the side and brought new contestants to the fore. The newcomers included newly rich individuals, sometimes people who had amassed wealth because of personal connections in exotic lands and then returned to Western Europe looking for investments. Among the most prominent: Ernest Cassel, good friend of the British royal family; Baron Maurice de Hirsch; Saemy Japhet; Jacob Schiff. Some of these never entered banks; their money did the talking, and the banks handled it for them.[7] Others, such as Schiff or, later on, André Mayer, took over established firms and transformed them.

Meanwhile, the typical turnover of merchant banks continued. Every crisis brought its array of losers, its family splits, its personal secessions. Every boom brought in newcomers: Seligman, Goldman Sachs, Lehman, Lazarus. Like the older houses, these typically had their specialties of trade and geographical purview, their preferred allies and collaborators. Their multiplication reflected the needs and opportunities of growth and globalization. (They did not call it that then, but that is exactly what was going on.)

Such elements of novelty did not entail a systemic transformation; rather a change in the dramatis personae. But as we have seen in the Rothschild story, the appearance of joint-stock banks, with and without limited liability, promised/threatened a revolution.

Banking, after all, was traditionally a private, personal business. People with money or access thereto lent it to those who needed it, and made money thereby. A few banks, typically national and central in scope, were organized as joint-stock entities, usually with limited liability for inactive investors or for all participants. Such firms usually required governmental authorization and were constrained by custom and expectation to such relatively safe activities as re-discount and limited-note issue. As of the 1870s, such firms could push their way into the profitable sphere of state finance—but only so far. The older merchant houses occupied the strategic positions because they enjoyed personal connections to men of state and power. The French liberation loans of 1872 and 1873 were the testing ground of the old and new financial powers, just as the liberation loans of 1817 and 1818 had been in their day, and now as then, the old private banks (Rothschilds and company) won handily.

Yet now as then, the victory was something of a nostalgic consolation. The joint-stock banks continued their rise, the more so as their hospitality to small depositors brought them further usable funds; while the merchant banks, however rich and well connected, succumbed to the diversions and temptations of success. Partners died or retired; heirs found more congenial uses for their money, the more so as they found it possible to sell out to the joint-stock banks. This was especially true in Germany, where rapid industrialization, new technologies, increasing scale, and overall growth enabled the bigger joint-stock banks (the so-called universal banks) to combine successfully the prudence of commercial banking with the risks and rewards of investment banking. And similarly in the United States, rich in space, land, industrial resources. By the turn of the century, Morgan's found itself an exceptional example of successful private banking, in part because of opportune alliances with such corporate firms as the First National Bank and the New York Life Insurance Company; and engaged in friendly (?) competition with the Rockefeller group: Standard Oil, James Stillman of the National City Bank, Jacob Schiff of the firm Kuhn, Loeb, and Edward Harriman.

Life insurance provided particularly important support. These companies were overstuffed cashboxes, full of money from patient waiters on death and only too happy to join in investment projects. At the turn of the century, their assets were growing rapidly—from $1.7 billion in 1900 to $2.7 billion in 1905. Clearly, new patterns of saving were taking hold. In the United States, nearly half of the latter sum was held by the top three companies: Mutual of New York, Equitable, and New York Life, and these firms and others were looking for banks, especially such cozy private houses as Morgan's, to serve as links to securities-issuing corporations. Sometimes, as with George Perkins of New York Life and Morgan's, the same person served both sides. These businessmen had no trouble with this double duty, saw no conflict of interest. On the contrary, they preferred cooperation to competition and acted as though there were nothing to defend or explain. But these sweetheart arrangements troubled government officials, so that in 1906 the New York legislature, followed by other states, prohibited life insurance companies from underwriting the sale or purchase of securities, barred them from investing in common stock and collateral trust bonds, and prohibited their officials from taking a personal interest in the financial transactions of their firms.[8]

Life insurance behavior was only one of several areas in which the growing size and power of business enterprise clashed with political populism. Matters came to a head during the administration of Theodore Roosevelt, scion of a long line of Dutch landed gentry on the shores of the Hudson, alpinist, adventurer, politician, organizer and leader of the regiment of volunteer cavalry known as the Rough Riders, governor of New York State, vice president under McKinley and successor to the presidency upon McKinley's assassination in September 1901, a man as versatile and proactive in politics as J.P. was in business. Teddy was the leader of the campaign to assert government control over big business, to defend the natural environment, to tame the plutocracy; whereas J.P. promoted and financed mergers, acquisitions, and similar scenarios of business versatility, concentration, and collaborative exploitation. For J.P., trees were there for the cutting, land for the digging. The two men, for all they had in common socially, were bound to clash.[9]

Ironically, the clash came to a head when J.P. reached the peak of his stature and power, when, in response to the financial crisis of

1907, he led the small group of entrepreneurs and enterprises that sustained and saved those companies whose loss of credit threatened to unleash a general panic. It was J.P., George Baker of the First National Bank, and James Stillman of National City Bank who summoned the lesser lights and put together the emergency cash and credits needed to still the fears; and it was J.P. especially whose prestige and financial ingenuity carried the day. No one refused his invitation, and hardly anyone turned down his advice. His style was not to negotiate but rather to set the task, suggest a solution, and let the principals thrash matters out while he played with his rarities and antiquities.

On these last, J.P. was, even as a student, a collector of objets d'art, of memorabilia. And when he became a hugely wealthy banker, there was no holding him back. For one thing, these rare and beautiful objects were tickets of contact with and access to people of the highest rank and status. No one would refuse an invitation to see and touch. To be sure, William Valentiner, the Metropolitan Museum of Art's first curator of decorative arts, did not agree. J.P., he said, did not need this kind of boost: he was already a member of the elite, had wide-ranging artistic and antiquarian interests, and did not go after the most popular collection items, namely, oils. And insofar as he did acquire paintings, he liked the less fashionable masterpieces of the early Renaissance. The man had esoteric tastes. Moreover, he was not merely a collector; he was a connoisseur, and in matters of value and authenticity, he knew more than most of the professionals.

He started with books, manuscripts, letters. Then coins, tapestries, fabrics (crimson damask from the Chigi palace in Rome), gold and silver vessels, ivory pieces, jades, porcelains, enamels, pottery, bronzes, armor, paintings. Napoleon's watch, Catherine the Great's snuffbox, Leonardo da Vinci's notebooks, Shakespeare first folios. And on and on. He did not like to dicker. What worked in business would work with art. How much? Add 10 or 15 percent, and that was that. Early on, he decided that he had to buy full collections in order to have the collection of collections. He had his passions of the moment—now Greek, now Egyptian, now Renaissance. He hired agents and stationed them strategically for long periods, the better to get what came along. *Carpe diem, carpe rem.* He printed lavish, gilt-encrusted catalogs and sent copies to European royalty to let them know that the United States and capitalism had produced, or at least had acquired, their equal.[10]

BACK TO BANKING AND POLITICS, with one more example of "Morganatic" leadership. At the end of this eventful October 1907, New York City found itself so short of funds that it could not meet its payroll—in effect, it found itself within forty-eight hours of bankruptcy. This, on top of a local banking crisis, could mean general disaster. Once more, Morgan into the breach. The answer at first approximation had New York City issuing bonds; but then, who would buy them? It was J.P. who found a solution. The banks in the syndicate would buy the bonds, turn them over to the Clearing House, which would pay for them by issuing certificates, which would be credited to the city's accounts at the First National and the National City banks; and so the banks would remain liquid and the city could pay its bills. This still left Morgan's feeling that some way should be found to bring in cash from abroad, preferably in the form of gold. England proved a dry well, with the Bank of England determined to keep gold from leaving, in spite of appeals and pressure by Morgan's and Rothschilds. So Jack Morgan, Pierpont's son, was sent to Paris to tap the Banque de France. His efforts met with disappointment: the Banque wanted the U.S. Treasury to guarantee the loan. But at this point the Treasury did step in and issued bonds and certificates that could back new issues of banknotes. The money supply eased.

The crisis was over. The whole thing was an exercise in the value of collaboration in the pursuit of obvious goals. But such collaboration is not to be taken for granted. As we have seen, it takes leadership. Some cynics would say that no good deed goes unpunished. The very success of J.P. and consorts' efforts troubled those who saw here proof of the power of money and its alliances. These early years of the new century saw a renewal of attacks on the "money trust" by writers and politicians. Collaboration between Morgan's and Rothschilds in defending the dollar encouraged anti-Semitic attacks, by farmers particularly, denouncing President Cleveland as a tool of "Jewish bankers and British gold." In a speech to Congress, William Jennings Bryan asked the clerk to read Shylock's bond from *The Merchant of Venice*. The historian Richard Hofstadter has described these attacks as paranoid. I would think "alarmist" or "alarmed" more accurate, because some of these concerns were not without basis in fact. I am referring here to bank power, not to anti-Jewish prejudice. Bank power was indeed a potential weapon against people and democracy—powerful and irresponsible.

Congress decided in 1912 on a committee of inquiry, called the Pujo inquiry after the committee's chairman, Democratic congressman Arsène Pujo. The chief interrogator, Samuel Untermyer, himself a successful investor and speculator, had made his fortune and would now redeem himself by disarming and discrediting the villains. The exchanges between him and J.P., it must be said, verge on the ludicrous—like something out of Edward Lear's nonsense poem "The Owl and the Pussycat"—two people talking past each other. They both speak English, but they are located in separate realms of discourse. Biographer Chernow speaks of J.P. as "spouting gibberish." It was more and less than that. Example: Untermyer wants to get J.P. to admit that the power to name boards of directors for one-year terms makes it impossible for those directors to act independently. J.P. dismisses this, with phony politeness: "My experience is quite otherwise, sir." Untermyer cannot believe his ears. "Really?"

"Yes, sir."

"The people who name the board have less power than those who have no part of naming them?"

"Very much so, sir."[11]

The same for Untermyer's assumptions that combination and concentration spelled control, or that Morgan's exercised great power. J.P. told him, for example, that he preferred competition. (In fact, he had long done his best to avoid or prevent competition, in railway construction especially—too many wasted resources.)

"Even if a potential competitor to U.S. Steel appeared on the scene?"

"Yes."

"You would welcome competition?"

"I would welcome competition."

"The more of it the better?"

"Yes . . ."

And further: "You admit you have [vast power]?"

"I do not think I have."

"You do not feel it at all?"

"No, I do not feel it at all . . ."

"You do not think you have any power in any department or industry?"

"I do not."

"Not the slightest?"

"Not the slightest."

And further: "Your firm is run by you, is it not?"

"No, sir."

"It is not?"

"No, sir."

"You are the final authority, are you not?"

"No, sir."

Lies? Denial? Mockery? Or offhand dismissal? I can say anything I please, even arrant, manifest nonsense. Or more than one of these? J.P. left the witness stand thinking he had done well, that he had shown up and put down that insolent ass of a prosecutor. And many of his banker friends seem to have agreed with him; at least that's what they said. But J.P. was left exhausted, and the bankers had lost the argument. Congress and the government saw them as the major force for destruction of competition, for they wanted and worked for order and stability in every industry they handled.[12] The result of the inquiry was a sequence of laws and administrative decrees designed to save the United States from private salvation à la Morgan et Cie, the most important of which was the introduction of the Federal Reserve System by act of December 1913.

J.P. felt burned out, and he prepared to take one of those European-Nilotic yacht trips that had always done so much to revive him. The ocean crossings alone afforded weeks of peace, homage, and stimulation. In a conversation with George Baker before leaving, he asked his old friend to assume the role of final pundit in the event that he, J.P., did not return. He was not feeling well. And indeed, his premonitions were justified: he made some of the sightseeing excursions he so much enjoyed but found himself worn by alternating moods of nervous fatigue and misleading revival. Going up the Nile in early February 1913, he suffered an acute breakdown. A physician friend, Dr. Moses Allen Starr, found him very tired mentally and physically but felt confident that these symptoms would pass. If the aim was to use encouragement as medicine, it did not work: J.P. kept going downhill, and in a characteristically moribund reaction, he stopped eating. On March 31, 1913, he died in his sleep.

His family, colleagues, and the media attributed his death to the Pujo inquiry and the Untermyer interrogation. His physicians insisted he had no organic problems, only a deep loss of nervous vitality that had robbed him of his powers of recuperation. As his protégé-partner Thomas Lamont put it a quarter-century later, his illness came "out of a seemingly clear sky" and he died "from no particular malady."[13] However discreet his illness, though, his death was an affair of state. The greatest nations and most powerful institutions vied to honor his memory and to facilitate the transport and interment of his remains.

J.P.'s diversions, combined with British obligations, health problems, and an addiction to long, educative vacations, posed a problem to bank management. Who would take charge while the boss was away? He had to find family partners or collaborators, and the latter were presumably abler, and easier to handle. To be sure, J.P.'s sense of dynasty and continuity made him save a special place for Jack, Jr. But there was no way Jack could handle everything, and from early on, J.P. was appointing as partners those people he saw as suitable. He was an elitist in these matters, and his taste took hold with his successors. As one observer put it:

Everything there must be in good taste. They have exquisite taste as people, in conduct, in personal appearance, in clothes, in the appearance of the offices, in the artwork. . . . People at Morgan are well groomed, not like those at IBM or Merrill Lynch, where it is a result of deliberateness, but rather by birth. They pride themselves on not being *nouveaux riches* like some of their competitors. . . . Until recently, and even now, Morgan people were not interested in money, but in elegance of conduct.[14]

And not only by birth. J.P. liked people from good schools, but he had no objection to self-made men, so long as they had the right looks and manners. George Perkins was one of these. He had made his name in insurance, then come over to Morgan's at J.P.'s invitation. So far as one can tell, he did an uneven job as banker, but a good job as promoter of social causes dear to the boss's heart. Perkins comes down to us as the man who met and rebuffed a "visionary nitwit" named William Durant. Durant wanted financing for car manufacture and told Perkins in 1907 that one day soon there would be as many as fifty thousand autos on American roads. Shouting "Impossible!" Perkins drove the fool from his office. Big blunder number one. So Durant went to the banker Seligman, who accepted his fees in General Motors stock and saw that stock rise to $850 a share by the end of World War I. J.P. would not have made this mistake.[15]

Thomas W. Lamont was another of J.P.'s choices. He was a young and promising banking exec when J.P. invited him to become a partner in Morgan's.

"What could I do for you?" Lamont asked.

"Oh, you'll find plenty to keep you busy. Just do whatever needs to be done."

Lamont saw this as a blue-ribbon opportunity but told J.P. he wanted the permission of his boss and sponsor, George F. Baker. Sure, said J.P. I've already discussed the matter with him. That was the way J.P. made such moves: the ground was already prepared.

Lamont had noticed that many Morgan partners worked very

hard when necessary, but took long vacations. He wanted to do the same and raised the subject with some trepidation; he wanted three months a year. Why, of course, came the answer. Take as much time as you like. J.P. suggested a trip to Egypt. "Charter a boat and spend a few weeks on the Nile. You'll want to go again and again."

"But the kids: we have four children."

"Nonsense, take along a couple of nurses and you'll be all right. That's what I did with my children when they were young."[16]

Other partners worked around the calendar. They enjoyed their jobs and had no desire to take three months off. J.P. gave them their head. It took all kinds to make a working bank. And it took an especially loyal crew to make a working bank an expression of personal family enterprise.

RETURNING TO BUSINESS: the ejection by Perkins of Will Durant might well have come down to us as one of the greatest business blunders on record. Durant, we shall see, was onto something monumental: the manufacture, not of a standardized auto model like the Ford, but of a range of vehicles and accessories for all purses and tastes. His General Motors declared in 1916 the largest dividend in New York Stock Exchange history. This gave the aforementioned Thomas Lamont the idea of financing Henry Ford's genteel retirement. He misjudged his man. Ford was an entrepreneur, a technician, a willful mover and shaker, and he had no intention of retiring and turning his company over to others, especially not to strangers. He had a particular dislike for bankers and did not need money. Lamont was spitting into the wind. Blunder number two.

But if there is a rule in business, it is that sooner or later, everyone needs money. Which means that everyone needs a banker. Durant, a smooth-talking charmer—he could coax a bird out of a tree, said Walter Chrysler—was a hapless manager and a habitual gambler. Thomas Lamont once said that Durant tossed millions around as though they were billiard balls. And when, in 1920, Durant needed some $64 million for a postwar expansion of GM, he turned to J. P. Morgan and Company.[17]

Why Morgan's? Because Morgan's was doing transatlantic banking for Pierre du Pont, and the du Ponts not only made paint and varnish—just the sort of thing one needed to decorate automobiles (unless, like Henry Ford, one gave customers any color they wanted so long as it was black)—but also had come out of the war with big profits. Their primary product was munitions and explosives, and du Pont was using these wartime earnings to buy up shares in General Motors. By 1919, du Pont owned 23 percent of the firm.

Yet 1920 was a bad year. One might have thought that pent-up consumer demand would have done well by the auto industry, but the economy went into a nosedive and cars piled up at dealers. Ford slashed prices. GM could not easily follow, the less so as Durant had in effect mortgaged his vehicles to secure loans. GM stock plummeted, and Morgan's and others had visions of another 1907. Frantically, Morgan's summoned Durant, made him sell his stock at a slasher price of $9.50 a share, hardly 1 percent of what it had been only two or three years before. That was less than the market closing price, but probably more than Durant could have gotten from a panicky exchange. Pierre du Pont was ready to let Durant stay on, but the Morgan partners insisted on his resignation. They were there to make money, not to be sentimental or charitable. Whatever Durant had left, he lost much of it later on in the 1929 crash, sank ever lower, and died poor and almost forgotten in 1947. Meanwhile, "overnight, the du Ponts and J. P. Morgan and Company had kidnapped an industrial empire."[18]

Back to George Perkins. He had big ideas, big ambitions, and these may have struck J.P. as pretentious and potentially dangerous. His Riverdale, New York, estate included swimming pool, ballroom, and bowling alley. In 1906 he bought a custom limousine, the biggest of its kind in the world—clearly expressing self-esteem and a lack of deference. He mocked J.P.'s son Jack behind his back (he wanted people to understand that he was smarter), and he made important bank decisions without consulting J.P. These may have reminded J.P. of his own youthful conceits, but he clearly had more patience for himself than for others. Perkins was forced to resign.

His place went to Harry Davison, Henry Pomeroy Davison to be exact, small-town son of a Pennsylvania dealer in farm tools, poor relation in a small-scale banking family. Davison made a good impression: cool demeanor, steely look, a smile the more potent for its rarity. He caught the eye of P. T. Barnum, circus impresario, then of George Baker, friend we saw of J.P. and head of the First National Bank. Davison organized Bankers Trust in 1903, helped in the negotiations to deal with the panic of 1907. J.P. liked what he saw and said later that he always believed what Davison told him—which added considerably to Davison's authority. This found expression in, among other things, the recruitment of other top managers. It was Davison who brought Thomas Lamont, Dwight Morrow, Ben Strong, and John Davis into Morgan's top ranks.

After J.P.'s death in 1913, the firm needed outside talent more than ever. As of July 1, 1923, one counted thirteen managing partners, not including son John, Jr., as follows: Edward T. Stotesbury, Charles Steele, William H. Porter, Thomas W. Lamont, Horatio G. Lloyd, Dwight W. Morrow, Edward R. Stettinius, Thomas Cochran, Junius Spencer Morgan, Elliot C. Bacon, George Whitney, Thomas S. Gates, and Russell Cornell Leffingwell. Some of these men came from modest origins; some were relatives of the Morgan family or well-to-do connections. Some brought legal or financial experience with them. Almost all of them stood tall, lean, haughty, and handsome. All of them became rich and important, and many saw their children rise to high rank after them. A partnership with Morgan's could be the peak of one's career or an entry ticket to a distinguished government job. It could also be the starting point of a dynasty.

This dependence on partners and managers, so different from Rothschilds, was reinforced by a process of morganatic genealogical decline. J.P. had matched, even surpassed, father Junius. John, Jr., was not in the same class as his father, and his sons were simply not cut out for business. John succeeded his father on J.P.'s death; the old man was a victim of too much smoking, drinking, indulging. Even with all his money and doctors, J.P. could not get away with so much pleasure and self-abuse.[19] John, Jr., was not cut to his father's jib. Even so, he could not be simply a figurehead; he had too big a slice of the bank's capital. And he represented name and fame and continuity. Insofar as Morgan's bank continued to play a familiar role as source of funding and counsel, Jack's presence had much to do with it. Family still mattered.

Jack himself seems to have known that the firm had better businessmen than he. As the author Frederick Lewis Allen put it, he did not have the "colossal personal force" of the old man. "He was an attractive young man, by reputation solid and reliable; he inherited his father's patrician spirit and tastes, his father's scorn of the common herd, and his father's blinding temper; but his capacity for personal leadership had not been tested."[20] Just about the first thing he did after taking over was drop the "Jr." from his name. Correct usage, but a little swift. He went to England to help settle and liquidate his father's estate. The visit was not all work: "Morgan spent considerable time being a country squire at Wall Hall, dropping in at the Morgan London office for an hour or two from time to time, or going through his father's papers. . . . There were shooting parties at Wall Hall or at Six Mile Bottom or house parties at the country houses of his friends."[21]

The man had apparently recovered quickly from his grievous loss. At the start of the next year, Jack surprised the financial world by resigning eighteen directorships, mostly railways. He felt that Morgan's should be concerned primarily with commercial credit and very occasional flotations. Enough of mergers for the moment. He also took it as his role to check the partnership accounts.

In one thing, Jack resembled his father. Neither of them liked Jews.[22] For the Morgan bank, that was perhaps the one tacit, unmentionable constraint on the choice of associates.[23] If anything, Jack was more candid on this point than his ancestor. He was outraged that the lawyer Samuel Untermyer—a rich Jew no less, the worst kind—had given his father so rough a time during the Pujo hearings of 1912–1913, and as we saw, he and his colleagues blamed Untermyer for J.P.'s collapse and death. Another enemy for Jack was Louis D. Brandeis, jurist and author of *Other People's Money and How the Bankers Use It,* a book that did much to discredit the rich and mighty and continued to influence political judgment in this area for a generation.

For Jack, it was as though people had lost a sense of place and taste. In New York City, in exclusive clubs, one could control encounters. (That's what clubs are for.) But Jack traveled a lot and felt uncomfortable meeting Jews on ocean liners and in the more expensive hotels and sharing table or common rooms with them. He was not actively anti-Semitic, just proactively. His prejudice and distaste shaped his social and commercial preferences.

Jews were not the only targets. When Ferdinand Pecora gave the Morgan bank a hard time in congressional hearings in 1933, Jack dismissed him as a "dirty little wop." That was the difference between someone whose family had come to America in the seventeenth century and an immigrant from Sicily. Had Pecora been appropriately submissive, the words would never have been spoken, though the latent sentiment would always have been there. No thinking required. Jack would have been hard-pressed to define or defend a rational, consistent policy.[24]

BY THE LATE NINETEENTH CENTURY, J. P. Morgan and Company was organized as a partnership, with first J.P. at the helm, then John, Jr. The statutes were explicit on this score: John, Jr., had the last word, and all partners were careful to defer to the bearer of the dynastic name. But John understood that having the last word was not the same thing as using it. Over time the partners took on more and more of the responsibilities of management, and John, who loved life too well to let business interfere, was happy to yield the initiative. His biographer John Douglas Forbes put it this way: "Morgan was a team player and submerged his own personality in the firm, where he managed with consummate skill to hold together a group of highly skilled and individualistic partners and make maximum use of their separate gifts to achieve very substantial results. Possibly it helped in directing the energies of prima donnas not to compete with them."[25]

Why should he not yield? The man was monarch in his kingdom. His huge 250-acre island estate off the shore of Long Island was almost sovereign territory. It required the services of a small army of full-time gardeners, who lived, alongside other domestics, in a village of cottages. The master's forty-five-room mansion was grander than anything J.P. had known or needed. Inside the columned entrance, portraits by Rubens, Gainsborough, and Lawrence greeted visitors with their own message of pride and hospitality. That was country living. In England, John had a London town house in Grosvenor Square, a short walk from everything that mattered; but nobody walked. But in England, too, the major residence was a country mansion, Wall Hall, three hundred acres north of London, with artificial lakes and gardens and its own tenants' village, church, cricket ground, tennis courts, bowling greens, public house, dance hall, cinema, and on and on, plus rent-free houses, registered milk delivery, free medical care, and old-age pensions. And I have surely omitted.

So much for the employees and servants. John himself traveled to vacation places, distant hearths where he enjoyed hunting, drinking, and playing cards. He shared with Eric Hambro—good banking family—a lodge in Scotland, where they and distinguished guests massacred up to ten thousand birds a year. Each hunter was attended by his own butler, to help with the guns and the prey. So much for some people's idea of gentility. How much killing John did is hard to say, for he himself was a fussy man. Killing has to be messy, even with butlers. Still, the fashion called for an abundance of easy victims. When, in August 1939, John had the pleasure of hunting with George VI—British royalty with American "royalty"—he had no trouble complaining about the shortage of birds.

This man was used only to the best. He lived in a gilded cocoon. Rather than remove his top hat every time he got into a car, he had his cars built with especially high roofs. (The Japanese did the same.) His various houses, lodges, and estates in Britain and the United States (he liked England better, because the Brits did not see him as an enemy of the people) and his personal yacht cost a fortune to maintain—armies of servants and a fifty-man crew for *Corsair IV*. Just an idea of size: after his death in 1943, the yacht was sold to a major steamship line and used for public cruises, with accommodations for eighty-five passengers.[26]

John enjoyed taking on airs of paternalistic authority: once a week he gave a black-tie dinner for the entire family (sixteen grand-children by 1935) in his hotel-size house at Matinicock Point. He was obsessive about time; clocks all over the place. At Wall Hall, someone came in every week just to wind and set them. One of his favorite gifts to partners and friends: rare gold watches. What other kind? Needless to say, like his father, he could not abide contradic-tion: since he detested Franklin D. Roosevelt, especially after the Glass-Steagall Act of 1933, he was said to have clerks go through the morning papers and cut out any photos of that class traitor; he could not abide to look at him.

In England, meanwhile, Morgan's followed the same path toward open partnership banking as in the United States: family in charge, plus managers to help run the show. Junius had been the early master there, followed by J. Pierpont in association with resident partners. And then by John, Jr. (Jack), who we saw was happier in England than in his native United States. London, after all, was the world's leading financial center, and British royalty adored bankers and wealth. The king himself found Jack so elegant a gentleman that he could barely keep from rising when this com-moner entered the room. Needless to say, Jack found reports of such esteem the greatest of compliments and the sorest of temp-tations.

But that was later. In the beginning, the Morgans' associates in London were relatives by marriage, American at first and then British. When Mary Burns, a cousin of Jack's and sister of a bank managing partner, married Lewis Harcourt, the first Viscount Har-court, the way was cleared for a stream of talent directly descended by the female line from great founder Junius. Jack himself was as-signed to the London bank in 1898. He was not happy at first, but his father tried to ease the adjustment with lavish gifts: two conjoined town houses at 13-14 Princes Gate; walls adorned with oils by Velázquez, Rubens, Rembrandt, Turner, and other world masters—paintings so precious that the housekeeper dusted them only if she felt steady enough; also social introductions galore. A Christmas gift in 1901 was a sum of money so large that Jack used part of it to buy a portrait by Sir Joshua Reynolds. At the same time, Jack rented, then bought in 1910, a country estate furnished with turreted house, phony ruins, and animals comparable to those of the king. Among the neighbors: Earl Grey (of tea fame), Florence Nightingale, Henry James, Sir James Barrie, and Samuel Clemens.

All of this gracious, even ceremonial, living left little time or energy for Jack to manage the business. The office manager was a certain Edward C. Grenfell, a smartly dressed, sharp-tongued bachelor, well schooled (Harrow and Trinity), politically conservative, well connected (father and grandfather MP's and directors of the Bank of England). Grenfell was the British firm's main contact with the British Treasury and the Bank of England. Grenfell then brought in a cousin, Vivian Hugh Smith, personal friend of Jack Morgan. Smith had a plain name but a bright lineage: Eton and Trinity Hall, Cambridge; father a governor of the Bank of England and member of one of England's most prolific banking lines, the so-called City Smiths of Nottingham origin. (When one has a name like Smith, some further designation is always useful.) Among Smith's marital connections: the Hambros, whom we met as hunting partners, German-Danish-Jewish in origin but, from their new start in England in the 1830s, unambiguously committed to Gentile gentility.[27] When Jack returned to the United States in 1905, he left Grenfell and Smith running the London show. In 1910 the London bank was renamed—changed from J. S. Morgan and Company to Morgan, Grenfell and Company. Thus did family firm become another managerial partnership.

All that money, all those connections were bound to yield an abundant social harvest. Grenfell was ennobled, becoming Lord St. Just; Smith became Lord Bicester; another partner, Tom Catto, became Lord Catto. Decidedly, peerages were in long supply. The problem with such promotions is that they drew the beneficiaries away from the firm, away from useful business, typically into important public banking slots, where they could no doubt help Morgan's but where they could no longer play the entrepreneur. As Chernow puts it, this gave the bank "an inbred feeling, a genteel hothouse atmosphere, and a stuffy complacency that would make it dangerously ossified by the 1950s."[28] Lord Bicester, Chernow tells us, "indulged a mad passion for steeplechase horses" and gave much time and money to this pointless (my opinion) diversion. Other partners had their own hobbies. These were the kinds of distraction that John, Jr., not managing partners, could afford, though in truth no business is so forgiving in this regard as banking—up to a point. By comparison with the American house, Morgan, Grenfell was reduced, indeed lulled into a state of pretentious inaction, though connections with the royal family induced the later Elizabeth II to confide an important part of her huge personal fortune to their care.

Unspoken compromises among colleagues, such as those between Jack and all those partners, are intrinsically fraught with hazard. Who could be sure that Jack knew enough to avoid misunderstandings and misstatements on important matters of bank policy? Who could be sure what was policy? Take the gold standard: an article of faith; gauge of stability; no surer guarantee of banker's honor and dependability. Everyone at Morgan's knew as much.

But faith was changing. The end of the 1920s brought England and the West to a crisis of business confidence. After years of carefree speculation, prices began falling, trade contracted, protectionist measures sought to defend national markets against price-cutting competitors. Politicians sought shelter in devaluation, particularly in suspension of the gold standard and even repudiation of established commercial commitments.

Like other paragons of financial virtue, Morgan's loved gold and the gold standard. So the bank had played a key role in returning England to gold in 1925, lending money to the British Treasury that the gold-friendly U.S. Federal Reserve was not allowed to provide. (It was allowed, though, to lend to the Bank of England.) That seemed like a major achievement, yet return to gold was not a good idea. As politicians and some economists (including the great Keynes) warned, a gold-standard pound, hence overvalued, raised the price of British exports and pushed British manufacturers to wage cuts by way of compensation; and wage cuts led to labor strife and social disorder. So the gold standard was no sooner restored than subjected to second thoughts. Within a matter of years, a preponderant mass of power and opinion called for its abandonment.

Not everyone agreed. Authoritarian ideologues such as Montagu Norman of the Bank of England and Benjamin Strong of the U.S. Federal Reserve Board were not used to rethinking their convictions. But merchant bankers were in business to make money and could not allow religion and idolatry to interfere with practice. A house such as Morgan's, moreover, cherished its tacit alliance with political authority. So the managing partners, nose to the wind, quickly reconciled themselves to a new order. Gold standard: finished, fini, finito. Montagu Norman was on an ocean liner returning from Canada on September 21, 1931, when Britain went off gold. Upon landing, he made a tempestuous irruption into Bank of England headquarters, on Threadneedle Street, where his associates finally calmed him: he would have done the same had he been there. (But of course he hadn't been, and that did make things easier.) Britain was followed by twenty-five other countries over the next few years. Governments had to be able to defend themselves, to manage money, the better to reverse deflation.

With Morgan's, however, monarchical structures interfered. No one had to tell Jack that Morgan's stood for gold, stability, honor, dependability, and all the other virtues that made this the bank of banks. They took him for granted. Yet when England went off gold, Jack defended the move to journalist interviewers. Partner Thomas Lamont was aghast. Morgan's had enlisted more than a hundred private banking houses to save the gold standard. And now the boss was giving the lie to the whole achievement. Thomas wrote Jack a careful, apologetic letter to chide him gently for his betrayal of years of good bank policy, concluding with "Much love from us all." Some would see this soft reprimand as evidence that the Morgan family had lost its absolute power in the bank. I see it as an expression of the mixed character of a family partnership. In the meantime, Lamont was learning—and this was one time the boss was right. So Lamont followed up with an apologetic phone call to Jack: no reproach was intended, and he would have done the same in those circumstances.

IN GENERAL, official policy was an ever-present trap: the orthodoxy of today could easily become the heresy of tomorrow. This was only to be expected: the government and its minions were concerned with power; the bankers, with money. Politics, for all its reliance on ideology, is inherently fickle and improvisational; banking tries to be adaptably stable. The rise of Nazi Germany in the 1930s, and the threat it posed to the peace of Europe, was just the kind of challenge that separated the realists and idealists on the one side from the businessmen and money powers on the other.

The Morgan banks found themselves on the horns of more than one dilemma here. The London house was ready to deal with Germany in order to shelter its clients from the consequences of changes in boundaries and sovereignty—and this if necessary at the expense of the clients of the bank in New York. Thomas Lamont was furious at this financial appeasement, but too prudent to make his vexation public; which did not prevent London partners at the firm Morgan, Grenfell and Co. from communicating these American reservations to British authorities.

In the meantime, on the political level, Lamont and most of his colleagues in the bank wanted to keep the peace. Lamont learned to use "appeasement" as a good word: What could be better than to avoid war? He became a close personal friend of Lady Nancy Astor, vivacious wife of the master of lavish Clivedon manor, magnet headquarters for pacifists and Germanophiles, and herself a strongly isolationist member of Parliament.

Meanwhile, Morgan's found friends wherever friendship paid, on both sides of the political axis. The bank cherished and cultivated its long affection for Britain, and particularly the royal family, but also stood ready to help the new Germany find money. This was not always easy, not only for political reasons but also because Germany had concocted a new principle of international finance, to the effect that it should not have to pay interest on debt except to countries with which it had a positive balance of payments. It was not easy to lend to a borrower who set the rules to suit convenience, but somehow Morgan's managed it. Morgan's also made money handling transactions at both ends of the transatlantic, pro-Allies axis. As did other merchant banks. The only exceptions were those banks of German origin and German loyalty, and not all of them.[29] Special difficulties arose once the Germans defeated France and occupied Paris. Morgan et Cie (the French bank) had anticipated this possibility and shipped all manner of assets to quiet shelters in the provinces, but the Nazis appointed plunder committees to search for and grab vulnerable assets—Jewish holdings, for example. Morgan's found resistance to these demands impractical: "It seems doubtful whether any bank could have operated during the occupation if it had resisted these efforts too strenuously."[30]

Ironically, although Jack Morgan, thanks to his anglophilia, got the political and banking story of the 1930s straighter than his partners—he understood the German threat—the Morgan family interest in Morgan's multinational weakened over those years. Jack himself lacked the passion required to hold on to the reins. Now he was ready to let go, and his children were even more indifferent. He had fathered two sons, both of whom he wanted to see at the helm of their ancestral firm, and neither of whom was equipped for or attracted by the task.

The older, Junius Spencer, Jr., became a Morgan partner in 1919. Easygoing and friendly, Junius was much too nice to be a Morgan or a banker. His real dream was to be a marine architect, and he did become a commodore of the New York Yacht Club. Pierpont would have been revolted.

Harry Morgan, the younger son, had a typical Morgan résumé as shaped by his father: commodore of the New York Yacht Club, trustee of the Metropolitan Museum of Art, a director of General Electric, overseer of Harvard University. His estate on the north shore of Long Island included a manor house, cottages for the help, a swimming pool (of course), and an eight-car garage. A smaller version of the residences of his ancestors.

He wanted to bring his son Charles into the firm, naturally. The other partners were reluctant. A partnership was worth a million dollars or more a year, and this young man had neither interest nor aptitude. But his father owned a treasure, the right to the Morgan name, and he threatened to take it away from the bank unless it took his son in. So Charley Morgan became in effect office manager: checked the phones, went over the blueprints, called in the plumber. It was too late to assign him to correspondence, as the firm Duncan, Sherman had done with Pierpont; they had typists for that. And the bank now owned the name. But when Charley's younger brother John was put forward, too, the partners rebelled and invoked an anti-nepotism rule never meant to be used against members of the royal dynasty. Enough. Ironically, John proved more capable than his brother and made a career for himself with other banking houses.

In the meantime, Morgan, Stanley had been taken over by the managerial partnership gang. Their aim in life was to get around the constraints imposed by federal legislation (the Glass-Steagall Act), which had compelled the bank to split into two units, J. P. Morgan and Company (commercial banking) and Morgan, Stanley (investment banking); and, in contrast to the best tradition, to seek and find customers among capital-needy businesses and capital-rich idlers. The old rule was that bankers should never hunt; the game should come to them. In fact, the rule was now honored more in the breach than in the observance. Good bankers were attentive to opportunity. Death in rich families, for example, yielded heirs to help and cherish. So good bankers kept an eye on obituary notices and an ear out for useful medical gossip.

In this way, a merchant bank such as Morgan's was able to con-fine itself to rich clients, and the richest got personal phone calls in-quiring about physical and monetary health. To say nothing of dinner and hunt invitations or opportunities to share in the beauties and mysteries of personal collections of art and old manuscripts.[31]

Meanwhile, the clients, however touched by these marks of so-licitude, were looking for and finding cheaper sources of finance. Ambitious execs were always seeking ways to prove their useful-ness. Banking competition was keen, and new, more enterprising credit promoters moved in. These were often one-man shows, run by individuals well trained in money and banking, well connected personally (including to royalty), uninhibited by tradition and the constraints of collegiality.

More threatening to the old merchant houses, however, was the rise of joint-stock banks to parity and then superiority. Once conde-scended to, these omnibus credit merchants took all comers, poor as well as rich, and as economies grew and flourished, they had a lot more to work with than the fussbudget merchant banks. Not only more money, but more effective human capital. The 1950s and '60s proved to be a period of active merger and concentration: National City took over George Baker's sedate First National; Chase tried to swallow Morgan's and when turned down, took over the Bank of the Manhattan Company; Chemical merged with the New York Trust; and Manufacturers Trust with Hanover Bank; and then Chemical with Manufacturers Hanover; then this last with Chase Manhattan, and then with J. P. Morgan–Chase in 2000. Over a third of New York's banks disappeared. These fusions were the only way for banks to stay big enough to handle and compete for business.[32] Needless to say, mergers gave rise to internecine struggles and maneuvers. In Morgan Chase the winners were known by some as the "Chemical Mafia," since many of them had gotten their start at the Chemical Bank.[33]

Morgan's, then, was not immune to these merger schemes, the more so, remember, as the firm had been obliged to follow the op-posite course and divide, splitting commercial from investment banking. This was the banking fruit of the New Deal, the first Democratic administration since Wilson. The aim was to reduce and humble the money powers, which were seen by many, in the anti–Wall Street populist tradition, as a threat to democracy. J. P. Morgan and Company, who were symbolically and literally the main target of the legislation, remained as a commercial bank, while investment activities were hived off to the new, much smaller Morgan, Stanley and Company.

The hope—indeed, the expectation—of Morgan's was that a formal dissolution would not prevent the firm from remaining what it had been: a unified enterprise inherited from days of yore. To this end, the successor firms did try to work together, especially abroad, where the United States government had no jurisdiction. But such unity does not accord with human nature. Even within a single firm, competition for place breeds trouble, and one of the advantages of a family-run enterprise is that usually genealogy determines hierarchy and prevents internecine warfare. For better or worse, Morgan's was now three separate houses (the London branch also having broken off), and the best intentions of the group eventually yielded to personal strategy and advancement.

Insofar as one of the firms carried the flag, it was J. P. Morgan and Company. The name told all. They had a good team of partners, men who moved easily between business and government, and who found the name and record of Morgan's a valuable asset. Within the walls of the firm, they established their own little dynasties. The symbols became terribly important: how one dressed, ate, spoke. Morgan's prided themselves immensely on their cultivated spirit and genteel ambience. Many of the partners had joined through inheritance or marriage, but whatever their origin, they were expected to be gentlemen, members of a new money aristocracy.[34]

A sense of superiority can be a source of contentment and gratification; it can also be an advantage in business. While other firms thought only in terms of the short run, J. P. Morgan and Company built long-term relationships and capitalized on them over generations. Over time, however, selectiveness in customers can be poison to business decisions and choices, and eventually Morgan's found itself losing ground to more enterprising newcomers. So the moment came in the 1980s for the partners in Morgan's to think once again the unthinkable: contemplate absorption via merger, by way of adding resources and improving their competitiveness. Inevitably, other firms began to eye Morgan's as a potential prize.

Morgan's pride and pretension, though, got in the way. After all, in 1991 it was still considered "the strongest commercial bank in the country, if not the world."[35] But money is the most democratic of measures, and the price of Morgan shares kept falling, even in prosperity: from May 1999 to the end of the year, J. P. Morgan and Company went down 12 percent, while Morgan Stanley and Goldman Sachs went up 37 and 35 percent, respectively. Morgan's chiefs knew that the firm had to grow to survive, but one deal after another broke down or never got off the ground. For starters there was the name problem, because name signaled to all who was buying whom. And should they keep the Morgan with the J.P., or would just "Morgan" do (cf. Morgan Stanley)? Let workers go? Which workers? Should they specialize in one sector? Which potential partner would give the best fit? And culture? Who would set the tone and call the tune?

Ironically, of all the candidates, the most desirable was Goldman Sachs, once scorned for its lowly Jewishness, foreign accents, and peddler style. That was all gone now. De-Semitized and de-Deutschified, full of piss and vinegar, manners and tone, Goldman had made its promotional fortune in new branches and such traditionally humble sectors as retail trade. Even so, a marriage to Morgan's would be more than a promotion; it would be a kind of coronation. And yet, after some give-and-take that led Morgan's to believe they had a deal, Goldman Sachs dropped them at the last minute. Morgan's, it felt, with its inherited dynastic tradition, simply cost too much. J.P., had he been alive, would have slaughtered the lot.

Ultimately Morgan's allowed itself to be bought by Chase Manhattan, a large retail omnibus bank that would accept small sums as well as big. The price: thirty billion dollars. The partners smiled, stiff upper lip, but they were not really happy. As the old Goldmans and

Sachses, not to mention the Rothschilds, could have told them, mixed marriages are a chancy, uncomfortable business. One of the big issues: What to call the new combination? In this case, Morgan won. The name of the new bank would be J. P. Morgan Chase. Order counts. Besides, what would "Chase Morgan" have sounded like?

Then, in 2004, J. P. Morgan Chase announced a merger with Bank One, Chicago-based and a specialist in consumer banking. The combined company has some 2,300 branches and $1.1 trillion in assets, making it the second-largest bank in the United States. Big business is bigger than ever.[36]

On the brokerage side, Morgan Stanley has gone through similar merger pains. It found a partner in Dean Witter, a major brokerage house, so that Morgan Stanley, with all its stock and bond flotations, had a ready-made distribution arm. Here, too, "Morgan" got name priority, but it was Philip J. Purcell, chief executive of Dean Witter, who got the presiding chair. The story was that after five years, John J. Mack, chief of Morgan Stanley, would take the reins. But four years later, Mack left to enjoy the fruits of money management, and Purcell denied that there had ever been a commitment to transfer power. As of that date, Mack owned more than five million shares of Morgan stock, worth some five hundred million dollars, and he was part owner of a private golf club in Purchase, New York, the better to enjoy retirement. Both men denied a contest for power, although others roundly challenge this. "The ordeal, which has lasted for about six months, has resulted in a lot of bodies piling up," according to a Goldman Sachs report.

We've come a long way from J. P. Morgan, from family heir to take-charge dynasty to international financier to mixed partnership to managerial takeover.[37] This ending is what happens when the founding family loses interest and control, and bureaucratic managers take charge. But here the results aren't all bad from the family perspective. The Morgan name survives and serves as a continual source of prestige. The business itself is strong, very powerful, and stable. And most of the Morgan family has done quite well. Most likely J.P. would be pleased.

Part Two

AUTOMOBILES

PROLOGUE

*T*he successful banks we've examined were founded by shrewd businessmen: persistent, ambitious, discreet. The early years of the automobile industry were very different. The founders of car companies tended to be inventors, mechanical geniuses who were passionate about building new machines. Intense and brilliant, these were men whose obsessions were often scoffed at by their families, not to mention by the general public. To be sure, many failed. Those we are about to look at succeeded so brilliantly that they have become household names around the world.

Early on, nearly all car manufacturers were individual or family enterprises. In Europe at the turn of the twentieth century, for instance, there were literally hundreds of independent car makers, most of whom produced a small number of luxurious vehicles, customized for their purchasers. Some of these names remain with us today, such as Renault, Daimler-Benz, and Peugeot (whom we'll meet in chapter 6). Others, such as Maybach, Horch, and Bugatti, built beautiful cars, lasted a time, and then vanished.

Many, if not most, of these inventors saw themselves as the founders of dynasties, and they attempted to raise their children as successors. Members of this second generation were often appointed to positions of control within the companies, despite lacking any of the technical training or inclination of their fathers. That said, car-making families also brought in outside expertise more readily than families in many industries. Unlike banking, developing an automobile line required much more than personal connections and the trust of clients. Successful auto firms needed knowledge, innovation, and business acumen. These broad needs quickly forced most automakers to expand beyond the capabilities of a single family—and yet many of these families have maintained leadership and control over their companies.

As early as the eighteenth century, man began experimenting successfully with independently powered road vehicles, although theoretical designs had been drawn up much earlier, by Leonardo da Vinci and Isaac Newton, among others. As soon as the steam engine was invented, inventors tried to adapt it for road use. The first successful automobile was an enormous beast created in 1769 by Nicolas-Joseph Cugnot, who designed it to haul French artillery pieces. In England, that precociously busy nation, Richard Trevithick brought out a steam carriage in 1801, and within twenty years one saw steam stagecoaches—cumbersome affairs weighing several tons—lumbering and puffing and beating the roads, and even regular coach services operating at speeds of ten to fourteen miles per hour.

These vehicles met with sharp opposition in England from those invested in horses and horse-powered transportation, who attempted to confine powered land transport to the railroads by imposing prohibitive tolls and driving regulations. Thus a British law of 1865 required that there be at least three people driving every motorized vehicle, in addition to a walker with a flag who had to precede the "locomotive" by sixty yards to warn those ahead and calm frightened horses; that the speed be limited to four miles per hour in the country and two miles per hour in populated areas; and that the engine be prohibited from blowing off steam; among other constraints. In theory, these restrictions applied only to heavy transport, but the British courts decided that they applied to every kind of self-propelled vehicle, down to light motorized tricycles. It was not until 1896, a century into the industrial revolution, that the speed limit for "light road locomotives" (autos) was raised to fourteen miles per hour, and the requirement of a walker warner was eliminated. All of this seems absurd for an advanced industrial nation. But the British worshipped horses, and when the British cherish tradition, they do so to a fare-thee-well.

Overcoming vested interests in horses was a challenge to the auto industry everywhere. But let's face it: horses are a nuisance. They are mass producers of organic waste and of the disease-breeding organisms that thrive in such an environment. We have data for New York City at the turn of the nineteenth century: every day an estimated 2.4 million pounds of manure and sixty thousand gallons of urine flooded onto the streets—two thirds of the city's filth and litter. Not surprisingly, it was livery stable keepers and employees who contracted most of the diseases, including tetanus, diarrhea, and typhoid fever. The foul odor of stables caused horse owners to keep their mounts and drays far away from their homes, and to hire drivers to bring them as needed. Traffic was often obstructed by horses that dropped dead in their tracks from heat and illness, and approximately fifteen thousand dead or crippled beasts had to be removed from the streets every year. Cumulatively, the estimated maintenance cost to the city ran to one hundred million dollars a year.

Back in England, the love affair with the horse and the steadfast dedication to tradition made Europe's leading industrial nation do without an auto industry until the start of the twentieth century. Before then, those Brits who wanted cars bought them from foreign makers, particularly the French.

Meanwhile, Germany had taken the technical lead with Nicolas Otto's Gasmotoren Fabrik Deutz of 1872, which hired Gottlieb Daimler as manager. In 1876 they brought out a new four-cycle gas motor known as the "silent Otto," which was a huge improvement over the oversize vehicles of the past. Otto and Daimler tried to protect their invention by patent, but the courts ruled against them, and by early 1886 another motor builder, Karl Benz (later of Mercedes fame), built a large motorized tricycle that is generally seen as the first gasoline-powered automobile. The vehicle left much to be desired. Its motor turned slowly and yielded only two-thirds horse-power for a motor weight of ninety-six kilograms, and the electrical ignition worked uncertainly. Benz could not sell even one of his cars for a couple of years.

Little by little, engines got smaller and turned faster, achieving greater horsepower, and the world inched closer to mass production and ownership of cars. Here the bicycle, an industrial product of the 1860s, showed the way. It made its start in France, but it was in Britain that the so-called safety bicycle, the chain-propelled two-wheeler as we know it, made its appearance in 1885. Before then, cycling was a specialty of acrobatic gymnasts. Now it became a sensible means of locomotion and transportation. This practical application justified the growing taste for self-controlled vehicles, and encouraged hundreds of engineers, mechanics, and handymen to try their hands at building mechanically propelled machines.[1]

In many respects, Europe was the pioneer, and its aim was to produce the best possible cars for discriminating, well-furnished buyers. Autos were objects of luxury consumption, of thrilling adventure, of self-advertisement. The United States took another path. America, a frontier nation, was big, and its inhabitants were used to movement. American society, moreover, was historically and temperamentally innovative: the response to need or opportunity was to find a new and better way of doing things. Much of this interest and initiative turned to improvement of transportation—canals and then railroads and then smaller, private horseless vehicles. There was no question of squashing or cramping the new industry as Britain had done; even moderately successful people assumed that the auto was a necessity, and the inevitable way of the future. While Europe had a clear class structure, America was a society of widely distributed income, an assemblage of pretended equals unwilling to accept a division into haves and have-nots.

So it was in the United States that the industry found expression in mass production of standardized, uniform, cheap-as-possible vehicles. Those who had the money and the inclination could import elegant, costly cars from abroad. Most Americans, more populist, were ready to drive about in the same standard model their neighbors owned. One could buy larger cars as well as smaller, more or less fashionable; there was variety within and between makes. Henry Ford, as we shall see, was the one exception; he thought all Americans could and should drive in the same black vehicles, year after year. He did very well with that belief, until increases in personal income permitted buyers to be choosy. The managerial giant General Motors set the standards for the industry in the 1920s, producing lines of vehicles aimed at every economic stratum. These two firms present opposing case studies: family and dynasty on one side; managerial incorporation on the other. Both have been very successful for many decades, with Ford still a dynastic enterprise with the control largely in the hands of the Ford family, and General Motors a model managerial company. Both are running into trouble today from Asian competition.

Autos became the great industry of modern times, the marker of modernity. Consider the statistical data. At the end of the nineteenth century, some thirty American makers produced some six hundred cars; a decade later, in 1909, 150,000 cars rolled off the production line; the next year, 200,000. In 1935, in the depths of the Great Depression, the United States made almost four million cars, and by 1950 the number was eight million. And no industry did more to win World War II. Between 1940 and 1945, automobile firms made almost twenty-nine billion dollars' worth of military equipment, a fifth of the national product. They made some 2.6 million trucks and 660,000 jeeps, along with 60 percent of the tanks, all the armored cars, and half of the machine guns and carbines used by American forces.

The next-largest producer during the first half of the twentieth century was France, working not only for its national market but also for export. The French were leaders in auto fashion and publicity, and they built demand through public auto races, periodic shows and sale displays, and mouth-watering journalism. Their emphasis was on the auto as a device for self-assertion and display, an accessory to manliness and sex; or, as one American observer put it in 1896, the French auto was the "car of Venus and Cupid."[2]

So it was that in the early years of manufacture, the top French makers could not keep up with orders, and purchasers waited months, even many months, for delivery. Some provincial makers specialized in simpler vehicles for the country doctor and other door-to-door practitioners, the makings of a market for the auto as a useful means of transportation. Among the pioneers here were the Peugeot family, experienced in the manufacture of machines and bicycles. They took quality seriously, did not neglect repair and maintenance, built a network of dealers, and in so doing set an example to other firms in the industry. They had a keen sense of who they were and how their business ought to be run, and have developed that family and brand identity carefully over the years. Their success continues to this day, a clear example that generations of industrial enterprise and dynastic traditions matter.

Since its development, the automobile has been a great object of entrepreneurial endeavor. With the emphasis on a combination of technological mastery and taste, the car has lent itself to the inspirations and accidents of genius. In every producing economy, manufacture was primarily in individual hands, and the names of the car models signaled the role of the auto-making heroes. Note that many of these were founders of dynasties, indeed made a point of forming their descendants as successors and appointing them to positions of control—this in spite of their technical shortcomings. Industry in general differs here from banking in that hereditary limitations compel more frequent recourse to extrafamilial competence and managerial performance. In banking, as we saw, family and persons, connections and trust, matter more than anything. In industry, knowledge and know-how dominate. The auto industry, more than most, responds to a combination of both elements.

Four
FORD

WHEELS FOR EVERYONE

HENRY FORD (1863–1947)

I was once asked by a national newspaper to contribute to a millennial project. For a review of major achievements of the last thousand years, I was to select the person I saw as the leading industrial entrepreneur and innovator and write a mini-biography. I thought hard about this and decided that, given the changing rate and impact of technological change, the pool of candidates should be limited to figures of the last two or three centuries. And I chose Henry Ford. The newspaper was not happy and decided not to publish my piece. The editor said that all the other contributors had found their examples in the first two or three centuries after the millennium. Why did I have to spoil things by picking someone so recent?

I suspect the newspaper's refusal to publish my piece had less to do with the time frame than with our current vision of Ford the man. Henry Ford has not aged well. For the longest time his cars looked primitive; his product line, unimaginative. His company lost ground in his latter years. His persona was unfriendly and unattractive; his political and social opinions were addled, prejudiced, primitive, and noisy—to the point where it is apparently impermissible to praise him. But we should credit him with his achievement: the vision of mass production and mass markets, of personal transport for the multitude, and of the technology that would make such a revolution possible. Bravo!

Ford's genius and vision—and yes, his political and social stubbornness—found expression in his running of the Ford Motor Company. In the story of this corporation we have an extreme example of a dynasty in which the founder overshadows his successors, nearly to the point of ruining the firm. We have already encountered similar examples of daunting predecessors—N. M. Rothschild and J. P. Morgan, for instance—who cast long shadows over their business enterprises. But in this respect, Henry Ford outdoes them all. And even after his death, as authority passed to later generations and the company diversified and sold a share of ownership to outsiders, the family retained its control.

The first Fords came to the United States from Ireland in 1832. They were Protestants from a Roman Catholic countryside, participants in an immemorial British occupation—so, warriors in a hostile environment. They needed the preparation. In the New World, they went west to seek land, to have cheap and to hold dear, and set out to cut and tame the forest. This was Indian territory, and while most of the aborigines had pulled away, some remained to provide hazard and uncertainty.

Henry's grandparents left Ireland in 1847, at the depth of the potato famine. All around them, people were dying of hunger and disease, and by disease aggravated by hunger. The Irish did not know how to fish, and no one was bringing food in as needed. The Irish could not have paid for it anyway. How these Ford grandparents paid for passage is not clear; presumably they sank their savings into a flight to deliverance. On arrival they borrowed some $350 (perhaps from relatives already there) to pay for eighty acres in the Dearborn area, near Detroit, where smoking chimneys signaled the arrival of local industries. The Great Lakes were serving more and more as passage for industrial materials and products, in particular a huge volume of copper ore from the upper Michigan peninsula to the mills of the East. The oldest Ford son, William (later Henry's father), hired himself out as carpenter to the railroad to pay off the family debt. This was a land of opportunity to those with the will and the skill.

Henry was born in 1863. His father, by then a prosperous farmer, introduced the children to the world around them: the animals, the trees and plants. Henry kept and cherished a love of nature for the rest of his life. This was not the same thing as a love of farming. He did his chores, but his mind and heart were elsewhere. He had two precious assets: wondrous hands and a head for tools and machines. His father was not happy. To him, it was the land, the farm, that mattered. To William Ford, all these industrial activities were accessory issues; besides, he wanted Henry's labor.[1]

Henry always wanted to know how and why things worked. His father, with reservations, let him set up a workbench in the house. His brothers made it a point to keep their toys from Henry, for he would invariably take them apart, sometimes to their definitive demise. He would take the long walk to Detroit just to visit hardware stores. Clocks fascinated him: Was there ever a more complicated, more ingenious object? A neighbor is said to have remarked, "Every clock in the Ford home shuddered when it saw him coming." We have no better assurance of his talent and his forbidding personality: a man who could scare a clock could scare anything.

By the time he was sixteen, Henry had had it. He went off to Detroit and found a job with a machine shop, the kind of place that made and did just about anything in metal: valves, gongs, whistles, fire hydrants. When he found they did not pay him enough to cover the rent, he earned extra money of evenings repairing watches. A lesson there. After some three years in Detroit, he went back to the land, but made more money repairing farm machinery and tools than working the soil. He courted, got married, received from his father the gift of eighty acres to clear and plow. For Henry, the cutting, sawing, and selling of timber made the task interesting, the more so as much of the work could be mechanized. Then, when he had just about exhausted the timber, he decided to go back to Detroit. His wife, happy on the land, was surprised; but she loved her Henry and went with him. Henry had found employment as a mechanic engineer with the Edison Illuminating Company at forty-five dollars a month, beginning September 1891. This was good pay and his kind of job, because once he had the generators working properly, he had lots of time to fiddle with his own gadgets.

At this point, we must pause to contemplate the special difficulty of establishing the circumstances and facts of Henry Ford's life and work. Normally, a historian relies on the records and relics of the past, and in Henry Ford's case, we have access to voluminous material that he himself saved, recovered, and reconstructed. But that's just the problem: he wanted to build a past to suit his view of himself and his role in history, and he had no trouble suiting and fixing the facts to his purpose. So everything—his relations with family, friends, and business associates; his business activities and achievements; his political and social values; his hopes and intentions—has to be questioned and verified if possible. Not an easy task. We shall never have complete agreement on who and what Henry Ford was.

Henry did very well with Edison Illuminating. He was Mr. Fix-It, and it wasn't long before he became chief engineer at more than double his starting salary. It was during these years that he came to know the work that was going on in Europe on internal combustion engines and in the United States on automotive vehicles, usually powered by steam. The first American gasoline-powered car was probably the one built by the Duryea brothers of Springfield, Massachusetts, in 1893.[2] Within a year, there were enough automobiles rolling and sputtering around to organize America's first car race—on Lake Michigan in a wild snowstorm. The winner, made by Duryea, averaged six and two thirds miles per hour.

This race was followed by many others, typically accompanied by spectating enthusiasm, and one may well ask why so much ado about these competitions. Part of the answer lay in the selection process. Racing provided a test for performance and endurance, and auto technology learned thereby. But more important was the publicity. Winning translated into sales, because many would-be drivers thought of themselves as sportsmen and of cars as serious toys, to say nothing of symbols of style and wealth.

Racing has continued to be a feature of automobile prestige to the present day, as has the virtual, imaginary derring-do of ordinary usage. Just look at television ads: the cars are shown in the wildest poses and places, climbing dangerous mountain roads, speeding and sliding around curves, jouncing and bouncing, violating all the rules of good driving behavior in a world of overcrowded streets and highways. But always spotlessly clean. The auto remains fantasy and dream. Such publicity, needless to say, makes for bad drivers, encouraging road races, daredevil conduct, and the follies of road rage. But the makers and dealers think it sells cars.

Henry Ford, in his early auto phase (late 1890s, early 1900s), was a racing driver, operating his own cars built for his own use. He won a number of major competitions, eventually setting a record for the measured mile. Much of his success was due to the ingenuity and reliability of his machines; and much of it to his personal toughness, honed by years on the farm. But he also owed much to his sense of what an automobile was about. He built light vehicles—light but tough—and he gained efficiency thereby. Most cars in those early days were built heavy—horseless wagons and carriages for the well-to-do. Ford's cars were more like motorized tricycles and four-wheelers. He thought of them as a practical help to farmers, not as luxury transport.

Henry sold his first car in 1896, for two hundred dollars. He had become one of the sights of Detroit, tooling around in his homemade vehicle. His boss was beginning to fret at a hobby become a business. Besides, he did not think the gasoline-powered auto had a future. Electricity, maybe. Gasoline, no. But Henry had found his calling. In 1899, he gave up the chance to be general superintendent and quit Detroit Edison to devote himself full-time to automobiles. He began with the newly established Detroit Automobile Company, but left after nine months. His bosses, he felt, wanted only to sell cars, improvising and making as they went. Henry wanted to give some thought to design and to the assembly process.

The Ford car was a success from the start because Henry Ford understood the potential of the market. When he began his company, automobiles were primarily luxury toys and status symbols. Ford aimed instead at the utilitarian market, seeing that cars could fill needs for all manner of professional and commercial people. By the end of March 1904, the company had sold 658 vehicles, at a profit of almost one hundred thousand dollars. Henry got twenty-five thousand dollars of this, and he had not put up a penny. As production increased, the company had to move to bigger quarters, where it turned out an average of twenty-five vehicles a day. Henry was too busy to attend to his mail, and important bills and checks were left unopened. All that interested him were the shop and the design of improvements, such as a better, cheaper carburetor. If he could have, he would have stopped half the vehicles on their way out for last-minute retouches. Fortunately for the company's bottom line, he had hired an office whiz named James Couzens, who made it his business to keep the cars moving and the deliveries going. The two men made a good team, and Couzens would play an important role in the company for many years.

The firm's first significant internal conflict came between Ford and Alex Malcomson, a coal dealer who was the largest partner in the business, with a share equal to Henry's. Malcomson understood and appreciated Ford's mechanical brilliance, but he wanted to build heavy luxury automobiles for a bourgeois clientele, which would yield a substantially higher profit per vehicle, just as SUVs do today. Ford wanted no part of this. As he said in 1903, "The way to make automobiles is to make one automobile like another automobile, to make them all alike, to make them come through the factory just alike, just as one pin is like another pin when it comes from a pin factory."[3]

How to solve the problem? Henry decided to buy out Malcomson, but Malcomson was not ready to sell. So Henry decided to push Malcomson out, using a tactic that may have been suggested by Couzens, and that certainly would not pass legal scrutiny today. He created a new firm, Ford Manufacturing Company, to make the engines, gearing, and sundry other parts for Ford automobiles. Ford Motor Company then began purchasing all of its parts from Ford Manufacturing at inflated rates. Henry thus shifted all the profits from one corporation to the other.

Malcomson reacted furiously. He would have had a good legal case for conspiracy, but instead he chose to fight fire with fire, setting up a new car assembly company to compete with Ford Motor. This put him in the awkward—and slightly ridiculous—position of competing with himself. A Ford lawsuit called for his resignation. He resisted, but after a few months decided to sell out his share in Ford, taking with him several other major shareholders. Since Ford's articles of association required any shareholder wishing to sell shares to do so to another existing shareholder, this meant the transfer to Henry Ford, directly or indirectly, of absolute control. Ford Manufacturing was then absorbed, and the Ford Motor Company became what it was to remain: a Ford fiefdom.

Henry Ford was now truly free to call the shots, and many innovations flowed from his keen technical curiosity. Further, he was an astute observer of his competition: at a race in 1905 he had occasion to examine a French car that had been wrecked, and he marveled at how light yet durable its parts were. He inquired and learned that the French were using an alloy of vanadium unlike any made by American smelters. He found a stateside steel shop that was ready to experiment. Their first attempt was a failure, but the second yielded a steel with more than twice the tensile strength of ordinary steel. By the time Ford received the first commercial shipment in 1907, the tensile strength ran ten times what Carnegie Steel was getting in its armor-plate experiments.

The first Ford car to use vanadium steel was the Model N, which was released in 1906 at a price of six hundred dollars. Ford had planned to sell it for $450 but did not yet have the technology to keep the cost that low. Still, the popular car was as cheap as anything on the market and offered better value. It was a tremendous success, which owed much to Ford's development of the steel alloy. Seeing this as a lesson in the value of knowledge and innovation, the company set up a metallurgical research lab. Of course, Henry Ford—a militant plebeian—did not shop for talent in the universities. He took a former floor sweeper, sent him off for three months' schooling, and put him in charge of the lab. It worked: the Ford labs remained for many years among the best in the country, and vanadium steel found company in nickel, chromium, and molybdenum alloys.

It was at about this point that Henry bent his attention to the design of a new car that was small, light, strong, reliable, fast—and, most important, affordable to the average man. Eventually this quest would yield the Model T, the car that made Ford world famous. When advance circulars of the new car went out, dealers could not believe them: the car sounded too good to be true. When the first Model T went on the market in October 1908, for $825, orders poured in and quickly exceeded factory capacity. The price was no small sum—almost twenty thousand dollars in today's money—but for its time, it was a bargain: "No car under $2,000 offers more," went the Ford ad, and this was certainly true. Further, unlike most vehicles at that time, the Model T was made to stand up to the rutted, unpaved roads of the day. Most car makers of the time aimed at rigidity; Henry at flexibility.

From the moment it went on sale, Ford's Model T was the most popular car on the planet. Demand for the Tin Lizzie, as it was affectionately known, grew rapidly—18,664 cars in 1909–1910; 34,528 in 1910–1911; 78,440 in 1911–1912—which forced Ford to shift his focus toward increasing productivity. First, he instituted the use of interchangeable parts and the precise machine tools that went with them. Henry and his engineers aimed at tolerances of one-ten thousandth of an inch, and whenever they found a better tool, they scrapped all the old ones. The managers grimaced, but by 1910, all filing and adjustment of inaccurate parts was a thing of the past.

A second major innovation was the simplification and routinization of tasks, thanks to the use of an assembly line, a concept Ford took from competitor Ransom Olds and then improved dramatically. The process developed in three stages. First, teams of assemblers moved from chassis to chassis, or assemblers simply stayed with their chassis while others brought them tools and parts as needed. With this method, the average time for the completion of a Model T chassis was twelve and a half man-hours. Then came line production: a rope or cable winch pulled the chassis along while teams of assemblers moved with it, picking up parts from bins strategically placed along the way. The progress was jerky and irregular, but the average completion time was cut dramatically, to just under six man-hours. In the final evolution, the workers were placed in carefully calculated stationary positions along the way, while the moving chassis ran along at waist-height, while overhead carriers and gravity slides brought subassemblies as needed. Best time: ninety-three minutes. Henry rejoiced: "Save ten steps a day for each of 12,000 employees, and you will have saved fifty miles of wasted motion and mis-spent energy."[4] Output more than doubled in 1912–1913 and doubled again the next year, while the workforce actually shrank. By the end of the First World War, almost half the cars in the world were Model Ts. Ford had made more than fifteen million of them by the time it shut down the line in 1928—almost a million a year.[5]

What was the larger economic significance of these new ways? Consider Ford's supply needs. In 1913, the company required one million lamps, eight hundred thousand wheels, eight hundred thousand tires, ninety thousand tons of steel, the hides of four hundred thousand cattle, nearly two million square feet of window glass, and twelve million hickory billets for wheel spokes. It took thirty-five thousand freight cars to ship the finished autos. Ford also needed continuous flows of coal, iron, nickel, brass, rubber, lubricants, and gasoline, among other things, brought in from all over—the Mesabi Range, West Virginia, Canada—and all delivered on time. And that was just Ford. Nothing like the auto industry had ever been seen: a swarm of manufacturing plants, suppliers, shippers, agents, road builders, sellers, and repairers, all devoted to supplying and servicing a costly and complex object that everyone wanted.[6]

The moving assembly line soon became central to the manufacture of many goods throughout the world. Henry Ford, with the aid of a remarkable team of collaborators, had effected a revolution in production technology.

Not surprisingly, the new technology posed a problem for labor morale in Ford's older plants. Repetitious work was dull and thus fatiguing, and the employees were under constant pressure to raise productivity ever higher. Henry Ford's solution was an economic one: he pushed the workers hard and rewarded them with higher pay. Instead of paying them based on the number of vehicles produced, which was the prevalent method in Detroit, he switched to a daily wage. To ensure a diligent, reliable workforce, he set the bar high, paying five dollars a day, two to three times what workers for other automakers made.

Nothing did more than this pay raise to enhance Ford's reputation as a statesman of industry and a model of employer wisdom and generosity. Newspapers all over the country carried the story, and would-be workers lined up outside the factory gates by the thousands, far beyond the hiring possibilities of even this most promising of young companies. One newspaper headline summed it all up: "God Bless Henry Ford."[7] In addition to the wage increase, Ford instituted a sociological department at the company, charged with inculcating moral virtue in the workers, both on the job and at home. Ford was also ready, far more than most, to hire black workers as well as immigrants (whom the firm taught to speak English), ex-cons, and disabled people—even the grievously handicapped—for whom he charged his staff to find jobs.

Through the first decade of the 1900s, Henry Ford was at the peak of his powers; he was aggressive, imaginative, technologically visionary, and extremely popular. It was just at this point that he found himself attacked by a would-be cartel of car producers, the so-called Association of Licensed Automobile Manufacturers (ALAM). The ALAM was the legal heir to a patent taken out in 1879 and renewed in 1895 by George B. Selden. The patent covered gasoline-powered vehicles, and had been purchased from Selden by a group of foresighted investment bankers. The patent itself had no basis in fact. Selden had invented nothing, just claimed the idea, which went back in Europe a decade or more, and the U.S. Patent Office had no business granting him rights. But the banking syndicate that had bought the rights did well at first, pulling in car makers who felt that surrender was cheaper than litigation.

But unlike the others, Ford went to court and challenged Selden in 1907 to produce a workable automobile. Court officers, lawyers, and car makers gathered for the fateful trial. Selden's machine coughed into life, rolled five yards, and stopped cold. That should have decided the matter, but the judge thought the failure irrelevant. Selden, he said, had not claimed to have invented a mechanical device, but rather to have brought together preexisting elements into a new "harmonious whole." On that basis, the judge upheld the patent in 1909.

Other car makers jumped to join the ALAM, among them the new General Motors, comprising Cadillac, Buick, Oldsmobile, and other makes, which agreed to pay the ALAM a million dollars in back royalties. Meanwhile, the ALAM threatened everyone in the industry: manufacturers, dealers, owners. Henry Ford dug in his heels and stood firm. He put up twelve million dollars in bonds to indemnify any Ford dealer or customer who might be sued by the ALAM, changed lawyers, and shouted his continued resistance to what he saw as a phony claim. In January 1911, the appeals court ruled in Ford's favor and condemned the ALAM in such categorical terms that there was no point in the group's fighting on. The ALAM dissolved, to the intense joy of most of its own members, who were themselves unhappy about paying royalties.

Thus Henry Ford almost single-handedly freed the American car industry from an outrageous piracy. Biographer Robert Lacey lauds Ford's "lone crusade" against the motor trust, seeing it as a key moment in Ford's rise to prominence in the public imagination: "Innovator, giant-killer, and tribune of the people, a new American folk hero was beginning to stand revealed."[8]

Ford's non-automotive activities soon grew, and he became a public figure, hobnobbing with the rich and powerful. In photographs we see him sitting with Woodrow Wilson, leg thrown over the arm of an easy chair, buddy boys in a club. He brought an unabashed populist Midwestern point of view to the Eastern establishment. He became particularly outspoken about the war raging in Europe, a conflict he believed tragically stupid and wasteful.

By this time he had more money than he could possibly spend, and because of his populist business practices (especially the wage hike), he was approached by a steady stream of pacifists who sought connection to his prestige and funding. Among them was a Jewish Hungarian named Rosika Schwimmer, who proposed a plan to stop the war by sending a delegation of pacifists to Europe on a chartered "Peace Ship." Ford was enchanted with the idea, and he organized a group to book passage. Before he set sail, he granted an interview in which he proudly boasted, "We're going to stop the war. . . . We're going to get the boys out of the trenches by Christmas." The crusade captured the public imagination briefly, but ultimately it proved a colossal fiasco; the journey had no strategy beyond idealism, and Ford had no vision other than a belief that if he could personally gather the heads of all the warring states in the same room, he could get them to see the folly of their ways.

The ship docked in Oslo, Norway, in the dead of winter, 1915. Ford gave one highly confusing speech, in which he stated that it would be wiser for the munitions factories of Europe to produce tractors instead of weapons (not coincidentally, he had recently released a new tractor on the European market). Soon after, Ford himself gave up the project, and returned home as soon as he could, leaving his fellow Peace Shipmates behind.

This was his first exposure to monumental failure, and it galled him. Many laughed at him, in the press and in person. Ford found a scapegoat for his own failure through the anti-Semitic beliefs that had been developing within him for several years. In fact, he had even told Rosika Schwimmer during their journey, "I know who started the war—the German-Jewish bankers."[9] He had imbibed and internalized a casual, habitual anti-Semitism from childhood, but after the Peace Ship debacle, his anti-Semitism became increasingly virulent, taking on even stronger elements of paranoia.

From a business perspective, however, the Peace Ship project had its virtues. It had cost about half a million dollars—say, ten million in today's money—but Henry argued that as a fee for penetrating the European market, the cost was a bargain. Besides, he noted, at least he had tried to promote peace. Meanwhile, the war raged, and Ford Motors made a fortune supplying vehicles and equipment to the Allies. Ford himself would have been just as happy to do the same for the other side—as a highly profitable proof of his impartiality.

Peace returned with the end of the war, but Henry never forgot his animus against Jews, and it is no coincidence that the passing years brought him the company of people with similar convictions, including Charles Lindbergh, the American hero who later became a friend and proponent of the Nazis, and Father Charles E. Coughlin, a clerical spokesman for anti-Jewish views going back to the Crucifixion. In 1919, Ford purchased *The Dearborn Independent,* a small weekly newspaper that became the medium through which he could disseminate his views and turn his private prejudice into political expression. His numerous activities included writing and publishing the regular column "The International Jew: The World's Foremost Problem," publishing and defending *The Protocols of the Elders of Zion,* financing fascistic anti-American parties, and publicly defending the Germans in the 1930s. The only thing that gave him pause in these attacks was that his outrage at the Jews had negative consequences for Ford auto sales. Ultimately, he signed a public apology—which he is said never to have read—but his private opinions never changed. In 1938, he was vain enough to accept with pride a German medal of honor, the "Grand Cross of the German Eagle." (His successors at the helm of the company have struggled to make amends, but the bitter memory of anti-Semitism has remained, and to this day many Jews avoid Ford products.[10])

With time, Henry Ford became increasingly stubborn and autocratic, both in politics and in business. This grated on some of his colleagues, in particular his old associate James Couzens, general manager and guardian of the company accounts. Couzens was strongly patriotic and, with America's entry into the European conflict in 1917, pro-war, a position that clashed strongly with Henry's pacificism, and which led to clashes between the two men. For Couzens, Henry was turning out to be two personae, one friendly and sweet, the other harshly autocratic, even paranoiac. The occasion for their final confrontation was a fierce attack Henry wrote for the company newspaper, condemning American loans to Britain and France. British foreign secretary Lord Balfour was then coming to the United States with a delegation to ask for more funds, and Henry wanted them "kicked off the dock." Couzens, vice president and treasurer, stopped publication of the paper. This infuriated Henry, who reminded Couzens that he owned 59 percent of the company stock and could say what he wanted. True, said Couzens, but then I resign. His departure left Henry entirely in control, for better and for worse, of his own fiefdom.

Couzens's departure left no one significant in the corporation who was prepared to stand up to Henry, and what evolved is an example of one person's wielding total control over an organization. Henry's vision, arrogance, and autocratic nature shaped the corporation, molded the family and its business, and overshadowed both his descendants and much of the industry for many decades. He became increasingly intolerant of even the hint of contradiction by his partners and employees. It also pained him to share the company's profits with the shareholders, whom he saw (and spoke of) as parasites. From his perspective, they had already gotten their money back over and over.

Among those who felt his wrath were the Dodge brothers, longtime suppliers of parts to Ford, and minority stockholders in the company. John Dodge was a member of the Ford board of directors, but in 1913 he resigned and gave notice of the Dodges' intention to manufacture their own car. Vexed at this lèse-majesté, Henry responded by eliminating shareholder bonuses and cutting dividends, so as to deprive the Dodges of resources they were counting on to finance their factory. He also kept cutting prices for the Model T as demand grew; by August 1916, the car that had once cost $825 was down to $345. (No wonder the 390,000 cars Ford made in 1915 amounted to 45 percent of the whole industry's output!) Meanwhile, *The Wall Street Journal* suggested that the introduction of the five-dollar workday had had a similar motive behind it. And anything left, Henry announced, would go to finance Ford development, in particular a new plant on the River Rouge. In November 1916, the Dodges sued to compel Ford to distribute 75 percent of its cash surplus. The case went to trial and through numerous appeals until a final decision was handed down in February 1919, ordering Ford to pay out over $19 million to shareholders, plus $1.5 million in interest.

Despite the fact that Ford owned most of the company, and would therefore be paying most of the dividends to himself, he was furious. He detested outside interference, and he preferred to deprive himself rather than enrich unworthy others. He began a series of maneuvers, all with the intent of prying shares of the company back from investors: he announced his own retirement and the installation of his son, Edsel, as president of the company, and he announced his intention to start a new company to build a new car that would sell for as little as $250. It was the Malcomson coup all over again, and it worked, though not to the same extent. This time, Henry had competitors. A number of canny investors offered substantial sums to the Dodges and the other minority shareholders for their stock—not as much as the shares were worth, but enough to make Henry understand that he could not "steal" these holdings.

Over time, Henry managed to buy back all 41 percent of the outstanding shares. The payoff was very good for the lucky few. James Couzens's sister, who had put in one hundred dollars "way back when," got $262,000 for her shares, along with $95,000 that she had received as dividends over the years. Couzens himself had invested $10,900, and now received $29,308,858, over and above dividends of $10,355,000. The Dodge brothers got slightly less per share, making $25 million, plus accrued dividends of $9.5 million, for the $12,500 they'd put in. All told, Henry paid a fortune—almost $106 million for the 41.5 percent of the company owned outside the family. It was a bargain, as Ford Motors was worth a lot more than $250 million, and indeed a few years later a syndicate offered him a cool billion for the company.[11]

There was nothing like it anywhere: one family owning 100 percent of a billion-dollar corporation. Henry Ford could now do as he pleased, without concern for others' reservations, and without fear of contradiction. He was sitting on top of the world, and he began to find autos less interesting than before, if only because, in his grandiosity, he'd begun to see all commercial competition as an act of implicit disrespect from his competitors. But he could not stand boredom: "The unhappiest man on earth," he once said, "is the one who has nothing to do."

He began to focus less on the business and more on politics, public causes, and plain self-indulgence. Nothing was too big for him. He bought a railway. He manufactured airplanes. He built worker housing. He financed a hospital that he himself had designed, and he worked closely with the doctors. He tried to take over, for a song, dams, factories, and powerhouses at Muscle Shoals, along the Tennessee River. He sought to promote the cultivation of soybeans, the better to feed people and profit American farmers. He played the country squire on his estate in Georgia, visiting the farms, checking the soil, destroying the residents' moonshine stills, draining the swamps, opening a medical clinic for the poor, financing agricultural experiment stations. He ferociously opposed disrespectful labor unions—so much so that his workers came to see him as a ruthless capitalist exploiter. Through it all, his anti-Semitism grew, such that he took on the Jews as enemies of mankind.[12]

He ran for Congress and narrowly lost. He sought support for his candidacy for president of the United States, seeing Warren G. Harding (as many did) as a corrupt disgrace. And he continued his attack on Jews as the enemies of mankind. On the personal side, he even took up with a secretary thirty years his junior and may well have fathered her child. Henry's wife, Clara, found out, but learned to live with the arrangement. She knew that Henry would never leave her.[13]

Henry Ford's willful personality was beginning to hurt him in business. To be sure, the Model T was selling in the millions, representing over 90 percent of the output of low-priced cars. But more and more people were buying autos, and numerous aspirant manufacturers were offering innovative models in competition with Ford. The General Motors offering in particular, from Cadillac at the top to Chevrolet at the bottom, challenged Ford leadership, the more so because these cars changed every year and proposed new devices and accessories that made driving easier and more pleasurable. From 1924 to 1926, Ford's output went down by 400,000 units, while Chevrolet's went up by 350,000 and Dodge's by more than 70,000. Ford's share of auto output fell from 48 to 30 percent.

Ford Motors was not blind to this new trend, but Henry was so convinced of the virtues of his immortal achievement that he resisted novelty. His competitors had gone over to the foot-pedal accelerator; he was still using a hand throttle. GM offered five hundred lacquer colors and upholstery choices in the new Cadillac. Fords were available in red, green, blue, and black—mostly black. To be sure, Ford cars were cheap, but by now half a dozen other makes were also selling for under a thousand dollars. At most, Henry accepted some indispensable improvements as extras.

The best example of auto novelty was the self-starter, first installed on the Cadillac in 1912. Next to such body changes as the windshield, this was probably the most important advance since the gasoline engine and the pneumatic tire. Henry Ford resisted: he knew how to crank a motor. But he had to yield here, because the self-starter made all the difference between chauffeur-driven and owner-driven cars, between male and female drivers. So he allowed his customers to order one as a supplement. And in 1923 he adopted low-pressure balloon tires and made available closed weatherproof bodies with two front doors.

The negative effect of Henry's reticence is best measured by the developing race between Ford and General Motors. In the early twenties GM was running hard to compete with Ford, but before the end of the decade it had become the biggest, most profitable automobile manufacturer in the world. General Motors was in character and personality the very opposite of Ford. Ford Motors was the product, achievement, and property of an individual (and highly individualistic) entrepreneur and was to remain for another two generations a family-run enterprise. General Motors started that way but quickly became a managerial company. As we have seen (in chapter 3), the company was founded by Will Durant, a visionary who lacked only money and who, unlike Henry Ford, had no problem asking banks and bankers for help. And he needed it, because his way of growing was to buy up promising companies such as Buick Motors. Meanwhile, one of the top executives of DuPont, the Delaware explosives manufacturer, a man named John J. Raskob, smelled promise here, and in 1914 he persuaded his "daddy," Pierre S. du Pont (that's what Raskob called him), to buy a small bundle of GM stock.

That was a good tip, because GM made lots of money in the Great War (as did DuPont), and the value of the stock shot up. By 1922, the DuPont company had invested eighty million dollars in what had come to be known as the General Motors Corporation. As part of the new venture, Pierre du Pont brought in Alfred P. Sloan, business planner and organizer extraordinaire, who turned the company into the very model of rational, efficient management, an example to other big firms, including DuPont itself. With Sloan at the helm, General Motors pursued the multi-brand model of auto production begun by Durant, a hierarchy of cars for all purses and all stages in life. There would be six brands in all, each with its own range, each with its market appeal. The Chevrolet, for example, would not attempt to compete with Ford at the bottom—no chance of that—but rather at the top of the lowest range. As Sloan put it, "It is not proposed to compete with the Ford grade, but to produce a car that will be so superior to the Ford, yet so near the Ford price, that demand will be drawn from the Ford grade and lifted to the slightly higher price in preference to putting up with the Ford deficiencies."[14] Those deficiencies were by then something of a scandal.

Sloan was betting on rising incomes and a growing appetite for motor transportation. Ford, with its limited offering, could not compete. Before the decade was out, GM had pushed Ford into second place and had a net worth of billions.[15] By 1937, toward the end of the Great Depression, GM held roughly 45 percent of the American car market and was making almost four fifths of the industry's profits—far better obviously than Ford. Throughout the Depression years of the thirties, the company was making 18 percent on its investment. It could easily have had a bigger share of the market, but Sloan felt that that would simply invite an antitrust prosecution.[16] Besides, better to take the dependable cream and leave the ups and downs to the competition. That was the name of game: making money.

Edsel Ford was the only child of Henry and Clara Ford. Born in 1893, when his father was thirty, he grew up in a busy, busy family. Even so, his father doted on him in an absentminded way, buying him the latest mechanical toys, taking him on outings and errands, proudly showing him off on bicycles and in early cars.

Edsel never went to college. Henry did not see the need, the less so as he himself had never gone and had destined his son to a life as heir to the Ford Motor Company. Edsel went into the firm as a teenager and moved around to different departments, learning as he went. It was no doubt premature of Henry to turn the presidency over to Edsel in 1919, when the young man was only twenty-five; but, then, Henry would still be around to oversee things. That was the problem: Edsel was at best a figurehead and never knew when he might be reversed or overruled. And everyone in the firm was aware of this contradiction in power.[17]

Edsel was very different from his father. For one thing, he was not a mechanical genius. He knew cylinders and chokes, but he could not show workers how to do things better or walk through the shops as though he belonged there rather than in an office. For another, he had the sweetness and patience his father lacked. His very limitations encouraged an open mind—an awareness of competition and the shortcomings of the immortal Model T. It was Edsel who worried about body design and dashboard at a time when appearance was becoming increasingly important. It was Edsel who pushed for new Ford cars in the 1920s, while Henry dug in his heels. (Also for innovation was William Knudsen, who was forced out of Ford in 1921 for his temerity and went over to General Motors, where he enjoyed his revenge cold.) As Henry put it, this was his business, and he intended to run it as he pleased. And that meant no nonsense about love.[18] Or a phony presidency.

In the end, it was the market—the declining Ford sales, the success of Chevrolet et al.—that forced Henry's "technological senility."[19] Sales went up into the mid-twenties, rising to over two million cars a year in 1923–1925. But share was falling. In 1925 the Ford share of the popular car market fell from 57 to 45 percent; in 1926 down to 34 percent and still falling. And share told everything. So did the letters of complaint and disparagement. The Ford car made too much noise. It was too slow for paved highways. Suspension was uncomfortable. And it needed a modern gear shift. Many former Ford buyers left it because they were just plain bored, or as their careers advanced and their incomes rose. But Ford left no room for realists. These complainants, many of them Ford dealers, did not understand: they were insulting Henry Ford in the inmost fiber of his being.

Still, there was no arguing with the market. The Model T was tearfully abandoned, and Ford closed down while arrangements were made for production of a new car, the Model A, equipped with all that had been lacking. The new model was initially a wild success, the answer to all the needs and desires of the Ford family. But these were bad times for the economy as a whole. Depression was freezing the hearts and emptying the pockets of potential customers, while competitors brought out new and better cars. This was particularly true of Chrysler, which had devised a new motor suspension that sharply reduced engine vibration and noise and gave the relatively low-priced Plymouth the smooth feel of a six- or eight-cylinder luxury car. A generous, proud Walter Chrysler drove one of his new cars out to Dearborn to show Henry and Edsel what he would be offering customers. Charles Sorensen recognized the advantages of Chrysler engineering, but Henry Ford would not hear of it. "For no given reason," recalled Sorensen, "Henry Ford did not like it, and that was that."[20]

Meanwhile, car output in the United States fell from 4.59 million in 1929 to 2.79 million in 1930; 1.97 million in 1931, to 1.14 million in 1932—down 75 percent. The only car to sell more in 1932 than in 1931 was the Plymouth, whose share of the low-priced majors went from 7.8 percent in 1931 to 24.1 percent in 1933. In that year, Chrysler overtook Ford for second place in this category—"an achievement without modern parallel," to quote *Fortune* magazine.[21]

Ford was now compelled to lay off much of its workforce, and labor issues took center stage for the next decade. This boded ill. Henry, for all his faults and obstinacy, understood much about machines and engines. But he had little understanding of the men who labored in his mills and plants, and less and less patience for their troubles. He thought depression was good for them, good for the United States, good for the soul. He had no use for his son's compassion in these matters, and instead turned over much of the responsibility for labor control and discipline to an aide who can only be termed a thug, Harry Bennett. Bennett, an ex-navy man, was a semiprofessional pugilist who could and did beat up men twice his size. Henry Ford took to this bullyboy to the point of preferring him to Edsel, whose sweetness and politeness drove his father crazy. And given a free hand, Bennett installed a kind of mafia at Ford, made up of cons and thugs from inside and outside the firm. When labor union organizers made Ford a target, Bennett brought in his goons and summoned conniving police authorities to attack, even kill, some of these courageous men in order to intimidate the rest. All of this in the face of the pro-labor New Deal administration. Unsurprisingly, Henry Ford did not like Franklin D. Roosevelt.

Edsel and Harry Bennett did not get along. Understandable: to Edsel, Bennett was an intrusive interloper and brownnoser, intriguing for the succession. Meanwhile, Henry Ford backed Bennett and liked him personally, but Bennett understood that the old man would never give up his dynastic commitment. Henry kept telling himself that his policy of toughness would shape his son to the task. In fact, Edsel was tougher than his father, and drove himself to exhaustion and illness in the face of repeated contradictions and scoldings by an old man who ran the show from retirement and gave a free hand to Bennett and his goons. Edsel gave particular attention to accounts and car design, but found himself ever thwarted by those employees who sought irregular advancement.

The result was despair and death. Henry nursed the belief that Edsel had made himself ill by drinking alcoholic beverages, but everyone else in the family, including wife, daughter-in-law, and grandchildren, knew who was at fault. Benson, Edsel's second son, went into a rage: "Grandfather is responsible for Father's sickness, and I'm through with him!" Edsel kept himself alive through undulant fever and stomach cancer until he could see his youngest son come home from the Hotchkiss School, then let himself die in May 1943, aged forty-nine. On the day of the funeral, the Ford factories were shut down for all of five minutes. Henry had his moments of guilt: "Maybe I pushed the boy too hard." But he was a master of denial. In the meantime, Harry Bennett actually persuaded Henry to add a codicil to his will, stipulating that on his death, the company should pass for ten years under the control of trustees, among them Charles Sorensen, "cast-iron Charlie," and Charles Lindbergh, Henry's favorite Jew-hater and Germanophile isolationist. "Jews—that's all they talk about," said Bennett, who would be made secretary of the board.

Henry would have replaced Edsel as president with Harry Bennett, but at this point the Ford women, who controlled nearly a third of the voting stock, made their presence felt. Normally docile and discreet, Edsel's widow, Eleanor, accused Henry of killing his son, and Clara quietly agreed. Embarrassed, Henry decided to take over the presidency himself and, with a view to the future and the substantial stockholdings of Edsel's family—Eleanor was threatening to sell them to the public—made Edsel's oldest son, Henry II, vice president. Also a factor was the federal government's concern: no one was ready to see a major war contractor fall into the hands of thugs, crooks, and fixers. So in August 1943, Henry II, then a naval ensign, was released from the service to join the Ford Motor Company.

Henry II began by walking around and visiting the works. He was stunned to find that the company was as decrepit and senile as the old man himself. Ford Motors, the car branch, had not posted a profit since 1931 and was losing millions of dollars a month. One aircraft department was still making trimotor propellers for a plane that had been out of production for years. Organizationally there was no effective management: no cost controls, no materials scheduling, no engineering of any significance. The company as a whole was making money thanks to wartime government orders, but it did not deserve what it got.

Henry II was determined to confront the problem that was plaguing the company: vetoes and interference from the old man and the Bennett crew. As he moved toward control of the company, he prepared to confront his grandfather. Once again, the women had their say. As Eleanor put it, "He killed my husband, and he's not going to kill my son." When Henry challenged his grandson, Eleanor responded by again threatening to sell her stock to outsiders. Clara added her own quiet pressure, and on September 20,

1945, a fateful family meeting was held. Henry I passed the presidency to Henry II, and Henry II, in accepting, made clear what was on his mind: "I told him I'd take it only if I had a completely free hand to make any changes I wanted to make. We argued about that; but he didn't withdraw his offer."[22] Henry Ford II took control of the company with the goal of major reorganization. Some might even have called it a purge. Henry II and the rest of the family were particularly determined to rid the company of Harry Bennett.

Henry II was not typical top-notch management material. Jowly and overweight, he had lived an indulged childhood marked by mediocre school performance and unlimited funding. Because of a cheating episode in his senior year, he never got his Yale diploma. He had his virtues, however—in particular a willingness to respond to his own mistakes and an ability to enjoy life that was seemingly absent in the rest of the family. He was an auto man by inheritance, not by passion, but he was keen enough to know that he needed help: he had inherited an enormous financial mess, one far beyond his own capacity to solve. He found the help he needed right after the war ended, in the form of a group of air force logistics experts headed by Colonel Charles "Tex" Thornton. There's nothing sexy in logistics, but after all, supplies, production data, and schedules pose the same problems in any industry; only the materials are different. For Ford, however, this emphasis on logistics—on actually keeping records and tracking accounts—was something new. Old Henry had no use for such exercises. If he could have, he'd have banished the accountants altogether, and indeed he tried. The company usually made money, and it had no outside investors to answer to. How did Ford know how much it owed? Measure the stack of bills and multiply by a reasonable approximation of amount due per inch. It was primarily taxes that made it necessary to count. As University of Michigan history professor David Lewis, a Ford family expert, put it, before Thornton came on board, "Ford couldn't tell you whether they were making money or not."[23] Thornton's team of ten became known as the "Whiz Kids," and over the next ten years they completely transformed the corporation, returning it to profitability.

But good accounts and organization are only the surface. The heart of a successful auto manufacture is the quality and excitement of the product, the sex appeal of the model. Does it turn the consumer on? Appearance counts; speed counts; even the sound of the door closing makes a difference, because the user, who cannot understand what lies under the hood, thinks it proof of solidity and workmanship. Henry II used to have himself picked up each morning in a different model so he could do his own sound test.

In theory, the money men and the auto production men were teammates. In fact, though, they often found themselves at loggerheads. The money men wanted to save; the auto men, to spend. Top Whiz Kid Robert McNamara, the company controller in the early 1950s, made it a point to deny whatever the auto men wanted. The goal was to make them sweat, to force them to prove their case twice over, then cut their request in half. When Lewis Crusoe, general manager of the Ford division, sought to renovate a factory in Louisville in which the aisles were too narrow to get a forklift through and the ovens too cool to get modern paints to dry properly, McNamara stalled by insisting that piecemeal modernization was logically unacceptable, that the state and needs of all plants should be reviewed. Crusoe thought that would take six months. In fact, it took much longer; whatever evidence Crusoe came up with, McNamara wanted more. Meanwhile, the company could not meet the demand for the 1952 model.

In the end, the finance men won. They talked better and faster, dressed better, knew how to use calculators and throw figures around. And it is always easier not to spend, especially when spending entails dependency on outside money sources, which at Ford were always defined as the enemy.

Many of these differences ended in Henry II's lap. He presided over the strategy meetings and inevitably was asked to decide those issues that surpassed debate. In extremis, he sought for Solomonic solutions that would not leave either party vexed beyond recall. But the long-run result was clear: Henry II needed the money men, talked to them more easily, found them intellectually more congenial. Slowly but surely, the auto men found themselves pushed toward the sidelines.

The tension increased as the habit of wealth led Henry I and his descendants into the ways of prestige and enjoyment. The founder himself, as we have seen, found himself drawn into political and ideological diversions, to the cost of the firm. He also pursued his own program of collecting mementos with a view to rewriting history. Moreover, in spite of a desiccated appearance and ascetic manner, he had his self-indulgences. With all that money and power, temptations abounded.

Henry II and his brothers largely eschewed the political, but they found their own amusement in social engagements, where they naturally played a leadership role, and in such cultural pastimes as art and collections, along with a tireless pursuit of tireless vacations. The women played a role here. Clara had happily remained house- and family-bound. And Eleanor, with all her Hudson rearing, had her hands full with Edsel and their children. But Anne McDonnell Ford, Henry II's wife, was an active socialite by training and predilection and expected her husband to do his bit at her side. The motor company was only a part of her life, a subordinate part. Eventually the two went their separate ways, because Henry II, in the best Ford tradition, suffered from ocular distraction, carnal temptation, and uncontrollable appetite. This surrender to pleasure was said to have been influenced by social contacts with his Italian counterpart, Gianni Agnelli, heir to Fiat. Agnelli was a spectacularly busy, blatant, and successful womanizer, with partners and playmates ranging from noble damsels, to Hollywood starlets, to other men's wives, to just plain whores. For Henry II, this exposure to the opportunities of glamour and wealth was a revelation: "So *this* is what running a family car business is all about!"[24]

Henry II was also a serious drinker, the kind that manages to swill into the small hours, catch a little sleep, and then get to a meeting that morning with a controlled appearance of sobriety. The old man had been a teetotaler, but this penchant for drink was a family trait: Henry II's brother Benson died an alcoholic, and Benson's children escaped only by having the sense to flee into Alcoholics Anonymous.

By most accounts, Henry II led the company quite well for many years. The Ford Motor Company remained throughout a family firm, but no longer an absolute monarchy. For Edsel, the company was his father's. His father had made it, and his will was law. But for Henry II, the company had an identity of its own, embracing all manner of participant interests: from management to dealers and repairers to car buyers and users, and eventually shareholders, including the so-called Ford Foundation, a major recipient of Ford family largesse. But Henry II was not his grandfather, and while he fought to preserve his personal primacy, he needed many skilled collaborators to make and sell cars and to manage the firm. This meant men of enterprise and ambition, and such men are inevitably potential rivals. Even Henry Ford I, the grand old man, had run into one in his protégé Harry Bennett, although Bennett had thought better of trying to displace the founder. But when it came to Edsel, or Henry II, why not? Bennett was still on the scene when Henry II took over, and the new boss dealt with this threat quickly. Firing Bennett was one of his first acts as president.

Henry II's most serious challenger was Lido "Lee" Iacocca, son of hard-driving Italian immigrants and ambitious to the point that he drew up a calendar of his own anticipated promotion. Iacocca was born in Allentown, Pennsylvania, in 1924. His father, Nick, raised him with high expectations and with the male chauvinist, money-powered attitudes he had learned in the old country.

Young Lee Iacocca went to work for Ford as a trainee engineer in 1946, but quickly realized that this was not the path of rapid advancement. He expected, he said, to be a vice president by age thirty-five. So he got himself a job in the field, in sales. He learned to know his merchandise and his dealers and, even more important, to talk fast and hard, with no concessions to doubt. He got so good at it that he was quickly promoted to teach other salesmen, and he even wrote a handbook on the subject.

In 1956, after a decade of labor in the boondocks, Iacocca got the idea that set him soaring. He figured that a 20 percent down payment plus monthly installments of fifty-six dollars would pay for a new Ford, then introduced the slogan "56 for '56" in the Philadelphia area. Then, by way of finding customers, he sent salesmen to parking lots to look for well-cared-for older Fords and put purchase offers on the windshields: "Would-ya-take . . . ?" The campaign was a huge success, and Philadelphia became the bestselling district in the country. Robert McNamara so liked what he saw that he extended the approach to the other sales areas and calculated that the campaign helped sell seventy-five thousand additional units. Iacocca was reassigned from Philadelphia to Dearborn, and the company paid to send him to learn speech and confidence at the Dale Carnegie Institute.

In 1960, Iacocca was summoned by Henry Ford II to learn that he had been put in charge of the Ford Division, the most important unit in the company. McNamara had gone off to Washington to serve in Kennedy's Cabinet, and his absence gave Iacocca a chance to move up. It was a good time to be promoted, although Iacocca did have some regret that, having just turned thirty-six, he had missed his own deadline for advancement.

Iacocca's weakness was that, for all his engineering training, he was not really an auto man. He had to rely on the skills and imagination of the technicians. On the other hand, he understood the appeal of style, whereas the product men "thought a guy buys a car purely to be able to get from here to there. They didn't understand that a guy wants to be *seen* going from here to there."[25]

Iacocca easily picked up the habit of giving orders and imposing duties from above, as McNamara had. He watched the sales figures, understood that publicity mattered, relied heavily on his own taste and instinct, set schedules and goals and expected his people to meet them. His two big coups were the Mustang and the Pinto. The Mustang was presented at the New York World's Fair in the spring of 1964. The car cost only $2,368, but it looked twice the price. It conveyed a sense of speed, play, youth, and excitement. Young people loved it, and older people bought it to feel and look young. The splash got Iacocca simultaneous cover stories in *Time* and *Newsweek*—great press for Ford, and great inflation for Iacocca's ego. The Pinto came out toward the end of 1970. It was light and cheap and oh so sporty.

Both cars, however, embodied the weaknesses of finance-driven, thrifty production. Iacocca wanted these cars to be compact and light, European style, because every increase in weight called for further increases in engine size and power, and thus an increase in cost. The Pinto in particular aimed at a "2,000/2,000" goal: two thousand pounds, two thousand dollars. It was up to the production men to find ways to meet these demands.

Obviously, the easiest way to cut costs was to cut corners.[26] One formula for lightness was to use fewer parts by making one part serve two purposes. That philosophy was all right in the realm of body ornament, but potentially perilous when applied to structural or mechanical elements. In the Pinto this proved extremely dangerous: the gas tank was squeezed in at the rear between bumper and axle, and the floor of the trunk did double duty as the top of the gas tank. In an accident, the filler neck to the gas tank was easily torn loose, and the tank would blow up; meanwhile, the light body frame tended to crush around the doors, which then jammed and made exiting very difficult.

This pursuit of economy was a recipe for death. A conservative estimate suggests that gas tank explosions from rear-end Pinto crashes killed dozens of people. Another source bumps the estimate to more than nine hundred fatalities. And although the histories and court records primarily mention the Pinto, there is good reason to believe that the same design flaw was already a shortcoming of the Mustang. Ford engineers had been aware of this problem from their own crash tests and those of government and industrial laboratories. But the power of the top-down management structure at the company was such that no one dared speak of this problem to the impatient higher-ups. Better to get the car ready in time, weigh it, and sell it. What was a human life worth, after all? (No more than a court would make the company pay.) Thrift has consequences—or, as Iacocca liked to say, the American people want economy, no matter how much it costs them.[27] The sad truth is how incredibly simple and inexpensive it would have been to save those lives. After enough public outrage over the Pinto, Ford finally modified the design to fix the problem by adding a small plastic protective casing to the gas tank. Cost: one dollar.

Despite these troubles, and some public perception that held him largely responsible, Iacocca gained power and popularity at Ford, and ensconced himself as the number two man: a boon to the corporation in many ways, but a significant threat to Henry II.

Henry Ford II's mother, Eleanor, died in October 1976. He was overcome with grief and began to rethink his life and work. He decided to extricate himself from the presidency and to retire. Before doing so, however, he'd have to ensure that the company was in good hands—*family* hands. This brought up many problems, the largest of which was how to get rid of Iacocca. Henry could see another Ford taking his place at the helm, or possibly even a meritorious outsider. But not Iacocca, whom Henry II neither liked nor trusted.

He first tried to get the board of directors to fire Iacocca, but they were reluctant, and it appeared he would have to do the dirty work himself. He then tried to find some illegal or discreditable behavior to hang on Iacocca. To this end, he spent a small fortune on investigators and spies, all without success.[28] The only bit of paydirt they found was Iacocca's role in the Pinto scandal, but Henry himself would most likely have been implicated as well, and he chose not to pursue that tack.

He then changed tactics and attacked Iacocca's support base, isolating him by getting rid of all his allies, even when it meant firing some of the company's best men. Then, in April 1977, Henry II announced a major change in Ford management. In accordance with the suggestion of outside consultants, the firm would now be run by a triumvirate: Henry, Iacocca, and Philip Caldwell, an experienced executive who had had great success running Ford International, the biggest money-maker in the company. Caldwell, he made clear, would be vice chairman, in effect, second in command. Iacocca found this hard to swallow—first the symbolism, then the implications. But he got the message: "In 1975," he said later, "Henry Ford started his month-by-month premeditated plan to destroy me."[29] Iacocca saw it as a dynastic response by "King Henry" to the prospect of mortality. Here is how Iacocca gauged Henry's rationale: "He turned animal. I imagine his first impulse was: 'I don't want that *Italian* interloper taking over. What's going to happen to the family business if I get a heart attack and die? Before I know it, he'll sneak in here one night, take my name off the building, and turn this place into the Iacocca Motor Company. Where does that leave my son, Edsel?'"[30]

Iacocca's first thought was to hit at Caldwell, but he soon found that Caldwell had his own constituency and could hold his own. Besides, Iacocca's fight was with Henry II. Iacocca sought allies among the directors, but even the ones who sympathized with him were not about to take on the Fords. He tried to win over Henry's long-alienated brother Benson, but when the chips were down, Benson, for all his tears, sided with his brother and the family. As Henry had tried with him, Iacocca sought grounds for Henry's impeachment. He collected what he could on Henry's womanizing and partying, but quickly realized that even indiscreet moral turpitude and childish behavior did not matter to the family, the board, or even the shareholders.[31]

As one outside director remarked, Iacocca's quixotic campaign was "an act of insanity; he just didn't have the cards."[32] Iacocca made a last-ditch attempt at a coup in June 1978, when Henry was away on a trip to China. As Ford executive Walter Hayes tells it, Iacocca took a company plane to see directors George Bennett in Boston and Joseph Cullman III, chairman of Philip Morris, in New York. With them he argued, to no avail, that Henry II was senile and not up to the job.

This kind of maneuvering can be self-defeating. One of the directors warned Henry about Iacocca's machinations, and Henry decided that the time had come and that he indeed held all the best cards. He went to a subcommittee of the board and gave them the choice: "It's me or Iacocca." Not surprisingly, it was Ford all the way. They held no vote, but sentiment was unanimous.

The next day, in the company of his younger brother William Clay Ford, Henry told Iacocca that his services were no longer wanted. Iacocca pleaded his case eloquently and hard, with four-letter words as needed. Henry was unmoved. William Clay told Iacocca that he had won the argument. Iacocca agreed, adding, "But I'm dead, and you and he are still alive." The Fords gave Iacocca an office in the Parts Distribution Center to work in until he found another job. There he found cracked linoleum and only broken plastic cups to hold his coffee. His secretary wept. He *was* dead, at least at Ford.[33] (He did, however, go on to a new career as head of Chrysler.)

This prolonged battle between Henry and Iacocca is not unique in the business world, where struggles for power at both high and low strata are an integral part of most job descriptions. This is a compelling example, though, of the kinds of battles that threaten dynasties. Iacocca's ascendance was the greatest individual threat to family supremacy Ford has encountered. He had been remarkably successful and had helped lead the company back into both profitability and a special place in the public mind. In many ways, he was a logical choice to succeed Henry II. He was not family, though, and he was too dynamic and ambitious to be controlled by family. When he became too powerful, he had to be forced out.

Shortly thereafter, Henry II resigned as chairman. He remained, however, head of the finance committee of the board of directors, and in that capacity he was able to keep an eye on whatever he wanted. This was a replay of his grandfather's tenacious surveillance in retirement.

It was outsider Philip Caldwell who took Henry II's place as chairman, but Henry was not pleased. This was a company that had always been headed by a Ford, and Henry liked it that way. But now the family seemed incapable of generating the administrative talent required, in part because the male heirs had taken for granted that they would always be able to get well-paid posts with the company and did not have to improve or prove themselves—as their mediocre college performances showed. This, it should be said, is a major shortcoming of dynastic enterprise, as it is of any culture that treats its males as privileged princes from childhood on. Meanwhile, Ford family ties were breaking down. Fights were breaking out among the cousins of the fourth generation, with the women unexpectedly combative and articulate and their husbands mixing in.

These were hard times, on the auto side and the family side. Whose the fault, the old regime's or the new? What matter? The old regime took responsibility and did its best to hold on to power. But even old friends and allies were beginning to pay attention to ability and qualifications. Henry II would have liked to pass on the chairmanship to his brother, but the other directors would not hear of it. There was too much at stake here to let family pride and incompetence get in the way. Years later, when Henry was asked by a journalist how he could have let these outsiders lay down the law, he gave an unassailable excuse: "I married the company." That was the only thing more potent than his own hereditary claim to preeminence. The man held his job by royal descent. Under the circumstances, he had no patience for reporters or biographers. Historian David Lewis interviewed him and asked where his personal papers would be housed. Nowhere, came the surprising answer; he was busily shredding them. No wonder Victor Lasky chose as title for Henry II's biography *Never Complain, Never Explain*.

Yet things had changed since the founder's time. The company head now had to sacrifice all to complex service, to give up all the other things and make the company number one. Henry did his best, but later in life he skipped the board meetings, left management to subordinates, and made up for some of the indulgences he had missed out on earlier—as his grandfather had. That kind of thing can hurt a company, though not necessarily. But it also makes it easier to lose the leader when he passes on.

After Henry's brother came his son Edsel II, whose painful graduation from Babson was the occasion of a grand fête. Edsel planned to join the company, aiming at the marketing side. "I'm not really very mechanically minded," he confessed. "I could change the spark plugs or the oil, but I'm not much of an engineer. . . . Unfortunately it isn't like it was in the days when a Ford just walked into the company. I'll have to go out and prove myself, which I really want to do. I hope some day to run the company, but if I can't, I can't."[34]

It was managers who took over now, business bureaucrats. These were not car people, and the quality of Ford cars now left something to be desired, as warranty records proved to those execs who paid attention. All the evidence showed Japanese cars to be superior, while the Japanese were able to pay substantially lower wages. What's more, Ford was paying the top managers extravagant bonuses, which would not make it easy to push the workforce to lower wages and salaries. Between 1980 and 1982, Ford showed losses of $3.3 billion, 43 percent of the company's net worth. Shareholder equity fell from $10.6 to $6 billion; the debt-to-equity ratio rose from 19 percent to 79 percent; the credit rating fell from AAA to BBB. At this point, irony of ironies, Ford sent missions of inquiry to Japan to visit Japanese auto plants and learn how to make cars. Somehow the Japanese had learned to increase output and still retain simple, human production and team relations, whereas Ford had accumulated layers of bureaucracy. To quote a plant manager, "The games we played were amazing. We'd sabotage the other's projects. We'd freeze the other side out of discussions, swear, blow up, ignore people, or simply not show up at meetings."[35]

So ill run a company might easily have been swallowed by a competitor, likely a Japanese competitor. But the Fords found in Henry II's nephew William Clay Ford, Jr., someone to run the show, or rather to serve as front man. And a manager to take charge: Jacques Nasser, an Australian of Lebanese origin, one tough guy who, like Iacocca, felt there should be no limit to his ambition or his rise. Meanwhile, young Ford was learning, had served in nearly two dozen increasingly important posts with the company, represented some 40 percent of voting stock, and clearly aimed at assuming the role of his uncle.

Not easy. The old-timers resented what they saw as rule by inheritance. Many found William Clay too goody-goody, especially in matters of environmental responsibility. Ford people (most businessmen?) liked profits more than virtue.[36] Virtue is for heirs. For some heirs. In short, outsiders and bureaucrats had changed the company. Alexander Trotman, chairman from 1993 through 1998, thought passion for the product was not the essence of car leadership: "I think it is important, but not vital. I'm very wary of people who profess to have gasoline in their nostrils and all of that. I'd like them to have shareholder value in their nostrils more than I would a passion for gasoline. I'd rather somebody tell me I'm going to deliver the right return for the shareholder than I'm going to produce the greatest Mustang that ever hit the street."[37]

But product clearly matters. Look at the excitement produced in Germany by the new Ford Mondeo in May 2001. The Germans rated the car as the best in its class, ahead of the Volkswagen Passat. We must wait for sales figures, but first signs are promising.[38] To be sure, Germans are more open to facts than other Europeans. But the history of the car industry has often been a story of models—of appearance, performance, reliability, comfort, style—and these are the work of hands-on car people. However, such achievement is now less the work of individual genius than of committee collaboration.

In the end, Nasser had to go: the company was not doing well (losses of $5.5 billion in 2001 alone); he spent money like a drunken sailor; and besides, one cannot have two bosses so different in background and attitude. Indeed, one cannot have two bosses. And as before with Iacocca, Ford had the votes. Even those relatives who had their reservations took the family's side, and most of the family shareholders were only too delighted to see "that man" go. Why had Bill Ford, Jr., waited so long?[39]

That still left the problems of design, marketing, and competition. In 2001 and 2002 the public prints were full of gloomy announcements of closings and firings, of debts and losses. One even hears talk of imminent bankruptcy. Founder Henry must be spinning in his grave.

Since its beginning, the Ford Motor Company and the Ford family have been nearly indistinguishable. And while the company recently dropped to third among the world's automotive manufacturers (with Toyota taking over the number two spot), there are few other examples in which a single family exerts such control over a corporation of this size. Ford Motors is a case study in family/dynastic enterprise and corporate managerial manufacture, and its history is a major chapter in business history, an excellent introduction to the larger story of the twentieth century's major industry.

Five

THE AGNELLIS AND FIAT

THE LATIN PATTERN

GIANNI AGNELLI (1921–2003)

*T*here has always been more to Fiat than automobiles. Alan Friedman, author of one of the most intimate histories of the Agnelli family and the Fiat car manufacture, tried to get an interview with Gianni Agnelli in preparation for his book. He was refused in no uncertain terms. According to Friedman,

> [W]hen Agnelli and his men at Fiat found out that I was writing this book they were not pleased. In a letter that was written to me on 25 March 1988, six months after my first request for an interview, I was informed of Agnelli's view that a meeting would be

"neither opportune nor desirable." Fiat's hostility then became uncompromising and it ran the gamut, from a criminal lawsuit that was lodged (before publication) against me and my newspaper, the *Financial Times* of London, to a Fiat official who was quoted in *Le Monde* saying that I was variously a "neo-colonialist, racist, Mossad agent or stooge of the extreme right wing of the Pentagon."[1]

This vehement protection of name and reputation fits the Agnelli legend, and reality, perfectly. Fiat is no mere family business; it has been the very embodiment of twentieth-century Italian capitalism: "highly political, Byzantine, [and] wary of outsiders."[2] Gianni Agnelli, the family's flamboyant patriarch through the latter half of the twentieth century, wielded incredible power, both economic and political, in a way more reminiscent of kings than of CEOs. And while there have been many powerful examples of businessmen from managerial corporations, Agnelli's influence and completely unapologetic stance flow directly from the very personal, family nature of this enterprise.

The Agnellis were local gentry. Their home village, Villar Perosa, lay some thirty miles from Turin—just the right location to enjoy agricultural tranquillity within easy distance of courts and politics. The name Agnelli goes back to the Middle Ages, but the direct lineage is singularly undistinguished—not a bad thing probably in a world of arbitrary rule and unpredictable violence. But the family in its quiet way must have been prospering, because in 1853 it was able to buy the seigneurial villa of the local count, a large residence that remained thereafter a kind of titular family headquarters.

Giovanni Agnelli (1866–1945), the patriarch-founder of the modern clan, was given military training and became a lieutenant in the cavalry. It was in this station that he made his early career: a life of dress uniforms and formal rituals, of pomp, pride, and pretense. What took him into automobiles was an accident of fantasy. He was fascinated by mechanisms and devices, and he and some friends thought at first to invent a machine that would yield perpetual motion. That's how far he was from reality in such matters. But this foray may have prepared the way for a second and more realistic project: the building of a horseless carriage. In 1898, Agnelli joined forces with another visionary, the Count Bricherasio di Cacherano, who was looking for investors in a new company, the "Società Italiana per la costruzione e il commercio delle automobili Torino," later renamed the Fabbrica Italiana di Automobili Torino, or F.I.A.T., soon known as Fiat. (One word will always beat unpronounceable initials or lengthy labels.) Agnelli became managing director.

The early history of the company is not easy to follow. Output seems clear enough: by 1903 Fiat was making 135 cars; three years later, 1,149 cars. But ownership and direction are something else again. Somehow—we shall never know how—Agnelli got some of the early partners to sell out, including the Bricherasios, whose idea the company was in the first place. The Bricherasios neither forgave nor forgot. Fat lot of good it did them. At one point, in 1908, the state prosecutor of Turin charged Agnelli and associates with manipulating the share price—sucking small investors in at phony highs, then pushing them out at phony lows—and with falsifying balance sheet and accounts and mulcting investors big and small. Agnelli was forced to resign. But he survived trial and retrial, possibly because the evidence of crime was insufficient; more likely because he had more friends in Turin than the prosecutor had. That was the nature of power in local Italian jurisdictions. Agnelli resumed his post as managing director in 1909, and from that point on, the firm, although nominally a public company, was a family fief.

These experiences taught Agnelli that friends matter, and he made it a point to build bridges from Turin to Rome. Among his political contacts: Giovanni Giolitti, also from Piedmont, who was to become prime minister. Who paid whom for what is impossible to say. In 1907, Giolitti made Agnelli a *cavaliere,* and when Italy went a-conquering in North Africa in 1911, Fiat received lucrative arms contracts. Then Agnelli spotted another comer, by the name of Benito Mussolini, publisher of a noisy newspaper *Il Popolo d'Italia.* Agnelli and Fiat gave financial and political support. Mussolini paid them back with friendly publicity (so much for social Fascism) and, later, with all manner of monetary rewards.

By 1914, Fiat was making more than four thousand vehicles a year—cars, trucks, ambulances—to say nothing of guns and air-plane engines. The fifty workers of 1899 had become four thousand in 1914, ten thousand by end of 1915. During these years of war, the company jumped from thirtieth to third largest in the country. Agnelli rewarded himself accordingly; his salary was equal to that of two hundred workers. Some politicians—he didn't have everyone in his pocket—and shareholders thought this excessive, especially in time of hardship and shortage. (Food riots in Turin in August 1917 cost twenty-four lives.) One prominent investor noted that "not even the prime minister has such a fabulous salary [what did that prove?] . . . it is not fair that these privileged persons show them-selves colossally greedy, while we watch the less privileged endure terrible sacrifices." Such pious lamentations could not touch Gio-vanni Agnelli: ". . . the conspicuous earnings of the directors repre-sent a natural compensation for the increased responsibilities they have assumed in order to contribute to the success of our armies."[3] *Honi soit qui mal y pense.*

Giovanni Agnelli ruled over a company whose success owed much to the quality of its skilled workforce, and even more to the ex-ploitation of political connections for fat orders and protective tariffs. His contemporaries thought him arrogant—he was—but also effi-cient. He would walk through the shops telling the workers to turn the lights out when not needed, by way of saving money and remind-ing them who was boss. Needless to say, the workers did not take kindly to Giovanni's airs and multiple tyrannies. They tried strikes and sit-ins, but the old man had authority and force on his side.

Fiat was not the only company under attack. In the early 1920s, Italian politics and government foundered on irreconcilable hostili-ties, aggravated by the ambitions of the new Communist Party and Mussolini's Fascist response. Huff, puff, and in 1922 the parlia-mentary house came down. Big business, including Fiat, welcomed the Fascisti, who spelled order and profits. For Fiat, they also spelled the end of a government commission looking into excessive industrial profits during the war years 1915–1917. Also—but this the Agnellis could not foresee—they brought irremediable disaster and national humiliation.

In the meantime, patriarch Giovanni had a family to raise, to his standards and taste. He had a son, Eduardo (1892–1935), the only male heir, designated successor to the direction of the auto combine. Unfortunately Eduardo was not made to his father's measure. Autos were fine to ride in, not to make. He gave his heart to the Juventus football (soccer) team, another Agnelli enterprise, and to the development of the Italian Alpine resort of Sestriere, where he was famous (notorious) for lavish, intimate parties of après-ski. He enjoyed life and love, but not work and duty, and for this he died. He was supposed to attend a board meeting in Turin in 1935, but he was having such a good time in the family-financed resort in the Alps that he chose to cancel the car that came to take him there, enjoy a few additional hours of pleasure, and fly back instead. The plane crashed and thereby changed the history of Fiat.[4]

Eduardo left a wife and seven children. His lady was Virginia Bourbon del Monte, Princess of San Faustino—because once the Agnellis made all that money, only the bluest blood would do. The princess, half American and thus relatively emancipated, indulged her own appetites with the ease that comes from an abundance of domestic help, and this with a clear conscience given her husband's amorous adventures. She too became a victim of her recreational diversions. Ten years after Eduardo's untimely demise, Virginia died in a car crash in the company of a male friend. The Agnelli family let it be known that she was strangled like Isadora Duncan of old, whose scarf had caught in the wheels and choked her to death. In fact she was amusing the trouser-less driver, who lost control in the wrong place and at the wrong time.

Of Eduardo's seven children, the one who came to matter most to the family enterprises was the second, Giovanni (1921–2003), better known as Gianni. He was a chip off the old block: handsome and irresistible, easy but proud, self-indulgent but inclined to rigor and severity with others. He had something of his father, something of his grandfather, and something of both. Friedman writes of him that he "was destined to enlarge the empire that he inherited, to become as great and as powerful as the Savoys, the Medici, the Gonzagas, Sforzas, Viscontis, or any other dynasty from the pages of Italian history."[5]

But all of that lay in the future. As a boy, Gianni was reared by an English governess, who dressed him in elegant sailor suits that changed color with the seasons, indulged him with postprandial sweets, and never failed to remind him that he was an Agnelli. With that kind of spoiling, he grew up to be something of a rascal and a pest. His idea of a joke was to snatch the bag of a school chum and toss it onto a passing truck. Whether that bothered the school more than the insults he proffered his teachers is hard to say. He was demoted, but so what? His sister Susanna, today a politician, tells of the time she told Gianni she was in love: "In love? How is that possible? I thought only servants fell in love."

To be sure, Gianni hardly needed friends. The mansion in Turin was outfitted with a gym, a movie theater, and a huge library. When the children were not at home, they were enjoying themselves in villas by the sea, sailing yachts, driving cars without a license—they could afford to compensate victims—fraternizing with the great soccer players. Also accompanying their elders on visits to important people, where Gianni could learn manners, and manner, from his grandfather. In those days, Fiat was making the most of its closeness to the Fascist regime, to solicit not only Italian orders but also German. Why not? The whole point of making cars was to make money. Fiat would have courted the British and Americans just as eagerly.

When World War II came, twenty-two-year-old Gianni did his duty. That is worth mentioning these days, when so many important political figures have not only found ways to evade military obligations, but have somehow managed to persuade the public that cowardice (the French *lâcheté* is better) is not relevant to character; or that draft dodging may even be a sign of moral virtue and intelligence. The young Lieutenant Agnelli served in Russia, where the Germans pushed the Italians around; and later in North Africa, where the Germans pushed the Italians around; and still later in Italy, where the Germans beat up the Italians but where he had the satisfaction of being on the winning side.

The war was also an opportunity to readjust the family's political alliances. Here, Gianni made a sharp contrast with his grandfather, who may or may not have been a faithful Fascist but had been seen as such and had made it a point to cultivate Mussolini's friendship. This was long an asset, but Italy's reverses in combat destroyed the regime and made old ties valueless. In the final months of the war, il Senatore Agnelli withdrew to the family home in Villar Perosa, a bitter man who wondered aloud whether his whole life had not been an error. He died in December of 1945, an outdated relic of the old order.

The picture of grandson Gianni at this juncture is somewhat contradictory. On the one hand, he used the time he was still in the army and his impeccable English to build connections to Allied officers and prepare himself, if not the firm, for a drastic change in government and connections. Alliances and friendships interested him more than making cars, but in Italy the two went together. On the other hand, he did not like the hardships of a war-torn country. As soon as he could, he left Italy for the comfort and pleasure of his villa at Beaulieu, on the French Riviera: lots of servants, playmates, pals, cruises up and down the Côte d'Azur, parties, gambling, imaginative couplings. Fiat? He left it in better hands, those of Vittorio Valletta, once a professor of banking, a full head shorter than Gianni, but meaner and more capable.

Valletta had run the show for Grandpa Giovanni. He owned little stock, but he liked his job and did much to build the multiple empire that the first war and government connections had made possible. With that kind of upward fidelity, he made the ideal manager. During the interwar years, Fiat had continued to concentrate its manufacturing in Turin: automobiles and all the preliminary operations on iron and steel (electric furnaces, foundries and forges, rolling mills, wire and cable drawing, shaping and stamping); railway equipment and rolling stock; airplanes; tractors and trucks. The Turin conglomerate rose to Italian industrial leadership: output of some ten thousand units in 1922, thirty-seven thousand in 1925, forty-two thousand in 1929, equal to 85.5 percent of the national auto make, with exports amounting to 90 percent of those of the entire industry. Fiat held in effect a national monopoly.[6] To be sure, monopoly is not good for you, and Fiat's technology left something to be desired. But in the 1930s, confronted by a population of limited purchasing power, it moved in the direction of smaller, cheaper cars. Success came in 1936 with the introduction of a two-door model, the Fiat 500, nicknamed the Topolino, or little mouse. Fiat was able to double output in the space of a year.[7]

In addition to automobiles, Fiat owned or held a controlling share of a variety of subsidiaries, some commercial, some industrial. These manufactured ball bearings, farm tractors, military vehicles—you name it. Further, Fiat held interests in road and air transport, naval shipyards, and hydroelectric power. The company also owned the major newspaper *La Stampa*. The Agnellis' economic power thus reached far beyond the realm of automobiles and into the society itself. Nor was Fiat limited to its home country—in 1934, in order to get around French tariff restrictions, it opened an assembly plant outside of Paris and manufactured a six-horsepower Fiat model much like the popular Peugeot 201 (the Simca Six), thus becoming an important player in the French market. Nonetheless, Fiat was the quintessential Italian company, both reflecting and shaping the political and social culture of the land.

Valletta, that experienced and tough manager, enjoyed running the factories the way Gianni enjoyed hosting his fast crowd—jet-setters such as Errol Flynn, Anita Ekberg, Rita Hayworth, Doris Duke, and Prince Aly Khan—in La Réserve hotel in Beaulieu or in the Agnelli villa. Postwar Italy was suffering desperate hunger and poverty, but Gianni's crew knew nothing of such infelicities or embarrassments, opting instead to pursue recreation, glitz, and amorous connections. Gianni received a great deal of attention, and not just from the women in his circle; he was a celebrity, an international playboy, and the newspapers breathlessly reported his every move.

In 1953, Gianni Agnelli got married. His wife, Marella Caracciolo di Castagneto, daughter of the Duke of Melito, was both beautiful and stable, a fashion photographer by profession (and so a fixture at fashionable events) and possessed of the longest neck in Europe, just made for jewelry. Marriage, everyone agreed, settled Gianni down some and made him somewhat more discreet, though it did not cure him of his sensual wanderlust.

This new, more serious Gianni even tried his hand at management, tentatively presiding over Fiat's manufacture of ball bearings, which he saw, in his layman's way, as the truffles of the automobile. Then, in 1959, he became chair of the Istituto Finanziario Industriale (IFI), the holding company that voted the family shares and effectively controlled the vast and varied Agnelli interests. His contradictory personality led his adversaries to underestimate him. *L'Unità,* the Communist Party newspaper, offered this description of him in 1959: "Manicured nails, refined habits, deft in four languages, absolute indifference to finance or to the problems of industry."[8] In 1963, Gianni became managing director at Fiat, and he got three years of direct executive experience before Valletta finally retired in 1966.

The Valletta era had seen Fiat grow from 3,260 cars a year at the end of 1945 to well over that number every working day. Sales totaled $1.5 billion a year. The company was growing more than twice as fast as the European average. Valletta ruled the company with an iron hand. When labor showed signs of interest in unionization, he dismissed some two thousand potential troublemakers. To be sure, he made up for tyranny by building worker housing, medical facilities, retirement homes, and nursery schools. These he offered and gave. Workers were not there to demand or take; workers were there to listen and work. Small wonder that Valletta expected to have the final say about his successor.

But if Valletta knew cars, he did not really know business. When Gianni Agnelli told him that he expected to succeed him as chairman, Valletta was stunned but helpless. Gianni may not have been ready in 1945, but he felt he was ready twenty-one years later. One of the first things he did was institute strict retirement rules, so that more than a hundred Valletta executives were simply forced out. This was not merely succession but revolution. And it was Gianni who got the credit for subsequent expansion. As one woman employee tearfully recalled at his death some thirty-six years later, "He created work; he gave us jobs."

Revolutions do not lend themselves to easy management. Valletta still had his nostalgic and frustrated adherents in the company, who were not easy for Gianni to master. This huge conglomerate would not get consolidated accounts until 1980. How do you run a puzzle?

Gianni, though, had ambitions. Fiat had just passed Volkswagen as Europe's biggest car maker. Now to pass Chrysler and become number three, after General Motors and Ford. The answer: absorb another producer. No firm in Italy was big enough to fit the bill. Fiat's choice: France's Citroën, which seemed a perfect match. Fiat made small cars, Citroën bigger ones. Fiat had a good truck division; Citroën, a mess. Fiat built simple cars; the front-wheel-drive Citroën was famous for its all-too-cunning engineering.

The merger promised great things for Europe, in the fresh throes of economic union. It stumbled, however, on the hurdle of French pride. Fiat assumed that it would absorb its new partner, but Charles de Gaulle could not bear the idea of national surrender, and to those Fascist losers no less. Besides, the structures and philosophies of authority differed widely from the one firm to the other. In Citroën, no one was happy. They thought Fiat engineering elementary, whereas they took great pride in their own cleverness and ingenuity. They would be damned before they passed on their know-how and secrets to those ill-trained foreigners—especially when business began to pick up again in the early seventies. Five years, and that was it.[9]

Those were not easy years for Fiat. After the retirement of Valletta in 1966, the firm needed comparable technical leadership. They brought in Carlo De Benedetti, experienced manager of a family business, but he was too independent of manner and method. Valletta had known his place better. Gianni Agnelli is said to have advised Benedetti to relax and enjoy himself. No use. Of Jewish descent, from a family classified by the Fascists as Jews in spite of conversion and marriage to a Catholic, Benedetti was in too much of a hurry. The "Tiger," as he was called, had no patience for lazy old Fiat managers. So Benedetti lasted a hundred days and went on to a bright career with Olivetti.[10] But Fiat found useful replacements, particularly with the appointment of a true successor to Valletta. This was Cesare Romiti, a bull of a man of stentorian voice, *il Duro*, a transferee from state industry in Rome. He came in good time, because the decade of the seventies brought mixed results to the auto industry. Romiti not only got to run Fiat's production, but he also represented the company in negotiations with the Italian government and parliament. The big issue in 1985–1986 was to keep Ford from coming into Italy as a competitor, and to constrain the government's desire to build Alfa Romeo as a serious commercial rival to Fiat. The very idea startled and enraged Gianni Agnelli and the Agnelli family, who saw their privileged market position as sacrosanct. This was not their public position; butter wouldn't melt in their mouths. But they could play the *beau rôle,* while Romiti did the dirty work. And in the end, Fiat simply acquired Alfa and got Ford excluded.[11]

In the years that followed, Fiat prospered, grew, and diversified. Romiti took over most of the practical running of the company, becoming chief financial officer, then president, and finally board chairman when Agnelli retired, taking on the title of honorary chairman of the Fiat Group. Over this time, Gianni Agnelli became, for all intents and purposes, Italy's new king. He was appointed senator for life, and was called *il Re* by many Italians.

It is rare that a family business finds an outsider to run the firm well and loyally, and Fiat had somehow achieved the miracle twice. In Valletta and Romiti, the Agnellis had found brilliant, resourceful, and capable outsiders to manage the business without trying to take it over. This was a triumph of property over enterprise. The Agnellis retained their economic and political power by creating and perpetuating—through acumen, intelligence, and force—an aura of familial legitimacy. This contrasts strongly with the more typical story of the Fords, where outsiders and family members repeatedly clashed over control.

To be sure, the family enjoyed a good deal of luck, too. The luck to have three successive generations of talent and energy. But then the luck ran out. For one thing, the family kept marrying up, into ever higher social circles. That kind of thing is poison to commercial commitment; there are so many more enjoyable ways to pass the time. Thus Gianni's son, Edoardo, had neither interest in nor talent for business. Not that Gianni didn't try. After sending the boy to an American university called Princeton—which the Italians apparently thought, perhaps from Edoardo's residential preferences, to be located in New York City—Gianni apprenticed Edoardo in the family holding company (the IFI), the better to know how rich he was, and then placed him with Lehman Brothers in New York, under the watchful eye of Italian-American financier Mario D'Urso, a close friend of the family. Then Edoardo did a stretch in a family-owned cement plant, and went from there to the presidency of the Juventus soccer team. Football is more fun than cement.[12]

As for Edoardo's potential role in running the family holdings, he was clear on the question of division of labor and responsibility. Economic and technical matters called for special competence and should be reserved to technicians. "But managers should not feel authorized to decide alone the large basic, strategic questions, which fall to the owners. There has to be a division between management and property."[13] Such statements did not win Edoardo points with the managers. Romiti especially, *il Duro,* made his displeasure known. In a television interview a few weeks later, he condescendingly declared, "Edoardo has no role in any part of Fiat, not on the board of directors or anywhere else. If he wishes to come and speak with me, I shall be happy to do so, provided I have the time."[14] Take a chair.

Edoardo knew better. He owned a big piece of the company. Besides, his mind and heart lay elsewhere. He preferred to live apart, ascetically, the better to keep in touch with himself. The Italian public came to know him first for his defense of astrology against the "scientism" of the director of the astronomical observatory of Trieste. He was drawn to oriental philosophies, spent time in India sitting at the feet of mystics, marched in antinuclear demonstrations, lamented Western materialism. Withal, he had not abandoned Christian concerns: the Nicene creed, the nature of the Trinity, the possibility of other prophets after Jesus. Edoardo was also apparently a homosexual. In macho Italy more than elsewhere, such leanings expose people to embarrassment, make them vulnerable. They seem to have hurt Edoardo, who in November 2000 was found dead under a bridge near Turin, an apparent suicide.[15] From fortune to misfortune.

Gianni should have made more male children. Daughters would not do, because Italian values leave no room for capable, combative women entrepreneurs. To keep the business going in family hands, Gianni had to look to collateral lines. These he saw as family, but not immediate family. And there, his luck ran out. His nephew Giovanni, son of Umberto, the one who seemed best suited to succeed him, came down with incurable cancer and died in a New York hospital in 1997 aged thirty-three. Another possibility, John Philip Elkann, born 1975, son of Gianni's daughter Margherita, joined the firm's board of directors at age twenty-two. His face has nothing of the severity of Gianni's intimidating stare. Nor his well-burnished, haughty persona. But Elkann is learning. He is of Jewish ancestry, but here, as with Benedetti, the family has intermarried and adopted the Catholic faith. No matter, as with Benedetti. For his purer Agnelli relatives, he will always be Jewish. (But not for Jews; his mother wasn't Jewish.)

Meanwhile, the family enterprise has grown in fortune and complexity. The auto branch became only one of a number of major enterprises, ranging from tourist facilities and real estate to insurance, banking, French wine, department stores, paper, and telecommunications, plus that leading soccer team.[16]

Can the dynasty continue to run a business of this size and complexity? Can it juggle its many debit accounts, reassure worried stockholders and investors? From a peak value of nearly forty-five euros in 1998, by mid-2002 the value of a Fiat share sank to less than thirteen. Gianni was not inclined to open his worried heart to the public. But his sister Susanna had already admitted at a news conference in 1995 that "This is a very bad moment for Fiat."

So Fiat has started selling assets. Most strikingly, in 2000, it sold 20 percent of Fiat Auto to General Motors in a $2.4 billion stock swap. GM saw the deal as an opportunity to affirm its foothold in Europe, where it had already bought Saab and Opel, and in South America, where Fiat had plants mostly in Brazil and Argentina. But the deal gave Fiat a put option—the right to sell at a specified price a specific number of shares by a certain date—from 2004 to 2009, whereby it could require GM to buy the rest of Fiat Auto, which option it might very well exercise, given the poor returns of recent years. (In 2001, Fiat Auto and GM Europe had combined losses of $1.3 billion. And the Italian market itself has been hard hit by the decline of tariff protection.) Yet could Fiat really do that? If Fiat dumped the rest of the auto branch, the very raison d'être of the enterprise would disappear. And would such disengagement reassure investors? We might have an act of entrepreneurial suicide.

Besides, GM had not been doing well and was by no means ready to honor the agreement. It announced that it would go to court if necessary to avoid the merger. Such a threat might have amounted to a veto, though likely an expensive one.[17] Fiat refused to back off. In such matters, stubbornness pays. Final result: GM paid two billion dollars to be relieved of liability.[18] A fortune, but probably worth it.

Meanwhile, how can a managerial enterprise like Fiat come to terms with hereditary monarchy? Will shareholders, including family members, put up with generations of interfering, incompetent rois fainéants? (They cost, even if they do nothing.) Yet Fiat is Agnelli, and Agnelli is Fiat, and Agnelli and Fiat spell Italian industrial grandeur. So Fiat has sold two of its money-making businesses—

insurance and aerospace components—and kept those ancestral automobiles, losers though they may be. The hope is that the cars will start making money again in 2007.[19] These vehicles symbolize Italian industrial potency, and Fiat is still a national monument of achievement, with output and turnover representing almost 4 percent of Italian GNP. The popular slogan has it: "What's good for Fiat is good for Italy."

So Italy gains from Fiat's gains. That applies to buying and selling: when Fiat wants something, the state turns it over at a bargain price; and when Fiat is stuck with a lemon, the state develops an irresistible taste for lemon juice. Thus Fiat turned its loss-making steel business over to the government for a sum that has remained secret. That gave rise to scandal, even in Italy. Carlo de Benedetti chided his old associates: "In our country a number of families have dominated events, and in my opinion they have destroyed the capitalist system inasmuch as they have held on to that which serves them and have unloaded that which they consider useless onto the State."[20] The minister of foreign trade was not intimidated. "A wise government," he said, "must take into consideration what the biggest private company in the country thinks. Helping Fiat is in the interest of the entire country."

Maybe the Italian government will now buy Fiat, if only to resell it to bloodier businessmen. They will not necessarily sell it to an Agnelli, because Gianni's last direct and ready male descendant, Umberto, died in May 2004. To be sure, there is the chic John Elkann, whom we met as an Agnelli by the female line, but the Italians see him as "far too young to take the position. They are missing a rung on the generational ladder, and I don't know whom they will come up with as chairman."[21] Or as ex-CEO Luca di Montezemolo put it, "What I try to do is try to let John [Elkann] grow up." Wise words from another outsider.

Will the auto dynasty continue or move on, as it is already doing, to other fields? Yes and yes. Does Italy need an auto industry? That's hard to say. But insofar as it has one, it has been, up to now, the work of a single family and its liege supporters.

Six

PEUGEOT, RENAULT, AND CITROËN

FRENCH CAR DYNASTIES

LEFT TO RIGHT: ROLAND PEUGEOT (B. 1926), JEAN-PAUL PARAYRE (B. 1937), AND PIERRE PEUGEOT (1932–2002)

*I*n France the venerable Peugeot name is a symbol of national pride and success, viewed much the same as Italians view Fiat. Peugeot is also the oldest surviving manufacturer of automobiles, by which I do not mean that they invented the engine or chassis, but that they built and sold entire vehicles.[1]

The Peugeot family can be traced back hundreds of years, to the fifteenth and sixteenth centuries, largely because the Protestants of the Pays de Montbéliard (interior Burgundy) made it a point to register births carefully, long before government practice made such recording routine and even compulsory. They were peasants and oc-

casionally soldiers to start with; what else was there in the late medieval, early modern countryside? But early on, they developed an
interest in industrial and commercial occupations; the descendants
are described as nail makers, tool makers, carpenters, clockmakers,
barkeeps, innkeepers. Note a precocious affinity for metalwork; this
leaning remained a family tradition. That such diversions from the
land (or more accurately, contributions to the land) proved a success
is shown by the continuity of these pursuits. The Peugeot made good
in the modest way possible in modest towns and villages. Some of
them were chosen as mayors, and most of them counted as what
contemporaries would call *notables* or *coqs de village.*[2]

The modern industrial history of the family dates from the eighteenth century with a certain Jean-Jacques Peugeot, who married
Suzanne Mettetal and her family flour mill. This was followed during
the revolutionary years by a second mill, better located, more efficient.
Another descendant, Jean-Pierre Peugeot, without mill, went into textile manufacture. The big commercial fabric then was what the French
called *indiennes,* a cotton print imitative of the original Asian version.
The new technique had already implanted itself in England, Germany,
and Switzerland, and now France wanted to move in. To this end, it instituted prohibitions on importation, and these caught the village of
Hérimoncourt in no-man's-land, even though it had just become
French territory. Peugeot sought and obtained permission to make and
sell the new fabrics, subject to proof that the product was his and not
contraband. This was one tenacious enterpriser.

It took time to secure permission, so Jean-Pierre took up oil
making, setting mills to breaking linen and hemp and a battery to
beating grains. When the new revolutionary regime began selling
national properties (*les biens nationaux*), Jean-Pierre bought a couple of nearby forests. He knew he would need timber and wood, for
everything and anything. In 1802 he asked permission to start up a
fulling mill and set about founding a paper factory. The latter project failed, but Peugeot held on to the land. He died in 1814, but he
left his four sons a diversified industrial patrimony worth some two
hundred thousand francs. A small fortune for the time.

Two of these sons married Japy girls. Who were the Japy? Another versatile Protestant dynasty of the region, given especially to clockmaking, beautiful preparation for the most demanding mechanical work. The two families were destined to great achievements and esteemed each other's prospects and the advantages of well-chosen alliances.

These years were not only revolutionary politically; they saw major transformations also in industrial technology. In Britain, the industrial revolution was well under way, and now the continental nations wanted to catch up. Cotton printing was fine and profitable, especially when protected by the state; but the Peugeots saw even bigger opportunities in machines and their applications, particularly devices to spin cotton and other yarn. Every textile manufacturer needed cheap yarn. Two of the Peugeot brothers traveled to Paris to study the new machines in the Conservatoire des Arts et Métiers, which was there to promote technology. They then brought the secrets back to the home county, hired a British expat (his compats would have killed him at home) to help with technique, and built a factory that took the manufacture all the way from the raw cotton wool to finished yarn, including the actual building of machines and spindles. Around 1819, the two Peugeot spinning mills were turning out fifteen to twenty tons of yarn a year. An extraordinary achievement.

Yet the Peugeot future did not lie with textiles. The managing brothers were swept away by typhus, and their children lacked their enthusiasm and talent. That, of course, is one of the weaknesses of dynastic enterprise. Genes count, but they are not foolproof. Also money diverts and distracts. But the Peugeot children had cousins, and these moved ahead in metallurgy, first as craft, then as manufacture.

The founder of this branch and the man from whom one generally counts the modern family line was Jean-Pierre Peugeot II (1768–1852). Taking over management of the family flour mill, he turned it into a steel foundry. Very quickly, though, it was clear there would be less trouble and more money in making final products—

not raw steel, which called for lots of coal and iron ore, but rather saws, springs, and even fine springs for clocks and watches. Also corset bones and stays, which, thanks to fashion and masculine taste, would provide good demand for a century, not only in France, but also in Switzerland (horology) and Italy (women's styles). This metallurgical firm diversified and prospered, increasing its labor force, acquiring bigger and better equipment, and buying ever larger quantities of raw steel from suppliers in coal areas nearby. Through luck and ambition, the Peugeot had hit on one of the most promising growth opportunities in the economy.

What's more, the family had the personnel and ability to deal with these matters. This is another of the uncertainties of family enterprise: Does the clan produce enough people and talent to continue running the show? At this turn in their fortunes, the Peugeot were well provided. Jean-Pierre, the oldest of the brothers, fathered eight children, three of them sons; while Jean-Frédéric, his younger brother, married a cousin, Suzanne Peugeot, who gave him four sons. Thus seven boys in the third generation of the metallurgical branch. Jean-Frédéric died early in 1822, but his widow was up to his measure. (She died in 1836.) She dressed like a peasant but dealt on equal terms with bankers, creditors, and suppliers and took in a third of the profits, some twenty-five thousand francs a year. One cannot help but wonder how much was lost to capitalism by the traditional division of labor by gender.

By comparison, her son Fritz, the precocious inventor and technician, drew a salary of 1,200 francs, and his brother Charles, less talented, earned 420 francs. The Peugeot made it a point to limit executive salaries by way of avoiding worker jealousy and dissatisfaction. But they understood well how to use associated companies (distributors, for example), well paid by the mother house, as vehicles for quiet reward.

The years that followed were marked by family rearrangements: by abandonment of the textile business by cousins apparently bored with factory industry; by the eventual conversion of the yarn-making mill to toolmaking; by a number of joint ventures with members of the Japy clan, and then separations; by building new plants; by disagreements among cousins leading to reorganizations. Insofar as money was needed for new equipment (turbines, steam hammers, rolling mills), the family borrowed in Switzerland—more discreet than French sources. (Whereas in France borrowing was frowned upon, the Swiss lived to lend.) The range of products grew with changes in custom and fashion. The 1860s and 1870s were decades of hoopskirts, which survived in the countryside and abroad long after Paris had gone on to other garments; also of saws, chisel blades, springs, and a variety of tool blades; but also of coffee mills and hair clippers (big in the army); and hooks and pitchforks and other hardware.[3] Steel came in everywhere as king.

And locally the Peugeot clan reigned as a kind of royal family. The members were elected as mayors, because they were rightly seen as people of influence on the larger departmental and regional scene. They made it a point to build housing, provide low-cost retail and food outlets, and offer education and training to the children of a workforce that by the end of the century numbered thousands and built its own Peugeot-connected lineages. And greater days were still to come.

For Peugeot and French industry the birth year of the bicycle was 1885. Various versions of velocipedes had appeared earlier: two-wheelers, three-wheelers, four-wheelers. But now the curious and rare became matter for industrial output and fiscal attention. The French government began to tax these machines, and who taxes, counts: 256,000 in 1895; 981,000 in 1900; 2,697,000 in 1910; 3,552,000 in 1914.

The Peugeot, well traveled and metal tried, saw an opportunity. The pioneer here was Armand, son of Emile, who had learned about bikes during an engineering apprenticeship in England. He persuaded brothers and cousins to retool one of the plants: eight thousand bikes in 1892; twenty thousand in 1900. The hundreds of workers there were paid more than those in the other Peugeot factories: a five-franc, ten-hour day for the men; three francs for the women, 1.5 francs for the children.

Along with continuing improvements in shape and weight, the introduction of pneumatic rubber tires made an enormous difference in riding comfort and control. These were the pioneer days of Dunlop and Michelin. Was such coincidence of innovation a happy accident? Or rather a larger response to opportunity and need? Because almost immediately, on the heels of man-powered vehicles, came the development of the internal combustion engine and the launching of the automobile—the most popular and productive vehicle of the twentieth century. And here, too, Armand Peugeot saw his chance and that of his family enterprise. Automobiles were remarkably complex machines to build, but Armand was already well positioned, having a wealth of technical and human resources, as well as a strong reputation.

Peugeot joined forces here with Panhard and Levassor. They would build the motors, Peugeot the bodies. They debated at first where to put the engine. P&L wanted it in the rear; it stank too much. Armand wanted it in front, where it made for better balance. Armand won the argument, partly because balance made a huge difference to safe driving, partly because Peugeot learned to make its own motors. Thanks to ball bearings, theirs were smoother and less smelly and noisy than the original Daimler internal-combustion model. From there it was a simple matter to dispose of fumes via pipes to the rear. The first Peugeot car, an auto engine on a quadricycle, came out in 1890.

But in his fixation on the new product, Armand ended up quarreling with his cousins, who cherished the older lines of manufacture and were intimidated by the risks of this new, capital-intensive adventure. In 1897 he left the Société Peugeot Frères and founded S.A. des Automobiles Peugeot, with factories at Audincourt and Lille. The first still lay in the old home district of Montbéliard, but Lille was almost foreign territory, at the northern tip of the country. Armand found himself there close to coal, in a region long devoted to heavy metallurgy. He brought his technicians with him, designers and inventors, with an endless task of emulation and amelioration, the more so as he decided to build trucks as well as cars. Why not?

Why should the road not serve as the locus of goods traffic, into and from areas not served by rail? To be sure, that posed a new task for public works. Railway concessions held by private enterprise built track as opportunity offered. But roads would depend largely on public initiative and investment. Failure to build and improve could spell isolation and self-impoverishment.

However much Armand's cousins opposed or feared his auto-mobilistic ambitions, they had to salute his successful new enterprise and the prizes his cars won in competition. So having said no, they now said yes and proceeded to lend him money, and to build their own vehicles—first motorcycles, then small cars. This was not easy, because the early motors outstripped the car bodies, grew big and heavy to meet the high-speed competition, and made it hard for even high-placed drivers to see over and beyond them. Such monstrosities may have fascinated the public, but they lent themselves poorly to adoption by ordinary timid mortals. They were made for show-offs. They suited European societies, with their big gap between a few rich and many poor. American society, we saw, was something else. Here Henry Ford set the example—building not for the exceptional car fancier but for the safe and slow user. Over time this revolutionized American infastructure and society and made the car a necessity.

Family cooperation played a role here, as the cousins focused on smaller vehicles, so as not to compete directly with Armand's larger cars and trucks. In this competitive world, it was hard to maintain the distinction between Armand's product and that of his cousins. To the public, these were all Peugeots. What's more, Armand was running into financial problems—historian René Sédillot tells us he was on the edge of bankruptcy—and needed a transfusion urgently. So in 1910 a family agreement restored unity with the merger of the two enterprises under the name S.A. des Automobiles et Cycles Peugeot. Meanwhile, the older manufacture of all manner of metal objects continued: bicycles, corset stays, pitchforks, all kinds of springs, pince-nez, etc., made mostly by the cousins under different corporate names, but only until the Great War, when fashions changed, in part because of the arrival of American forces. *Adieu les buscs, les corsets, les parapluies hommes!* No matter. Mechanical razors alone gave Peugeot a market of tens of millions of blades every month. And such metal objects were a mere addendum to the big business of motor vehicles, winner of wars, with its trucks, tanks, and command cars, all with their multitude of parts, their assemblies of related equipment, their frequent demolition and rapid depreciation.

Here the American example was stimulus: Ford, with almost fifteen million Model Ts in nineteen years; GM, with more than sixty factories making a changing range of models. By contrast, France was a country of small car makers—a hundred of them on the eve of the Great War. Almost all of these car makers relied on their own financial resources, theirs and those of relatives and friends. Banks for the most part stayed clear. They knew from often unhappy experience that the availability of funds was a stimulant to appetite. And the manufacturers in turn mistrusted the banks. As one of the Peugeot execs put it, "A banker is someone who reluctantly lends you a parasol when the sun shines, but refuses an umbrella as soon as it starts to rain." As automaker Louis Renault said dismissively, "Bankers are not philanthropists; they are dealers in money. One must, as much as possible, never have anything to do with them."[4]

Take the case of France's most ambitious automaker. This was André Citroën, engineer by training, the kind of person who had the nerve, intelligence, and knowledge to do something important in the new industry. He was in many ways self-made. His father had committed suicide when he was only six. His mother died at forty-six, when he was still a lad. When he decided to try his hand and focus his technical imagination on autos, he turned to Ford and GM; neither would help. The banks shunned him. So he took his personal fortune, went for loans to relatives (his family were the leading diamond dealers of Paris), to his wife's family (Italian bankers), and to his classmates in the Polytechnic (whom the French call the "Xs," after the algebraic unknown). He remained the sole shareholder until 1927. At that point he needed more help. His weakness was a penchant for the latest technology. He built the finest factories, and these cost money. So he turned to the Banque Lazard, backed in turn by Morgan's: 300 million in capital, 150 million in bonds, 160 million in straight loans. In return he granted the Lazard banks three seats on the board, one of which went to Paul Franzen, Lazard CEO.

This did not mean a power shift. André Citroën held only 25 percent of the capital, but his shares enjoyed special voting rights, so that he controlled 70 percent of the votes in the general assembly. So when Lazard tried to make their influence felt, Citroën sent them packing—for "disagreements with the CEO." He replaced them with his personal buddies. Who says bankers run the world?

Yet loans are loans, and debts are debts. Citroën spent the early thirties spinning in every direction, trying to get banks and French government agencies to give him the credits he needed. Also gambling: he loved cards and could practically make them talk. And yet, for all his wealth and open pockets, he lived outside the luxury of his industrial milieu. No yachts or châteaux or vacation resorts for him: he liked his money liquid, available for investment in new techniques and equipment.

No use. Those were bad times, and even a good, pathbreaking car such as the *traction avant* (front-wheel drive) had trouble selling. Given the precariousness of his funding, Citroën was drawing on every potential source of money, including suppliers and dealers. By 1934 the only question was how to liquidate and reorganize without André Citroën. Even so, the auto firm remained a family enterprise—now, however, in the hands of Michelin, tire makers extraordinary. Legend has it that once they took over, they never uttered the name of the founder.

In March 1935, André Citroën entered a fashionable clinic—in France those who can afford it avoid hospitals—where he died some three months later. *L'Univers israélite*, in its obituary, attributed this early demise to an "inexorable illness," his financial difficulties, and perhaps the death of his infant daughter in 1925. The official funeral, at the Montparnasse cemetery, took place without the military honors normally due to a *grande-croix* of the Legion of Honor. The family refused, vexed perhaps by the earlier reluctance of the government to help the auto company. (Very different from Italian practice and official support for Fiat or Alitalia.) But the Great Rabbi of Paris recited the prayers. Edouard, James, and Henri de Rothschild attended, as did other Jewish dignitaries; also General Gouraud, military governor of Paris; also the director-general of the Crédit Lyonnais; also Eugène Schneider, the iron and steel magnate; and Louis Renault, Citroën's auto competitor. Nasty legend had it that Renault came to make sure that Citroën was really dead.

The media did not make much of his death. But a number of people of distinction took occasion to note that he had been a good Frenchman who, although of Dutch birth, had served in the armed forces in the Great War. And Georges Clemenceau stressed the fact that Citroën, although a Jew, had been a good Jew. "There are good Jews," he generously conceded. "They did not all crucify Jesus Christ."[5]

The successor company kept the name, which continued to appeal to French auto buffs. But with almost no exceptions, Citroën's children and relations had nothing more to do with it. The oldest son, Bernard, obviously very bright, was also a graduate of the Ecole Polytechnique, as was his younger brother Maxime, and he went from there to government service. (That is France's way of honoring but also wasting talent.) Bernard also spent a few years representing the Engrenages Citroën (Citroën Gearings) in Spain along with some other private business. But his greatest pleasure came from writing and poetry. He had escaped the perils of German occupation, French collaboration, and Jewishness by volunteering service in the British Royal Air Force, where he earned the *croix de guerre* and became a *commandeur* in the Legion of Honor. His younger cousin Louis also did Polytechnique—this was one smart family— and handled trade matters for the plant at the Quai de Javel; but he, as well as other members of the family, was arrested and sent to Auschwitz, where he was murdered.

Dynasty interrupted.

THE LEADING FRENCH CAR MAKER at that time was Louis Renault, a born mechanic and tinkerer who had made his start in the best French fashion: by winning car races. His brother Marcel also raced and won the Paris-Vienna of 1902, a long and tedious achievement that brought fame to their marque; but then Marcel died the next year in the Paris-Madrid, missing a curve while trying to pass a competitor, which showed that automakers do better to let their employees do the running. Louis had a further surprise when he learned that Marcel had willed his shares in the company to his *chère amie,* Suzanne Daveney. Not a man to share, Louis bought her out with an annuity and a new car every year. In those days, a year was a reasonable auto lifetime.

In 1902 the company began making some of its own engines; in 1903 all of them. By 1905, it had its own foundry, body shop, and repair shop; had some eight hundred workers; made some 1,200 cars; had risen to become the third- or fourth-largest firm in the industry; and Louis and his brother Fernand were each clearing some 2 million francs in profit on 8.2 million in sales—a huge sum for the time. Among the bestsellers: taxicabs. These were having trouble getting accepted by Parisians, who particularly disliked negotiating charges with the cabbie. (This can be more painful in France than elsewhere.) At this point, a couple of resourceful inventors perfected the taximeter, which made all the difference, at least within Paris boundaries, where legal rates applied. (Even now, that is still the definition of the A zone.) When World War I began, about three to four thousand Renault cabs were operating in Paris. They later became famous as the *taxis de la Marne,* the vehicles that rushed French troops into combat to hold the line and protect the capital.

Large orders for taxis made Renault number one in the industry in 1907 and thereafter. By 1912 sales were up to some fifty-nine million francs and total profits nineteen million. All this money might have tempted lesser men to retire to ease and pleasure. Not Louis. He was an abstemious man (though not a Calvinist) and plowed most of his cash back into the business. That is the way of good personal and family enterprises: the first generation lays the foundation for those that follow.

But family enterprise, as we know, is dependent on the accidents of reproduction and mortality. In 1908 brother Fernand died after a long illness, leaving Louis in sole charge of the business. Not that he minded. If he missed his brother, his associates would not have known it. This was one authoritarian, tough-minded, short-tempered guy. How short? Just read this list of reproaches to his mistress, Jeanne Hatto, actress and singer:

Absent from Herqueville [his country house] Sunday 18 May 1911. [You] returned Monday without giving an account of activity while away.

[You went] off to sing in Strasbourg instead of passing Sunday at Herqueville, as did all the friends who care about me.

Received so-and-so in your loge, without my permission.

Interrupted me to talk theater with Briand [a top politician] when I was telling him about the beginnings of my little shop.

[You] came to the factory without permission on December 14th. I don't want any woman in my factory.[6]

Small wonder the two split up, although Renault's biographer tells us they remained friends. Maybe. In 1918, Renault married the daughter of a Parisian notary, who in 1920 bore him a son, Jean-Louis. So might he have the basis of a dynasty. A daughter would not have filled the bill. No women in his factory.

In spite of fruitful contacts with American makers, especially Henry Ford, in the years before the war, Renault was slower than others to move into mass production—not until the mid-twenties. He waited first for the French military to pay its bills for vehicles furnished during the war. That took some years. Governments, we know, are lazy payers, unless of course some of the money goes to functionaries. In 1922, Renault converted the company into a joint-stock corporation. He bought in 81 percent of the eighty million francs of initial capital, leaving a little room for friends sure not to offend or talk back to him. Further increases in capital came in 1928 (40 million francs) and 1940 (120 million francs). He took almost all of these additional shares, so that at the latter date he personally held 96.8 percent of the company's capital. Among the few outside stockholders was the Mirabaud group—a good old member of what the French call the H.B.P., the Haute Banque Protestante. Renault got rid of them all in 1926, because they had the nerve to mix into management.

There is no question that Louis Renault, for all his self-assertion, counted on passing his enterprise down in the family, but just at the point where his son would have entered the business as apprentice (Jean-Louis assumed that even as son of the owner, he had to justify his presence by learning), the war came. A political conservative with connections to Marshal Pétain, Louis Renault would no doubt have collaborated with Vichy of his own accord, the more so as his chief associate, François Lehideux, was committed to the new regime and Renault's health was failing. But such predilections aside, no major auto- or truck maker could refuse to go along with French government plans and programs, especially not in wartime.

Whether the firm was equally compelled to work with and sell to the German Nazi regime is another matter. In any event, once the war was over and the Allies victorious, the government of the Liberation, in its pursuit of what it defined as treasonable behavior, confiscated the Renault auto manufacture, arrested Louis Renault, and revived the company as a national enterprise (régie). Renault himself died in October 1944, and his family received only a fraction of what they might have expected in other circumstances. Strangely enough, the French government, while proclaiming Renault's misdeeds, kept his name for the nationalized firm and its cars, reasoning that memories of past successes would help sell the new postwar models.

Family enterprise interrupted.[7]

THE END OF WORLD WAR I ("The Great War") and defeat of the Germans found Peugeot in bad shape. Even though Paris had been liberated, the Germans had time to pillage northeastern France, and the bulk of the company's workforce found itself cut off from production units. Meanwhile, the French government made a point of reducing damages by half to take account of the dilapidated condition of plant and equipment. And even then it took a couple of years to remit compensation.

Yet Peugeot was determined to keep up, to catch up. The big men here were Robert Peugeot (1873–1945), "Monsieur Robert," followed by Jean-Pierre Peugeot (1896–1966) and his vice president, Maurice Jordan, graduate of the Ecole des Mines and adjunct CEO in 1933. These were calm, cool businessmen, careful in their decisions and decisive in their execution. Their sense of the future was based on experience: aim at a professional clientele—doctors, lawyers, functionaries, retirees—and build them solid, dependable middle-class cars. So well did Peugeot meet these standards that dealers complained they were not getting full use of repair facilities. The reason for this solidity: Peugeot was the French automobile enterprise that assigned the largest proportion of workers to verification. Most of their cars needed no attention during the guarantee period. In the words of Jordan, "Quality is the only seed to sow that will pay in the future."[8]

Yet strangely enough, after successfully running the company for so long, in the late 1920s Robert fell momentarily under the influence of Louis Rosengart, a financial operator who had helped competitor Citroën find the money to mass-produce cars when it had faced bankruptcy several years before. Rosengart came to Peugeot in 1927 and performed a similar feat. His methods were questionable. Essentially, he would create an associated firm to hold the Peugeot stocks (supplies, equipment, parts, cars), borrow against these stocks in the form of drafts on this firm, then rediscount these drafts with the Bank of France. In short, he turned the company's short-term debt into long-term debt.

It was the kind of maneuver that looks good when it works but can pose serious risks. Because the market for automobiles was growing so quickly, it worked for Peugeot, and Rosengart became a director of the house. For better or for worse, his success then went to his head, and he undertook other ventures: an assembly plant in Milan and a factory for making automobile canoes (motorized boats). These projects did not do well, and Rosengart left Peugeot in 1928 to operate on his own. For the automaker it was a timely, easy rupture. Rosengart lost himself in the mists, but Peugeot endured.

The Rosengart venture was the family firm's first significant experience with outside/inside financial aid. It was not to be the last. In 1930, on the eve of the Great Depression,[9] Peugeot found itself short of cash. In this crisis, the family decided to sell some 30 percent of capital to the Oustric bank, a firm of speculative habit and dubious solidity. Oustric proceeded in May 1930 to issue some sixty million francs in new Peugeot stock, a small fortune, all of which was lost when the bank went under shortly thereafter. Peugeot had to stop payments. The firm was saved by two events. First, their newest design, the Peugeot 201, was an extraordinary success. Second, and more important, was a heightened sense of family solidarity. Robert, president of the automobile enterprise, agreed in 1938 to lend the company some twenty-five million francs of his personal funds, interest free. This type of loyalty in time of crisis is one of the great strengths of family firms. It's hard to image the CEO of a major corporation putting up his or her own fortune for the company, and yet this happens time and time again with major family firms. Remember Thomas Baring in 1890, for instance.

In the decade that followed the armistice, golden postwar years, Peugeot reorganized its system of production, locating the factories in such a way as to minimize the costs of assembly. For many years the company had focused on making each car a unique product, fitted to the client's desires and taste. Clearly this model would no longer work if Peugeot wanted to compete in the ever-expanding market. The time had come for standard models, visible on showroom floors, ready for delivery with a minimum of distinctive gimmicks.[10]

Modernizing the firm and shifting into a major factory-manufacturing program called for a great deal of extrafamilial help. Here

Peugeot outdid itself. Calling on personal connections, sometimes with old school classmates—the competitive *grandes écoles* did a good job of merit selection—they were able to find loyal and able managers and technicians, most notably Edouard Arnaud (graduate of the Ecole Centrale) and Maurice Jordan, an engineer who was promoted to adjunct CEO in 1933, at thirty-four years of age. And while the company was at it, it found new banking support, of untouchable solidity, in the Bank of France, the Crédit Lyonnais, and some of those quiet Swiss houses. The lenders were reassured by a long history of industrial success and tenacity.

The Peugeot also did a remarkable job of locating outside executives who were loyal to the firm. When one looks at similar high-tech family enterprises, the entry of top-flight outsiders is almost invariably a threat to family control. To be sure, much of the internal/external dynamic depends on the strength and talent of family members, as well as the degree of unity within the family; outsiders can easily profit from discord. Managers, even old schoolmates, have their own differences in personalities and attitudes, and are quite capable of nursing rivalries. Peugeot and its top managers tried to deal with such friction by separating people, by posting them to different plants and assigning them diverse tasks. Such strategies did reduce conflict, but they also facilitated disobedience and insubordination. Overall, however, there was relatively little warfare inside and outside the family, in comparison with the experience of other major family firms. The long-run success of Peugeot shows that conflict is not inevitable; rather, that managerial functions and teamwork can coexist effectively within a family-owned structure.

For one example, look at the career of the afore-mentioned Maurice Jordan, CEO. Historian Alain Jemain sees him as indispensable. Without him, "Peugeot would never have celebrated its fiftieth anniversary."[11] On two occasions, once after the Oustric debacle and again after the destruction of 1945,[12] it was this "cold, rough, and distant Protestant, of superior and rigorous intelligence, who saved the firm from disaster." Jemain gives us a capsule photo of Jordan: "Tall, always very straight and thin in his strict suits, his face frozen in the mask of a Spanish grandee, ever biting on a cigarette holder, Maurice, Napoléon, Robert, Charles Jordan is a natural dominator. His faith lies in making on-the-spot practical decisions by way of avoiding the pains and costs of uncertainty."[13]

Jordan was the youngest of six children and heir to a family tradition of achievement and connections. His grandfather was from Montbéliard and so was part of the Peugeot world. He was a graduate of the reputable Ecole Centrale, worked as an engineer, and eventually became president of the coal mines of Denain-Anzin, and then later vice president of the Comité des Forges (the high command of French iron and steel manufacture). Young Jordan volunteered for service at the time of bloody Verdun, won a *croix de guerre* for initiative and bravery, and rose to the rank of second lieutenant. In 1921 he entered the Ecole des Mines in Paris (another *grande école*) and graduated as a civil engineer. He then applied for a job with Michelin.

With that pedigree, Michelin was interested. But the company had developed the habit of subjecting officer candidates to a questionnaire thirty pages long, calling for information on leisure activities, food preferences, hobbies, weekends, vacations—just about everything but sex and defecation. Jordan was used to more respect, had no patience for these indiscretions and *enfantillages,* and told Michelin to get lost. At this point, Michelin decided that he was a real prospect, but Jordan would have none of it. He walked out the door.

A doctor friend and relative who had married a sister of Robert Peugeot told Jordan to apply to the auto manufacturer. Peugeot liked what it saw, and only three years later, Jean-Pierre Peugeot, building a new team to help him take over after his father, named Maurice Jordan administrative director of the Sochaux plant. Jordan made himself indispensable. Two years later, he was named general-secretary of the corporation, and it was in that capacity that he set about repairing the Oustric bankruptcy mess by mobilizing bankers, dealers, and suppliers in a common effort to save the firm. He took an interest in the cars as well, working out the production of the 202 model and its derivatives, smaller versions of their top-of-the-line 402 that were designed for the middling bourgeois. By 1933, Jordan had been raised to vice-CEO, and Jean-Pierre Peugeot—who addressed him with the familiar *tu* rather than *vous* (which was an even bigger deal then than it is now)—consulted with him on every decision.

Jordan was exact, meticulous, a zealot for detail. His memory for figures made him a living calculator. Six in the morning found him at work, in summer as well as in winter. He had a small office adjacent to that of Jean-Pierre, and the door between the two was always open. An avid smoker, he finished a minimum of three packs a day. He kept his office clear of papers, but always had the telephone within reach and a bell to call the errand boy. His exits were as meticulous as his entrances: come 6·00 P.M., he shut down, always reserving his evenings for his family.

The essence of dominant management lies in mastery of time. The boss watches and bends himself to the minutes and imposes his temporal obsessions on everyone else. For Jordan, that meant no lagging or dragging: he demanded quick answers and quick application. He forbade communication with the outside; there lay the enemy in wait. For Jordan, Peugeot was at war, always fighting. A Peugeot may have ridden at the firm's head, but Jordan was the constable, the chief enforcer.

He had no use for theories, big programs, or generalities. He preferred to pay attention to detail, payments, expenses, and customer evaluations and relations. He had no use for adventures; what mattered was good sense, practicality. All of this, though, did not keep him from cherishing dislikes (bankers) and phobias (the labor troublemakers of the Paris area). One especially counterproductive animus: he did not like to export vehicles, feeling it was too hard to collect payment.

Meanwhile, he took care to make his own money, to hold a big block of stock in the Peugeot credit company, to own a major agency in the provinces and the firm that held the exclusive right to import Peugeot vehicles into Tunisia. Despite his ambition, and his great influence, he never thought to push aside or neglect the Peugeot clan, in the way that Iococca did at Ford. On the contrary, his immense loyalty to the Peugeot family was remarkable. He even put together a large group of lesser bureaucrats and inculcated in them a similar sense of loyalty to the Peugeot founding fathers.

BACK IN 1936, when family patriarch Robert was sixty-three years old and held undisputed authority, he presided over a family luncheon every Sunday in his mansion on the heights above Valentigney. The clan that assembled there was formidable: his three sons and two daughters came with their spouses and offspring, some fourteen grandchildren. Conversation at table dealt with current events and honors at school—never business. Such topics as the hopes for a new model, financial dealings with bankers, promotions, and recruitment were reserved for the men alone, after the coffee, in the billiard room.

One of Robert's chief preoccupations was avoiding dispersal of the family fortune. This is what had happened to the Japy, their close Protestant friends and preferred marriage partners. So Robert drew up a set of rules:

Shares in the enterprise would be passed only to sons, never to daughters or sons-in-law. Since French law dealt with inheritance differently, reserving shares for women as well as men, the company was charged with buying the women out. One daughter of Robert, Marthe, who never married, went to court and fought for sixteen years to claim her share; she was clearly a troublemaker. She ended up leaving France and settling in Switzerland.

All members of the family must reinvest earnings from the company in the company. There was no question of simply enjoying the income at the expense of the enterprise. Black sheep had to be put aside, where they could not make trouble.

All the Peugeot should have enough collateral income to be able to live up to these terms. In other words, they would have to work in order to make enough money to reinvest. There was no stipulation that they had to work in the family firm, but if they were capable and wanted to work there, they could count on united family support to maintain them in key posts.

All the sons would be given a place on the board of the family partnership, Les Fils de Peugeot Frères. Their voting power would be partial to start, but would grow as they got older and gained experience. It would grow faster for graduates of one of the competitive *grandes écoles*. The aim was to ensure a well-educated pool of descendants.

Executive managerial officers of the company were explicitly forbidden to engage in political activity other than local. In other words: no distractions, however attractive.

These matters settled, Monsieur Robert reigned as absolute monarch over firms and family. Every day, wrapped in his cape, he visited the workshops. There were to be no secrets; he wanted to know everything.

Outside of the actual Peugeot family, the firm strived to treat its workers with greater generosity and privilege than other automakers, and thus created a broader sense of family and family loyalty. Among the benefits were low-cost housing, medical facilities and care, company stores that sold at below-market prices, and death benefits for workers' families. There were also clubs for children and parents: scout troops, sewing circles, gardening and music groups, even a football team with funds to recruit professionals to play in national competition. There was a company newspaper, filled with news of company-sponsored activities such as the annual Christmas parties, helpful advice such as "Don't chew your fingernails," and a serial called "The Worker and His Children"—an inspirational morality tale of the rise of the Peugeot clan.

The workforce was recruited almost entirely locally, and company buses made the rounds to pick up employees and take them back home. Many of these were the children and even grandchildren of Peugeot personnel. Medals were generously awarded for good work. Workers were encouraged to save and to place their savings in the company-affiliated bank in Montbéliard, allegedly the most prosperous of its kind in the entire country.

The executives, of course, received rewards appropriate to their responsibilities. They drove Peugeot cars bought at favorable prices, wore the team beret, and swore by the company. Their fidelity brought end-of-year bonuses, shares in the firm, and a chance to acquire agencies or other concessions on good terms.

This emphasis on a caring family environment remained a firm characteristic throughout the twentieth century. In a sense, we see here a company with socialistic ideals competing successfully in a highly competitive, highly capitalistic marketplace. The company reaped (and continues to reap) many benefits from this approach, most notably very low turnover rates. Its retail shops were now organized as cooperatives and sold all the necessities, mainly food and clothing.

Throughout, the Peugeot family and firm made it a point to be discreet and unobtrusive, but *en famille,* in the company of members and agents, they liked to stress their special familial character and the example they offered their countrymen. Thus, at the banquet closing the Salon de l'Auto of October 1935:

> Does it not seem clear to you that the example of our great industrial family deserves attention? Like France, we have had our hard times, and if we have been able to re-establish our situation, it's because our industrial principles were good and solid. These principles, which have been the force of our house in the past and ensure our future, are they not applicable to our dear country as a whole? This magnificent country, which some would divide or send into dangerous adventures, could it not find once more balance and health in work, honesty, and unity? I should be proud to see the image of a great French house like ours serve as model to all the French.[14]

WORLD WAR II changed lots of things. Gasoline was so scarce that from September 1940 no one in France was allowed to drive except on public duty and with official permission. By the end of the year, less than 2 percent of gas pumps were fueled and the maximum ration was set at ten liters a month. In effect, the French learned to live without cars. The ordinary citizen made do with bicycle or public transport. The Peugeot and their execs were patriots, volunteering for military service and making it a point to get authorizations for vehicles that could be used to move arms and food to resisters or to take injured and wounded to the hospital.[15] They saw a company work stoppage as a social tragedy—"the annihilation of our national wealth."[16]

The Germans were not good for one's health. Robert Peugeot suffered several heart attacks. Much diminished, he could no longer get around without a wheelchair and in 1941 was replaced as president by his son Jean-Pierre. The outside execs such as Jordan were still around and made all the difference, and Peugeot continued to reward them in kind.

These war years saw the firm scramble for orders: cycles (of course), airplane parts, even some cars and trucks for military service. Of the big three French automakers, Renault, as we saw, sought to make money by dealing with the Vichy regime and even the Occupation authorities. Mistake: come the peace, the government nationalized Renault. That left Peugeot and Citroën as the great exemplars of family capitalism, though Citroën was now a piece of Michelin. The "traditional builders," they liked to be called. Some thought the two were made to be married, but marriages do not always follow a rational logic. Instead, Peugeot found Renault a more congenial partner, and although the usual exchange of shares was not feasible, they learned to work together, to the point of becoming Europe's number one automaker of the early 1970s.[17]

The oil shock of 1973 hit Citroën especially hard, bringing it to the edge of failure. The long-abandoned idea of marriage with Peugeot returned to the drawing board. Michelin, tire maker extraordinaire and restless entrepreneur, brought its big banks (Paribas and Lazard) into the negotiations, along with the government functionaries involved in Renault. Peugeot correctly saw this as an opportunity for capital reinforcement, 750 million francs from the Michelin group, which sold

Berliet to Renault for 450 million to help raise the money; plus a billion lent by FDES (Fonds de Développement Economique et Social). In December 1974, Peugeot acquired 38.2 percent of Citroën, and September 1976, after the necessary ratifications, saw the birth of a new conglomerate, PSA Peugeot Citroën. With all that, the Peugeot family kept its majority control of the overall firm.

And that was not all. While these legal and financial procedures were under way, the American firm Chrysler, with its own financial difficulties, offered to sell Peugeot its three European branches: Simca (Chrysler France), Rootes Sunbeam (Chrysler UK), and Barreiros (Chrysler España). Together, these three were making some eight hundred thousand cars a year, about as many as Peugeot. In August 1978, Peugeot agreed to pay $230 million for Chrysler UK and Chrysler España, plus 1.8 million shares in PSA, to be created. All of this came from company funds and left Peugeot with 41 percent of the new group, against 15.5 percent for Chrysler and 7 percent for Michelin.

At this point the second oil shock hit the Peugeot group (Peugeot, Citroën, and Chrysler Europe—Talbot by its new name) especially hard. Sales in France fell from 42.6 to 30.3 percent of the market from 1979 to 1982; sales in Europe, from 17.2 to 12 percent.

What to do? The Peugeot general staff decided that production would have to be modified along Japanese lines (*sic transit*), but since this would cost much money at a tough time, once again they needed a potent outsider to save the day. The man chosen was Jacques Calvet, an "Enarque" (graduate of the Ecole Nationale d'Administration), former cabinet director for Valéry Giscard d'Estaing, ex-minister of Finance, and former boss of the BNP (Banque Nationale de Paris). The choice showed the Peugeot family's determination to keep the firm going and its ability to find and win the right person. First task: a major pruning of the workforce, by 30 percent in ten years—not a simple matter for so paternalistic an enterprise. Second: a significant increase in capital, even at the expense of the Peugeot family and its two new allies, Chrysler and Michelin. Calvet put together a bank syndicate to help with all this, including

Chase Manhattan, First Chicago, Morgan, BNP, Crédit Lyonnais, the Société Générale, and Paribas.

One unexpected result was a growing share of Peugeot paper held by American institutional investors, mostly pension funds. No problem there; these were people who knew how to mind their own business. But as a sensitive, super-chauvinistic nation, the French were beginning to worry about this new financial dependency. Anyone else would have been happy to get the use of the money.

At this point, end of September 1997, Calvet retired and was replaced by another blessed outsider, Jean-Martin Folz, polytechnician and mines engineer, organizer of a new production technique designed to promote the possibilities of making varied models from a common platform. This represented a distinctive strategy. The other makers sought variety via purchases of or mergers with the makers of other kinds of cars. Folz did not agree, preferring independence and joint ventures with useful partners where desirable. "The key to succeeding in this car market is to produce cars quickly and make them as varied and attractive as possible and at competitive cost." (Also to change what one says from one year to the next.)

The Peugeot family agreed with him. To be sure, one heard occasional reports of dissension within the clan, prompting rumors of a sell-off. Pierre Peugeot, family patriarch, denied these categorically: "The family," he said at a news conference, "is completely united." Peugeot did its work within, and without. So well did it do, and so happy were the design choices, that in 1999 the Peugeot group found itself the sixth-biggest car maker in the world, reaching three million vehicles by 2001. Not only was it growing in volume and share, but its profit margins ran more than twice those of the sometime European market leader VW. That kind of success can go to your head.

The Peugeot retained control, but the production process lay in the hands of managers. These were people the family approved of—the family had the shares and the votes—and left to their devices. The result might have been a reduction of the family to rentier gentility. The business days, centuries of family business, might have been over. But no, the Peugeot made it a point to avoid such an out-come. With dividends restored at the turn of the century, the family found itself in a position to rebuild its share in the enterprise, to 26.5 percent of the capital and 40 percent of the votes, a return by 2001 to the levels of 1986. At the same time, a new generation of heirs found positions in such departments as Innovation and Marketing; among them, for the first time, a woman: Marie-Hélène Roncoroni, daughter of Pierre Peugeot, elected member of the board.

But being a Peugeot has its negatives. Wealth and success are an ever-present temptation to evil. Witness the kidnapping in 1960 of Eric Peugeot, a sweet kid of four years, son of Roland, grandson of Jean-Pierre, and some day likely heir to the auto kingdom. Eric was playing in the game park of the Saint-Cloud golf club, social stronghold for businessmen and politicos living in the tony western reaches of Paris and environs. He was visiting his grandfather, who had confided the boy to a governess and chauffeur. What could pos-sibly go wrong? That must have been what the *nurse* was thinking: she was sitting in a family car (a Peugeot 403), allegedly reading a book. The chauffeur seems to have been distracted or inattentive. Anyway, a man came up from the far reaches of the park, took Eric by the hand, and gently led him through a breach in the outside wall and to a waiting car. The man must have said the right reassuring things, because the boy never uttered a protest. He was used to caretakers and servants.

Near the swing, the kidnappers had left a ransom note, in all caps, warning against failure to pay the sum demanded: 50 million old francs, equaling 500,000 new francs, or $100,000. Not much, but in France it was a lot of money. The kidnappers' warning took the form of an imaginary newspaper report: "Young Peugeot died after suffering horrible torture, because his worthy parents refused to pay up or talked too much to the police." Then another word of warning: "I wouldn't want to have to confide your son to the special attentions of my friend Dédé. . . . Dédé's OK, but a little crazy. You have forty-eight hours to raise the money, and we'll tell you what to do."[18]

So Roland did as he was told, and a day later Eric was released, crying but uncomplaining. The two men, he said, had been friendly and kind. A year later the kidnappers were arrested. They never had a chance, were effectively asking to be found. They had spent the money too freely, to the point of arousing the suspicions of people around them, and one or more of these reported them for the reward.

For the Peugeot family, the lesson was obvious. No attention; no notice; no danger. The cars were one thing; the family, another.

Automobile historian Jean-Louis Loubet is lost in admiration when speaking of the Peugeot. At the start of the twenty-first century, he writes, the automobile industry seems to show that family capitalism is still thriving, at least in several instances. The pattern followed by the Peugeot—from successful family enterprise to a managerial arrangement, with or without family executive participation (cf. Morgan's bank)—has proved to be a normal, natural consequence of success, especially in complex industrial operations that call for technological knowledge and imagination.

The insiders need the outsiders. Even so, Loubet sees Peugeot as a special case, as the last general automaker to remain a family enterprise. For example, the Agnellis, he writes, despite their current focus on their car division, have become a case study in diversification: industry, but also finance, distribution, tourism and hotels, even professional football. Loubet could find other examples, of course. I would argue that both Ford and Toyota are still primarily family fiefdoms in which the day-to-day operations are run by outsiders. Toyota is still owned and supervised by the Toyoda family, managed by an array of proud and loyal technicians, building and assembling the full range of cars and trucks, and running factories and agencies all over the world. Ford has managed to survive systematic and repeated subordination without losing family dominance of a multinational enterprise specializing in auto manufacture. But even compared with those two firms, there is something about the cohesiveness, unity, and conscious decisions to nurture a familylike environment within the workforce that sets Peugeot apart.

Seven

TOYODA

Toyota and the Rise of Automobiles in Japan

Akio toyoda (b.1957)

The story of the rise of Toyota automobiles as well as of the founding Toyoda family, is akin to that of the Peugeot. Both families made their name and initial fortune in textiles, with both making significant contributions to the textile industries in their nations. Further, both created a strong sense of familial loyalty within their workforces. For Toyota, this sense of extended family included the factory workers—a truly remarkable development, and one essential to the firm's success. Their stories also highlight significant differences in how Western and Japanese societies view both family and business, yielding a model of dynasty that blurs the line between insiders and outsiders in the structure and leadership of family firms.

The founding father of Toyota, currently the world's second-largest automobile manufacturer and pressing hard for first, was Sakichi Toyoda.[1] As with the Peugeot (and the Schlumberger, as we shall see), the patriarch of the Toyoda got his start in the textile industry. He was born in 1867, the son of a carpenter in a remote country village in Shizuoka Prefecture, located on the Pacific Coast, some 110 miles south of Tokyo. In this largely agricultural area, women earned additional income for the family by weaving cotton cloth for market, and most homes had a handloom.

From a young age, Sakichi was fascinated with the challenges presented by these looms. Watching his mother's constant frustration with broken thread and inefficient design, he set himself to making improvements—much to the despair of his father, who felt his son should stick to carpentry. Sakichi had his own ideas. In 1890 he traveled to Tokyo to visit an industrial exposition that showed him modern mechanical marvels he had not imagined, including Japan's first electric tram. A year later he patented a new wooden handloom that he claimed increased productivity by 40–50 percent. He soon moved to Tokyo, where he shifted focus from handlooms that offered a real, but small, increase in efficiency over the traditional methods, to a power loom, which would truly alter the dominant mode of production.

Sakichi struggled in Tokyo. His marriage failed, and he moved back to his home village, leaving behind his wife, but taking his children. He then divorced and remarried, and his second wife, Asako Hayashi, reared his son Kiichiro, who, as we shall see, became a world-class entrepreneur as an adult.

Through this period, Sakichi continued his efforts to develop an efficient power loom. He also began producing fabric on his own account, using some sixty steam- and water-powered looms of his own invention and construction. His machines cost substantially less than German and French imports, and caught the attention of Mitsui, a giant Japanese mercantile corporation, which agreed to act as sales agent for Sakichi's machines worldwide.

Here we see the complexities of the traditional Japanese family system (the *ie*) at work: Sakichi's eldest daughter had married Risaburo Kogama, whose family ran a major branch of the Mitsui empire. In Japan, the sons-in-law are often brought into a family with all the rights of a child by birth. When contrasted with a strict patrilineal society (for instance, that of the Rothschilds), it's clear that this structure radically changes the dynamics of inheritance and status. Through marriage, Risaburo, who was ten years older than Kiichiro, took Toyoda as his last name and became, in effect, Sakichi's eldest son and first heir to his fortune.[2] This would make a big difference later, when the family moved into automobile manufacturing.

Back in textiles, Sakichi's looms tested better than his German and French competitors, but never quite so well as the best British makes. This only stimulated him to work harder: "It is impossible to create an innovative product," he wrote, "unless you do it yourself, pay attention to every detail, and then test it exhaustively. Never entrust the creation of a product to others, for that will inevitably lead to failure and cause you deep regret."[3]

Eventually his tireless efforts and insistence on quality were rewarded; the war stimulated a growing market for cheap mass-produced cloth, and also generated nearly constant orders for military uniforms. Toyoda Spinning and Weaving Company, Ltd., was soon keeping busy some thirty-four thousand spindles, one thousand looms, and one thousand workers. In 1924, Toyoda invented the Type-G Toyoda automatic loom, which was a groundbreaking invention that offered a number of new features, such as automatic thread replenishment. In the past Sakichi's looms had been largely imitations of British models; now he was a true leader in innovation. These new looms found a ready market abroad, but instead of continuing to expand the company's cloth and loom business, Sakichi made a radical choice. In 1929 he sold the patents to his automatic circular loom to Britain's Platt Brothers and Company, Ltd., world leaders in the loom industry, who were primarily interested in keeping Sakichi's loom out of the Western market. The sale brought in the 1929 equivalent of one million yen, which became the seed money for the Toyota Motor Company.

Sakichi himself was too old to undertake auto manufacture, but a visit to the United States convinced him that cars had a mighty future. He saw this as a suitable task for his son Kiichiro, whom he admonished: "I devoted most of my life to inventing new kinds of looms. Now it's your turn. You should make an effort to make something that will benefit society." He challenged Kiichiro to "build a Japanese car with Japanese hands."[4]

While Sakichi had been a simple country-boy inventor, Kiichiro had rigorous formal training in mechanical engineering at Teidai, Tokyo Imperial University. After graduation, in 1921, he went on a tour of the textile mills in Europe and the United States, which yielded much useful information for his father's company. In 1929, he accompanied the representatives of Mitsui Bank on the mission to England to negotiate the sale of Sakichi's patent rights to Platt Brothers. This trip proved even more influential for the young man, as he spent very little time exploring textiles. Instead, he visited automobile plants and took copious notes on what he saw and heard.

An observant and perceptive man like his father, Kiichiro was much impressed by what the automobile was doing for the more technologically advanced Western societies. He accepted his father's charge, seeing in automobiles a new path for Toyoda that was also a natural extension of the company's experience.

By 1933, Kiichiro felt ready to get started, and he asked his brother-in-law and adoptive brother Risaburo Toyoda, who headed the family textile business, to call a meeting of the board to approve a new automobile department.[5] Given his status as "eldest son," Risaburo[6] was named first president of the automobile division of Toyoda Automatic Loomworks. Kiichiro, however, would be the main force behind the company in the early years.

The other "son" who would play a major role was Sakichi's favorite nephew, Eiji, whom Sakichi made sure to send to university to study engineering. This emphasis on formal education for both boys had a significant impact on the company's success, and on the history of automobile production throughout the world.

At this point Japan had no true automobile industry, even thirty years after major companies had been established in Europe and America. In fact, the Japanese of the pre-Meiji era (nineteenth century) were not much given to wheeled vehicles in general, other than light rickshaws and the occasional beast-drawn wagon for heavy objects. Japanese roads were badly rutted and pitted, and did not lend themselves to automobiles or their predecessors. Most Japanese vehicles were more amusements than industrial products—in 1929 the nation of islands had all of 436 hand-built licensed units.

Despite the scarcity of vehicles, Japan soon had the highest rate of accidents and injuries in the world—which is particularly impressive given the very elaborate precautions governing road use that were put in place, such as the little yellow flags provided to pedestrians at intersections. Japanese drivers, it seems, saw roads as test strips for masculine courage and preening.

The average Japanese driver of the time got his car from assembly kits shipped in by Ford and General Motors: eight thousand by Ford, ten thousand by GM, by the late 1920s. These imports left the Japanese government and military worried and unhappy. The government found the purchase of kits a huge drain on the balance of payments and the buying power of the yen; the army found dependence on foreign suppliers an implicit threat to Japanese power and autonomy.

To combat this threat, the state appointed a committee to look into developing a national automobile industry and urged a trio of producers, Nissan, Isuzu, and Toyoda, to design a standard chassis for trucks and buses. For all of them, this was the easy part. The big problem was the engine, and here Kiichiro had the advantage of metallurgical and mechanical understanding from his university instruction and his earlier work on looms.

His university training had left its imprint. He eschewed intuition for methodical trials and practical comparisons; made small test engines before going on to larger models; sought out the best available technicians, including university professors and researchers; and gave their best students good jobs at Toyota. In short, he understood that he was creating not only products but an industry and a new system of production that reflected the particular conditions in Japan at the time. This understanding of the importance of developing successful processes lay, and still lies, at the center of Toyota's success.

Kiichiro quickly saw that it would take special steels to stand up under the heat and friction of high-speed movement, particularly within the engine. As a result, he decided to establish the Toyoda auto works at Nagoya, a center of Japanese industrial manufacture. Construction of the new factory got under way in 1933, and included a steel mill to make metals that were unavailable from other manu facturers. A casting specialist was hired to design a plant that could start with prototypes but move on to mass production. Yet with all this planning, preparation, and focus, Toyoda still took a year to bring out its first real automobile engine, a copy of a Chevrolet model with six in-line cylinders that yielded sixty-five horsepower. Many of the parts had been reverse-engineered from foreign models; many, especially the combustion chambers, had been changed, tried, and tried again. The result was an engine so exact that it could accept Chevy replacement parts, a major advantage when the inevitable breakdown occurred. Then, in the spring of 1935, the first passenger car was completed, a streamlined model styled after the current Chryslers.

Toyoda's Model A1 was promising but premature. Japan at the time was a very bellicose country, stronger than its neighbors and aiming to exploit the advantage. The army was engaging in and preparing all manner of military operations, and the army wanted trucks, not cars. A "Bill Concerning the Manufacture of Motor Vehicles" passed the Diet (Japan's governing body) that very year, setting trucks as the Japanese auto industry's official priority.

Simultaneously, the government went about the task of indigenizing the automobile industry. The army pressured the government to end what it saw as the precarious dependence on foreign vehicle imports by simply expelling Japan Ford and Japan GM. (It may be that the military was already anticipating the possibility of war against the United States.) The government refused to go that far, fearing U.S. reprisals, but it did place higher import duties and punitive exchange regulations on Ford and General Motors, giving the American companies a strong incentive to pull out. In 1936 (the year the auto company changed its name to Toyota) a law was passed calling for any company making more than three thousand vehicles a year to be licensed, and stipulated that no firm could be licensed that was not at least half owned and directed by Japanese nationals. Such companies would get generous exemptions from taxes and import duties, and would receive other forms of assistance. Ford and General Motors could not compete on this tilted playing field. Both made efforts to merge with Toyota or Nissan, but by 1939 they gave up. International relations and emotions were not favorable. The Japanese were gearing up for trouble.

Through all of this, Toyota got the message. If the state was going to designate certain firms for protection and favor, it wanted to be on that list. And if the state wanted trucks, then trucks it would get—so, for the time being, Toyota scaled back its proud plans for passenger cars. Kiichiro ordered construction of a plant outside Nagoya with capacity for producing 500 cars and 1,500 trucks a month. The site had its virtues: lots of flat land in a country that was otherwise all hills and gullies; easy access to water; and a local mayor who made it his business to get the land for Toyota at a bargain price.

Kiichiro also began to experiment with new systems of supplying materials: he cut back on traditional cash outlays by deliberately decreasing warehouse capacity. The goal was to produce vehicles on order and to use the proceeds to pay for materials and parts as needed. He also invested in conveyor belts and multitasking machines in order to reduce workers' movements, and thus to reduce the space needed for manufacturing.

Kiichiro's idea of cutting back on storage was theoretically excellent, and it presaged what eventually came to be known as "lean production." It assumed, however, the ability to sell the cars and trucks as they rolled off the line. But during the first months of production, Toyota's vehicles were so plagued with quality problems that they piled up unsold. This massive accumulation of new vehicles would be a problem on any showroom floor, but to a firm whose main strategy for survival was efficient turnover, it was a disaster. Toyota found itself on the verge of collapse—until war intervened. Fighting broke out, and the military bought up every truck they could lay their hands on. Toyota was saved.

But saved for what? As Japan went from conquest to conquest, the ambition of the military knew no measure. No one in the east Asian and western Pacific areas could bring killing power to bear so quickly and effectively. But from the very beginning, there were shortages and hardships on the Japanese home front. Japan was a small country geographically, poor in natural resources, and had always depended extensively on imports. As trade was disrupted by the war, the essential materials from abroad became harder and harder to secure. Only a stoical, hardworking, and ingenious people could have put up with the resulting hardships and scarcities so long. The government issued orders against hoarding, but even the most patriotic Japanese found themselves scrambling to locate and hide supplies—to trade, if not to use. One resource that became particularly scarce in the embattled land was labor, for the most able workers were the first to go fight. As more and more people left for military service, employers took their workers wherever they could find them: nuns, geisha, criminals, and invalids.

The needs of the military demanded urgent actions, and as the war rolled on, every effort was made to stretch resources. Toyota reduced vehicles to their barest essentials: trucks rolled off the line with one headlight instead of two, with brakes on rear wheels instead of on all four; with wooden bumpers and a single bar instead of a radiator grille. These were downright dangerous modifications, but in the middle of a brutal war, accidents with automobiles were only one of many ways to die.

Toyota continued to produce, and the Japanese war machine

continued its aggression through Asia and the Pacific. In the first years of the war, Japanese domination was near total. But with time, the tide of the fighting shifted. Despite all the hardships to which they had become accustomed, neither the Japanese armed forces nor the civilian population was prepared for defeat. The Japanese had a tradition of victory, and their eventual recourse to suicide air strikes and other hopeless attacks was seen as evidence not of desperation but of spirit and courage. War spread to the United States, and while the effort was successful at first, it quickly became a case study in jingoistic madness and denial.

Changes at Toyota reflected the state of the battle: some trucks were made of light parts, ready to be disassembled and carried across streams and through jungles to drivable terrain. Other engines were used to power plywood boats to be loaded with explosives and sent against enemy naval vessels. All of this ingenuity in destructiveness testified to the growing desperation of Japan's wartime condition. Even the atom bombs dropped on Hiroshima and Nagasaki made little impression on the other parts of the country—but the generals and admirals understood their meaning and conveyed the painful facts to the emperor. So Hirohito, himself an instigator of and accomplice in madness, finally announced the need to "endure the unendurable," and accept defeat.

Surprisingly, many Japanese were so caught up in dreams of endless victory that they were completely stunned by the news. Toyota workers, who, unbeknownst to them, had barely escaped a murderous bombing scheduled by the American command for the next week, wept at their machines.

Denial aside, the outlook for Toyota was grim. The company had barely managed to make 3,275 trucks and buses (and not a single passenger car) in the last year of the war, while their plant was equipped for eight or ten times that number. Logic suggested that this was the end of the business. But the resilience and ingenuity of management and workers were extraordinary, and they transferred their manufacturing efforts to focus on subsistence. Employees were set to work planting vegetables, and the company built a flour mill, bakery, and charcoal plant to take care of food and cooking. Kiichiro had his cousin Eiji join with potters in the neighborhood to set up a chinaware business, while other Toyota units set to making pots and pans. Kiichiro also sent his son up north to learn what he could about making fish paste, a possible business opportunity. This was a family that did not know the meaning of "quit," and tirelessly continued seeking income in those activities that were linked to survival and everyday living.

Fortunately for them, the American occupation authorities soon found that to survive in Japan, they needed transportation. They asked Toyota to start making trucks again, and the motor company responded with alacrity. Kiichiro understood the task. The company would have to make the most of their accumulated stockpiles; to learn to live and work small; and to anticipate the future by designing the kind of car that would meet the needs of a famished economy. To offset these great challenges, Toyota had, for the time being at least, a large and reliable client in the United States military, which purchased as much as Toyota could make.

Still, this was a very difficult period for Toyota. Kiichiro's first instinct was to have a group belt-tightening, replete with wage cuts and layoffs. Not surprisingly, workers found this a demoralizing return for their years of devotion and commitment. In an effort to calm the staff, he asked for voluntary retirements. This also went over poorly, and produced angry work stoppages in a company that prided itself on its sense of loyalty. Kiichiro's peculiarly Japanese response was to resign as president, symbolically setting the example to staff as a father might to his children. This gesture of sharing their fate seems to have helped. More people offered to leave than had been asked for, and Toyota did its best to find them other work. Labor peace returned, and the company returned to production, if not prosperity.[7]

At one point in 1948, Toyota debt was eight times capital. Why would anyone lend? And then, in the 1950s, the company was momentarily rescued by the Korean War. America needed friendly manufacturing might in Asia, and Japan was in the perfect position to give it. In July 1950, the U.S. Defense Department ordered a thousand trucks; this number rose to almost five thousand by March 1951. Between 1950 and 1954 nearly three billion dollars in industrial contracts flowed into Japan, and Toyota took its share. The United States, Japan's lethal enemy only years before, was suddenly her savior. As Prime Minister Yoshida put it, the war contracts were a "gift of the gods."[8]

This gift was life's blood to Toyota, but it was only a temporary salve to a recovering economy and to an automobile company that had always lived on government subsidies. In the long run, the company was saved by acknowledging that it would have to abandon dependence on official favor and compete in a free market. Even before Korea, Kiichiro, toward the end of his presidency, had pointed to this problem in a memo that became something of a moral call to arms: "The Japanese auto industry has been fostered and protected in a controlled economy and has never braved the rough waves of a free-market system. It is like a hothouse plant. Moreover, viewed impartially from a global standpoint, Toyota is far from being a first-class company. Because of Japan's defeat in the war, we see ourselves as something like a third-class auto company."[9]

Ultimately it would not be Kiichiro who was able to change this view. But change it would, over time, and through the efforts of many people, both Toyoda family members and outsiders. Kiichiro's abdication left his cousin Eiji as the most important family member active in the firm.

Eiji had been with the car maker since his graduation from university, even though his father, Sakichi's brother Heikichi, had hoped Eiji would follow him into the textile business. (Heikichi was so dedicated to the firm that he made his family home inside the spinning factory.) In essence, though, Kiichiro had claimed the young Eiji for the automobile side of the family business, and given the strongly hierarchical Japanese social structure, Eiji and his immediate family quickly acquiesced. During the thirties, Eiji had earned his place by devoting particular attention to the quality of the company's cars, which for many years had left much to be desired. He was also noted for his ceaseless hunt for reliable parts suppliers.

Soon the company decided that a learning trip to the United States was imperative, and Eiji was selected to visit the factories of the major automobile makers. He was given only three thousand dollars for expenses, including airfare, but fortunately his American hosts were hospitable and fed him. Who could dream that a Japanese car maker would ever be able to compete with an American giant? At the time (1950), Toyota was making forty cars a day; Ford, twenty thousand. Eiji learned much of value and returned with a report on American manufacturing methods. More important, he returned with the sense that nothing he'd seen in America was beyond Toyota's ability.

But despite his family position and his many years of experience, Eiji was seen as too sweet a personality to run the show at a time when the firm had to be aggressively preparing itself for bigger and bolder competitors. The official presidency of the firm was therefore handed over to an outsider, Ishida Taizo.[10] The real power in the company, however, resided with Taiichi Ohno, a professional manager and mechanical engineer who had gained his experience at Toyoda Spinning and Weaving.

Ohno was a martinet. He prowled the shop floor endlessly, observing the lines and the workers, and tirelessly asking questions. His favorite was "Why?" As Toyota historian Ed Reingold puts it, "He terrified everybody who worked for him, drove them unmercifully, criticized them, belittled them, threw things at them, kicked them."[11] His subordinates did their best to avoid him, although many are said to have appreciated his strictness, which was certainly possible in a culture where rigor and discipline were highly valued. What he lacked in managerial and interpersonal skills, Ohno more than made up for in vision. It was he who developed and implemented Kiichiro's idea of "lean production" into a system that became known as TPS, or the "Toyota Production System," which could be used in making not only automobiles but all manner of complex industrial products. TPS was perhaps the most important technical innovation since Ford's successful implementation of the moving assembly line, and it has transformed manufacturing throughout the world.

The aim was to waste neither time nor space. Lean and mean. As with a standard assembly line, workers didn't need to move about, and materials were delivered to them. There were, however, key differences. For one, materials arrived only when needed, or "just in time," which cut down considerably on waste and avoided any interruption of flow. Much of what Ohno wanted ran against deep-rooted Japanese habits of hoarding against feared shortages. But his sense of opportunity and rationality was shaped by a visit to the United States in 1956, where he experienced the phenomenon of American supermarkets. They filled their shelves to meet anticipated demand, which changed with the seasons. Customers took for granted that they would find what they needed when they wanted it, and so they had no need to hoard goods in their homes. Lean manufacturing also emphasized a more collaborative team approach to production, which squared well with Japanese cultural traditions and has now been implemented in factories worldwide.

Ohno's lean manufacturing process took several decades to develop and perfect, so the great benefits were not clearly visible at first. This was right about the time that the Korean War ended, giving the company, which owed its steady business to the war effort, reason to fear the worst.

But the company was again saved by war—this time, the spread of the cold war. The Americans had no particular intention of supporting the Japanese economy, but the Communist victory in China in 1949 changed the geopolitical dynamics completely. With Chairman Mao in power, America turned to Japan as an ally against the further spread of communism in Asia. Many war debts were forgiven, and various foreign markets were opened to Japanese products. This was a period of major growth for Toyota. From 1955 to 1961, production scaled up tenfold, beginning in 1955 with the Crown, the first entirely Toyota-developed car. By the early 1960s more than two hundred thousand cars were rolling off the lines annually. Output continued to grow as Ohno perfected lean manufacturing, with its extremely efficient parts-delivery system.

In the late 1960s the company underwent other major shifts. The immensely popular Corolla model was launched in 1966 and quickly became the bestseller in its lineup (which it would remain for the next thirty years). And in 1967, Eiji Toyoda—finally getting his chance—took over as president and chairman, the first family member by bloodline to hold the position since Kiichiro.

Growth continued at a rapid pace, as it became clear to the world that Toyota had outgrown its position as an exotic minor player in the world automobile market. In 1972, the company's annual production hit the two million mark; by December 1980 it was three million. With this precipitous growth came the need for expanding markets and greater (and even more efficient) production capabilities. Simply put, the company was getting too big for its economic britches. Early on they began looking for opportunities to produce abroad as a way of getting around commercial barriers. In January 1958 the first such foreign factory began operations in Brazil; in September 1962 a second opened in South Africa; and in February 1984, Toyota joined General Motors in a joint venture in the United States: NUMMI, the New United Motor Manufacturing, Inc. Several other major joint ventures and production agreements were forged in the following years, and by the early 1990s, Toyota could compete with anyone on equal terms.

One of the most promising areas of opportunity for Toyota has been China, with its huge population and spectacular economic gains—now catching up after hundreds of years of lost opportunity. Present plans call for construction of dozens of plants from the coast deep into the interior, producing by 2005 some 250,000 vehicles a year, about 10 percent of the vehicles Toyota and affiliates are making outside Japan today. The man in charge will be Akio Toyoda, great-grandson of the founder of Toyota Motors, appointed with a view to training and promotion within what is still a family enterprise. By 2010 the company hopes to be selling a million vehicles a year in China, which figures to be a key element in the goal of 15 percent of the world market—the share that General Motors holds today. Culture counts, and the Japanese take continuity seriously.

MEANWHILE, good was never good enough. The company's motivational slogan was *kaizen:* continuous improvement. Workers were rewarded for finding glitches and suggesting remedies. PDCA (plan, do, check, action)—why stick to verbs so long as one arrives at quick decisions. Here *beya* (big room) meetings help, bringing together engineers, designers, marketers, and suppliers to develop and improve new models. Meanwhile *pokayoke* (mistake-proofing) sensors alert workers to missing parts or mistakes in assembly, while management keeps pushing to reduce cost of components and GBL (global body line) reduces the number of braces required to hold frames together from fifty to one. And when rival Nissan came along with its "cost killer" and began saving billions, Toyota replied with CCC21 (construction of cost competitiveness, twenty-first century). As always, the aim was to save money. Turn down the heat in company dorms during working hours. Cut down the parts in door handles from thirty-four to five, which also made it possible to slash installation time to three seconds. Squeeze suppliers to near-death, but not all the way.

Migration and globalization required a reconciliation of Japanese and foreign cultural values. Toyota, we have seen, has always thought of itself as a family. It was not ready simply to hire and fire. To find the right human material, it engaged in extensive, time-consuming, costly tests and interviews—dozens of hours per candidate. The company gave the people it hired clothing bearing the Toyota name and logos. It wanted them to be proud of their affiliation and wanted others to know they were proud. And the company made it a point to go beyond shop arrangements and provide the kind of toilet and shower and recreational facilities that would meet worker needs. That sounds simple enough, but it took deliberate effort to learn and adapt to the expectations of other cultures. The question of gender was a special puzzler: Did American rules of nondiscrimination require common men's and women's toilets?

Toyota also exerted itself to meet the passionate objections and ideological demands of its neighbors. One might have expected less trouble. After all, the company brought jobs and prosperity with it. As a local official in Derbyshire, England, put it, Toyota came as a godsend, not only for its outlays on construction but for the stimulus it gave other businesses in the area.

And yet such a mundane calculus has little effect on nature lovers. So Toyota planted some 350,000 trees around the English factory site and created surface water fields to preserve wetlands habitat for lapwings, peewits, and swans. The plant was built to minimize noise; the paint shop instituted emission standards well above official requirements. Just about all (99.9 percent) parts packaging was reused; wastewater was recycled; exhaust gases were used to preheat other processes. To be sure, the very size of the operation interfered with TV reception; so the BBC was persuaded to relay its signal into the area from a new direction. Meanwhile, the company made contributions to local arts and education and encouraged employees to participate in community activities. Henry Ford would have been flabbergasted.

The success of this strategy shows in the data. Since 2000, the global output of autos has risen by three million vehicles to some sixty million; of that increase, half has come from Toyota alone. This increase reflects consumer confidence above all: the quality of the finished product and the reliability of customer relations, which are too good for need. Toyota bears witness to Japan's obsession with flawless yet improving performance and Toyota's ability to transmit such cultural attitudes to foreign employees. "As Japanese carmakers steadily overhaul America's Big Three, it must be a chilling thought that Detroit's nemesis is working on ways to improve its performance."[12]

And the Toyoda family?

Through all this, the Toyoda family continued to play a major leadership role, with Eiji continuing as president. In 1981 the leadership was further consolidated when Kiichiro's son Shoichiro Toyoda was named president of Toyota Motor Sales, the firm's distribution branch. In 1983 the manufacturing arm and the sales arm were united for the first time as the Toyota Motor Corporation. Eiji was named chairman, and Shoichiro became president and CEO. At the time a *BusinessWeek* article quoted a Japanese economist as saying the return of the Toyoda family to power was a "restoration of the bluest of blue blood."[13]

Part Three

TREASURES OF
THE EARTH

PROLOGUE

The development of natural resources in the form of raw materials such as timber, metal ore, and petroleum is another sector in which family firms have thrived. Unlike banking, where business connections and reputation are paramount, or automobiles, where personal relations between producers, intermediaries, and consumers are a top consideration, with raw materials luck, and the ability to identify and seize opportunities as they present themselves, are central. Who owns the land that holds the treasure? Who knows of the existence of mineral wealth on, or in, that land? Who can obtain rights to those materials? And what changes are occurring in the larger economy that will affect the value of a given raw material? As we shall see in the following chapters, each of these considerations has a critical impact on the evolution of lasting dynasties of enormous wealth and power.

On the most fundamental level, wealth in raw materials is centered on the issue of land ownership, and the discovery of exploitable assets on that land. Over time, individual landowners have gotten a hold of these raw materials and have built fortunes, which they've been able to pass on to later generations. The Wendel, French iron-makers, built their empire little by little, developing lands that had been in the family for generations, then seeking out new regions to purchase, which provided key resources in making iron and steel. In this world of raw materials, the development of one resource or property tends to lead to the next, and family fortunes are compounded.

Historically two categories of natural materials in particular have led to the accumulation of great wealth—materials used for creating armaments and tools, such as metal ore, whence the fortunes of the Wendel and the Guggenheims (who began there and then diversified), and materials used as fuel, such as coal and oil, upon which the dynasties of the Rockefellers and the Schlumberger are founded.

In ancient times, workable, shapeable materials were important. At first it was wood that was essential. Gradually it gave way to metals, as new technologies (heat, and rudimentary tools for metalwork) allowed them to be shaped with greater accuracy and ease. Craftsmen came to value copper and alloys such as brass and bronze. Bronze was especially useful; resistant to wear by water and oxidation, it was the metal of choice for arms and armor. And as we have seen both in banking (particularly with the Rothschilds and Barings) and to a lesser extent the automobile industry (particularly Toyota), war shapes the commercial environment.

The Middle Ages saw Europe, especially the British Isles, move toward greater reliance on iron, above all its relatively carbon-free forms of wrought iron and steel. Steel was the most desirable of these, as it was harder and potentially sharper than any other metal, and also less vulnerable to rust than carboniferous cast iron. Steel made great swords, hammers, and arrowheads. And as we shall see in the chapter on the Wendel, there was an enormous commercial difference between low-grade iron ore, which has plagued French metallurgy, and ore that could yield high-quality steel, such as that found in the British Isles.

Fuel, the raw material that yields energy for work and heat, is both indispensable in the cooler climates and essential for powering industry. Early on, man learned to burn wood and to use fire for all manner of work, causing primitive "industry" to be centered in forested areas. (And we'll see that wood charcoal provided an essential source of fuel for more contemporary industry as well, powering, for instance, the Wendel forges.) The next major advance was the use of coal as fuel. This also affected the location of industry; while coal can be moved, to do so takes effort and resources. No surprise, then, that the new fuel-intensive industries were clustered near coal mines.

Nature has also provided man with liquid fuels, the most abundant and important of which is petroleum (literally "rock oil"). In one form or another, this substance has been used since prehistoric times. While the liquid forms were initially undesirable, some of it took the form of bitumen, a mixture of burnable oil, pitch, and asphalt that proved especially useful in such treeless environments as the Tigris-Euphrates delta. People learned to use the messy mix as caulking material for ships and walls, and as fastener and glue in tools and weapons. Arabs and Persians eventually learned to use these oils as a source of light. They brought the technique to Spain, whence it passed to Northern Europe.

It was as an illuminant that petroleum became increasingly valuable in Europe from the Middle Ages and into the Renaissance and modern times, as people began to read more and do other types of work that called for clear sight and measurement. Oil also proved useful as a lubricant for the growing numbers of mechanical devices. These uses alone made it a valuable resource, though not yet the object of passionate desire and worth that it would become in the twentieth century. Naturally occurring oil slicks and pools (known as "seepage") remained a convenient but messy source, and new deposits were being found regularly, usually in lands colonized by European interests. Meanwhile, new techniques for distilling coal yielded kerosene, which was so convenient and comparatively clean burning that it increased the demand for oil. Sometimes, contrary to what economic law might lead us to expect, a rise in supply can lead to an even greater rise in demand.

In the mid-nineteenth century, go-getters began drilling for underground oil, and in August 1859, the first such well came in, some seventy feet deep, in western Pennsylvania. This was the beginning of a new age, one of search and discovery, oil fields and oil refineries, and an ever-growing and diversifying technological world based on liquid and gaseous fuel. Since the discovery of oil and its first industrial use, this new resource has been so valuable that men have fought and even killed for it. As one historian put it, "Oil was a subject not just of commercial competition, but of outright war; and oil warfare, in the latter part of the last century and the first two decades of this, was not an activity which can be judged today, by ordinary people living ordinary lives, according to any accepted, civilized standards."[1]

Oil has been the source of some enormous private fortunes, such as those of the Rockefellers and the Schlumberger, whom we will meet shortly. The big winners in this industry have been the oil refiners, the well owners, and the engineering companies: individuals and firms who made their fortunes by putting together luck and business acumen, and sustained those fortunes by using their clout to reap favorable policies from governments hungry for fuel. In the stories of these raw material powerhouses, we'll meet some of the shrewdest, toughest, most ruthless, and, ultimately, most successful businesspeople in our survey. Awesome and a little frightening, their success shouldn't be surprising considering how desperately the modern world needs what they possess.

Family fortunes have grown enormously quickly in some of these cases, particularly the Rockefellers' and the Guggenheims', for whom nearly untold riches accrued within two generations. This wealth was easily passed on to future generations, and while their businesses have been transformed into more diversified managerial models, the fortunes themselves, and their management, growth, and use, have become dynastic enterprises in their own right.

Eight
THE ROCKEFELLERS

LUCK, VIRTUE, AND PIETY

JOHN D. ROCKEFELLER (1839–1937)

The Rockefellers are an interesting case study in any examination of dynasties. Everyone *thinks* of the Rockefellers as a dynasty; everyone knows the Rockefeller name and is aware that Rockefellers remain active and powerful in business, politics, and philanthropy. When it comes down to it, though, the Rockefeller story is really that of the meteoric rise of one person: the patriarch, John D. Rockefeller (1839–1937). He took luck, combined it with hard work and remorseless business acumen, and became the richest man in the America of his day. He unquestionably loved money, but he was never completely happy with it, and he spent much of his later years trying to find worthy ways to give it away.

He was a brilliant but difficult man, and perhaps it ought not to be surprising that a person of his drive, ruthlessness, and emotional miserliness did not inspire a passion in his descendants to take command of the family enterprise as he had. Nonetheless, these later generations have made the most of the opportunities that the family's wealth has brought them, and Rockefeller remains one of the most celebrated names in America's industrial history.

John D. Rockefeller's luck came from time and place. He was born in 1839 and grew up in an America Midwest that was just opening to agriculture and trade. The Cleveland of his early years was a small boomtown, a place that favored energy and ambition, and John D. (who always isnsisted on using his middle initial) had plenty of both, along with cleverness and cunning. Part of this was due to his upbringing. "I cheat my boys every chance I get," his father, William A. Rockefeller, bragged. "I want to make 'em sharp. I trade with the boys and skin 'em and I just beat 'em every time I can." John D.'s father was a lecher and seducer who made an irregular living by selling folk remedies to gullible yokels. But he was not entirely without conscience: getting ready to desert his little family, he gave money to John D., then eighteen, to pay for construction of a house downtown. John D. undertook the project so earnestly, getting bids from eight contractors and supervising every detail, that the builders actually lost money on the job. When the work was complete, John D. assumed that the family would live in their own house free of charge—but no. The old man wanted rent; after all, he'd put up the money, hadn't he? This cold, hard materialism taught John D. fortitude and shrewdness. It also freed him of any sense of obligation to the paterfamilias.

His father's lessons paid off. John went to work as an office boy/bookkeeper and caught the eye of his employers as an intelligent, punctilious, and zealous young man. In 1858, feeling underpaid, young John D. left their employ to begin a mercantile partnership. For this he needed a thousand dollars, which his father was ready to lend him at 10 percent—above the then-prevailing rate. But John was happy to take it. At nineteen he was his own boss, and he felt as if he were on top of the world. He went down on his knees and begged the Lord to bless his new enterprise.

Still in his teens, John D. met with much success because he was patient and methodical; he did not push, did not try to get rich by rapid or devious means. His strong faith in Protestant Christianity helped here, teaching him the importance of honesty and morality and bringing him invaluable personal contacts. Moreover, bank loans came to him more easily because lenders saw his piety as evidence of reliability. John D. was the very model of an ascetic Protestant entrepreneur, à la Max Weber. His life aim was to get money—honestly—and then use it as wisely as possible. The pursuit of wealth, then, was a sacred calling, with philanthropy and virtue as the rewards. Wealth was a sign of God's grace, and poverty the sign of heavenly disapproval. John D. believed that he would be rich, and believed that this was because God wanted him to be. This Protestant ethic, as Weber termed it, bred successful businessmen. And John D., as biographer Ron Chernow describes him, "was the Protestant work ethic in its purest form, leading a life so consistent with Weber's classic essay that it reads like his spiritual biography."[1] Rational, thoughtful, systematic, committed, and diligent, he also cultivated an intense curiosity, a spirit of calculation, and an attention to opportunity. His competitors and associates were amateurs by comparison. He saw them for what they were, but never let his self-assurance get the best of him, always maintaining politeness and civility and preparing his coups with prudence aforethought.

The partnership that John D. formed with Maurice Clark, Clark and Rockefeller, bought and sold meat, grain, and produce by the carload, and advertised its readiness to deal in water, lime, plaster, salt, legumes, and other goods.[2] Business was great, the warehouse was bulging, and profits climbed to seventeen thousand dollars in 1862. Yet all of that was nothing compared with the riches that oil would bring young Mr. Rockefeller. Talk of luck: John D. did not look for oil; the oil came to him.

Why oil? Because the latent demand for artificial lighting, especially in urban areas, was enormous and growing, and the known sources of illuminant were increasingly inadequate. Artificial lighting had long been a prerogative of the rich. Unconsumed candles were worth a fortune, to the point where the candle perquisite of the servants of the British royal household financed the creation of what later became Harrods department store. Supplies of sperm oil and animal fat were inelastic, as were those of tallow and cottonseed oil. Coal oil from shale had possibilities. But petroleum had them all beat.

Here science stepped in. People had long known that rock oil was abundant in western Pennsylvania but looked on it as a nuisance; it stained the water and spoiled the ground for cultivation. But in the 1850s a certain George Bissell, surely one of Dartmouth College's greatest gifts to the nation, came to the idea that rock oil might outdo coal oil as an illuminant, and he sent a sample to Professor Benjamin Silliman of Yale with the request that he analyze the foul stuff. The answer came back positive: not only could the kerosene in rock oil provide light, but the oil would yield a number of other useful components. That was all it took. Bissell found an agent, Edwin Drake, to prospect the area, and the oil rush was on.

Now the merchants of the region were confronted with a new commodity just waiting to be turned into money. The question was, how to move it and in what form. Here Clark and Rockefeller got lucky, because Samuel Andrews, an industrial chemist who knew how to "cleanse" oil with sulfuric acid, just happened to come from the same Wiltshire town as Maurice Clark, and frequented with John D. the Erie Street Baptist Church in Cleveland. Andrews visited his acquaintances in their Cleveland office and talked up the possibilities of their investing in industrial refining. Who caught the vision is hard to say—John D. credits Clark, and Clark, John D.— no matter; the result was a major shift in the content and direction of the partnership and the beginning of a revolution in American enterprise.

The story of oil was in large part a story of transportation. Early movement was by horse-drawn wagon, but this was costly even for short distances. The better choice was railway and lake-and-river water shipment, and the best, pipelines. These last, however, encountered violent resistance from the teamsters who hauled the barrels from pithead to refinery and refinery to port. The oilmen who first installed the lines hired armed guards to defend them, all of which raised the cost and delayed the final move to a rational system.

In the early years, the key mover was the railway, not only because tracks could be laid through wilderness but also because this potential ubiquity minimized the need for costly transshipment. To be sure, a new technology was required to move the oil on swaying, jolting cars. Barrels splintered and spilled, and were replaced after the Civil War by pine tubs mounted on flat cars; and these in turn gave way to iron tanks. Railroads, moreover, typically enjoyed freedom to set rates to their measure and pleasure. Profits for refineries, then, were a direct function of the ability to extract favorable freight charges from some of the biggest economic powers in the country. Anyone who looked at this situation *ex ante* would have declared the railways the inevitable winner, squeezing producers and refiners within an inch of their survival.

Yet that is not what happened. For one thing, local laws usually forbade the imposition of onerous railway tariffs. For another, railroads were dealing here with some of the sharpest businessmen around. Not the oil producers, but the oil well owners, whose uncertain returns intoxicated them. These men found an alternation of rich and poor days, boom and bust, as is always the case with mineral treasure. Many if not most finished penniless, but at least they had fun doing it. One of the most memorable, "Coal Oil Johnny," lit big cigars with hundred-dollar bills, tipped bootblacks a similar amount, gave diamonds to the ladies who pleased him. He threw away at least half a million, went broke when his well went dry, and ended as a baggage clerk.

The oil refiners, though, the big men, facing high costs for equipment and overhead, were looking for steadier results, and they got them. John D. gave nickels and dimes for tips. A nickel, he reminded one recipient of his generosity, was a year's interest on a dollar bill. The man was a walking calculator, a wonder for negotiation and persuasion, and he just kept getting richer. He was not alone, of course. He had Andrews and a new associate, Henry Morrison Flagler, the son of a minister and a young, handsome fellow. (John D. was also young, twenty-seven when the new partnership was formed, but he was old and wise before his time.) John D. had a liking for associates of pious tutelage. Long on wit and expectation, Flagler added an almost irresistible drive to the combination. John D. loved Flagler (as much as the former was capable of love) for his work and his mind and his dreams. Flagler liked to say that a friendship founded on business beat a business founded on friendship. John D. could not have agreed more.

Flagler in these early days matched John D. for thrift and caution. It was hard, but "I would rather be my own tyrant than have someone else tyrannize me." As these axioms show, Flagler was a master of words and especially of legal language; in the give-and-take of negotiation, John D. found him superior to trained lawyers. John D.'s only reservation was that he found Flagler sometimes a shade too enthusiastic. But that was what John D. was there for. The man was a walking cold shower.

The idea was to elicit discounts and rebates—not only on one's own shipments but on those of competitors; better in your pocket than theirs. And what could be better than to have your competitors working for you? Especially when the railways raised rates to cover the cost of rebates to Rockefeller and company. Rockefeller won on every count.

Published railway tariffs, after all, were for the small man, not for major shippers who could play one railroad against another while promising steady cargo. Such favors to the big boys seemed wrong, nay, outrageous, to many, the more so as the railways secured their concessions and rights-of-way from the state, and the democratic state could hardly be permitted to connive at economic favoritism. (Leave aside the private deals and secret stipends to co-operative officials and officers. Where there's money to be made, someone will offer and someone will take.) John D. of course defended such arrangements on the grounds of the reliability and regularity of fat cat shipments. It made sense to the railways to accord them preferential prices.

But these were seen as not ethical, so that in the long run, federal and state legislation made preferential rates illegal. By then, however, the game had long been played out. Rockefeller succeeded in "persuading" just about every refiner of importance to join his cartel. That was the only way they could obtain good rail rates and compete with him. Typically he bought them out, whether with cash or shares in the holding company that operated the cartel, the famous/infamous Standard Oil Company.[3] (We shall see more of this firm later.) He spoke softly, but much of what he saw as friendly advice was taken by the refiners as warnings and threats. The stubborn holdouts went under and died hating him. The wise ones sold. Most of them took cash. The smart ones took stock and became rich. John D. told them to do that. Good advice. Even so, they hated him.

In all this, John D. deserves credit for vision—the vision of what could be if only the industry could be gotten under control. Where others could think only of quick profits and fast living, he thought of restraint, organization, rationality, frugality. In all this, he felt, he was acting not as a greedy monopolist but as a kind of angel of mercy, come to help helpless refiners, come to bring order, stability, long-term prosperity. John D.'s greatest asset was a nose for money and profit. He could fairly smell opportunity. In a lifetime of successes, his one significant error was a failure to appreciate the potential contribution of pipeline oil transport. How could he? Why should he? Standard dominated the rail network that moved the oil from wells to refineries, could fairly dictate charges. Who needed a system that would cut costs to less than even Standard had been able to extract? Or one that would hurt inland centers such as Pittsburgh and Cleveland (Standard strongholds)? (It was then mistakenly assumed that pipelines could not move oil over long stretches.) The competition by the new mode of transport soon reduced itself to a political issue: Would the states be willing to grant pipeline companies the same rights of eminent domain that had long permitted and encouraged the construction of rail lines?[4]

In such matters, Rockefeller money and connections worked to thwart pipeline aspirations and pro-pipeline legislation. His associate Flagler did the coaxing, suborning, and bribing, and did well, but only up to a point. In Pennsylvania, he could not get an outright rejection, but managed to obtain quashing, effectively nullifying amendments. In New York, though, something went wrong. Flagler's efforts failed, and by now the issue had drawn so much attention and Standard had aroused so much resentment that the governor did not dare veto the bill.

Besides, pipelines were simply too promising to prevent, and in the late 1870s a firm called Tidewater Pipe Company went about purchasing a right-of-way from central Pennsylvania to the coast. Standard did everything it could to stop the intruder. In vain. At one point, it sank a large sum into buying a broad north–south band of land to block the pipeline's eastward march. Tidewater found a chink in the wall. Standard spread tales of the unreliability of these pipes; they might leak and ruin the land around them. It bought up or leased just about any refiner who might be a Tidewater customer. The one thing John D. did not resort to was violence: pious virtue has its disadvantages.

This was one instance in which John D.'s normally impeccable instinct deserted him. When his associates urged him to begin his own network of pipelines, he dismissed them. But he was smart enough to learn. Once oil from the Pennsylvania field began pouring through the pipes into Williamsport at a tireless rate of six thousand barrels a day, that was it. John D. did an about-face, and tried to buy control of Tidewater. Refused. He set about squeezing the independents, cut Standard's gathering charges to a nickel a barrel, had the railroads move the oil at fifteen cents a barrel, less than even the pipelines could afford to charge. But there was no money in such concessions. John D. and Flagler now recognized pipelines as the way of the future. When the railroads refused to join him in a new collaborative program, Standard simply took such low rates as it could get and began building its own pipelines, first into Cleveland and Buffalo, then along railway rights-of-way. What could be more convenient? Now Tidewater, once so saucy, began hinting at an alliance with Standard. When the dickering was over, Standard had acquired a controlling interest in Tidewater. All those mistakes, now cured by money. John D. never bragged of this victory.[5]

In his own quiet, irresistible way, John D. was capturing and incorporating what was destined to become the strategic artery and fuel pump of the American economy. The oil poured in, was refined, and was turned into gold. This rush of riches—not his business coups—posed ethical problems to this pious predator, whose religious upbringing laid great stress on the dangers and temptations of wealth. Matters were complicated by growing hostility to a man seen as a pirate and villain. In an effort to justify himself, John D. saw to it that he received a trivial salary, twelve thousand dollars in 1875, thirty thousand in 1900. What matter? His annual income from the shares he held in Standard Oil amounted to millions. Public versus private persona. He also made it a point to keep his refineries punctiliously neat and clean, very different from the foul mess that characterized the rest of the industry. That was the way he had his servants keep his homes. And that was how he himself dressed—so sparely that his family had to remind him to get a new suit when the current one got shiny. How close to godliness can one get?

All his life, he underspent for personal needs. He had grown up in parsimony, had worn his older sisters' dresses as a child by way of saving money. His wife was if anything even stingier, making do with two dresses patched as required. He could hardly conceal his rapidly growing fortune, which if anything tale and rumor exaggerated. But he did his best in the cause of discretion, and he liked business associates to do the same. Not easy in an age when plutocrats preferred to flaunt success. John D. prided himself on his abstinence and taciturnity. When a business competitor showed himself equally tight-lipped, Rockefeller was impressed: "That's the kind of man I'd like to go fishing with!" Not much talk in fishing.

Some of this preference for silence and modesty was business related. In his campaigns to secure a dominating position in divers markets, Rockefeller often resorted to cushy buyouts; butter wouldn't melt in his mouth as he offered large sums and generous perks. (His clincher was to offer the "victim" a look at the books of Standard. In one instance, a potential seller was dumbfounded to learn that Standard was able to sell at less than his own cost of production. They could kill him whenever they pleased.) But, then, it was important to keep such contracts confidential, for fear of arousing the expectations of other targets. Keep this deal secret even from your wife, John D. told one man. When you start making more money, don't let anyone know. No fancy new house, no stylish fast horses, no betting or carousing.[6] One time, riding the train to Cleveland, a colleague of John D.'s spotted a handsome house on a nearby hillside. Whose house? he asked. That's the Hopper house, John D. said. He makes barrels for us. He's obviously making too much money. Back at the office, he checked, decided that Mr. Hopper was indeed making too much at their expense, and terminated all contracts. A business lesson, but a moral one, too.

One of his great fears was that his children would be corrupted by money—it was so easy. So he invented a make-believe market economy for the home. His wife was named "general manager" and saw to it that the children kept careful accounts. They were paid to do chores, earning two cents per fly killed (some remember a dime a hundred), ten cents for sharpening pencils (in those days with a penknife), five cents an hour for music practice, two cents a day to abstain from candy plus a dime bonus for every consecutive day, a penny for every ten weeds pulled from the vegetable garden. John, Jr., got fifteen cents an hour for chopping wood, and one of the girls was reimbursed for every saving on gas consumption; she made sure that unneeded fixtures and lamps were turned off. And the old man did his bit by saving the paper and string from every package received.[7]

And then abstinence—aside from candy. The children were limited to one piece of cheese daily. One day one sister tattled on another, who had taken a second piece. (Nothing like privation to bring out the best in people.) John D. was shocked. All that afternoon, whenever self-indulgent (or was it hungry?) Edith came within hearing, the father would intone his condemnation: "Edith was greedy." Another time, brother John, Jr., and sister Alta announced that Edith had taken the biggest piece of something. So Father chided again, repeating singsong, "Edith was selfish." How much money does it take to compensate for that kind of embarrassment cum torment?

Well into their lives, the Rockefeller children were kept in ignorance of the family's fortune. Like his father, John D., Jr., as a child was dressed in his sisters' cast-off (outgrown) dresses. The children went to costly private schools but thought this the normal path to education. Nothing in their father's behavior could have clued them in to his means and status. In an age when a certain embonpoint was the sign of success, John D. offered a lean and mean silhouette. (A turn-of-millennium doctor would have loved him.) His idea of gastronomic indulgence was bread and milk in the morning and a bag of apples at night. When business cares promoted tension, he resorted to celery. Most people who eat oranges eat oranges; John D. thought a piece of orange peel before breakfast a bracing tonic. He went to work on the Sixth Avenue el, five-cent fare; wore suits, we saw, until they shone and his wife, Cettie, jogged him into buying a new one; never entertained; read only works of spiritual uplift; bought a house in New York (he was already one of the richest men in the country), but then kept all the previous owner's furnishings, however little they pleased his taste. In general he led a life of such abstemiousness as to make one wonder at his incentives. His brother was not that way; nor were his business associates. John D.'s children envied their cousins, who were allowed to have parties and enjoy life. Once Cettie asked John D. to buy her a new four-wheel carriage. John D. was aghast; we can't afford it, he cautioned, unless we trade in the old one.

Not that the old man did not know how to spend money. He had his personal indulgences. Oh, nothing like the yachts and mansions enjoyed by the Carnegies, Fricks, and Schwabs. But he enjoyed riding and trotting horses and spent some tens of thousands for a Rockefeller stable. And he hired a copious staff of secretarial and household help and ran telegraph lines into the house, the better to stay abreast of business while away from the office. Above all, he found effective executive associates to handle those transactions that called for bloody-mindedness. Later on, when interrogated by congressional or judicial committees about the alleged misdeeds of Standard Oil, John D. could play the innocent. Who, me? It was those other guys. He may have been telling the truth. He had at once a hard and easy conscience—no better prescription for peace of mind.

Valuable raw materials, as we noted earlier, are a treasure, and therein lies the danger. Those who find them and own them, sell them and end up swimming in money and drowning in self-indulgence. The great advantage of Rockefeller, as we have seen, lay in his resistance to temptation. He had the soul of a bookkeeper, the abstinence of a good dieter, the vision and energy of an entrepreneur, the rationality of a good economist. Where others took what they could get or grab with no thought to the morrow, he bought at bargain prices the wealth that tomorrow would bring. In later life, enormously wealthy, he liked to brag that he had no use for credit or moneylenders. In fact, his early successes owed much to extensive, vehement reliance on bank loans. Good credit, he knew, rested on prompt and punctual repayment and the spreading of risk. Bankers love dependable debtors. No one was more dependable than John D. Rockefeller. Or more attentive to appearances. At one point he needed some money in a hurry and had the luck—luck always matters—to run into a would-be lender. The man offered him three times what he needed. The Rockefeller answer: "I'll think about it and give you an answer in twenty-four hours." That was one of John D.'s cherished techniques: Don't take the money immediately. Line up the offers and then come around to collect. Make the lender feel that the borrower is doing him a favor. Unless the borrower was someone else and he the lender.

It was this push to control that led John D. in 1870, along with his friend and associate Henry Flagler, to transform their partnership into a joint-stock corporation to be known as Standard Oil. The very name was a pretension, a claim to uniformity and reliability. The firm was capitalized at one million dollars—perhaps the largest of its kind in the America of that day. It controlled about 10 percent of national petroleum refining, and included warehouses, shipping facilities, and a fleet of tank cars. In his pride of the moment, John D. predicted that the company would one day refine all the oil and make all the barrels. But his pride was more than just words. The organizers would receive no salaries; rising dividends and share prices would be reward enough.

Big as it was, the new corporate giant was not big enough. On January 1, 1872, the board, anticipating further acquisitions, increased capital to $2.5 million and then, the next day, in hasty reconsideration, to $3.5 million. New business allies came in, but John D. made it a point to maintain his share. The newly enlarged firm went on to a series of quiet coups: the acquisition of major refining, storage, and shipping facilities in New York; and the establishment, along with major rail allies, of a shipping cartel innocently named the South Improvement Company. The aim here was not only to secure low rates but, even more important, to obtain drawbacks on the shipments of competitors. This was hardly fair play, but who ever said business was fair? John D. of the tender morals certainly saw nothing amiss here. As we saw, he felt that big reliable shippers deserved favored treatment, and the very readiness of the roads to go along proved the case.

But wait a minute. Favoritism implied transgression. The railroads after all were privileged entities, sanctioned by the authorities on the unspoken premise that they would treat all customers alike. Unspoken but assumed. In the end, this premise found expression in law and rules. But in these early days, buccaneers such as Rockefeller and minions could get away with murder. Little more than a decade after the end of the Civil War, Standard and quiet allies (no point in promoting scandal) had come to control almost 90 percent of the oil refined in the United States and were able to treat with the biggest railroads as better than equals.

That was refining. What about producing? Well, initially it did not really matter. On the contrary, the competition among the well owners imposed a reasonable price for the raw material, while the monopolistic position of the refiners assured them high rates of profit. In the early 1880s, Standard Oil owned only four oil-producing properties—a trivial supplement to their business in transport, refining, and storage. Why look for more? But then in 1885 a small group of prospectors, looking for natural gas in northwest Ohio, found a patch of oil instead. The excitement was the greater because everyone had assumed that big oil was confined to Pennsylvania. A rush ensued, with some 250 derricks rising by the end of the year. Unfortunately, this "Lima crude" was not the same kind of oil as had been found in Pennsylvania. It stank, hence was ill suited to residences, and its high sulfur content just ate up metal. It also contained less kerosene, and this part, such as it was, deposited a film on lamps, quickly making them useless.

Most gave up. Not John D. His spiritual leanings helped here: he simply could not believe that God had created this resource to no purpose. The first thing he did was hire a German-born chemist named Herman Frasch to find a cure. Frasch, a difficult, hot-tempered man, had already done good work for Rockefeller, inventing a wax for British candle makers and isolating an ingredient for chewing gum. And then, in 1887–1888, he found a way to remove the sulfur and made possible a marketable oil. Rockefeller, in the meantime, was not idle and began looking for and pushing new uses—outside the household. He sent out teams of technicians and salespeople to persuade railroad men to replace coal by fuel oil; similarly for heating hotels, mills, and warehouses.

That kind of rationality was a Rockefeller strong point. Knowledge and technique could make bad good, and scientists and technicians could be found and hired. The lesson was not lost on others:

laboratory experiment and application came to be standard operating procedure in the industry. The next step was one of personal inspiration. It took some years, but eventually John D. persuaded his partners in Standard Oil to move energetically into the acquisition of oil-bearing properties. He did this by stating his willingness to hazard his own personal funds in the venture. If he was right, he said, the company would reimburse him. If wrong, he could take the loss. In effect, he shamed his associates into going along. In 1890, Standard bought up Union Oil and three other major producers, comprising over three hundred thousand acres in the older producing districts. By 1891 it had won control of the majority of the Lima fields. It now held a quarter of the output of American crude. By 1898 the figure peaked at 33 percent. Ironically, Standard had to market Lima oil products in the face of a legacy of mistrust, promoted by Standard itself in the days before it acquired these new fields. But this handicap eased before the changes in application. New uses were coming, and new users had less cause for complaint.

It was about this time that John D. chose to retire. I say "about" because he himself dated his withdrawal as somewhere between 1894 and 1897—and so what? Even after retirement, he still ran the show. But his daily rides on the elevated downtown and back ceased. He stayed at home or traveled to vacation spots; and his appointed successor at Standard, John D. Archbold, reported to him whenever something came up. Ordinary business routine bored him.

Besides, as we have seen, he liked the idea of using aggressive henchmen and playing tough. They could do the dirty work; he could play the innocent. John D. was a devoutly religious man, sanctimonious to a fault. But like most pious folk, he had no trouble living amid sin. (That's the point of the exercise.) When Henry Clay Frick ordered his Pinkertons to fire on striking workers at Homestead in 1892, John D. sent him a congratulatory wire. He had no trouble profiting from the weakness or ignorance of others. When interrogated on the witness stand about the actions of trusts in restraint of trade, John D.'s tactic was to parry every question with answers technically truthful but factually evasive.[8] He was asked by committee counsel if he had ever belonged to the "Southern Improvement Company," an egregiously bad actor in matters of competition. Answer: no. Counsel was startled: "There was such a company?" Answer: "I have never heard of it." "Were you not in it?" "I was not."

All technically true, for the actual company name was the South Improvement Company. John D. knew perfectly well where counsel was trying to go. But he felt no obligation to truth or virtue to help out. "I never undertake to instruct the man who asks me questions. . . . There is the record to stand on. . . . It was no part of my duty as a witness to volunteer testimony." So John D. kept his calm, read the mind of his adversary, spotted every trap. Samuel Untermyer, well-known lawyer, called Rockefeller "the ablest mind he had ever encountered on the witness stand."

Such cunning helped but hurt. On the one hand, no one ever nailed John D. for illegal behavior. Legally, he was untouchable. On the other, many people thought him an enemy of the people and were ready to believe the worst of him. No accident that an enormous body of critical, even defamatory literature on him appeared and found a large national audience.

It was under these unpleasant circumstances that John D. retired and gave himself up to a career of philanthropy. He had so much money and so little capacity for self-indulgence and enjoyment that giving money away became the key to happiness. This was good for recipients but often bad for the donor, bad for his character. The man had become unbearably self-righteous, a full-time fault-finder and censor, disapproving "both for himself and others of drinking, smoking, dancing, card playing, wenching, theater going, concert going, banqueting, idling, general socializing, and 'good fellowship.'"[9]

Besides, he did enjoy and cultivate problems of health, illnesses real and apparent, though as his eventual longevity shows, he knew how to avoid the kind of behavior that promotes illness and decay. No carousing or bilging for John D.; rather, as we saw, a diet of milk and crackers and fresh fruit. No fat. Trace carbohydrates (an anticipator of the Atkins diet). Golf and fresh air and lots of sleep. The old man's weight fell to under a hundred pounds.

Meanwhile, he was not needed in the office. His fortune grew by accrued interest, technological innovation, and economic growth. The automobile in particular exploded the demand for petroleum. When Rockefeller retired from Standard in the 1890s, he was worth about $200 million, an easy $3.5 billion today; twenty years later, in 1913, he was worth a billion, say $30 billion now. And auto growth was just beginning.

He could afford to "retire."

The challenge to the Rockefellers lay in their enormous wealth, too great to require further cultivation, too great to ignore or leave fallow. For all his expectations and achievements, John D. would not succumb to the temptations of grandeur. Standard was located in a modest four-story building, where Rockefeller and Flagler had shared an austere, somber office: black leather couch, four black walnut chairs, fireplace for winter warmth. From home, John D. continued to watch the pennies and the dollars, to the despair and occasional resentment of his associates. Frederick Gates, fighting negotiator for Standard in business dealings and manager of family wealth and philanthropies, quit over this and perhaps other issues. He was tired, overwrought, and keen to spend more, including more time with his family. John D. valued his judgment and tried to hold him to the job by spoken and written appeals, which did delay departure a few years (1912–1915); but his high judgment of Gates's value was not enough.

The point for John D. was not to arouse attention, jealousy, or hostility. An impossible goal. Criticism and opposition were bound to develop. One does not take over a major industry, push people around, obtain all manner of competitive advantages, and accumulate huge wealth without arousing the furies. Besides, both John D. and Junior cultivated antediluvian social attitudes, and so convinced were they of their virtue that, for all their discretion, they did not have the good sense to shut up. The so-called Ludlow Massacre was a case in point.

Ludlow was the site of mines owned by Colorado Fuel and Iron (CFI), a firm controlled by Rockefeller. The company proved to be a loser, which may have confirmed John D.'s resistance to and abhorrence of union organization by labor. John D. had no trouble paying good wages, the better to win the workers' love and loyalty. And Junior liked the idea of company stores, an instrument for control and favoritism and a means to exclude potential troublemakers. But the introduction of an outside party, a rival for authority, was something else again. The issue was one of managerial prerogatives and the privileges of hierarchy—in a deep sense, questions of order and propriety.

Way back in 1903, when Rockefeller had first bought its control of CFI, Junior set out his convictions on this subject: "We are prepared to stand by in this fight and see the thing out, not yielding an inch. Recognition of any kind of either the labor leaders or union, much more a conference such as they request, would be a sign of evident weakness on our part."[10] Junior here was simply echoing his father's sense of fairness. What were unions anyway, if not schemes to avoid work? They start beautiful, said John D. They put out promises of high principle. But then they show their true purpose: "to do as little as possible for the greatest possible pay." All these workers wanted was to spend and squander, go to picture shows, drink whiskey, smoke tobacco, and what else. The old man wanted to halt gifts to YMCA building projects using union labor. At his Pocantico estate, he fired workers who tried to organize, and he refused to allow the staff to take Labor Day off. What an irony: a work-free day called Labor Day.

Efforts to ward off a strike of CFI employees met with no cooperation from the Rockefellers. Junior ducked behind the agents in the field: "We'll stand by you to the end"—a foolish encouragement to intransigence. By the end of September 1913, more than eleven thousand of the fourteen thousand workers were on strike, and the stage was set for a shooting war. By the end of October, the prospects were so dire that President Wilson himself intervened; but why should good Republicans like the Rockefellers heed his partisan nonsense?

Wilson called for consultation and peace. The manager of CFI responded that nothing would persuade the company to recognize the union. "We shall never consent, if every mine is closed, the equipment destroyed, and the investment made worthless." And John D., Jr., praised the "energetic, fair and firm way" CFI was handling the battle.

Then, in December, the snows came. Strikers and their families, all of whom had been evicted from their company-owned housing, shivered in their tents. Spring followed, and one morning at dawn a squad of state militiamen and company guards started firing on one of the worker encampments, killing some of the strikers. A fire started (was set?), and the strikers fled. But some two women and twelve children hiding for safety in a trench were suffocated by smoke and died there in the dirt. That was the Ludlow Massacre.

It goes without saying that these events redounded to the shame and censure of the Rockefellers. Even Helen Keller, once a grateful beneficiary of their largesse, now condemned them publicly: "Mr. Rockefeller is the monster of capitalism. He gives charity and in the same breath he permits the helpless workmen, their wives and children to be shot down." Much of the difficulty derived once more from this familial conviction of virtue. For Junior there had been no Ludlow Massacre. He said so explicitly. The strikers had started the trouble by attacking the militiamen with overwhelming force. It was they who had put women and children into the pit and covered them so that ventilation proved impossible. Theirs the fault. Further efforts by President Wilson to promote conciliation encountered implacable resistance: the question of a closed shop was simply out of bounds, off the table. John D. saw the anti-union campaign as a replay of the Revolutionary War, a fight for rights and freedom. No arguing with that.

Much of the opposition took the form of official inquiries; much found expression in the public prints. The final decade of the nineteenth century and the opening years of the twentieth were the age of the so-called muckrakers, the uncoverers who brought awareness of the misdeeds, the everything-goes of competitive business or, worse yet, business in bed with politics. Some of the indignation found expression in fiction: the anonymous novel *The Moneymakers* (1888); Frank Norris's *The Pit* and *The Octopus*; Upton Sinclair's *The Jungle*; Thomas W. Lawson's *Frenzied Finance*; and many more. Much of it appeared in the new journalism: *Munsey's, McClure's, Collier's, Cosmopolitan,* even *Ladies' Home Journal.*

But all these revelations were as nothing compared with the denunciations of Standard and the great oil monopoly. For who was richer, who a bigger target? In 1894 came Henry Demarest Lloyd's *Wealth Against Commonwealth,* which Edward Everett Hale compared to *Uncle Tom's Cabin* in its impact on the public consciousness. Lloyd had inherited money, lots of help, and a huge accumulation of testimony in official inquiries. He saw "the rise and progress of the oil monopoly to be on the whole the most characteristic thing in our business civilization." His book was clearly aimed at Rockefeller and Standard, but Lloyd avoided naming names, perhaps for fear of libel action. By the same token, publisher Harper's took out the copyright in Lloyd's name; safer that way.[11] The result was a vivid, fervid image of a "cruel, greedy, and wicked" Standard—so strong and persuasive it would last for decades. This image, in turn, was reinforced by the data on Standard's profits: $55.5 million in 1900, $83 million in 1906.[12] For many, nobody could make that much money so fast honestly.

That was contemporary denunciation. For historian Allan Nevins, however, writing decades later, the Lloyd book was "full of prejudice, distortion, and misinterpretation." Many of its claims and assertions, he averred, were false or inaccurate, though many were true. "No present-day student of corporation history," he writes, "would trust the book at any point." Maybe so, but the fact that Standard Oil made no effort to refute the book enhanced the credibility of the charges. Silence here may be the haughty expression of ineffable virtue and resentment of unjust injury; but it also spared the company unwanted debate and revelations. As Nevins put it: "to do this would have involved making damaging admissions at various points, and for that they were not prepared. It would have dragged the Standard Oil leaders into direct controversy, which they were anxious to avoid."[13]

More harmful to Standard's reputation, such as it was, were Ida M. Tarbell's articles in *McClure's*, published in two volumes in 1904 as *The History of the Standard Oil Company*. Tarbell was the child of a loser in the oil wars and had personal reasons to dislike Rockefeller and Standard. She had already made a career as a magazine writer, focusing on the biographies of great men and women—good preparation for her inquiry into oil mogul villainies. The book, in its final form, offered 550 pages of text and 240 pages of appendix source material—a potent combination. The theme: "Rockefeller and his associates . . . had built up a combination which was admirable in its organized efficiency and power; but nearly every step in the construction of this vast industrial machine had been attended by fraud, coercion, special privilege, or sharp dealing, which had tended to debase the whole standard of business morals in America."[14]

The book "was received with an explosion of applause." Here, too, Nevins argues that "critical readers of today will detect the bias running through it, while at important points its conclusions are demonstrably erroneous."[15] Yet he concedes that "much of her indictment of Standard methods was absolutely irrefutable"; and that "her book was actually too mild, for she made less than she might have done [or than Nevins did] of the excessive prices and profits of the trust."[16]

And here, too, John D. refused to react or respond: "Not a word!" Junior did show "justifiable resentment" when Tarbell wrote a piece attacking his father personally and denouncing John D.'s ostentatious piety as hypocrisy. Admittedly, Junior had strong reservations about his father, but the old man, for all his shortcomings, was no one else's business. Most vexatious, Tarbell mocked John D.'s parsimony, even his healthful recreations: "There is little doubt that Mr. Rockefeller's chief reason for playing golf is that he may live longer in order to make more money." In a moment of rage, John D. called her Miss Tarbarrel, but then withdrew into wounded silence.

Nor could John D.'s many charities and philanthropies clear his reputation. For one thing, he insisted on discretion—charity was not meant for bragging—even where his associates thought a little publicity would help. For another, people saw these generosities as acts of contrition, attempts to fumigate illicit wealth. As Wisconsin governor Robert La Follette put it, "I read yesterday that Rockefeller has been to prayer meeting again; tomorrow he will be giving to some college or university. He gives with two hands, but he robs with many. If he should live a thousand years, he could not expiate the crimes he has committed. . . . He is the greatest criminal of the age."[17]

THE YEARS PASSED and Junior grew up. He could no longer wear his sisters' cast-off dresses. The time had come to send him to college. Yale was the first choice, but rumor had it that student life there was fast and immoral—unsuitable for an apprentice saint. So Junior went to Brown, then a fortress of Baptist piety. Even so, his mother and grandmother warned him to be vigilant and wary of temptation and rejoiced to hear that he was teaching a Sunday school class in Providence. His taste in extracurricular activities ran to music: the glee club, a mandolin club, a string quartet. His taste in fast food ran to graham crackers. And he kept to his self-discipline: no smoking, no drinking, no cards, no theater, no newspaper comics. Guests to his room got hot chocolate—the milky American variety. His thrift became legend: he mended his own clothes and dish towels, pressed his trousers under the mattress, sewed his buttons. In holding to his father's example and training, he kept an account of every penny, down to the two-cent stamps that allowed him to write home and the nickel sodas he bought for girlfriends. Some classmates thought him a hopeless prig, "without redeeming vice." But he was popular and important enough to be elected junior class president, which gave him further opportunities to replace traditional indulgences by virtuous abstinence.[18]

His elders were delighted, even though he was beginning to enjoy the first worrisome cracks in his shining armor. He went to England in his sophomore summer, and there in London he saw his first plays: *Two Gentlemen of Verona, A Midsummer Night's Dream,* and—comic indulgence—*Charley's Aunt.* I wouldn't have done it at home, he wrote his mother, but in London nobody knew me, and after all, a chance to know Shakespeare . . . and Brandon Thomas.

The next step was dancing, always a source of contact and temptation. But it took more than that to lure this young man. For him dancing was exercise and a case study in socializing and friendship. Even when he found the young woman of his dreams, he was afraid to presume and propose. The lady in question was Abby Aldrich, daughter of the United States senator, a self-made man rich in favors from rich businessmen and indulgent with his children as John D. never was. Abby was personable, sweet, and semi-pretty and knew early on that the junior Rockefeller was the man she wanted. But the customs of the time and milieu dictated that she wait for him to take the initiative, and that shy fellow lacked the nerve. So Abby waited and Junior dithered, more than four barren years. Junior prayed for divine guidance every night, and the young couple passed six months apart as test of their conviction and commitment. Only when Junior got up the courage to ask his mother what she thought of Miss Aldrich and Cettie took cognizance of her son's hesitation did she tell him to get on with it. Only then did he undertake to propose—first of course to Abby's father, painstakingly informing him of his financial prospects. Senator Aldrich, who must have thought the young man hopeless, hardly had the patience to sit through the obvious and assured Junior that all he, the father, wanted was the happiness of his daughter. She was already twenty-eight, almost a decade older than she had to be. Some things are worth waiting for. Still, there is one citation in her biography that gives one pause. "Do you know, John," she told him shortly after their honeymoon, "that if you should ever strike me, I should leave you?" The very idea astonished him. But it was not likely "apropos of nothing at all." In any event, Abby said she wanted to warn him of what would happen if ever he did. The marriage seems to have been a rhapsody in harmony.[19]

As father of the bride, Senator Aldrich made the kind of wedding that rich people make for rich friends—no corks plugged, no holds barred. It did not have the modesty and sobriety that John D. and mother Cettie considered proper. No matter. The Rockefellers made the concessions required (they had always refused to attend parties where liquor was served) and may even have enjoyed themselves. After all, it is not every day that one sees the son and heir married and anticipates the prospect of little Rockefellers coming along. Which they did, beginning in 1903 with Abby (known as Babs to distinguish her from her mother), followed by John D. III (1906), Nelson (1908), Laurance (1910), Winthrop (1912), and David (1915). Five boys, one girl. Immortality almost assured.

Junior didn't have the same taste for business that his father did; by age thirty-six, he had stepped aside from many of his duties with Standard Oil and its associated companies to add his efforts to the family's philanthropic work. Still, he remained his father's son. In 1915, he was offered a chance to acquire the best Chinese porcelains in the collection assembled by the recently deceased J. P. Morgan. The cost: over a million dollars (about twenty million today). Though not a poor man, Junior had nothing like that kind of cash, so he wrote his father to ask for a loan. John D. turned him down cold. But Junior was now past forty, and he felt that he was entitled to more consideration from a loving father for whom a million dollars was small change. So he wrote John D. another letter to stress the care and thought that went into this seeming indulgence: "I have never squandered money on horses, yachts, automobiles or other foolish extravagances. A fondness for these porcelains is my only hobby—the only thing on which I have cared to spend money. I have found their study a great recreation and diversion, and I have become very fond of them. This hobby, while a costly one, is quiet and unostentatious and not sensational."[20]

This time John D. not only relented but offered the purchase price as a gift. Junior was overcome. He wrote back: "I am fully conscious of the fact that I am in no sense worthy of such munificence on your part. Nothing that I have ever done or could do will make me worthy."

This contretemps served as a reminder to John D. that he had to start thinking about the disposition of his fortune. Junior had a net worth of about twenty million dollars in early 1917—no small sum, but one that yielded small income. His combined salary and allowance amounted to a few hundred thousand, a fortune to ordinary mortals but hardly enough to cover the cost of well-served if careful Rockefeller living. Grandson David wrote later that his grandfather had long had reservations about Junior's ability to handle money. But now increases in the inheritance tax provoked in the old man an urgent sense of confidence. John D. began transferring large blocks of stocks and bonds (for example, sixty-five million dollars in Liberty bonds at one stroke), accompanied by terse notes of conveyance signed, "Affectionately, Father." These gifts left Junior speechless (although it should be noted that the two men were not much given to conversation, anyway).

Between 1917 and 1922, John D. gave almost half a billion dollars to his children, almost all of it to Junior. The daughters were not left penniless, but it was Junior's duty to carry on his father's role as philanthropist. John D. saw it as proof of his own virtue that his son could take up these duties as he laid them down. After all, only a good tree brings forth good fruit.

In his later years, John D. retained the values and habits of his boyhood; rich as he was, he still watched the pennies. One day, scrutinizing the logs in his fire, he decided they were too long—all of fourteen inches. Let's try twelve, he told the butler. From then on, the wood was cut precisely to one-foot lengths. When Junior wanted to get him a Rolls-Royce for his birthday, John D. asked how much it would cost. Fourteen thousand dollars, Junior replied. I'll take the money, John D. said. He continued to follow the market, to speculate in stocks, to get the latest quotes even on the golf course. His memory remained sharp, and he could quote his holdings share by share in spite of constant turnover.

John D. turned ninety in 1929 and was caught by the Crash. His cash cushion of twenty-five million dollars shrank rapidly to seven million—much thinner than he was used to. He considered charging Junior $3.5 million for his share of the money spent on the Rockefeller family office, but then thought better of it.

Meanwhile, neither the old patriarch nor Junior was doing anything to familiarize the next generation with the oil business.[21] It seems that the men who built the dynasty failed to influence their descendants in any way other than by encouraging a commitment to thrift and philanthropy. This is striking, especially now that we have met families such as the Rothschilds, or even the Peugeot, who kept the family business growing and growing over many generations. The Rockefellers demonstrated no such inclination; accordingly it should come as no surprise that this is where the most dramatic business successes (and narratives) of the Rockefellers end. As with the Guggenheims (whom we'll meet shortly), the third generation did not take up the family business with an entrepreneurial spirit; that urgent money-making impulse was lost, as was the sense of the family business—as opposed to merely the family *fortune*—as something to be protected and nurtured.

The family remained very much in the public eye, but in different ways, as the third generation took advantage of the family's resources, advantages, and prestige and graduated to higher callings. Junior's five sons differed sharply in looks and personality, but all were bright and serious. Administration of the family's affairs was a complex enough task to require professional handling, and each grandson was rich enough to go his own way, to do his own thing.

Nelson Rockefeller turned out to be the most visible and publicly active of the next generation. His ambition was no less than the presidency of the United States, and with his money and connections, he might well have made it. Ultimately, he served four terms as governor of New York State, where he was the first in that post to maintain a permanent office in New York City. Among his larger projects was the formation of a Commission on Critical Choices, composed of serious scholars assembled to consider larger questions of public policy. Where should the United States be going? The man clearly wanted to prepare himself for the highest station in the land. This gubernatorial apprenticeship was followed by a long stretch in Washington, including a term as vice-president of the United States when Nixon was forced out of office. At that point, Gerald Ford stepped up to the top post and chose Nelson to be his vice-president. Ironically, this promotion proved a source of frustration. Nelson was used to running the show, and he did not take well to waiting for cues and instructions. But he consoled himself with the thought that Ford would be departing in 1976 (or, worst case, in 1980), and then it would be his turn. Ford decided not only to run in 1976 but, on the advice of his inner circle (Donald Rumsfeld in particular) to choose Senator Bob Dole as his running mate. This decision fairly crushed Nelson, who saw his presidential ambitions as dashed forever. His brother David tells us, "[T]hwarted when the greatest political prize seemed within his grasp, he [became] an angry and deeply bitter man."[22]

Nelson brought his frustrations back with him to New York City and the Rockefeller family office, expecting to be received by his brothers and cousins with the deference due a man who had once been second in command of the country. He announced immediately that he was going to redesign the offices in Rockefeller Plaza and take over the top suite. Once again, David says it best: "He seemed to have lost his political skills, or perhaps he felt he didn't need to apply them in dealing with his own family. In pursuing his objective of control he quickly succeeded in offending both his cousins and his siblings, most particularly our oldest brother, John." He adds, "The contest between Nelson and Johnny was no contest at all; Nelson manipulated his older brother cruelly, and successfully."[23]

Nelson's younger brother Winthrop actually worked a time for Chase National and Socony-Vacuum Oil (the old Standard of New York), but he was better known for his nightclubbing and womanizing. In 1948, he married "Bobo" Sears, the blond daughter of Lithuanian farmers. His father and mother boycotted the wedding, feeling the marriage was something of a black eye for the dynasty, which was not yet ready for commoner in-laws. The marriage lasted scarcely a year, during which time Junior tried occasionally to reason with his son, to steer him in the right direction, but Winthrop found these remonstrances vexatious. "By God, if I ever have children, I'm going to *talk* to them, not just make an appointment to see them and then get up after five minutes to go get a haircut."[24] Winthrop eventually became governor of Arkansas, and died of cancer in his early sixties, in February 1973.

The eldest of the third generation, the aforementioned Johnny (or, more formally, John D. III), was best known for his philanthropic work; passionate about international development as well as Asian art, he served on several important councils on development, and put together a formidable art collection. Sister Babs also served on boards of various foundations, but largely stayed out of the public eye. Laurance Rockefeller helped launch Eastern Airlines and was an early investor in some of today's most prominent high-tech companies, but he is best known as a supporter of cancer research and environmental causes.

In a way, the member of that third generation we know both best and least is David. His memoirs reveal much about the inner workings of the family, but also take care to soothe feelings and to maintain secrets. David went into banking when his uncle Winthrop Aldrich urged him in 1946 to join Chase, then the country's largest bank. While David had some initial reservations about the field, it was a logical outlet for his enterprise, money, and connections, and he met with great success. In the highest levels of banking, one tries to do business with people one likes and trusts. Whom better to call upon than an engaging young Rockefeller? In his early years, he received a number of offers to serve in cabinet or ambassadorial posts. He never regretted refusing.

As David tells it, the primary concern of Rockefeller money management was minimizing (or, whenever possible, avoiding) taxes. High rates of return on industrial stocks mattered little once the government cut them down to size. The solution lay in real estate, which paid a far lower tax on earnings than other forms of income and offered its own prospects of capital gain. This proved particularly true of Manhattan properties, which cost a lot to buy, but appreciated enormously as they were developed into prestigious locations. Rockefeller Center was the best example: the very address became a source of prestige and an assurance of a company's quality—the higher the rent, the better the company.

By this time, the Rockefeller family was not so much a dynasty as a clan—or a rich gang—and the maintenance of its fortune was an exercise in placement, banking, and careful management. Tight controls on withdrawals and use of funds were designed to keep a growing number of descendants comfortable but thrifty, while foundations galore were founded and financed, both to improve the world and to provide activities and employment to descendants, spouses, and friends. Not everyone in the family necessarily agreed with the aims of these foundations, but the range of concerns provided food and room for all. Those who had little or no interest in helping undeveloped and developing nations—a difficult and sometimes hazardous task—could concentrate on music and fine arts, which could generate their own pleasures and capital gains. The old man, John D., would have approved. He got his kicks from following the markets and financial returns; his descendants, on a smaller scale and along somewhat different lines, could still do the same.

Nine

THE GUGGENHEIMS

TREASURES OF EARTH AND SKY

HARRY F. GUGGENHEIM (1890–1971)

*H*arry Guggenheim died of prostate cancer on Long Island in a luxurious house called Falaise (French: cliff), pretentious copy of European residential pretension, on January 23, 1971. He was the son of Daniel Guggenheim and Florence Schloss, grandson of Meyer Guggenheim and Barbara Meyer, great-grandson of Simon Meyer Guggenheim and Schäfeli Levinger—so, fourth American generation of a dynasty that went back to a small Swiss village called Lengnau, an unmapped place of incomparable ignorance and narrow-minded anti-Jewish prejudice in the valley of the Surb River. Harry was buried with appropriate services and prayers at Temple Emanu-El, Manhattan headquarters of well-to-do bleached and often apostate Jews. He probably did not know a word of the ritual, but such ceremonies are not for the benefit of the deceased.

The Guggenheims trace their roots back into the seventeenth century, and it's likely they took their name from an Alsatian village named Guggenheimb (or Gougenheim) in what is today Germany. (Hebrew names being difficult for Europeans to pronounce, Jews generally derived their surnames from locations.) They left when the village banned Jewish residence and moved to Lengnau, with the first record of the family in that city dating back to 1696. One wonders how much of an improvement was Lengnau. Only well-to-do Jews were allowed entry, to begin with, and once there, they could not live in houses with tile or stone roofs, only straw—the better to burn. If the building was shared with Gentiles, the house had to have two separate sets of entrances and exits. No Jewish marriages were allowed. Why? Because these authorities could not countenance free-and-easy reproduction for such religious reprobates. But as long as the weddings were neither free nor easy, that was a different story; authorities made exceptions upon payment of substantial bribes. Every once in a while, the synagogue burned down (or was burned down); graciously, the authorities allowed the Jews to purchase the permission to rebuild it.

All of this constituted systematic extortion, marginalization, and cultural repression. The Jews of Lengnau responded in the most positive way available to them: they took it as an incentive to excel in learning and enterprise. They were smarter than their neighbors. They had to be. And over time, they became richer.

Simon Meyer Guggenheim (1792–1869) had mixed feelings about his ancestral faith. He never contemplated leaving it, which many of the European Jews of the time did, but he might easily have done so. Not only did he scorn religious observance, but he explicitly deplored the isolationist effects of Jewish practice in Europe.

Still, when Simon Meyer—at this point, a middle-aged widower—found he could not get permission to marry his intended bride, a widow named Rachel Weil, even though both sides possessed substantial assets, he decided the time had come for him to leave Lengnau. Where better to go than the United States, where, it was reported, Jews had equal rights with other residents? Such fairness was scarcely conceivable to Simon Meyer, but this is what the Jews who lived in the New World told their friends and relatives in the old country. Simon Meyer and Rachel brought twelve children from their previous marriages along with them—a substantial loss to Lengnau, a gain for the United States.

The history of the Guggenheim fortune(s) starts with energy, shrewdness, and flexibility. Hence the family's success in the sale of textiles, clothing, spices, and sundries. Simon Meyer saw to it that the boys got their education and training in Europe, where the fabrics and other merchandise came from. And son Meyer had a nose for good investment and made a small fortune in railway stock coveted by Jay Gould to complete Gould's assembly of the Missouri Pacific Railroad. Such victories yielded a significant degree of comfort—near millionaire status, when a dollar was worth twenty of today's bills. Railway speculation in turn woke the family to opportunities in the West. Pennsylvania mining was a kind of a practice run. The big opportunities were to be found in the Rockies.

What made the family really wealthy was good judgment. Some would say luck. As family biographer John H. Davis has put it, "A single, sudden decision, taken in nearly total ignorance of what its consequences might be, which, on its face value, was nothing short of wild speculation, was ultimately responsible for what the Guggenheims became and what they are today."[1] The decision was son Meyer's: to sink money into the ground in the hope of finding copper, lead, and silver, then to branch out into other precious substances. The silver of course was money. But the baser minerals also proved immensely valuable thanks to unprecedented consumption of ammunition, heavy reliance on telegraph wire, and new demands due to technological innovation. It was a good time to supply these needs, and the Guggenheims were among the greatest beneficiaries. The more so as most other beneficiaries thought that the primary purpose of money was to help one enjoy life. The early Guggenheims understood that money was even better suited to making money.

Life in the mining towns of the Rockies was one round of spendthrift success, alcoholic failure, heavy disappointments, happy surprises. In 1880 a small town such as Leadville (pronounced Leedville) had 120 saloons, 150 gambling dens, 35 whorehouses, and one so-called opera house. Most prospectors went down the tubes and holes; their business partners quit richer or poorer—it made no difference. Mayor H.A.W. Tabor of Little Pittsburgh (or was it Leadville?), ex-owner of a grocery store (even miners had to eat), had a mine called Chrysolite. He'd bought it from Chicken Bill for a thousand dollars. Chicken Bill was thrilled. He'd found nothing, but he'd salted the pit with some real ore to fool the next sucker. Ten hundred-dollar bills for some dirt. But Tabor then dug deeper (he'd really been fooled) and took out fifty thousand dollars' worth of silver in a month. Tabor's partner in Chrysolite was a man named Marshall Field, another hopeful retailer. The partners sold the company for $1.2 million—say, twenty million of today's dollars—but then Wall Street turned around and capitalized the hole at ten million.

This was the game that Meyer Guggenheim entered. But he was not the ordinary long-distance investor. He went out to look. For the locals, this was a sign of desperation or exhaustion: "Even the sheenies are coming in now." They should have known better. Sheenies are not known to throw their money away. So far as one can tell, Meyer got involved by lending money to a Philadelphia business acquaintance with personal contacts in the mine fields; or maybe by refusing to lend and buying a share in a pit instead. The circumstances were sufficiently obscure to allow the Guggenheim offspring to invent and embroider convenient fables, which says something about Meyer's communication with his own children. What did they need to know about these things, busy as they were with silk embroideries?

What matter? They were the heirs. Meyer would not last forever and had done so well that before long the problem was not so much how to make money as how to spend it. Meyer never threw it around; on the contrary, he fought in courts and on the ground for every inch and penny. Every fee and charge he paid was an invitation to expansion and diversification. The smelters, he felt, made too much for the services they provided, not only charging for smelting but holding the refined ore at some predetermined price. Why should they have the speculative gains? Why shouldn't he have his own smelter, even charge others for this service? In some circles—in Philadelphia, for example—such grasping behavior by Jews, however legal and legitimate, might be seen as proof of ethnic greed, as a push for dominance. In the mining towns of Colorado, it just showed that Meyer was every bit as tough as his fellows, and smarter.

At this point, Meyer Guggenheim decided it was time to liquidate the embroidery and fabric business and concentrate on mining and smelting. This must have come as a shock to the family. Things were not going well in smelting, where he had suffered heavy losses, to the point of horrifying his children. Yet Meyer would not let himself be discouraged. Meyer summoned the boys, admitted the losses, but predicted a bright, limitless future. He offered to sell his mines if he had to; all his resources were at their disposal. They could never be much as lace importers. Meyer loved proverbs and mottoes: roasted pigeons, he told them, would not fly into their mouths. They had to find and swallow fortune. He meant what he said. His smelting partners were ready to sell out? He bought their entire half interest, cash on the barrel. The children took heart, bent to the task, looked for new fields to conquer. The United States first, but then the world.

The nearest and most promising target area was Mexico. The country was poor, a victim of self-indulgent, corrupt government and the kind of immigration policy that had poisoned Latin America. Keep the Protestants out! Keep the Yankees out! The natives showed the effects of mismanagement—by their meager stature, poor life expectancy, illiteracy. "These Indians, once the proud creators of North America's only genuine native civilization, had lost everything, their leaders, their arts, their riches, their independence, their gods. By 1890 they had fallen into a chronic, sullen indolence. Those who had once been lords of the earth were now 'cheap labor.'"[2] The descendants of Spanish immigrants, who sustained themselves despite genocidal imports of murderous European maladies, betrayed their privilege by a pronounced incapacity for productive labor. Why work if one did not have to? Why work if work is meant for common folk?

The country as nation had its own sources of unhappiness. Aside from what resentments may have remained from the Spanish betrayal of Montezuma and defeat of the Aztecs, more recent events—the successful revolt by Texas and the loss to the United States of everything north of the Rio Grande in 1848—had nurtured new grievances. The Mexicans did not like the United States or its people.

Yet the land was rich with treasure, which interested Americans, the more so as these last were light-years more developed economically and were correspondingly greedy. The Guggenheims, with their new smelter at Pueblo, were particularly drawn. How else to make use of unused capacity? But in 1890, in an effort to raise the price of silver and protect American interests farther north, the United States raised a protective barrier against imports of ore from south of the border.

Most refiners would have made peace with this only too natural fact of commercial life; but not the Guggenheims. They sent Daniel, the most enterprising of that second generation, to Mexico to reconnoiter and make connections. Daniel's mother worried about bandits, disapproved. But Daniel surprisingly found himself at home in Mexico. They may not have liked Americans there, but they did not consider him a gringo. A Jew to be sure, but they found Jews easier and more familiar than Protestants, especially someone who had learned European manners across the ocean. Daniel found himself invited to banquets and parties, and was allowed to meet and deal with Díaz, convinced as the president was that the future development of Mexico depended on foreign investment. By an agreement of December 12, 1890, Daniel got concessions for two new smelters and permission to undertake the exploration and exploitation of any mine Guggenheim might lease or buy. Even more, he got Díaz to allow any machinery brought in from the States to enter Mexico duty free. No small matter. Not that Mexico was making such equipment; but such duties would ordinarily have ended up in the pockets of worthy officials.

Daniel returned to New York triumphant and vindicated. The whole character of the family business was in effect transformed, and he was put in charge of that transformation. Isaac, the oldest brother, was left to oversee liquidation of the embroidery and fabric trade that had once been the heart of the matter, now passé. The other brothers got appropriate assignments; every male member of the family counted. And father Meyer jubilated. Now, he told his boys, their future was the entire earth, above and below—nothing less than control of all mining and smelting in North America.

Mexico first, Alaska next. For more than a hundred years Alaska had been the easternmost extremity of the tsarist empire, which stretched more than halfway around the world. The Russians there devoted themselves to fishing and furs and kept warm by consuming huge amounts of vodka. That was it. The place had the reputation of frozen wasteland, so that when the tsarist government sold it to the Americans in 1867 for $7.2 million, less than two cents an acre, the deal was decried and mocked in the United States as Seward's Folly, after the U.S. secretary of state who negotiated the purchase. In fact, the land was mineral rich, but the Russians had never bothered to explore its possibilities.

The Americans were made of different stuff. Very early, the United States Department of Agriculture conducted experiments in Alaska that showed substantial opportunities of cultivation and raising livestock. Even those lines pursued by the Russians were susceptible of development; pushed hard, the salmon fisheries came to furnish more than half the American supply. The problem was haste and waste, rush and crush: valuable animal species were pushed by the United States to the edge of extinction. Russian indolence had its virtues.

Meanwhile, prospectors scratched the frozen ground and combed the river bottoms and came up with intimations of gold. By the late 1880s, serious successes on both sides of the border, Canadian and American, drew increasing numbers. Gold has that effect: the merest glint is an irresistible magnet. The first Klondike claim in Canadian territory in August 1896 provoked an explosion. One estimate has output of Alaskan gold and silver jumping from five million dollars in 1880–1896 to more than thirty-two million in 1895–1901. And this is surely an underestimate: the most successful prospectors avoid boasting unless they are selling. One expert gave a figure of more than one hundred million dollars from 1880 to 1906. And this was just precious metals. Other minerals were turning up in abundance: copper, lead, coal, gypsum. And they were dense, rich: the first trainload of copper ore assayed at 75 percent, as against the 2 or 3 percent from the porphyry mines of Nevada and Utah. Digging was a killer: ". . . the copper ore was mined in wind, rain, hail, snow, and ice, torn out of the frozen mountain, heaped into steel buckets, and shot down the four-mile tramway to the waiting gondola cars in the valley. The work was arduous beyond all imagining and many a miner fell dead upon his pick."[3] Transportation cost a fortune in that godforsaken climate, but it was worth it.

The Guggenheims made a rule of talking and listening—mostly listening. Somehow Daniel, thousands of miles away, got wind of a green, treeless mountain on Kennecott Creek, allegedly all copper. Not of interest to gold prospectors, but to Guggenheim . . . Daniel sent his top assayer to explore and verify. It took the poor man some months to make his way to the treasure. The trip was well worth it. He reported back that the ore tested at 70–75 percent, untold millions of tons—surely one of the largest and purest deposits of copper in the world. Was he ever right! The so-called Bonanza Lode proved to be the richest in the world in its time. John Davis tells the story as no one has:

The difficulties of the undertaking were of staggering dimensions. First, a two-hundred-mile, $25 million railroad had to be constructed over vast river deltas, over moving glaciers, through deep, unexplored canyons, from the sea to Kennecott Mountain. Then a multimillion-dollar breakwater had to be thrown across the exposed bay at the marine terminus of the railroad, and a harbor built to accommodate large freighters. Then a steamship line had to be bought or formed to transport the copper ore to the Guggenheim smelter at Tacoma. To fuel the mining camp, the railroad, the harbor, the steamships, accessible coal mines had to be found, bought and developed. To construct camps and warehouses, make railroad pilings and scaffolding, build mining sheds, huge forests had to be bought or leased and cut down. And all this had to be done in one of the bleakest wildernesses on the face of the earth.[4]

And how to pay? Even Guggenheim resources and Guggenheim nerve would not be enough. Daniel needed help. From whom? The logical candidate was J. P. Morgan, he of the nose. Not that J.P. had any personal inclination in favor of a Jew such as Dan—on the contrary—but money was money. J.P. got up from his desk and met Daniel at the door with a warm handshake. The two men spoke for an hour, not a second wasted; Morgan asking questions, Daniel answering. A noted mining engineer who sat in could not get over Dan's ardor, but even more his knowledge. The engineer thought he knew Alaska; Daniel knew it better. When it was over, Morgan told Daniel to see his lawyer, who would write the deal in law-proof form. Morgan was ready. The two men brought in Jacob Schiff as third partner—ah, those Jews! Thus was born the Alaska Syndicate. Guggenheims put up a little more than one third of the capital and all the administrative and engineering know-how. In return, they would get the lion's share of the profits.

I wish I had the room to tell the tale of this superhuman construction achievement: the thousands of men brought in from Depression-pinched San Francisco, sleeping wherever they found cover, working for three dollars a day, paying a dollar a night for bunk, fifty cents a meal, working at sixty below zero, lashed by fifty-, seventy-five-mile-per-hour winds, seeking their footing on heaving ice, driving piles into frozen mud, caught by thaws more dangerous than freezes, holding tight against raging currents, fighting snow-drifts that overwhelmed trains and plows (more than a thousand de-railments in one fifty-mile stretch), racing to shacks every half hour to warm their limbs and swallow something, anything, hot. The last spike was driven in early 1911, just in time to beat the spring thaw. It was made of Kennecott copper; the mountain was already being mined and the ore molten and cast.

Each railcar carried twelve to fifteen thousand dollars' worth of the cheapest copper in the world. The first shipload for the smelter at Tacoma was valued at five hundred thousand dollars. By the end of 1912, Kennecott had yielded profits of three million. That was just the beginning. World War I brought a tremendous demand. By 1918, the Guggenheims had taken out ten times as much from Kennecott alone as the Russians had gotten from Seward for all of Alaska in 1867.

With that kind of money coming in, the Guggenheims just kept buying: copper, coal, iron, forests—everything they could lay hands on. Not only in Mexico and Alaska. Bolivia and Malaya held tin; the Congo and Angola hid diamonds—the world was a storehouse of treasure. The only thing that slowed this monumental strip job was the growing protest from conservationists. In the end, though, the Guggenheims won, thanks in part to the quiet but effective influ-ence of brother Simon, United States senator (by appointment) from Colorado. Besides, most Americans were too busy making money for themselves. When times were bad, they had to work harder; when times were good, they wanted to earn and spend. They had no time for paradise lost.

The success of the Alaska Syndicate was a measure of the Guggenheims' ability to work with others, even the most important, on a profitable basis. But one had earlier indications of this, which may have been what influenced Morgan to take these upstarts seriously. At the end of the nineteenth century (1900–1901), a rich group of smelters and refiners with Rockefeller connections decided à la Rockefeller that monopoly was the way to unlimited wealth. To achieve this market leverage, they decided, they would buy out their chief competitors, the Guggenheims. This called for money, more than they had initially envisaged, for the Guggenheims not only thought well of their assets but had systematically minimized them to the public. A question of prudence.

But prudence was one thing, sale another. The Guggenheims, deal in hand, talked a different language, swelled the value of their smelting facilities by shifting profits in that direction, asked for twice what the would-be buyers had contemplated and got it. Even more important, they had five of the brothers named to the board of the new company, ASARCO (American Smelting and Refining), and once there, they took control of the company. Daniel was elected to the new position of board chairman; Simon was named treasurer. The original organizers, who had thought to swallow the Guggenheims, paying for their smelting installations with an issue of new stock, found themselves simply displaced. Some quit in a fury. Others swallowed their pride and stayed on. The Guggenheims, meanwhile, held on to their mineral concessions, now worth more than ever in the context of their quasi monopoly of smelting.

OVER TIME, however, mines, minerals, and subterranean treasures lost some of their profitability and prestige. Harry Frank Guggenheim (1890–1971) had the insight to see underdeveloped countries as particularly amenable to mineral exploration and exploitation, but he did not anticipate counteractions and countereffects. There are those who see the whole policy as mistaken.[5] How could it not be? The sparkling richness of the Brazilian diamond harvest was more than even bribes could conceal. But Harry was apparently too busy enjoying himself to keep abreast of these tendencies and developments: Harry was always so busy with his horse breeding and racing, his aeronautical pioneering, his writing, his art museum overseeing, his public-service jobs, his cattle raising, his timbering, his foundation creating, his newspaper publishing, that he did not really have the time to consider where Guggenheim Brothers should go in the sixties and seventies.

Harry was not alone with these problems; the whole family had to figure out what to do with all its wealth. The answer, as for the Rockefellers, lay in philanthropy, which had the virtue of nobility, status, elegant company, and useful employment for Guggenheim descendants. (The business enterprises had long since been confided to outside specialists.) Hence an impressive array of foundations, museums, and fellowship programs only too well known in scholarly and artistic circles: the family had a gift for imagining and creating the needs and opportunities for talent and intelligence. Thus the John Simon Guggenheim Memorial Foundation, with its world-famous fellowships—the making of a multitude of creative and intellectual careers. Also art museums in New York, Berlin, Rio, and Bilbao, sources of joy, taste, and knowledge. The family is better remembered and appreciated for these than for its business achievements.

But not by all. In Brazil, a plan by the municipality of Rio de Janeiro to build a branch of the local Guggenheim museum at a waterfront site downtown has run into political opposition, especially from left-wing parties who see such projects as elitist, expensive, and condescending—a bow to the wrong people.[6]

Some of the Guggenheim descendants cultivated special hobbies: aeronautics in the early days of aviation; space travel in its turn. Such manifestations of man's mastery of nature may not have rewarded money and enthusiasm, but in any case it brought prestige and valuable personal contacts. Was such dispendious play the best use of the family's resources? Space travel in particular is an extraordinarily, almost supernaturally wasteful activity that takes for granted and makes much of its high mission and special legitimacy. Still, if we are to encourage enterprise, do we not have to accept the continuity of honest fortunes and the right of heirs to do (and play) as they will?

As they did—particularly in matters of love, sex, and marriage.

In the second generation, Isaac and his brothers married local Jewish girls, American or European, of comparably modest descent, although, as the Guggenheim fortunes prospered, there was clear evidence of social promotion. Solomon, the fourth brother, espoused a Rothschild—not of the great Rothschilds—but the daughter of a successful businessman of that august name. So what if strangers allowed themselves to be impressed? Benjamin married a Seligman—clearly an announcement of advancement. And the youngest sibling, Cora, married another Rothschild of the non-royal variety. All of these spouses were Jews; at this stage, the Guggenheims still knew who they were.

As we saw, dynastic founder, Simon Meyer of Lengnau, had mixed feelings about his ancestral faith. Son Meyer was made for assimilation. Not so his wife, of more traditional bent. For decades, the family made it a practice to gather every Friday evening, not for blessings or Hebrew songs but for warmth and good food and togetherness. In the same way, they attended temple services on the important Jewish holidays, not to pray for forgiveness or salvation but to keep company with their fellows, get the latest commercial and political news, learn and explore the personal connections that made for successful spouse hunting and marriage. But such commitment has to be seen as a salute to rationality: good matrimonial alliances promoted business relations, and a known Jew was worth any number of unknown Gentiles.

Not so later on. For one thing, the family as a family had no true religious commitment or conviction. Son Meyer even sent his daughters to the Convent of the Sacred Heart, reputedly the best private school around. One could not give a more ambiguous signal or better encourage eventual intermarriage. Besides, time brought success, success meant money, and money meant social autonomy. The Guggenheims (the Googs as Jewish and non-Jewish acquaintances dubbed them), because of the very nature of their business—prospecting in distant lands, partnerships with the Gentile practitioners of heavy industry, memberships in and visits to clubs that normally excluded Jews—found the kind of matrimonial opportunities that made for intermarriage. Because these new lines lived close by one another—the Hamptons on Long Island, town houses and elegant apartments on and near Fifth Avenue—religious rupture did not entail the dissolution of social and cultural bonds. But business disagreements and family feuds, the kind that blood ties can exacerbate to the point of hatred, made for lawsuits and personal boycotts that would have immensely saddened patriarch Meyer.

So the third generation was something else again. For one thing, the family, in John Davis's vivid term, almost "daughtered out." From one point of view, that should not have made a difference. Women can and do make good entrepreneurs. But the Guggenheims, as we have seen, did not think that way. For them, women were good for useful connections. Of all kinds. Eleanor May, daughter of Solomon, married Arthur Stewart, Earl of Castle Stewart. Her sister, Barbara Josephine, married a John R. Lawson-Johnston. The women—to engage once more in vocabularic invention—almost Gentiled out. Some of the males soon joined the pursuit; one cannot eat together, play together, dance together without discovering warm affinities, reinforced by the drawing power of wealth. Robert, alias Bob, son of Daniel, took as second wife Margaret Weyher of Scranton, a well-known horsewoman. The Guggenheim males were not particularly attractive, but they knew and could afford a good looker when they saw one. Family photographs show women who could hold their own in a beauty contest. The ameliorative physical effect on further generations was biologically inevitable.

Their cousin Marguerite, alias "Peggy," 1898–1979, became friend, patron, and interim lover to *avant-garde* artists and writers in a variety of countries. Her gallery in London (opened 1938) featured abstract and surrealist art by, among others, Brancusi, Kandinsky, Magritte, Picasso, and Max Ernst, whom she married and later divorced. Her plans for a museum in London was interrupted by the war, but finding herself in Paris, she announced her intention of buying a picture a day from artists eager to find ways to escape the German occupation; and she did in fact acquire thousands of canvases, which formed the basis of a world-famous collection. After the war she moved to Venice, where she pursued her art patronage. The world has come to know and admire her as the wayward Goog.

All of this—wealth, sex, play, social prestige—meant an end to active participation in the family enterprise. Why work, when the alternatives are so noble and enjoyable? The Guggenheim firms of today are in the hands of managers. From entrepreneurship to inheritance. The family is now many different families. Gone the Friday night reunions. Gone the distant memories or reminders of Jewishness. In every case of mixed marriage, the children have been reared as Christians. In John Davis's words, the family has "succeeded in liberating itself from its often inconvenient Jewishness."[7] The memories of earlier sufferings have simply vanished. The Guggenheim descendants now devote themselves to philanthropy, to supporting art, science, scholarship, adventure so well chosen as to be an assurance of prestige and honor. And gratitude.

Ten

THE SCHLUMBERGER SAGA

Brains, Luck, and Good Timing

Pierre Schlumberger (b. 1914)

*S*chlumberger is best known in America these days as an oil-industry powerhouse, but their colossal breakthrough into that business is a rather late development in the family's rich history. Indeed, their oil ventures were made possible by the family's success in trade over the two previous centuries. They leveraged that success to provide both the finest schooling for their ensuing generations and solid financial support for new ventures. Their business experiences also fostered both discipline and a sense of purpose, which served them well through the years.

Most of the dynasties we've looked at so far have been driven by enterprising patriarchs with outsize personalities to match their outsize success in the world of business. The Schlumberger offer us a different kind of narrative: one of steady, incremental growth and frugal practices in business as well as in life. The family dynasty is less a product of one dominant forebear than it is the result of familial and cultural values distinctly associated with their heritage as Alsatian Protestants. The Schlumberger offer us fewer tales of wild living and excess than many other families, but their journey over the centuries, from Alsace to Houston, is an interesting and instructive one.

The Schlumberger family traces its roots back to a small corner of Western Europe nestled between modern France, Germany, and Switzerland. This region, Alsace, was home to many important families and individuals, particularly in the fields of earth sciences and engineering. A politically fragmented region, it was at the crossroads of various peoples and religions, and the resulting tensions and opportunities helped give rise to a culture that valued education, hard work, diligence, and thrift. The region's impact on modern industry has been vastly disproportionate to its tiny size for this very reason; when sociologist Max Weber famously described the phenomenon of the Protestant ethic, he had Alsatian Calvinists and Jansenists such as the Schlumberger very much in mind.[1]

Briefly put, Weber argued that in the hierarchical structure of the Catholic Church, the impetus for work was the possibility of upward mobility in the Church and related society. As a result, many people worked hard, but for advancement, not for the work itself. In various Protestant sects stemming from Jean Calvin, however, the motivation was different. There was no hierarchical structure within the Church, or corresponding opportunity for social, or spiritual, advancement. Hard work, in these societies, was undertaken as a goal in its own right, and was seen as having spiritual significance. These societies quickly became more productive than their Catholic counterparts. Further, the Protestants began to see worldly success as an indication of God's smiling upon the righteous—and thereby reinforcing their worldly and business behavior. While in some cultures, ostentatious shows of wealth were common, the financial success of prominent Protestants was coupled with a value set of strict morals, frugality, and uprightness of character. The profits themselves were generally accumulated, or reinvested in business, which is essentially the model of modern capitalism.[2]

The Schlumberger dynasty stands as one of the clearest examples of the Protestant ethic in action. Over time, they and their spiritual and industrial brethren built up prosperous enterprises (textiles, primarily) and grew into a community-minded business elite.[3] Claus Schlumberger, a tanner, was the first of the family to arrive in the region, making his way to Alsace in the mid-sixteenth century. Within a century, the Schlumberger had become one of the largest families in the area and had firmly established themselves in the textile business.

The Schlumberger family, in its shifts of fortune, mirrored the political transformations of the region in the context of larger economic developments. Like the other businessmen of the area, the Schlumberger were *réformés,* Calvinist Protestants in a Lutheran and Catholic sea. Like the business entrepreneurs of Max Weber's *The Protestant Ethic and the Spirit of Capitalism,* they built their family fortune in trade and industry (the French in those days made little distinction between *négociant* and *industriel*), on work for the sake of work. Jean Schlumberger, member of the business dynasty and himself a novelist of merit, wrote as follows of these entrepreneurs:

> The virtue of these old bosses consisted above all in their Jansenist regularity. In the office from 8 in the morning to noon and from 1:30 to 7; no travel; no absences. . . . If one was to stay in business, one had to adopt this clockwork punctuality, which one could not think of violating without scandalizing the personnel and without a sort of impiety.[4]

The Schlumberger made and sold cotton cloth on the basis of putting-out and work in manufactories (workshops based on hand labor). Most of this cloth was intended for printing—*indiennes* after the originals from India. This was what some historians have called proto-industry, the prelude to mechanization and mass production.

And indeed, the Schlumberger, exceptionally, moved beyond spinning, weaving, and selling to the production of machines for the manufacture of, first yarn and then cloth. They were not alone in this shift; the British in particular had taken the lead in this direction. Still, such a self-transformation was not simple in France, which had to start from scratch. That is, France had to learn how to build the machines, invent them if necessary, because the British, in an effort to maintain a monopoly, forbade the export of these devices. It was easier to visit England posing as travelers and entice British mechanics to better-paid jobs in France. The story told in the family is that one of the Schlumberger brought back designs and plans by having them sewn in the lining of his cloak. Whatever. The family found ways to copy British inventions as needed, first for themselves and then for other textile firms in the region. This brought them a pioneering role in the French industrial revolution. They made money in machines as Alsace became a regional center of mechanized manufacture. And with the capital so acquired, they went on to take a leading part in the promotion and construction of the first railway lines in the area.

The family's enrichment owed much to enterprise and nerve: they were, as we have seen, ready to take up new lines, new fields, unknown activities. They were much assisted in this by reciprocal ties of duty and affection, the one as important as the other. This undoubtedly promoted the availability of resources, which grew disproportionately because of the ethic of thrift and modesty; one was not here on this earth to enjoy and waste. Even after a half-century and a century of enrichment, their clothing, houses, and manners proclaimed the virtues of abstinence. Our novelist Jean Schlumberger writes of his grandfather's house as follows:

> . . . an old, tall house, not ugly on the outside with its immense tile roof, but which struck from the moment of entrance by its

Spartan nakedness. No sacrifice to luxury or even to comfort. Not a good-looking piece of furniture; not an object bought as fantasy. It was an event when they installed a furnace in the glacial vestibule, lit in the evening by a feeble lamp. Not a work of art outside of a small Diaz . . . and a Saint Peter in the style of Ribera that apparently had come from the ancestor Dollfus.

As for his grandmother's room: "A small hotel for traveling salesmen is not more simply furnished. A big bed of walnut, a few chairs, bare walls covered by a somber leafy paper. Nothing that would betray the slightest feminine refinement . . . "

Along with this passionate thrift went equally sober, dedicated work habits. When Jean Schlumberger (not the novelist; this one, also known as Jean de Schlumberger, born in 1819 at Guebwiller) was summoned by his father, Nicolas, to abandon political ambitions and, like his siblings, join the firm, he acceded without question and remained a partner for sixty years—not bad for someone who did not like the textile business.[5]

In all this, Jean reflected the deliberate family attitude toward the use and cultivation of capital. We have the notebook of Jules-Albert Schlumberger, twenty-four years old in 1828—five years of working experience, already a man set in his ways and old in his judgments. He believes in careful inventories, systematically reduced so as to avoid all overestimates of results, any misapprehension of values. When he sees that the early cards are carried on the books at the high prices that then prevailed, higher than those for new and better pieces, he is shocked: Be warned! We think we are richer than we are; we are spending too much; we shall soon find ourselves on the edge of the abyss. And when, in 1829, the partners plan a new partnership, he puts forward a set of precautionary rules:

(1) No partnership agreement that does not require an annual inventory, rigorous and accurate. Equipment to be depreciated at 6 per cent; stocks (both raw materials and salable goods) at 8 per cent.

(2) Set the amount that each partner is allowed to withdraw each year.

(3) Partners must inform one another of anything of importance.

(4) Take or borrow no outside capital; and if one must, pay it back as soon as possible.

(5) No carriages or horses for the households of anyone on salary. (They can walk.) These must also pay for any supplies they take from the firm: oil, vinegar, wood, coal, sugar, etc.

This was a constitution for a family enterprise that took itself seriously—not a chance encounter, but a rational assemblage of capital and human resources. The Schlumberger were the kind of people who sought to learn by error and disappointment as well as by success, and to prevent the repetition of errors.[6]

But they had their outliers too. In Guebwiller, Nicolas Schlumberger (1782–1867) and Daniel Schlumberger-Bourcart (the French version of the ancestral German Burckhardt) were partners, and when Daniel died, the two remaining partners, Nicolas and Jean-Jacques Schlumberger-Bourcart, decided to bring their children into the firm. But then Jean-Jacques also died, and his children preferred to quit the enterprise, which became Nicolas Schlumberger et Cie. One son of Jean-Jacques, Jules-Albert, though a graduate of the Ecole Centrale and employed in his uncle's firm, never became a partner. He preferred a post as higher exec, a titular post, which his relatives thought appropriate, given his tastes, comportment, and self-indulgence—not to speak of his mad laughter. He spent a whole season hunting in Africa—just the kind of thing to turn off his puritanical brothers, who spent the whole day and much of mealtime in useful activity.

That was a strong point of the prolific Schlumberger: they had talent and devotion to spare. We have figures on results for 1850–1851 which show profits of something over 1.5 million francs a year—more than enough to pay for good housing and such good living as they wanted. The biggest gains came from the manufacture of cotton fabrics using the latest mechanized and steam-powered equipment; most of the rest came from the making and selling of new machines. When Nicolas died in 1867, he left his nine children some seventeen million francs in cash, over and above the two family factories, modestly estimated at about one billion. One paid less estate tax that way.[7]

IN THE SCHLUMBERGER CLAN, the great turning point came in the late nineteenth century, when Paul (1848–1925), son of the aforementioned Jean de Schlumberger and Clarisse Dollfus—nothing like good genes—left Alsace with his six sons rather than live and work under Prussian-German rule. This voluntary exile made a difference, placing the family in Paris, center of all action, political, intellectual, cultural. But however big that difference, the main break was the coincidence of family history with larger transnational intellectual and scientific currents. The Paul Schlumberger were in the right place at the right time.

Paul, in the best Alsatian Calvinist tradition, went to engineering school, then into business, where he came to hold some twenty-five seats on diverse boards of directors. His heart, though, was with science, and he sent son Conrad (1878–1936) to the Ecole Polytechnique, and son Marcel (1884–1953) to the Ecole Centrale des Arts et Manufactures in Paris—two high temples of French scholastic excellence, competition, and performance. There the young men were exposed to new areas of applied science, in particular electricity, and this experience of scientific novelty shaped an abiding fascination and curiosity. They were drawn especially to the uses of electricity in exploring and mapping subterranean features, the solids and empty spaces beneath the earth's surface. *Vive le Métro.*

This may have been curiosity and fun to begin with, but experience soon showed a correlation between features and substance: the presence of water, for example, or potentially interesting minerals. And the best was yet to come. In the meantime, the young graduates went on to the kinds of things French engineers did. Conrad, the older, entered the government Corps des Mines, went on to become professor at the Ecole des Mines in Saint-Etienne, and then, in 1911, ascended to Paris. Marcel went into private industry, working on light railways at the Decauville factory and bored stiff. He found automobiles more interesting and invented, long before its time, an automatic gear shift; then, in 1911, he took out a patent on a rotary internal-combustion engine, an anticipation again of later innovations. Reading of these achievements, one wonders why Marcel did not become a titan of the new industry. He had the imagination and the brains. Lack of friendly connections? Provincial isolation? Want of enterprise? Want of further interest?

No matter. In 1912, Conrad developed an improved method of under-surface electric prospecting and, with the assistance of brother Daniel, archaeologist, tested the technique at the Ecole des Mines in Paris—why not? where better to locate basements and subway tunnels?—and on a family estate in Normandy. The work seems to have been interrupted by the war, but in 1919 father Paul, impressed by his children's achievements, endowed their further research with a gift of up to five hundred thousand francs. The deed of gift is worth quoting at length.[8] It stipulated that in return for this support,

> . . . my sons will agree not to disperse their efforts, and to abstain from research or inventions in other fields. The field of activity is vast enough to satisfy their inventive genius by its investigation: they must devote themselves to it entirely. The scientific interest in research must take precedence over financial interest. I will be kept informed and will be able to express my opinion as to important directions and expenditures to be made or not to be made. The sums disbursed by me are a contribution on my part to primarily scientific and secondarily practical work which I consider to be of the highest value and in which I take an interest. Marcel will bring to Conrad his remarkable competence as an engineer and his common sense. Conrad, for his part, will be the wise physicist. I will support them.

THIS FAMILY COMMITMENT to intellectual and scientific activity was particularly characteristic of national and religious minority clans, people who were moved by cultural values and deterred by widespread prejudice from seeking assimilation into idle sociability. We may cite in this regard the Calvinist Koechlin and Dollfus family lines in Alsace-Lorraine; or the Boeing, come to Mulhouse after the German annexation of 1871 to buy up a French cloth printing plant, who sent one of their own to Seattle to go into aeronautics. The airplane that bears their name gives them a kind of immortality. This was the Schlumberger tradition and milieu.[9] Culture counts.

And so, in these post–World War I years, the Schlumberger brothers discovered copper in Serbia, iron in France, and then, in 1923, oil in Romania—in time to meet the automobile. With such prospects, Conrad quit his post as professor at Mines, and in July 1926 the brothers founded a Société de Prospection Electrique. Now they passed from surface soundings of subsurface to soundings conducted from subsurface probes—what the French call *carottage*—yielding a substantial gain in detail and accuracy. They essayed the first such probe on the Alsatian oil field of Pechelbronn: bingo!

But France is not rich in oil. The Schlumberger prospecting enterprise, Schlumberger Ltd., rapidly became international, took on missions for such oil giants as Shell, sent teams of engineers to North Africa, the Spanish Sahara, Katanga, the Dutch East Indies, Romania, the United States, Venezuela, the Soviet Union. For all that, the company was still small and suffered the contractions of the Great Depression, to the point of having to fire some of its engineers. The partners wanted for office support, and when they traveled, they watched every sou. We have the expense account of a trip by Marcel to the United States in 1926–1927: hotel, $6.05; taxis, $3.60; train Paris–Boulogne, $4.25. But Pullman car Houston–New York, $83.59 and tips, $10. You can work on a Pullman car. Passionate, penny-counting thrift in the best family tradition.

The company annals credit Soviet demand with saving the enterprise through the lean years. But by the mid-thirties, the growing capitalist economies and the rising demand for automobile transportation changed everything. The war also. In 1940 the brothers refused to work with the Vichy regime—very different here from

most French business interests during those years of German occupation and French collaboration. So they left their *patrie* for the
United States and sealed the transfer by adopting English as the
company's international language. For the French, no act of apostasy could have been more decisive. (That is still true.) At the same
time, the Schlumberger decided to separate ownership and management: specialist outsiders, presumably French, would run the
firm. This radical break with the past may have reflected changing
personal interests; it may also have been a preventive against intrafamilial quarrels.

In 1965, Jean Riboud became head, a tough, ironfisted, autocratic chairman who reigned for two decades. These years saw the
firm prosper as never before, in spite of some ill-timed and ill-advised
acquisitions. (It is hard not to buy when the money comes rolling
in.) More serious was a feud that broke out between Riboud and
Jérôme Seydoux, heir by his parents' marriage to some of the
Schlumberger fortune and seen by members of the family as a logical and legitimate claimant to Riboud's succession.

Riboud was dying. Like most business types of his day, he was a
heavy smoker, and his lungs had had all they could take. He wanted
to name his loyal lieutenant, Michel Vaillaud, as his successor, but he
did not have the time to make the appointment good. To be sure,
Seydoux had left the firm to set up his own multinational, all-purpose
business, Chargeurs Réunis, but in 1985, Riboud fought with the
Schlumberger clan over a plan to issue a special class of preferred
shares. He thought the family should not have them, but the family
won. The fight killed Riboud, who died within a month. The next
year was spent vainly chasing Vaillaud, and in 1986, the top post
went to D. Euan Baird, a Scot by birth and the first non-Frenchman
to head Schlumberger since its founding. He was a geophysicist by
training, M.A. from Cambridge, and had spent his career prospecting and testing around the world. That was the nature of the business: it was more important to find oil than to know what to do with
it. Just fill the tanks and motors.

So the years of prewar parsimony and reinvestment had paid off in rich profits, richer than old man Paul could ever have imagined. He wanted science; he got some of that, but above all he got the financial returns he feared would distract his sons from higher things.

Meanwhile, the other Schlumberger branches and interests flourished and diversified from generation to generation: banking, plastics, publishing, cinema, television, air transport, and what more. By way of explanation, Paulette Teissonnière-Jestin, assessing the dynasty's record of transgenerational success, stresses the Calvinist heritage: "We have first the Protestant faith and ethic, with their emphasis on the value of work, study, and thrift."

But just as success promoted diversity of interests (business first, of course), so it opened the way to a wider policy of marital unions. In the beginning, one found partners almost exclusively in Alsatian circles, then in other parts of France, and then abroad. In this next-to-latest generation, moreover, one had Dominique Schlumberger, daughter of Conrad, marrying Jean (later John) Dumesnil (alias de Menil), manager of the Schlumberger corporate headquarters in Houston, Texas. John was Roman Catholic by birth and faith, and shortly before the marriage, Dominique converted to Catholicism, much to the shock of her high-Protestant family. She later said she had been leaning that way.

Besides, when one is rich and worldly, one cannot continue indefinitely in narrow circles following tacit rules and constraints. Dominique had started right by doing math and physics at the Sorbonne. But then she somehow got a small movie job—the cinema is modernity's pathway of temptation—and in 1930 met Jean at a dancing party in Versailles. Such encounters change the definition of suitability. One meets new people, succumbs to emotions rather than submits to calculations. Family and dynasty will never be the same.

And luck: life's accidents make an enormous difference. In France the Schlumberger moved in closed circles in Alsace and Paris. Everyone who mattered knew everyone else who mattered. Marriages were, to use the French term, alliances. The de Menil were outside this bourgeois world, but not quite. The family had been honored (ennobled) for military service under Napoleon, and they remained an army clan. Not much money there, and Jean grew up poor because of his father's efforts to help out a bankrupt relation. He had to drop out of school, go to work in a bank, pursue his education in night classes. But in 1927 he met Dominique Schlumberger at this ball in Versailles, and four years later the two were married. That sealed his fate. In 1938, aged thirty-four, he joined the Schlumberger mining company and took up administrative work in their Romanian oil properties. And three years later, when the Germans had invaded France and effectively blocked fruitful work in Europe—Jean was risking heavy trouble by trying to sabotage the German war effort—the de Menils fled to Houston, where the Schlumberger had begun pumping oil. In 1962 the couple became American citizens. Jean had changed his name to John: no gender confusion. But when he traveled to France, he expected to be received as the nobleman he was—by recollection if not by civil status.

In Houston, the well-endowed couple gave themselves over to art collecting, exhibiting, and promoting; also to left-liberal political activities (anti–Vietnam War movement, civil rights, Black Panthers), with a special interest in Islam, Muslim institutions, and Islamic cultic exercises.[10] Most of this was a far cry from the interests and predilections of family and friends; also from their social pretensions in France, a nation of republican institutions but aristocratic leanings and yearnings.[11] Yet it brought them the company of artists, filmmakers, archaeologists, intellectuals, political militants, and other amusing types. The art collecting proved especially and literally rewarding. The de Menil had taste as well as money, and their canvases grew in value with time and the cachet of their ownership.

Even so, their cultural and political ambitions and aspirations often exceeded their means and personal resources—and their opportunities and availability for child rearing and loving. On occasion they borrowed money, or raised it from the Texas social elite, usually with fruitful educational consequences. And sometimes, principles clashed with aspirations. Dominique was reared a Calvinist and watched the pennies. She rode the New York subways and ordered half portions in inexpensive eateries. And once, she had a chance to bid for a van Gogh from the Henry Ford collection but could not make the auction unless she took the Concorde. Do you know how much the Concorde costs? she exclaimed to the chief financial officer of the Menil Foundation. Three thousand dollars! Not worth it. She was ready to pay a million for the painting, gave instructions for someone else to bid on it for her, but lost it by her absence.

When she died she was buried in a plain pine box and carried to the cemetery in a black Chevy station wagon. The eulogy was given by a black minister from the local Baptist church. So death transcended the sectarian boundaries of faith. Shortly before she went, her daughter Fariha, a convert to Islam, asked her if she was in pain. Answer: "Pain means nothing to me now. I am being shown such extraordinary things!"[12]

SCHLUMBERGER LTD. PASSED into the hands of managers. John Dumesnil, recruit by marriage, warned against family pretensions and claims:

> I have seen too many instances of businesses brought to ruin by a soviet of sons and sons-in-law, all extremely convinced of their right to equality, all fussing with everybody and giving orders left and right, the least experienced and the least active stifling the initiative and the authority of the better ones. I think the Company has reached the point of its development where a formal structure is imperative. It is perfectly normal that members of the family be brought into the enterprise in preference to strangers, but only on condition that their place in the Company be in accordance with their value to it.[13]

And so it was accepted and decreed: joint-stock incorporation replaced family enterprise. The Schlumberger continue to hold important blocks of shares in their eponymous creation, but they have sold off much to purchase other assets and pursue personal interests. Life is richer that way. But their ancestors would have been disappointed. Who said life should be rich?

Eleven

THE WENDEL

NOBILITY AND INDUSTRY

FRANÇOIS DE WENDEL (1874–1949)

*F*rench society has not historically been especially pro-industry, particularly in comparison with Great Britain and the United States. Simply put, by French standards there are so many more interesting and prestigious things to do than work in a shop or office in order to make money. Moreover, France is a predominantly Catholic country, and Roman Catholic doctrine is often unfavorable to pecuniary interest and materialism, which can only divert attention from higher, more spiritual concerns. For another thing, a history of pride and pretensions on the part of the nobility often found expression in scorn for "the newcomers"—*les nouveaux venus*.

There are of course exceptions, family dynasties that have flourished in this less than conducive business environment. One such family with a remarkable degree of success and longevity is the Wendel clan, whose prominence in the area of iron-making—as owners and operators of mines and mills—goes back to the early eighteenth century. Their history combines industry, business, and the affairs of state, as they have aligned themselves closely with governments and figures of power throughout.

Nowhere was this dynastic tenacity more evident than in those enterprises that rested on or entailed ownership of land, because land and the local mastery that goes with it was the traditional basis of power, authority, and prestige. Now among the oldest and most explicit links of land to industry are those found in such fields as mining and metallurgy. In France, the accidents of geography situated the richest and most inviting location of such resources in the northeast, in that borderland that became over the centuries an object of desire and contention between Gaul on the one hand and, on the other, that diversity of principalities and counties, towns and cities that eventually coalesced into Germany. And it is there that we find the great dynasties of ore barons and ironmasters. The most important of these was the Wendel clan, going back to the seventeenth and eighteenth centuries. Their mills and mines have been located now in France, now in Germany, then back in France after the German defeats in the great world wars. But they themselves have always remained French, by tradition, education, and personal preference.

The continuity of these metallurgical dynasties rested of course on the multiplicity of descendants and the availability of capable heirs. Thus Jean-Martin Wendel, the first ironmaster in the family line, had fourteen children, and while subsequent generations proved less prolific, the philoprogenitive pattern continued, yielding not only businessmen but officials, military officers, politicos, and members of the Académie Française and of the board of regents of the Bank of France. As for metallurgy, everything depended directly on the links between landownership and industry. The land held the raw materials, and land had always been the basis of power and status: French ironmasters were *seigneurs* who held power over labor. Some were nobles before they became ironmasters. Others were ironmasters who became ennobled, but the usual practice for these beneficiaries of social advancement was to remain active industrialists—unlike the typical pattern of hasty social climbers. Even those who entered politics made it a point to keep charge of mill and forge: one could find the necessary collaborators in either domain. Iron, that hard metal, was an honorable way of life, a way of living nobly.

The reason for all this lay in political rivalry and ambition. Ironmaking in Europe was an activity much cherished by local lords, for the obvious reason that it spelled the difference between being armed and being helpless. One can understand, then, why the technology kept moving ahead. The most important gains went back to the thirteenth century, in particular the move from the low to the high furnace (blast furnace). This called for powered blowers, which could also be used to drive hammers to pound and shape the metal. The energy needed to work these blowers typically came from falling water, and every drop in the level of water along rivers invited a forge. Even that was not enough, and smiths built artificial ponds to create and feed falls. With this equipment, the blast furnace would heat to 1,200 degrees, at which temperature the ore would melt, pick up carbon from contact with the charcoal in the fuel, and yield a melt of castable pig iron, which could also be refined to make wrought iron.

So it was that Martin Wendel, founder of the metallurgical dynasty and acquirer in March 1704 of the forges of Hayange in Lorraine, obtained in 1711 a post as *secrétaire du roi* and received, in 1721, letters patent conferring hereditary nobility. This was not taken as promotion above and outside industry; on the contrary. He and his many descendants were seen by the French monarchy as agents of development in an area closely linked to power and military success, as human resources to be called upon as needed. And so it was that the Wendel planted iron-making facilities not only in

Lorraine—a frontier area, hence uncertain after all—but also in Burgundy, including the beginnings of what eventually materialized as Le Creusot, later to become the locus and focus of the iron-making Schneider dynasty.

Martin Wendel left a widow who did not care much for industrial responsibilities. With all those children, she had her hands full running the house and family. She quit the forges and died some three years after her husband. In between, in 1739, their son Charles married Marguerite d'Hausen, the daughter of a royal tax collector, a most profitable occupation. Charles brought to the union the *seigneurie* of Hayange, land and forges, and some twenty-five thousand livres in cash. His bride brought a large dowry of sixty thousand livres and a prestigious name. The combination spelled an enduring future, the more so as Marguerite was good-looking and this may well have been a love match.

Like his father, Charles was a worker, resolute, committed to the enterprise, but he was bolder and less cautious. Where the old man conducted himself like an accountant and watched the pennies even in matters of personal comfort, the son played the industrialist and gentleman. That's the advantage of a generation's practice and habitude. Charles had large horizons. He equipped his factories with the latest improvements, to the point of straining his treasury. He also bought forests and cutting rights to woods nearby; in those days wood was the making of iron. But wood was in short supply, and ironmasters were running into hostility from domestic consumers of fuel. The answer was coal, which was beginning to make itself available; so that in 1768, Charles began substituting mineral for vegetable fuel. Within a short time he had the coal share of Wendel enterprises up to two thirds—a major achievement. Charles took more pride in plant than in profits. He also gave much to charity and built a new church for the people of Hayange.

Business, though, has its ups and downs, especially business with the government. The 1770s and 1780s brought a fall in prices, and Charles's position became the more precarious because the French Treasury was such a bad payer. One might have expected better, what with intermittent wars, especially French involvement in the American Revolutionary War and consequent demand for armaments. (The French have not forgotten Jeanne d'Arc and never want to miss a chance to do in the Brits.) But the same army and navy that were so slow to pay wanted quick delivery of finished goods, while the regime wanted immediate payment for raw materials. Charles was forced to borrow at high interest, and the Wendel enterprise found itself in deep trouble—which did not stop Charles from undertaking heavy contracts: he felt sure he could collect later if not sooner. Such worries could not have been good for his health: he barely outlasted the American war and died in 1784, aged seventy-seven, after forty-seven anxious years as head of the firm. Still, by eighteenth-century standards, that was one long career.

He left his widow, Marguerite, and their son François-Ignace in charge. François-Ignace Wendel, known as Ignace, was born in 1741 and grew up in Hayange, in the shadow and glow of the blast furnaces. He was an iron enthusiast, devoting time and intelligence to metallurgical technology. We would see him as an engineer. When his father died, he left his mother to run the firm, while he traveled at home and abroad learning whatever he could by direct contact with people, forges, and furnaces. England of course was a major field of inquiry and research. His big travels dated from September 1768, when the Duc de Choiseul gave him the order to learn the art of making iron; the king would pay. It was Ignace who assumed the *particule* and took the patently noble name of de Wendel, as did the other nobles of Lorraine when the province became French.

For noble *maîtres de forges,* the French Revolution was poison. The Revolution saw them all as traitors and enemies, but needed their output. So the government seized the Wendel plants and equipment, in spite of a sharp and sensible defense by Ignace's mother and pleas by officials who wanted to help her get the work done. The revolutionary tribunals also pursued members of the family as reactionaries and royalists, which they undoubtedly were. Thus Louis de Balthazar, great-grandson of Martin Wendel. This poor fellow almost escaped but was caught at the frontier when his dog barked and betrayed his hiding place. So he was guillotined. A family council decided that the young members of the family should leave the country to save the family; Marguerite would stay to save the house.

This she did, though to do so she had to survive a period of forced subordination to an imposed and incompetent government agent, followed by imprisonment and imminent execution, which she narrowly avoided thanks to the political turn at Thermidor. When they let her out, she found herself ruined, to the point of not having enough grain to make bread. She was saved by the kindness of sympathetic former servants; the Wendel had always done well by their employees. But she lost the family works, which were auctioned by the government and sold to outsiders. These went broke, perhaps because of overenthusiastic bidding, and a second auction in March 1804 saw the Wendel clan win the property back with the help of family friends and a Jewish banker by the name of Jacob Cahen, who lent them about half a million francs, say five million dollars of our money, and received some twenty-eight thousand francs in interest. That was an advantage of church doctrine: Catholics were not supposed to lend at interest, but they were allowed to borrow.

All these crises and misfortunes may have hastened Marguerite's demise. She died in 1802, leaving her descendants the example of her courage in the face of adversity. The firm would now be headed by François, son of Ignace, who may well be the most important in this long line of ironmasters because his values and career choices so well illustrate the social issues and dilemmas.

He was born at Charleville in 1778. At the age of fifteen, he was a student cadet at the royal school of Alès (Alais), which prepared future naval officers; so doing, he was following the normal career logic for young scions of noble parentage. But those were hard times. The Revolution that had begun in 1789, we saw, was turning bloody, with numerous executions of people of proud birth and royalist sympathies. The Wendel fled the country, and François, after a short, keep-busy stretch in Rhenish forges run by his father and uncle, enlisted as cadet in the army of the princes of Rohan, royalist opponents of republican France. He tried his fortune in a number of units, *hussards* and *cuirassiers,* setting the stage for a military career.

By the turn of the century, France had fallen into the hands of a Corsican "adventurer" named Bonaparte, who appealed to the expats (*émigrés*) to return and help their nation resume its place and historical destiny as European leader. François de Wendel leapt at the opportunity and returned to his home country of Lorraine, where he set up residence in Metz. It was there that he learned that the new French government, as part of a program of liquidating royalist residences and estates seized during the Revolution, would be selling the old Wendel property in Hayange. (The new government repudiated the Revolution, but was not above profiting by it.) François wanted this property, not in order to resume activity as an ironmaster but because it was the family home, the dynastic home. He was joined in this effort by relatives, and the group, as we saw, found the cash to make a successful bid.

Later on, in introducing his will, François would disclaim any interest in ferrous metallurgy. "I the undersigned," he identified himself, "François de Wendel, former cadet of the royal navy, officer in the regiment of hussars and cavalry, and now, against my will, ironmaster and owner of several industrial establishments that have prospered in spite of everything. . . ." Nothing better illustrates the paradox and contradiction of noble entrepreneurship.

"Against my will. . . ." Indeed.

But at the time, of course, François found himself deep in debt, and the only way to raise the money he needed was to make iron; and the sweetest way to justify such an effort was to link it once again to military achievement. So he determined to produce artillery, and wrote various functionaries recalling the earlier contributions of his father in this area—his father, *"ancien officier d'artillerie."* And while he was at it, this unwilling iron-master took the occasion to buy further iron-making lands nearby: mines, the forges of Moyeuvre, forests rich in hardwood. The sellers set different prices according to the time needed to pay—no mention of interest, but the price varied with the length of reimbursement. Even so, François had to borrow more, and this time he went to the good Catholic Seillière bank in Paris, where religious constraints did not apply. That was what Paris was for. The Seillière were specialists in collecting moneys owed by the French government. Such debts served as security for firms such as Wendel's.[1]

Meanwhile, François's brothers were giving him trouble, to the point of suing him for bigger shares in the property. François was disgusted and began thinking about liquidation. Even death, he felt, was better than this intrafamilial civil war. In the meantime, he sold the family's good furniture and his fancy coach and determined to save more than thirty thousand francs a year (say, sixty thousand of our dollars) and live modestly, with only one all-around servant, a cook, a maid, no more horse crew, as few outsiders as possible, and only local wines. No vintage indulgences. He would cut and sell wood, sell the house in Metz, give up farms, even one of the forges. He also fought to obtain better competitive and market circumstances for the iron manufacture: protectionist tariffs for finished metal, but low duties on imported raw materials.

The post-Napoleonic years saw the French iron industry grow and gain technically: when all is said and done, diversified production for industry beats boring production of cannon. By the mid-1820s, the Wendel works were making five thousand tons of wrought iron a year and six thousand tons of cast, of which six hundred by use of coke, without counting such specialties as *fer-blanc* and black sheets and plates. But François, like his mother, wore out early. He died in 1825, age forty-seven. He left his children a plant and estate valued at more than four million francs and a good reputation in the marketplace. But he felt himself a failure, largely because he had not been the sailor he would have liked to be.

A decade later (c. 1834), the Wendel firm ranked only ninth among French iron-making enterprises, with annual output valued at 3.5 million francs. (The biggest maker was the Cie des Hauts-Fourneaux de la Loire et de l'Ardèche: 7.3 million francs.) This represented barely 1 percent of French output, which amounted to some 340 million francs, and this despite heavy capital investment, almost twice as much as Loire and Ardèche. Something was clearly wrong. A generation later, in 1870, however, Wendel had pushed capital value from 7.6 million francs to 23.5 million, and the value of output from 3.5 to 31.6 million. In little more than thirty years, the quantity produced had been multiplied by almost thirty, representing 11.2 percent of national make. Wendel was now in first place and owed its growth to its willingness to invest in the latest equipment. It was helped here by family readiness to pitch in and by further assistance from the Seillière bank.[2]

During these decades, the big task was to catch up with Britain, which had moved far ahead of everyone else in ferrous metallurgy. In particular, the British advantage lay in the use of coal rather than wood or charcoal in iron smelting, which reduced substantially the cost of this first and fundamental step in the creation of workable metal. Note, however, that charcoal iron enjoyed higher purity and was preferred for certain high-quality uses—fine steels, for example. But these were the exception. Large-scale and heavyweight ferrous metallurgy made out well with coke-blast iron. And here the British had greater access to raw materials: good coal deposits and good ore. In France, the converse was true. The country was not rich in coal, though more so along the northeast frontier, and poor in iron. The British found much of their iron ore at home; the rest could be imported over water (low transport costs) from Sweden (50 percent iron content) or Russia (68 percent). By way of contrast, French ore ran 32–38 percent iron and that with too much phosphorus; hence the derisive name *minette*.[3] For François de Wendel, these handicaps were a constant source of irritation and concern, the more so as he made it his business to keep track of the British industry and learn what he needed in order to catch up.

For all his reservations, the records of the firm show a willingness to borrow large sums in order to equip the plants with the steam engines, rolling mills, and other heavy equipment required by the new technologies. This was easier after 1815 than before, because nonindustrial members of the French elite looked with favor on families such as the Wendel with their long and dependable credit record. If one had to lend because one had to put one's cash to use, better to lend to one's social equals, especially those with good security. Here as before, the Seillière bank played a major role, financing the equipment of the new Wendel plant at Stiring in 1846 and coming to the rescue of the firm during the business crisis of 1847. The Seillière were the heroes of French metallurgy in those times, helping not only Wendel but also the Le Creusot works of Schneider and the Fourchambault plant of Louis Boigues.

The metallurgical activities of the Wendel family were intimately affected by changing political and competitive circumstances in the late nineteenth and twentieth centuries. The French loss of Lorraine in 1871 hurt loyal French feelings; but moving the furnaces and forges into the German market did not hurt them as such; if anything Germany was pushing heavy industry and armament and thereby promoting demand for iron and steel. In the years immediately preceding World War I, annual growth was running a spectacular 20 percent, and the Wendel mills were described as overwhelmed by orders. Overall extraction in France of *minette* ore rose from 2.3 to 41 million tons between 1872 and 1913. Wendel, though, accounted for little of this increase. Its extraction went from 309,000 tons in 1905 to 763,000 in 1913.[4] The company had better sources.

Yet all was not easy success. German industry was working to higher standards: the railways, for example, would not accept anything but steel rails. The effect on Wendel rail output was brutal and abrupt: a drop from 50,000 tons in 1872 to 1,200 tons in 1883. And Wendel had to shut down its furnaces at Stiring because German railways would not deliver raw materials at the special prices that had been practiced by French companies. The town of Stiring-Wendel shriveled as the smiths left. Meanwhile, the family found it necessary to divide its industrial enterprise into two units. The German part, named Les Petits-Fils de François de Wendel, which included ancestral Hayange, Moyeuvre, the young installations at

Stiring (inaugurated in 1853), plus the coal mines of Petite-Rosselle, remained a family partnership with unlimited liability for partners. The contract stipulated that only direct Wendel descendants were eligible for shares. The family also made it a point to maintain its local authority by securing appointment to those German political posts that corresponded more or less to those they had held in French Lorraine.

On the French side of the border, cheek by jowl, the iron mines and furnaces and forges of the new plant at Joeuf came under de Wendel et Cie, a limited-liability joint-stock company shared half and half with the Schneiders of Le Creusot. Why include these strangers and competitors? Because the Schneiders had taken the initiative of securing French rights to the Thomas-Gilchrist process, the one way to turn the phosphoric iron ores of Lorraine into usable steel. The Wendel kept smiling, but not until the interwar years of the next century did they succeed in ridding themselves of these unwonted and unwanted allies. In the meantime, they kept their eyes on the long term and secured coal mines in northern France, the Ruhr, and even Holland. On the eve of the first World War, the two Wendel firms were mining 3.7 million tons of iron ore and making 1.25 million tons of pig iron, 1.1 million tons of steel, 892,000 tons of plate—more than a third of total French output and a goodly share of German production. The family employed twenty-three thousand workers, more than thirty thousand including the Ruhr and Holland. These employees were often housed in company lodgings and sent their children to company schools. Management aimed at cultivating the sense of one big industrial family. This was standard procedure in paternalistic French enterprises: family is family.[5]

For all the gains and opportunities in Germany, the Wendel rejoiced to see France win in 1918 and their enterprises reincorporated in the French industrial system. They had never felt at home east of the border, and nothing was so important to them as this sense of belonging to the country they knew as theirs. Henri de Wendel had sat in the Reichstag as a formal protester (*protestataire*), and that was all right. But when his nephew Charles tried to soften the family's principled opposition by taking Henri's seat and designating himself an autonomist, his relatives were furious, the more so as political opponents within France used this concession against the family. In effect, there was no way to satisfy everyone on these conflicting issues and goals, especially since German ambitions were by no means satisfied (the appetite grows with the eating) and republican France felt diminished by the new order of power in Europe.

The Great War, as is well known, was an extremely costly business. The French lost hundreds of thousands and would have been defeated again, as in 1871, had it not been for British and American intervention. The need for such outside help was itself a source of embarrassment and humiliation: Since when did Europe's oldest and greatest state, center of power, pride, and civilization, need allies to defeat this belated German coalition? Such mortification was a serious impediment to gratitude.

Still, it is better to win than to lose, and the Wendel had good reason to rejoice.

After the war, Lorraine became French again, and the Wendel were welcomed back with open arms. The land was returned to the family, and the forges were rebuilt using both family and government funding. Wendel firms were promoted by the French authorities as part of an effort to advance French industrial autonomy, particularly in defense and defense-related activities, and the family business returned to prosperity.

These were good years on the familial level as well, with strong leadership from various family members. Henri and his wife, Berthe de Vaulserre, produced three sons, François II (1874–1949), Humbert (1876–1954), and Maurice (1879–1961). François II and Maurice received polytechnical educations, of the sort the French do exceptionally well, and were able in later years to put their training to good use in educational visits to metallurgical installations abroad. Back home, they did not manage production, but they enriched and encouraged the whole process of technological emulation and modernization.

• • •

ECONOMIC AND POLITICAL RECOVERY came to an end in the 1930s, with the Great Depression and the advent of World War II. Once again Germany annexed the Lorraine and took over the forges. The war's end restored the Wendel family, but without the sense of exaltation or even optimism that had accompanied the victory in 1918. François II was approaching the end of a spectacularly diverse private and public career, first and foremost *maître de forges*. Industrial buildings had been devastated, the nation's morale and economy shattered. The French government began to regulate the steel industry, and pushed for greater efficiency and rationalization. In 1946 the Wendel coal mines were nationalized, and soon the government began to insist on company mergers in private industry. This accelerated selection and support of the most efficient steel-producing units, and the closure of obsolete centers. The screening process left the Wendel plants working, because by French standards they were better furnished with raw materials, capital equipment, and transport facilities.

But only by French standards. Over the course of the post–World War II worldwide campaign for global provisions and markets, France not only found itself losing exports but also was compelled to begin importing materials in order to hold its own in the finishing processes. For a hundred years and more, subject to political boundary changes, France had built its ferrous metallurgy on the *minette* of Lorraine. This ore, we saw, suffered the major disadvantages of low iron and high phosphorous content. As a result, yield and productivity were lower, regardless of the process used, which resulted in raised costs on the international market.

What is more, better deposits of ore were being discovered in distant places such as Brazil, while advances in shipping technology made it cheaper to move rich iron ore from Rio to Dunkirk than poor ore overland from Lorraine to anywhere in France.[6] In the meantime, new technology and better equipment elsewhere in the world outpaced the French factories and forges. In Europe, ironically, it was loser Germany that took advantage of reconstruction to build the newest and best installations. Even Italy had better plant than France; and outside of Europe it was Japan that led the rest. This trend, in conjunction with the general vigor of the West German and Japanese economies, might prompt some cynics to say that it pays to lose wars.

All of this made mastery of forges and furnaces much less rewarding than it had been. The modernization of the industry called for skilled engineers and professional managers, and little by little the Wendel began to extricate themselves from the iron and steel business. They did not disappear from the seats of authority that came with ownership, but their ownership became indirect. They were no longer ironmasters—rather landowning seigneurs of the kind they had tried to avoid becoming. Their marriages became less about iron and land resources and more about nobility and lineage, as they made it a point to collect blue blood: Noailles, Montaigu, Maillé, Montalembert, Montremy, La Rochefoucauld, and on and on. Meanwhile, the heirs retired to mansions and estates, there to enjoy good company, elegant alliances, sports, art collecting, scholarship, dignities, and amiable distractions.

In 1977, the 350 family shareholders voted unanimously to restructure their business. They sold off most of their holdings surrounding iron and steel production and began an investment pool. They are now a clan that meets annually to hear reports on their business holdings: electrical equipment, oil, abrasives, medical research. Gone are the iron and steel blast furnaces and forges. Where thirty blast furnaces were still working in Lorraine in 1970, making some two thirds of French steel, only two were left in 1995, and the regional industry was a memory. And insofar as Wendel descendants have continued to cultivate iron and steel they rely on managers, engineers, and technicians. They are too smart to attempt what they are not qualified to do. Besides, owning these companies is work enough.

Even Wendel is a memory. The limited partnership once known as Les Petits-Fils de François de Wendel et Cie changed its name to the Cie Lorraine Industrielle et Financière (Clif), shareholders limited to descendants of the founders, "as though the original name were now too heavy to bear."[7] And there is a Wendel Investment company, which quietly goes about the business of making money in a wide variety of undertakings: assets 1 billion francs in 1977, 2.5 billion euros in 2002—fortune multiplied by sixty in twenty-five years! Today the active members of the family hold eminent positions in government and bear other names than Wendel. These are sons-in-law who have entered the noble clan by judicious, well-chosen alliances. Thus the head of Wendel Investment is Ernest-Antoine Seillière, son of Renée de Wendel and Jean Seillière de Laborde, grandson of Maurice de Wendel and Andrée des Monstiers Mérinville, descendant thus of the bank that helped finance Wendel iron and steel back in the early nineteenth century.[8]

During these years of uncertain metallurgy, the surest Wendel role was played by the women, guardians of family identity and interest. Thus Berthe de Vaulserre, wife of Henri, represented and presided over the clan as he did the firm. She witnessed the creation of Joeuf, a milling town that was created out of nothing on the French side of the new German border. When iron ore was found there, refugees poured in and population went from under 500 in 1870 to over 13,000 in 1914. With this growth came the usual problems: housing shortages, school needs, inadequate health provisions. Mme de Wendel saw it as her Christian, Catholic duty to attend to these matters, to see to churches, schools, company housing, child care clinics, company farms. And when war came in 1914 and the Germans occupied French Lorraine, she fled to Paris and there established the Union Lorraine, a charity whose aim was to help refugees from those parts, whether or not they had worked for Wendel. To quote on this commitment Véronique de Wendel Goupy, herself a busy and tireless mistress of charity: "The sense of duty was always the first and foremost part of the Wendel way of life. This sense of duty was never separated from a religious commitment. This brand of Catholicism was in its effects not very different from Protestantism à la Max Weber."[9]

Berthe de Vaulserre died of the Spanish flu in 1918. Her successor as family philanthropist was Andrée de Montremy, wife of

Maurice, youngest of the three brothers. Mother-in-law and daughter-in-law did not get along. That's the trouble with matrimonial relations in high descent. The two shared a Paris town house, and Berthe had the unfortunate habit of visiting her son's conjugal bedroom to chat soon after the breakfast tray. Andrée found this an intrusion. She had firewood piled in the passage that linked Berthe's bedroom to theirs. Berthe was shocked, but she never mentioned the incident and never again insisted on her presumed right of maternal surveillance.

Andrée spent the interwar years running camps for the children of the Union Lorraine and organizing for the Red Cross. By the time she was ninety, the Wendel steelworks had been nationalized and the family had left Lorraine. The war and occupation brought them Fontlade, an estate in the south where the family began making wine. From one border of France, then to another. They sold the wine at a loss but used viticulture to employ worthy dependents. Meanwhile Andrée refused to leave Lorraine and spent her last years almost alone in Brouchetière, receiving and consulting with the local officials and dignitaries and sharing in ritual events. The only person she boycotted was the Communist mayor of Joeuf. For noble folk, feuds and honor are taken seriously. For French Communists also.

Because for noble folk, blood is blood. All the Wendel clan together are now preparing for or anticipating the three hundredth anniversary of regional ferrous and national prominence and familial prosperity. Berthilde de Wendel de Montremy, direct descendant of the dynasty, recalls visiting recently the tombs of her ancestors. How long, she thought, would they slumber under the gasps and rumbles of the family blast furnaces?[10] My wife and I recall dining as her parents' guests. Her father would wait at the door and have it closed the moment fixed for the start of the repast. No allowance for tardiness. We were always slightly early.

Concluding Thoughts

*I*n some ways, all dynasties are alike. They are structures of blood relationship, often reinforced by marriage ties and adoption. The essence of the relationship lies in the nature of paternal governance: father, later grandfather, rests his authority on age, love, the habit of accepted power, the advantage of experience, the legal possession and control of assets. In dynasties that work well, these considerations make for a system of reciprocal trust, duty, habit, and affection transcending legal and even personal obligations, surpassing time and cultural environment, and surmounting generations. As we have seen, however, such systems don't always work well, and can run into emotional difficulties. These emotional clashes seem to be almost unavoidable, gaining force from both success and failure (ya can't win and can't afford to lose!), and it is the family's ability to deal with such clashes within the structure of the business that helps determine their success.

Contemporary students of business history live comfortably with these strengths and weaknesses—in fact they largely ignore the struggles and successes of family firms because they assume family enterprise is merely a transitional stage model, if not obsolete altogether. They feel that sooner or later, depending on the nature and demands of the activity, the family must bring in outsiders—managers and technicians able to handle the business and deal with changes in methods and technology. This is particularly true of the more successful firms, growing in market and range. No one can reasonably expect a given bloodline, even one reinforced by happy marriages, to yield enough talent to achieve, cope with, and pursue growth indefinitely. Business dynasties, in other words, are seen as intrinsically inadequate, a thing of the past.

Alfred Chandler, Jr., in his distinguished work on managerial capitalism, has been the most influential spokesman for this point of view.[1] He points out that growth in both production and distribution creates problems and tasks that impose functional specialization (by the kind and requirements of the work) and thus compels recourse to appropriately trained personnel. Over time, even interested family members (holders of shares) prefer to leave such jobs to salaried middle and higher management.

The managerial model, initially called the "functional holding company form," was much facilitated in Europe by the organizational device of the limited partnership and its variants.[2] In the United States, the joint-stock company was the convenient form and found widest application at first in transportation (railroads and canals) and then heavy industry (mining and metallurgy). In the advanced industrial nations especially, this tendency toward the managerial structure continues to the present day, not only, we saw, because of the firm's search for competent and creative specialists but also because of family pursuit of alternative ambitions.[3]

Yet, as we have seen, this focus on the managerial form should not be deemed a valid dismissal of familial and dynastic enterprise. It does not mean that the family firm has become obsolete and useless. On the contrary, the creation of family firms continues apace, if only because the family is a nursery of knowledge and skill, an embodiment of trust, and a store of capital, in house or among relatives. Parents will continue to bring children into the business by way of using and training their talent and helping them to a life of earning and security.[4] Thus François Crouzet reminds us, quite recently, "We have perceived, a little late to be sure, that the huge majority of enterprises consists of family firms."[5]

These are firms whose familial character yields a kind of divine right of inheritance, but one *that is not to be taken for granted*. As the French silk manufacturer Alexandre Colcombet wrote to his children in 1894, "You would be making a mistake if you thought that my business, which I have from my father, which he had from his father, is a property that belongs to you by right of birth. . . . I shall leave you factories that will ruin you or enrich you, depending on whether you are ready to work diligently and tenaciously. It becomes your business; my responsibility ends."[6] These are firms, then, where the transmission of paternal authority promotes continuity but also undermines it by the strict and habitual character of this authority. Children of important people find it hard to take dictation even from these important people. And dynastic founders—such as Henry Ford and John D. Rockefeller—often find it hard to turn over the reins to eager children. Their reluctance is reinforced by that of inactive relatives, silent shareholders, who know, or think they know, the weaknesses of family members. Heredity alone, after all, is not a guarantee of competence. As a result, family business is family drama.

Even so, these family firms do distinctly better than their managerial counterparts: "One of the biggest strategic advantages a company can have, it turns out, is blood lines."[7] Aside from productivity, such firms have the advantages of secrecy, among other things, with regard to fiscal and legal obligations. Shady dealings are certainly not limited to family firms—managerial enterprises are equally ruthless in their avoidance of regulations. But family firms get away with more. And I would go farther in regard to the larger historical implications: even if the absence or desertion of heirs leads to dissolution of a family firm or its conversion to a managerial enterprise, the fact remains that it has found/made a place and exploited it, and that it has thereby played a part in the larger process of economic growth. In developing countries it is the family firm that has the resources and the mutual trust to make use of these resources boldly and effectively. Hence the role of "expat" immigrant families in such places as Southeast Asia and South America: they bring these assets with them. They can do what the native population cannot.

IN SHORT, NO ATTEMPT to understand the nature and methods of business enterprise while ignoring the family firm can be adequate to the task. Indeed, customers seem to understand this better than economists. They seek out the family firm as a token of personal success and prestige. Money is money, but as we have seen, borrowing from or investing with a house such as Rothschilds is evidence of acceptability and taste; not everyone can do it. In many instances, the family name as brand name is an assurance to buyers; thus Ford cars way back when, or Toyota cars today. Indeed family names are a salable asset, as the heirs are only too well aware. Remember here the Morgan bank and the sale of the name to the outside partners who had taken over its management; or Agnelli and their programs of diversification via brand purchases. Families matter, and the good economic historian will not omit them from the story, any more than he will the ambitious businessman. Studying dynastic enterprise is revealing for our understanding not only of economics and business behavior but of society, people, and culture.

Much depends on the nature of the business. Some activities lend themselves to centralized oversight and control and yield pyramidal personnel diagrams. A reasonably capable and numerous family, suitably defined and trained, can handle the ongoing activities and the opportunities for growth. But multiply the requirements at higher supervisory levels, open dispersed plants and make diverse products, and one needs a growing army of managers. Even at modest technological levels, such expansion entails the creation of administrative posts. An early study of large-scale retail trade offers a history of what may have been the world's first department store, the Bon Marché in Paris. The author, Michael Miller, who liked what he saw in that innovation, took me as a special target for criticism, denouncing what he felt was my tendency to equate family firms French style with conservative enterprise and slow economic development—very much the opposite of my optimistic interpretation here. And he went on to cite Alfred Chandler for his pioneering work on managerial capitalism—without, however, noting that Chandler's preference for the managerial form also implied an imputation of serious shortcomings to family firms.[8]

The fact is that the founders of the Bon Marché, Monsieur and Madame Boucicaut, wanted their creation to be a happy family affair and would certainly have passed it on to descendants had they been able to. But premature death wiped out their only son, and so the firm never achieved the limited nirvana of dynastic enterprise. In the meantime, my own work has led me to think better of these familial structures and their role in economic development. Also better of French economic performance, especially insofar as it has rested on dynastic achievement, as demonstrated by the Schlumberger, Wendel, Schneider, Dollfus, Koechlin, Gros, and other long-lasting and wide-ranging families of Alsace-Lorraine and other busy French provinces.

This reference to the work of Miller on the Bon Marché raises again the question what we mean by a dynastic firm. What is a dynasty? We have defined it as a succession of at least three generations of a family business, marked by continuity of identity and interest. Consider now what we have learned about questions of succession and durability: What makes for enterprise of such lasting power and continuity? Clearly, a major consideration is the availability of capable descendants and the readiness of those descendants to see the business as interesting and rewarding. Also their ability to work together, even to love one another in the face of differential rewards. One is not surprised to find founder and initial co-workers ready to devote all their time and energy to the office or shop. *BusinessWeek* puts it that family firms are more likely to have "managers [family members] with a passion for the enterprise that goes far beyond that of any hired executives, no matter how much they are paid." But what of the successive generations? To be sure, children and grandchildren often feel differently, especially if the wealth earned in the business permits all manner of sport and diversion, including privileged access to playmates. This dissipation is less likely if members of the founding generation are still around to approve and disapprove, to guide the heirs on the path of participation.

In that regard, some readers will feel that my numerous criticisms of commercial abandonment by family members and recourse to such diversions as art collection and media ventures are unfairly deprecatory. Such activities, after all, can generate important capital gains and more than compensate for business exits. But if one wants to understand the significance of familial achievement and the durability of enterprise, one has to see such diversions and departures as major changes in interest and direction, as subversions. They represent choices and thereby shape the nature of business activity and family character and status. Wealth in the purely monetary sense is only part of the story.

In exploring dynastic continuity, we also encounter the influence of culture—the values of the surrounding society and the possibilities opened by money. These, we have seen, were the enemy of continuity in societies such as Britain and France, where business was not deemed the highest form of activity, and money from trade, as against older, aristocratic sources of wealth, was seen as crass and inelegant. In such societies, land was the highest treasure. It was linked not only to income but to power, and it carried with it reminiscences of seigneurial connections and authority, as the noble titles of the greatest landowners testify. An early, exceptional addition was wealth acquired overseas in imperial ventures and adventures—thus West Indian sugar—for such fortunes also tasted sweetly of power.

Owing to this supercilious pursuit of status over wealth, the France of the Old Regime, for example, missed out on a great deal. The economist Jean-Baptiste Say suffered the pains of self-derogatory comparison: the British, he wrote, were commercial pathbreakers who saved and accumulated wealth; the French threw it away: "Under the French Old Regime, what hurt the increase of national wealth was essentially the foolish vanity of enriched bourgeois who bought noble status and with it wasted their savings on the excesses of the court. . . . It is the sum of wealth saved and capitalized that makes the difference between a rich nation and one that is not."[9]

But Say was too kind perhaps to England. Though England did better than France, was more keen for business and trade, it still thought of money as social means rather than an economic end—as a precious way to comfortable living, yes, but even more to social ascent and political power. The whole point was to use business as a vehicle, to use the business to promote oneself in style and status, to help oneself to meet the nobility and the local gentry and find the kind of marriage partner who could raise mere wealth to gentility.

And if not for oneself, for one's children. In nineteenth-century Britain, the whole point of what was deemed a good education was to avoid professional training, to eschew anything useful, to learn the empty poses of high and mighty pretense. Not so in France and Germany, where excellent and competitive technical and scientific education generated the talent needed to replace idle heirs. Nor in the United States, without a status aristocracy, with good public schools, with its democratic ideals and ideology, with land too abundant to be socially decisive, except in the cities. Americans were ready to look on schooling as preparation for doing, as a source of credentials. Eric Hobsbawm cites European data on the period before World War I: Britain in 1913 had only nine thousand university students, as against almost sixty thousand in Germany. Germany was producing some 3,000 graduate engineers per year, whereas England and Wales were turning out some 350 graduates with first- and second-class honors in all branches of science, technology, and math, and few of these were qualified to do research. Hobsbawm states that "this purely statistical phenomenon need not have been accompanied by a genuine loss of impetus and efficiency," but I think he is wrong there. Not only was the supply of knowledge and talent diminished thereby, but the data hint of and reflect larger anti-productive prejudices.[10]

Certainly the United States and other ambitious societies suffered from similar, if lesser, shortcomings. Every American city and town had its social geography, its good and poor neighborhoods, its mansions and its slum housing. Almost any newspaper worthy of the name had its society reporting, its announcements and accounts of elegant events. Besides, the role of politics in American life was if anything enhanced by the absence of monarchy and aristocracy. In a world of political parties and open competition for power, politics became a form of personal fulfillment, a pathway to prestige, a ticket to influence and money. And, conversely, the more successful the business enterprise, the harder to keep descendants from using money to achieve higher status, buy power, and multiply wealth. The career of the present American president, George W. Bush, heir to an oil fortune, is testimony to the process: remunerative business posts with firms seeking useful political connections; advance inside information to be exploited for personal advantage; privileged access to sports franchises; a ticket to office, appointive and elective.[11] Business in the United States has never conformed to the rational purity of liberal economic theory, or to legal prohibitions of inside maneuver. These last are enforced intermittently and selectively. (Ask Martha Stewart.)

Within this context, the gratifications of one generation may not be those of the next. We have seen how Rockefeller and Ford children of three removes from the founder came back from school filled with shame and regret for the alleged misdeeds of their ancestors—attitudes conveyed and cherished by envious teachers and fellow students; and how the very habit of wealth and authority, spoilage from above, encouraged them in their rebellious scorn and condemnation. This is the revenge of the have-nots or the not-yets, the more potent for the inability of wealthy fathers and grandfathers to find effective reply. On the other hand, school may suggest new and fruitful lines of activity, while marriage with people of virtue and prestige can alter a family, producing children who want to escape the money heritage (but of course not entirely) for what they see as more honorific.

Others are only too ready to push these deserters aside and take their place. One should not underestimate the interest and attractions of business activity. The pursuit of opportunity and the negotiation of deals can furnish endless excitement and amusement—such as courtship with money as the reward, and often sex as well. And the dull day-to-day details can be assigned to clerks and typists. Besides, as with the Rockefellers, Agnellis, Toyoda, and others, nothing constrains an enterprise to the specialty of the founders. On the contrary, money, connections, and imagination are invitations to diversification, and this more than ever in the period since World War II, our age of the so-called conglomerate.

The multicompetent firm, even if it starts as a family enterprise, builds on the diversity and availability of managerial talent and ambition to combine family and partners, and produce a multiplicity of outcomes. This very openness can lead to family withdrawal and conversion of firms to managerial corporations. It also can yield an increasing number of entrepreneurial dynasties: generations devoted to a changing array of remunerative pursuits. The founding family may keep an interest in its original area, may even cook the statutes in such a way as to ensure continued influence and preponderance of votes, all the while branching out into other enterprises (remember the Rothschilds).

Take the Wallenbergs, Sweden's first business family. They made their start in banking, with the Stockholm Enskilda Bank, founded in 1856 by André Oscar Wallenberg. From there they moved out into industry, founding or joining an array of the leading multinationals in their country: ASEA, Electrolux, Ericsson, Saab-Scania, SKF, Stora. At the end of the twentieth century, these firms made up some 40 percent of Sweden's capitalization on the exchange. The Wallenbergs would not necessarily hold a large part of the stock of these firms, but typically they held most of the votes because they knew how to lend. For the British review *The Economist*, the Wallenbergs are the outstanding European industrial dynasty, five generations of highly successful entrepreneurs. For their historian David Bartal, they are a Japanese-style family, Europe's most powerful of its kind, more discreet than the Agnellis and richer than the Rothschilds. Add up the sales of all the companies in the Wallenberg empire at the close of the twentieth century, and you will find that one had more than ninety billion dollars a year, ahead of British Petroleum, IBM, or General Electric. It was then Europe's largest private-sector employer by sales after Shell. But look for a "Wallenberg Inc." and you would be disappointed.[12] Discretion above all.

That kind of diversification demands, as we have seen, the support and assistance of henchmen: technicians and managers who have mastered or can master the special requirements of a given activity. This outside collaboration would characterize even a single firm, for technology does not stand still, and no family can count on finding among its own descendants and marriage partners the talent and knowledge required. Still, some do much better here than others. Thus the Koechlin of Alsace: Samuel Koechlin, founder of the first textile printing plant in the region, had sixteen children; three generations later, his descendants were still making an average of 5.2 children per household. We are talking hundreds of people. And Koechlin tradition and pride expected children to go to the best schools and get the kind of training that could be turned to productive and profitable use. Over the course of a century, they became a one-family industry, producing descendants as well as manufactures.

As noted, the need for outside help increases exponentially with variety, or what Michel Hau would call the reinvention of the business. It is this intrinsic dependency that has led students of the subject to argue that family enterprise is finished, kaput, and that any seriously ambitious business must assume, indeed must begin by assuming, the managerial form. I would not agree. The facts do not agree. Read if you can Hau's study of the Dietrich industrial dynasty in Alsace and the ability of that metalworking firm to alter its product mix and technologies over centuries. Here we have testimony to the ability of loyal family members cherishing the right values to resist the pull of alternative activities and lifestyles and to sustain the competition of modernity.[13]

Yet as numerous examples have shown, the two styles of enterprise can coexist, indeed, can even draw advantages from such coexistence. We saw this with Ford. There the task of corporate evolution was urgent. The initial attempt to move to a managerial model while remaining a family firm left the company between hither and yon, losing not simply profits but substance and fighting for survival. Over time, however, the Fords have won that fight and maintained family influence, if not complete control, while becoming a major multinational. But they could not have done so without the collaboration of growing numbers of trained outside execs. Recourse to managerial structure, in other words, while offering no guarantees, can make all the difference to new structures and new models, especially after initial family generations give way to less gifted and less interested successors.

Death, however, has a way of reopening the discussion: managers have less patience for successors they knew as children. But conversion to a managerial model is no assurance of good results. It may help; at least one has reason to hope so. But the examples of mismanaged managerial enterprises are legion—even among the stars. For one thing, the temptation to solve problems by appointing additional executives is almost irresistible; for another, it is only too easy to imagine or create problems by way of justifying personnel inflation. In contrast to Ford, take General Motors, once the model of efficient, effective governance. By the fifties and sixties, the swollen finance staff on the fourteenth floor of the headquarters building became a confusion of meetings and surveys and plannings and verifications, while operations people went mad with frustration. When the car parts finally came together on the assembly line, they needed all manner of retouches before they fit, and often it was cheaper to scrap them. Design and fashion changes found an uncertain, plodding response. "GM . . . was no longer able to maneuver responsively in the marketplace."[14] It took a couple of decades, into the 1980s, for the company to wake to the necessity of a revolution from above; and another quarter-century to recognize the desirability of a major purge of variants by way of standardizing final product.[15]

GETTING BACK TO FAMILY ENTERPRISES, much depends on reproductive capacity: how prolific the families are and on what level. The Alsatian pool, we saw, was huge and self-consciously distinctive and united. Well-chosen marriage there could make up for genealogical and commercial shortcomings. But these, as shown by the Chrysler story, can be fatal within a generation. Such outcomes are especially dependent on rules. Some cultures will not allow in-laws or even daughters into the firm; for business purposes they are defined as outsiders. Others are far more open, not only welcoming marital allies but permitting enlargement of the family by adoption.[16]

Take a quadricentennial case study: Saint-Gobain, maker of glass and chemicals, the oldest industrial firm in France.[17] It was founded by Louis XIV in 1665—noble antecedents—and was reborn as a private company in 1830. In the interwar years of the twentieth century, it owned half a dozen plants in France, Belgium, and Germany. It accounted for almost half of Belgium's glass and a fifth of the German make, was increasing and diversifying chemical output, kept growing, and financed all this by attracting new share- and bondholders, whose numbers leapt in the 1920s from two thousand to forty thousand. Withal, family control going back to 1830 was not lost, although other families that had joined via successive mergers now shared control. And although managing execs were hired to deal with new equipment and technologies, strategy and financing remained in the same hands.

It was the period after World War II that finally put an end to these comfortable, resourceful arrangements. Research and finance needed professional outsiders, while share ownership rose from 45,000 in 1945 to 180,000 in 1960. Diversification undermined harmony—too many experts—and such branches as artificial fibers and chemicals were having trouble holding their own with such international giants as Italian Montedison and British ICI. In an effort to rationalize, the company hived off the weaker branches—weakness is, we know, a great attraction to purchasers who think they can do better. None of this would have been possible without philoprogenitive reproduction and eager participation, and this in the face of bicentennial and longer social eminence. How many corporations in France could boast of a chairman named Armand de Vogüé? But all good things must come to an end.

Returning to the question of place in influencing the success of family firms, the laws that govern inheritance, tax arrangements, and similarly relevant institutions—that is, the institutions that help determine whether you can keep the money you earn—make some places more favorable to dynasties than others. Only recently, an article in *The New York Times* made much of a strong tendency for the power in Canadian corporations to remain with the founding family: "Family-controlled public companies exist in many countries, including the United States, but they are a particular hallmark of Canadian business." The United States, the argument ran, has a frontier tradition (still!) and expects individuals to carve out their own destiny, whereas Canadian fathers are said to have been indulgent and protective of their offspring.[18]

Place is thus defined by people, by the knowledge, values, and aspirations of the indigenous population as well as by legal regulations. In Western Europe, the United States, China, and Japan, the general level of knowledge and access to capital and resources is high and more or less equally distributed. Successful entrepreneurship can come from everywhere and nowhere, with a certain advantage to those social groups that encourage education and family support. In other places, especially so-called Third World countries, the mass of the indigenous population has neither the resources nor the knowledge and interest, nor the mutual trust, nor the wise and fair government, to pursue business consistently and successfully. Not coincidentally, that role is played largely by immigrants—in East Asia (the East Indies, Myanmar, Malaysia, the Philippines) by Chinese expats, in some parts of Latin America by American gringos.

These countries may show semirespectable gross income and production data, but distribution is disastrously unequal. The rich outsiders typically scorn and avoid mingling with the natives. They see them as stupid, lazy, superstitious, and dirty, yet are ready to employ them as workers in shops and factories and as servants in the intimacy of their homes. The logical consequence of this gap in status and wealth and of this condescension is an abiding resentment that often finds expression in violence and crime. Nor are the native police ready to pursue or punish those responsible for such misdeeds. What do these foreigners expect? Their very arrogance invites and deserves assault. As a result, the "visitors" are reluctant to invest in hard but vulnerable installations, preferring to export wealth to safe places abroad, thus substantially limiting the larger capacity for growth.

Read on this point the important, vivid account by Amy Chua, professor at Yale Law School and member of a Chinese Filipino dynasty, whose aunt was murdered by a thug with the connivance of two inside maids:

> My family is part of the Philippines' tiny but entrepreneurial and economically powerful Chinese minority. Although they constitute just one percent of the population, Chinese Filipinos control as much as 60 percent of the private economy, including the country's four major airlines and almost all of the country's banks, hotels, shopping malls, and big conglomerates. My own family in Manila runs a plastics conglomerate. . . . My relatives are only "third-tier" Chinese tycoons. Still, they own swaths of prime real estate and several vacation homes. They also have safe deposit boxes full of gold bars. . . . I myself have such a gold bar. My Aunt Leona express-mailed it to me as a law school graduation present a few years before she died.

Chua's aunt loved diamonds, bought them by the dozen, hid them in face cream jars on the bathroom shelf. One might think the motive for murder was theft and booty. But the police wrote only one word on the record: "Revenge." The two maids, having confessed, were simply released. The killer was never apprehended. No one was trying.[19]

As these reflections show, place and culture, linked and mutually reinforcing, count. They shape the ability of a population to work well and to work together. They also shape the choice of activity, whether by availability of raw materials, proximity to markets, or just plain climate. (Too much heat, for example, is a serious deterrent to diligence.) And less obviously, they help determine choice by genius and flair. It is no coincidence, for example, that France holds the lead in fashion manufacture: the French have made a specialty of such products and have persuaded the world that they have better taste.

The natural advantages of place (availability of raw materials, for example) can be compensated by modern transport and technologies of substitution; while national preferences can be countered by political and commercial (tariff) deals. So backward places can learn to catch up and compete with their predecessors, as long as they have enterprising people and the right kind of firms. But cultural advantages are another matter. They are not easily emulated, and the emissaries sent abroad to learn or the travelers who learn while abroad are not always ready to return home. Export of human talent can be more durable than export of capital or commodities.

Much know-how, of course, is transmitted by media of communication, which often suggest and stimulate voyages of exploration. Here, too, place matters. Anglophone societies have an advantage over other linguistic groups, because English is the nearest thing to a world language; and among the anglophones, the United States leads in the production of entertainment. No one can match Hollywood for action and excitement, or for the conveying of tacit messages regarding style and manners, to the point where manufacturers use and pay for films as a silent advertising medium. As a result, the United States exports styles and manners even to those nations that enforce strenuous protections against commodities. Thus anti-American crowds take such American chains as McDonald's as a preferred target. They see such hangouts as the instruments of cultural infiltration and imperialism.

We are talking pride here as well as anger, and we live in a time of heightened awareness and sensitivity; pride matters. The same France that exports fashion and wines spends a fortune promoting its national film industry and book trade, to say nothing of defending the national language and enticing tourists and visiting students. Even the French attitude toward British entry into the European Union has been shaped by the desire to establish French as the master language of the group; better that the Germans learn to speak French than English. At the end of the twentieth century, France was pulling in some sixty million visitors a year, more than any other country. The enterprises and monuments so endorsed and funded are typically either public institutions (museums and schools) or family business firms: hotels, restaurants, producers and sellers of antiques and "antiques," book publishers and sellers. In that way, France wins and holds worldwide admiration; and here, too, "backward" countries have learned and tried to imitate.[20]

For all the risks and mistakes of polyvalent and multinational enterprise, it unquestionably lends itself more to managerial than to familial structures. It is in this sense that the managerial form is the handmaiden of modern, global capitalism. Along with this goes a new geographical distribution of economic activity, one that takes account of the cost and availability of labor and local supervision. The gap in product and income is growing between places that lend themselves to new kinds of work and thereby find favor, and those that are neglected or avoided. To be sure, the rapid rise of longtime laggards such as China and India yields global statistics of overall world equalization: Asia, or at least some parts thereof, is catching up with the old-time leaders in Western Europe and overseas offshoots.[21] But the hard backward core—Africa, the Muslim Middle East, and most of Latin America—is falling ever farther behind. In all of these places we are talking about badly ruled, ill-educated populations marked by sexual inequalities and worshipful of machismo and associated empty virtues.[22] For such societies, globalization could be a huge gift, the fastest path to modernity. But why should rational managerial enterprise move there? The way I see it, these people *need* family capitalism. In a world of unequal development, the older forms that rest on personal trust and affection have enormous value.

All in all, it is hard to gauge the truth of the accepted distinctions between familial and managerial modes, or clearly to determine how well one or the other type of enterprise performs. Each has its advantages and limitations; each has its role to play. "It is almost a truism," Stanley Chapman tells us, "that the best small and medium-sized firms are the real growth points of the economy."[23] In contrast, Gordon Pitts, author of *In the Blood: Battles to Succeed in Canadian Business* (2001), says that the most successful business families have been those that have known how to step aside and turn the firm over to professionals.

Yes and no, then. There is a lot of work still to be done on this subject. In the meantime, the family firm is alive and well and continues often to pass the heritage down the generations. That is because it rests on human emotion and impulse that transcend and survive political and economic interruption and interference. It is, in fact, indispensable.

Notes

PREFACE AND ACKNOWLEDGMENTS

1. As we'll see in chapter 7, the family chose to change the business name to the familiar "Toyota" for a number of interesting cultural reasons.
2. In France, for instance, a recent report puts the figure at 60–70 percent, and states that more than half of the country's 250 largest traded firms on the Paris Stock Exchange were controlled by families or individuals. Quoted from "Multi-generational French Family Firms" by Christine Blondel and Ludo Van der Heyden, in *Families in Business*, April 2002.
3. Cf. François Crouzet, "Editorial," *Entreprises et histoire* 9 (September 1995): 6. An excellent source of information on business forms and numbers thereof is Jacques Marseille, ed., *Créateurs et création d'entreprises*. On the one third of the biggest five hundred and best performers, see *BusinessWeek*, 10 November 2003, pp. 100ff., which credits earlier research by Ronald C. Anderson and David M. Reeb published in the June 2003 issue of the *Journal of Finance*. More on these comparisons later.
4. For the early history of the German industry, see Peter Hayes, *Industry and Ideology* (New York: Cambridge University Press, 1987), part I.
5. Ibid., p. 3. For IG Farben, though, the highest duty was to the German government, and this turned out to be a poor and immoral ideal.
6. Ibid., p. 220. Sobel took this particular story from an economist named John Moody—no reference given.
7. *BusinessWeek*, 10 November 2003, p. 102. *BusinessWeek* itself is part of such a family firm. The parent corporation is McGraw-Hill, led by Harold W. McGraw III, grandson of the founder.
8. François Caron et al., "La question dynastique," *Enterprises et histoire* 12 (1996): 113.
9. *Les Schneider, Le Creusot*, Paris: Fayard, 1995 (pp. 146–47).

PART ONE: BANKING

1. "If the merchant fell out of favour, it was always possible for the prince to confiscate his property." Cf. Charles VII, who, "acting in what nineteenth-century Europeans would have almost universally condemned as an arbitrary and despotic manner," confiscated three mining enterprises in the Lyonnais and Beaujolais belonging to Jacques Coeur, "the most glamorous merchant of the fifteenth century." Nef, "Mining and Metallurgy," *Cambridge Economic History of Europe*, 1st ed., II, 485; 2d ed., II, 751. Jacques Heers sees this very differently: these were the king's mines.

2. *Encyclopaedia Britannica*, 11th ed., *s.v.* Medici. See also G. F. Young, *The Medici* (New York: Modern Library, 1930); and Christopher Hibbert, *The House of Medici* (New York: William Morrow, 1975).

3. On these high rates, cf. Braudel, *Civilisation matérielle*, III, 125. Only the poorest and richest could afford/accept such rates.

4. A superb analysis of this "irresistible rise of German banking" is to be found in Jean-François Bergier, "From the Fifteenth Century in Italy," pp. 116*ff*.

5. Cited in Ron Chernow, *The House of Morgan* (New York: Simon & Schuster, 1990), p. 20. Bagehot (1826–1877) was the son of a banker and maintained a close connection with banking for many years. He married the daughter of the first editor of *The Economist* and was himself for many years editor of that journal.

6. Martin Wiener, *English Culture and the Decline of the Industrial Spirit* (Cambridge: C.U.P., 1981), p. 127. An excellent survey of the influence of culture on social and national performance.

7. Lisle-Williams, "Beyond the Market: The Survival of Family Capitalism in the English Merchant Banks," in Mary Rose, ed., *Family Business*, p. 548. The article, p. 570, gives a list of thirty-six names.

CHAPTER ONE: THE BARINGS

1. Philip Ziegler, *The Sixth Great Power* (New York: Knopf, 1988), pp. 44–45. This is the major source for the history of the bank.

2. Ibid., p. 17.

3. Ibid., p. 23.

4. Ibid., p. 44.

5. Ibid.

6. From a letter of 1803 from Francis Baring to his son's father-in-law, William Bingham, in the United States, cited in ibid., pp. 44–45.

7. Ibid.

8. Ibid., p. 45.

9. Lord Erskine in *Gentleman's Magazine*, 1810, cited in Ziegler, *Sixth Great Power*, p. 51.

10. On Hamburg as a major center of trade and exchange, even in a period of French prohibitions and controls, see François Crouzet, *L'économie britannique et le blocus continental 1806–1813* (Paris: Economica, 1988), p. 225 and 40n.

11. J. E. Winston, "How the Louisiana Purchase Was Financed," *Louisiana Historical Quarterly*, XII, 2 (April 1929).

12. Ziegler, *Sixth Great Power*, p. 83.

13. Like royalty, the Barings entertained a limited choice of forenames, which complicates the task of the genealogist and historian.

14. Contrast the American house of William and James Brown and Co., whose Liverpool branch was an active supporter of British manufacturing firms in the Manchester area. They made good money in the 1820s and early '30s, but when the crisis came, Brown's found itself overextended. William Brown, senior partner, gave up: "Nothing can be worse than the news. It is quite certain we cannot sustain ourselves." John A. Kouwenhoven, *Partners in Banking* (Garden City, N.Y.: Doubleday, 1968), ch. 5.

15. Ziegler, *Sixth Great Power*, p. 124.

16. Ibid., pp. 272, 299.

17. Ibid., p. 187.

18. It was notable that he chose not to add to the family lands in Hampshire—eighty-nine thousand acres owned by various Barings, where the rich went hunting. The British fascination with mass animal slaughter is impenetrable to me: in 1887, a Baring hunting party set a family record, shooting 4,076 partridges on Lord Ashburton's land over a four-day stretch. Ibid., p. 188.

19. Ibid., p. 246, drawing on L. S. Pressnell, "Gold Reserves, Banking Reserves, and the Baring Crisis of 1890," in C. R. Whittlesey and J.S.G. Wilson, eds., *Essays in Money and Banking in Honour of R. S. Sayers* (Oxford: Oxford University Press, 1968), pp.167–228, and H. S. Ferns, "The Baring Crisis Revisited," *Journal of Latin American Studies* 24 (1992): 241–73.

20. Ziegler, *Sixth Great Power*, p. 253.

21. Ibid., p. 257.

22. Ibid., p. 270.

23. David Sinclair, *Dynasty: The Astors and Their Times* (New York: Beaufort, 1984), p. 284.

24. Ziegler, *Sixth Great Power*, p. 286.

25. Ibid., p. 339.

26. Ibid., p. 358.

27. On Tuckey, see John Gapper and Nicholas Denton, *All That Glitters: The Fall of Barings* (New York: Penguin, 1997), p. 3. On the World Bank contract, which owed much to Nicholas Baring's earlier employment and contacts there, see ibid., p. 100. Also on the last, unhappy years of the bank, see Stephen Fay, *The Collapse of Barings: Panic, Ignorance, and Greed* (London: Arrow Business Books, 1996).

28. Joseph Wechsberg, *The Merchant Bankers* (New York: Little, Brown, 1966), p. 121.

29. Gapper and Denton, *All That Glitters*, p. 114.

30. Judith H. Rawnsley, *Total Risk: Nick Leeson and the Fall of Barings Bank* (New York: HarperCollins, 1996), p. 140.

31. Leeson tried to flee to Europe but was arrested in Frankfurt and returned to Singapore for trial. He ended up spending a few years in prison. It goes without saying that he will never be able to pay the cost of his misdeeds. But he has written a book of memoirs and apologia, *Rogue Trader* (New York: Little, Brown, 1996).

32. See J. Treaster, "Big Dutch Insurer Sizes Up Potential Takeovers," in *New York Times*, 25 May 2001, p. W1.

CHAPTER TWO: THE ROTHSCHILDS

1. Wechsberg, *Merchant Bankers*, pp. 263–64.

2. Ziegler, *Sixth Great Power*, p. 13.

3. The term "ghetto" originated in Venice to describe the closed Jewish quarter there. The word is derived from the Venetian "geto," meaning foundry, as the first zone assigned to the Jews was near a new foundry, and was thus called "Ghetto Nuovo." The model of moving Jews into small enclaves spread throughout Europe until the French Revolution, an era that began a wave of Jewish emancipation. The term was put back into use by the Nazis in the 1930s.

4. Since writing this, I have learned that there is a Jewish doctrine that bars looking at others in this manner and calls for boarding up windows that permit prying and spying. So one might say that the burghers of Frankfurt were simply helping the Jews live up to their own rules.

5. There is an abundant library of material on the early history of the Rothschilds and on Jewish society and culture in eighteenth-century continental Europe. See especially Corti, *The Rise of the House of Rothschild*, and Berghoeffer, *Mayer Amschel Rothschild*.

6. Among the contacts, one proved exceptionally valuable, that with the family of Thurn und Taxis (the origin of our word "taxi"), hereditary postmasters of the Holy Roman Empire since the sixteenth century. From the 1780s on, Mayer Amschel lent the princes money and discounted their paper. In return, the princes provided the latest news and rapid courier service. Invaluable, and a characteristic feature of Rothschild performance in years to come. As they grew ever richer, the children of Mayer Amschel, with "Rothschild" now added to their name, spent a small fortune on couriers, coaches, sailing vessels, and uncounted bribes to move information and commodities across frontiers. Amos Elon, *Founder: A Portrait of the First Rothschild and His Time* (New York: Viking, 1996), p. 75; Joan Littlewood, *Baron Philippe* (New York: Crown, 1984), preface: "About the Rothschilds." All of it paid.

7. We have a library of work on British economic precocity. But see, inter alia, the numerous citations of eighteenth-century economic literature in the unfortunately neglected study by Rick Szostak, *The Role of Transportation in the Industrial Revolution* (Montreal and London: McGill-Queen's University Press, 1991). One would have thought the English and Scots were working in a world of their own.

8. For a closer approach to the decision to travel to Britain, see Niall Ferguson, *World's Banker*, pp. 51–52.

9. On the role of these Christian houses, see Louis Bergeron, *Les Rothschild et les autres* (Paris: Perrin, 1991).

10. Vansittart to Herries, 11 January 1814, cited in Derek Wilson, *Rothschild: The Wealth and Power of a Dynasty* (New York: Scribner's Sons, 1988), p. 53.

11. Anka Muhlstein, *Baron James: The Rise of the French Rothschilds*, p. 54, citing Gille, *Histoire de la maison Rothschild*, I (Geneva: Droz), p. 71.

12. Cf. Ferguson, *World's Banker*, pp. 78–79.

13. On the Mendelssohn clan: Heinrich Graetz, *History of the Jews*, vol. 5 (Philadelphia: The Jewish Publishing Society of America, 1964); and Sebastian Hensel, *Die Familie Mendelssohn* (Leipzig: Insel-Verlag, 1924). Also David S. Landes, "The Bleichröder Bank," p. 208.

14. Muhlstein, *Baron James*, pp. 75 76.

15. Some of this appears in ibid. Their daughter Charlotte later married Lionel, son of Nathan Mayer, and left correspondence, together with extraordinary diaries of the life of the family, in German. These are preserved in the Rothschild Archive.

16. To each according to taste and pretension. Cecil Roth, author of a Rothschild family history, also did a book on the Sassoons of Baghdad, *The Sassoon Dynasty* (London: Hale, 1941) claimants to descent from King David, whom he contrasts with such nouveaux riches as the Rothschilds. With regard to the marriages of Rothschilds, see the passage in Charlotte's journal devoted to daughter Leonora, nickname Laury, a hard-to-please adolescent. "Laury attaches much importance to a certain position in the world and would not like to descend from what she fancies to be the throne of the Rothschilds to be the bride of a humbler man. I begin to think that there is not much love left, not much love lost in the world. So much the better—at best it is a dangerous passion, dangerous in its results, in its influence over many years, the best years of a woman's life." Charlotte had Laury's Paris cousin Alphonse in mind, son of James, and it was Alphonse whom she married in 1857. Meanwhile, James, youngest of the five sons of Mayer Amschel and head of the late-born Paris house, had risen to such exalted status that eager stockbrokers saluted his gilt chamber pot when it was carried before them through the office to be emptied.

17. On these matters, cf. Niall Ferguson, *World's Banker*, p. 196. The family had room for anomalies. In her latter years, Adelaide Herz became

dotty and thought herself a teapot; and in Rothschild family circles, that is the nickname she is still known by: Teapot. Muhlstein, *Baron James,* p. 219, chap. 4, 14n.

18. This was not Hannah's first Gentile suitor. When the Prince de Clary asked for her hand during the lifetime of her father, Nathan not only sent him packing but also added a clause to his will that his daughters would be disinherited if they married without the consent of mother and brothers. Virginia Cowles, *The Rothschilds,* p. 94.

19. James to Nathaniel, June 29, 1839. I have relied mostly on the translation in Ferguson, *World's Banker,* p. 339, but also on Richard Davis, *The English Rothschilds* (Chapel Hill: University of North Carolina Press, 1984), p. 60, and have made a few emendations of my own.

20. James to Nathaniel, July 16, 1839. Once again, Ferguson, *World's Banker,* p. 340, and Davis, *English Rothschilds,* p. 60.

21. "He would be taught riding like all the Fitzroys, so that in later years he would have the seat of a born horseman." Robert Henrey, *A Century Between,* p. 75.

22. Ferguson, *World's Banker,* p. 345.

23. Nathan Mayer never had much interest in genteel country living. As his family grew, he decided to buy a suburban home near London, but was careful not to give in to show. For one thing, Herries cautioned him against display; he had enough trouble with jealous competitors, critics, and anti-Semites.

24. As any reader of the Bible knows, the horse is the mount of the autocratic, tyrannical ruler and his bullying henchmen. When one has a small elite on horses, one has a class-ridden society with equestrian masters above the divider and pedestrian masses below.

25. They are said to have been encouraged here by their mother, Hannah, who thought hunting good for one's health—one way to Judaize and justify this un-Jewish activity. Davis, *English Rothschilds,* p. 65. Nathan Mayer apparently did not discourage this anglicization—also on health grounds.

26. Russia was a special case. The big Western banking house there remained Hopes, and the Rothschilds, as always, disliked markets where they held a subordinate position. They would have liked to interest Britons and Frenchmen in the prosperity and stability of the Russian state, by way of preserving peace in Europe. But they wanted to do it inexpensively and safely—a small amount of debt bought outright, the rest on commission, returnable if unsold.

27. In a letter to his nephews in London, May 25, 1837. Project report to the Rothschild Archive, 28 May 2003.

28. These letters as cited in Gille, *Histoire de la maison Rothschild,* II, pp. 581–82.

29. Letter of 19 April 1849, ibid., II, p. 582.

30. Ernest Feydeau, *Mémoires d'un coulissier,* pp. 149–50, cited in Muhlstein, *Baron James,* p. 195.

31. On this revised version of the financial revolution of the mid-nineteenth century, see David S. Landes, "Vieille banque et banque nouvelle: la révolution financière du dix-neuvième siècle," *Rev. d'hist. mod. et contemp.* 3 (1956): 204–22.

32. On the Fould, see Bergeron, *Les Rothschild et les autres,* pp. 84–85. He writes: "The contrast is evidently striking between the achievement of social integration and the decline of the banking enterprise."

33. Ferguson, *World's Banker,* p. 554.

34. Ibid., p. 555.

35. On Bleichröder's, see especially Fritz Stern, *Gold and Iron* (New York, Knopf, 1977).

36. This was the Bank für Handel and Industrie, organized in 1853 by Gustave Mevissen, economist and projector (a little like d'Eichthal or Isaac Pereire), and Abraham Oppenheim of Sal. Oppenheim, Jr., and Company, of Cologne.

37. Gille, *Histoire de la maison Rothschild,* II, p.558; Myska, "La sidérurgie en Moravie et en Silésie," *Revue d'Histoire de la Sidérurgie* 5 (1964): 71.

38. Wilson, *Rothschild,* p. 132.

39. Understandably, Treasury officials wanted to diversify rather than depend on a single source. It was important here for the Rothschilds to be seen as both multinational and French. One of the primary considerations was to exclude German intermediaries, including the Rothschild houses in Frankfurt and Vienna. On the story of the indemnity loans: David S. Landes, "The Spoilers Foiled" 2: 67–110; Ferguson, *World's Banker,* chap. 22.

40. Letter of January 1872, cited in Ferguson, *World's Banker,* p. 736.

41. Ibid., p. 735.

42. He is not mentioned, for example, in Edmund de Rothschild's text or genealogical table. *Edmund de Rothschild A Gilt-Edged Life,* pp. 230–31.

43. Wilson, *Rothschild,* pp. 334–35.

44. Ferguson, *World's Banker,* p. 1018; also Cowles, *The Rothschilds,* pp. 11–12.

45. Cowles, *The Rothschilds,* p. 199.

46. Littlewood, *Baron Philippe,* p. 283.

47. See Suzanne Kapner, "Rothschild Prepares for Changing of Guard," *New York Times,* 11 February 2003, p. W1.

Chapter Three: The Morgans

1. On the early history of the family, see especially Herbert Satterlee, *J. Pierpont Morgan,* chap. 1.

2. Chernow, *House of Morgan,* p. 40. This has been my most important source. See also Jean Strouse, *Morgan.*

3. Chernow, *House of Morgan,* p. 114.

4. Ibid., p. 115.

5. Railroad investment doubled in that decade, from $5.4 billion to $10.1 billion. Vincent Carosso, *The Morgans: Private International Bankers, 1854–1913,* p. 247.

6. Cf. Charles Geisst, *Wall Street,* p. 115. Chernow, *House of Morgan,* p. 84, offers a somewhat different version.

7. These walking moneybags had their predecessors—in France, the Duc de Galliéra, Jean-Louis Greffulhe, the Demachy family. Some of these came to banking via the practice of law and notarial services. These last undertook among other activities the creation and monetization of paper debt instruments. On these houses and others, see Bergeron, *Les Rothschild et les autres.*

8. On all this, see Carosso, *Morgans,* pp. 530–33.

9. But to begin with, Morgan gave a big contribution to Roosevelt's 1904 campaign—big by political standards, but a trifle in return for financial favoritism, specifically the valuable right to participate in the merger of U.S. Steel and Tennessee Coal and Iron. The governor of Massachusetts, Thomas R. Marshall, called Morgan a tightwad. Strouse, *Morgan,* p. 666.

10. On this aspect of J.P.'s life, see Francis H. Taylor, *Pierpont Morgan as Collector and Patron;* Cass Canfield, *The Incredible Pierpont Morgan;* and Strouse, *Morgan,* pp. 606ff. and passim.

11. Excerpts from Carosso, *The Morgans,* chap. 18, and Chernow, *House of Morgan,* pp. 154–55.

12. Cf. Stanley Jackson, *J. P. Morgan,* p. 310.

13. Carosso, *Morgans,* p. 643.

14. On these questions of management style: Martin Vander Weyer, *Falling Eagle,* p. 208, who cites David Rogers, *The Future of American Banking* (New York: McGraw-Hill, 1992).

15. Cf. Steven Birmingham, *"Our Crowd,"* p. 349f.

16. Edward Lamont, *The Ambassador from Wall Street,* pp. 41–47. My presumption is that the bank paid for these outings, over and above salary and bonuses. Nothing was too good for such good men.

17. On earlier bank financing for Durant, by a syndicate led by J. and W. Seligman and Lee, Higginson, see Carosso, *Morgans,* p. 605. This was in 1910, after the turndown by Morgan's.

18. Chernow, *House of Morgan,* p. 224; Alfred D. Chandler, ed., *Giant Enterprise,* pp. 71–86.

19. But he had his lucky moments. He was supposed to travel to New York in 1912 on the maiden voyage of the *Titanic,* which was built with support from the Morgan bank and held an elaborate personal suite for J.P. that included, among other things, special cigar holders in the bathroom. (That is the test of an addicted smoker: he smokes in the bath.) But he had had to cancel and got an extra year of life for his disappointment.

20. Cited in John Douglas Forbes, *J. P. Morgan, Jr.,* p. 75.

21. Ibid., p. 78.
22. But Carosso, *The Morgans,* p. 452, stresses the respect that J.P. and Jacob Schiff of Kuhn, Loeb had for each other, in spite of their competition in business matters. Schiff was an observant Jew, and perhaps J.P. liked them better that way. Still, business was one thing, socializing another. As J.P. put it, "You can do business with anyone, but only sail with a gentleman." Naomi Cohen, *Jacob H. Schiff,* pp. 23–24. The first Jewish hire by the firm Morgan, Stanley took place in 1963: Lewis W. Bernard, roommate at Princeton of a son of a Morgan partner. By then Jack Morgan was long gone, and the company had fallen to strangers. Even so, some of the old-timers found such openness hard to swallow. Chernow, *House of Morgan,* p. 581. On the general exclusion of Jews from business and society—the Morgans had plenty of company—see Ferdinand Lundberg, *The Rich and Super-rich,* chap. 8. See also Chernow, *House of Morgan,* pp. 40, 214–17; and Forbes, *J. P. Morgan, Jr.,* pp. 114–17.
23. Chernow, *House of Morgan,* p. 257, says that the firm preferentially found places for members of the royal family ("23 Wall never had rules against nepotism"), but was otherwise meritocratic: "Any white, Christian male might qualify." One further constraint on choice and continuity of partners: no divorce. J.P. was a pious gentleman who saw no contradiction between wedlock and amours, but saw divorce as a sign of bad character.
24. Cf. Forbes, *J. P. Morgan, Jr.,* pp. 116–17.
25. Ibid., p. x.
26. Chernow, *House of Morgan,* pp. 408, 472–73, thinks this lofty living "frittered away much of the fortune that would have gone to his heirs." On the high cost of self-indulgence and its devastating effect on British family fortunes, see David Cannadine, *The Decline and Fall of the British Aristocracy* (New York: Vintage, 1999).
27. Bo Bramsen and Kathleen Wain, *The Hambros 1779–1979.*
28. Chernow, *House of Morgan,* p. 431.
29. Goldman, Sachs, German Jewish expatriates, had split over this issue in World War I. Henry Goldman, senior partner and passionate Germanophile, moved out of the office rather than work with or in the presence of his faithless relations. His sister, married to a Sachs, never spoke to him again. As the years passed, he became increasingly embittered, and in the early thirties he began looking for a suitable residence in Germany. Wrong place, wrong time.
30. Chernow, *House of Morgan,* pp. 452–53.
31. Morgan's were not alone here. One of the directors of the Hottinguer bank of Paris, a pillar in France of high-Protestant banking integrity, boasted that he could recognize on the phone the voice of each and every one of his three hundred personal clients. "That way I can salute them before they have the time to introduce themselves."

32. Chernow, *House of Morgan*, p. 530.
33. See Jathon Sapsford, "J. P. Morgan May Be Facing Real Change," *Wall Street Journal*, 19 January 2004, p. C1.
34. The house reeked with customs, genuine and invented. Chernow tells of a guest surprised to see the waiter dropping dirty ice cubes in his tea. Just in time, he realized that these cubes were not simply frozen water, but frozen tea. Lord, keep us from dilution. By the same token, the bank used to encourage attendance at partners' meetings by giving *jetons de présence* in the form of gold coins. That was money. But when such currency disappeared, ten- or twenty-dollar bills took its place. The remainder due to absences was customarily divided among those present. The only full house, we are told, came during a heavy snowstorm, when everyone thought he would be alone and take the entire kitty. (See Chernow, *House of Morgan*, p. 530.)
35. *Wall Street Journal Europe,* article by Charles Gasparino and Jathon Sapsford, 19 October 2000, p. 6.
36. *New York Times,* 15 January 2004, p. A1.
37. Patrick McGeehan, "Old Money Gives Way to Main Street," *New York Times*, 25 January 2001, p. C1.

PART TWO: AUTOMOBILES

1. Numerous devices and techniques developed for cycle manufacture found further application in the auto industry: ball bearings, chain transmission, various systems of gearing, pneumatic tires, and, most important, mass production of identical parts by specialized machine tools and appropriate assembly methods. This technology had already been developed in such fields as watch making and clock making, arms, and sewing machines, but it was cycle manufacture that taught it to the car makers. Indeed, many of them were veterans of the cycle industry. On this early history of the auto industry, see among others the essay by James Laux, "Genèse d'une révolution," in Jean-Pierre Bardou et al., *La révolution automobile*. Laux developed his essay into two full-length books: *In First Gear: The French Automobile Industry to 1914*; and *The Automobile Revolution: The Impact of an Industry*. See also the article by Charles Stewart Rolls (of Rolls-Royce), "Motor Vehicles," in the eleventh ed. of the *Encyclopaedia Britannica* (1910–1911), vol. xviii. Poor Rolls barely survived the piece. He was a pilot and died in an airplane accident in 1910.
2. E. J. Stevenson, "The Horseless Carriage in France and America," *Harper's Weekly* 40 (1896): 1075, cited in Laux, *In First Gear,* p. 68. Note that at that date, the term "automobile" had not yet become standard usage in the United States. On the early economic importance of auto races, see William Lilley III and Laurence J. DeFranco, *The Economic Impact of the European Grands Prix*.

Chapter Four: Ford

1. William Ford drew lessons from his own success. The great miracle of America, his daughter later recalled of him, was that this was a country where a man could own the land he lived on and worked. Rural life was clean and decent; the city, a place of filth and immorality. Ironically, his son Henry accepted these principles, which hardly conformed to his own life. Peter Collier and David Horowitz, *The Fords: An American Epic* (New York: Summit, 1987), p. 23.
2. Collier and Horowitz, *The Fords,* p. 31, give the date as 1889.
3. Collier and Horowitz, *The Fords,* p. 49.
4. Ibid., p. 109.
5. On all this, Robert Lacey, *Ford: The Men and the Machine* (Boston: Little, Brown, 1986), chap. 6.
6. On these larger aspects, see ibid., pp. 475–78.
7. Of course, a pay raise is only as good as inflation allows. The war brought a big increase in the cost of living, and Ford wages barely kept up, and then only fitfully. Wages elsewhere had caught up with and were passing Ford's, so that once again turnover became a problem. Meanwhile, Henry's natural impatience led to harsher discipline. The assembly line in particular had little leeway for diversion and conversation, the less so as timers continually sought for ways to speed the pace of work. Detroit became known as the "eight-finger city" because of the large number of digits lost to moving belts and machine parts. Spotters looked and spied, and workers learned to talk without moving their lips: the "Ford whisper."
8. Lacey, *Ford,* p. 102. For a more detailed history of this fascinating litigation, see Allan Nevins, *Ford: The Times, the Man the Company,* vol. I, chaps. 13 and 17, and William Greenleaf, *Monopoly on Wheels.*
9. Collier and Horowitz, *The Fords,* p. 101.
10. See especially Richard Bak, *Henry and Edsel: The Creation of the Ford Empire,* chap. 11; and Neil Baldwin, *Henry Ford and the Jews.* The *Protocols of the Elders of Zion* was a fraudulent document, cooked up by Russian anti-Semites toward the end of the nineteenth century and put forward as the work of a secret Jewish committee planning to take over the world. The very nature of the fantasy tells much about the psychology of the anti-Jewish fabricators and the tacit aspirations of their own credulous followers. This slander continues to circulate to this day in anti-Jewish circles, particularly in the Muslim world, where extremists look forward to a worldwide takeover by Islam—a goal that predisposes them to belief in and fear of such allegedly global conspiracies by others. Some of these Muslim groups have been receiving support from the Ford Foundation, which is theoretically not connected to Ford Motors but casts its shadow on the car manufacturer.
11. For these data, see Lacey, *Ford,* p. 176.

12. To quote Douglas Brinkley, *Wheels for the World*, p. 512: "He was a maniac on the subject of the Jews."
13. On Ford's alleged affair with Evangeline Dahlinger, wife of a Ford employee, and the son reported to be the fruit thereof, see Richard S. Tedlow, *Giants of Enterprise*, p. 459, 80n; and John Côté Dahlinger and Frances Spatz Leighton, *The Secret Life of Henry Ford*.
14. Cited in John McDonald, *A Ghost's Memoir*, p. 48.
15. On Raskob and Pierre du Pont, see Leonard Mosley, *Blood Relations*, pp. 286–93. On Sloan, see Alfred D. Chandler, *The Visible Hand*, pp. 459–62; also Alfred P. Sloan, Jr., *My Years with General Motors*.
16. On all of this and more, see the excellent chapter on Sloan in H. W. Brands, *Masters of Enterprise*. Also Sloan's autobiography, *My Years with General Motors*.
17. All of this in spite of the fact that the minority shares bought up in 1919 were assigned to Edsel, who thus held over 40 percent of Ford. But Henry held more than half.
18. Baldwin, *Henry Ford and the Jews*, p. 257.
19. I take the term from an excellent article by Stephen Fox on Walter Chrysler: "I Like to Build Things," *Invention and Technology* 15, no. 1 (Summer, 1999): 20–30.
20. Ibid., p. 28.
21. Ibid.
22. Allan Nevins and Frank Ernest Hill, *Ford: Decline and Rebirth, 1933–1962* (New York: Charles Scribner's Sons, 1962), p. 268.
23. Cited in *Detroit News*, "'Whiz Kids' Reinvent Automaker," June 9, 2003.
24. Lacey, *Ford*, p. 521. On the Ford-Agnelli connection, see Alan Friedman, *Agnelli*, p. 328, 18n, and the references cited there. Also chap. 5 in this book.
25. Herndon, *Ford*, p. 252.
26. Contrast that with today's mania for heavy SUVs, which sell more because weight means safety in accidents: better to kill the other guy. Besides, the makers can and do charge more.
27. Herndon, *Ford*, p. 246.
28. For a vehemently negative report on Henry's investigation, see Victor Lasky, *Never Complain, Never Explain*, pp. 163–71.
29. Lee Iacocca with William Novak, *Iacocca*, p. 111.
30. Ibid.
31. See Lasky, *Never Complain, Never Explain*, pp. 140–42.
32. This was Dr. Franklin Murphy, director since 1965. Lacey, *Ford*, pp. 600, 635.
33. Peter Wyden, *The Unknown Iacocca* (New York: William Morrow, 1987), pp. 119–21.
34. Lasky, *Never Complain, Never Explain*, pp. 152–53.
35. On all this, see Nitin Nohria, Davis Dyer, and Frederick Dalzell, *Changing Fortunes*, pp. 112ff.

36. Keith Bradsher, "A Ford Heir Struggles for Control," *New York Times*, 6 February 2001, p. C1.
37. Thomas J. Neff and James M. Citrin, *Lessons from the Top*, p. 305.
38. *New York Times*, 24 May 2001, p. C1.
39. On Nasser's dismissal, see Brinkley, *Wheels for the World*, pp. 749–50.

Chapter Five: The Agnellis and Fiat

1. Friedman, *Agnelli*. Further to the history of the Agnellis and Fiat, see Valerio Castronovo, *Giovanni Agnelli: La Fiat dal 1899 al 1945* (Turin: UTET, 1971; reissued Einaudi, 1977).
2. James Arnold, "Gianni Agnelli: A Troubled Tycoon," BBC News Online, Friday, 24 January 2003.
3. On this exchange, see Friedman, *Agnelli*, p. 28.
4. Cf. Lundberg, *The Rich and the Super-rich*, p. 763: "The airplane, it may be observed in this melancholy recital [*re.* the Kennedys], is a special hazard of the rich and affluent. Few plane crashes, unless upon buildings, ever involve lower-class citizens; many tycoons have already met their end in the skies."
5. Friedman, *Agnelli*, p. 31.
6. On Fiat output in the 1920s, see Valerio Castronovo, *Fiat*, pp. 441–44. Also Angiolo Ori, *Storia di una dinastia: Gli Agnelli e la Fiat*, p. 120. See also the report of 21 August 1934 by the French bank Crédit Lyonnais. Jean-Louis Loubet, *L'industrie automobile*, pp. 216–17.
7. Loubet, *L'industrie automobile*, p. 217, 23n.
8. Friedman, *Agnelli*, p. 54.
9. On these and other obstacles, see Joël Broustail and Rodolphe Greggio, *Citroën*, part 2, especially pp. 120–21; and Castronovo, *Fiat*, pp. 1170–74.
10. On Benedetti, see Friedman, *Agnelli*, pp. 280*ff*.
11. On Romiti, see Paolo Madron, *Date a Cesare* . . . (Milan: Longanesi, 1998).
12. On raising Edoardo, see Ori, *Storia di una dinastia*, chap. 45.
13. Ibid., p. 338. This in an interview with two Italian journalists.
14. Friedman, *Agnelli*, p. 314.
15. *New York Times*, 16 November 2000, p. A16.
16. For a reasonably up-to-date organigram of the Agnelli business empire, see the article by Alan Cowell and Danny Hakim, "Intrigue at the Palazzo Agnelli," *New York Times*, 7 July 2002, section 3, pp. 1 and 11. One is reminded here of the Ford ownership of a Detroit professional football team. Is there something that links autos to sport?
17. Cf. Danny Hakim, "Fiat Vows to Defend Its Right to Sell Car Unit to GM," *New York Times*, 10 December 2004, p. C4.
18. *New York Times*, 14 February 2005, p. C1; *Wall Street Journal*, 14 January 2005, p. 1.

19. See the report by Eric Sylvers, "Fiat Reports Improved Results, but It Is Still Losing Money," *New York Times,* 28 February 2004, p. B3.
20. Friedman, *Agnelli,* p. 323.
21. This from Nicolo Pini, a fund manager with Ifigest in Florence. Al Baker, "Umberto Agnelli, Quiet Member of the Fiat Dynasty, Dies at 69," *New York Times,* 29 May 2004, p. B15; cf. Eric Sylvers, "New Fiat Chief Puts His Mark on Ailing Car Unit," *International Herald Tribune,* 2 September 2004.

CHAPTER SIX: PEUGEOT, RENAULT, AND CITROËN

1. Their first vehicle was completed in 1890. Panhard and Levassor, with whom they collaborated, had finished their first car one year earlier, in 1889.
2. On the family history of the Peugeot (the French does not pluralize family names), the most convenient source is René Sédillot, *Peugeot: de la crinoline à la 404* (Paris: Plon, 1960). On the car, see Jean-Louis Loubet, *Automobiles Peugeot.*
3. Sédillot, *Peugeot,* p. 49.
4. On this and other aspects of the French auto industry, see the wise interpretive essay by Jean-Louis Loubet, "Capitalisme familial et industrie automobile: une autre exception française."
5. Cited in Sylvie Schweitzer, *André Citroën,* p. 209.
6. Laurent Dingli, *Louis Renault* (Paris: Flammarion, 2000), p. 32.
7. Two of the recent Renault biographies, by Chadeau and Dingli, throw considerable doubt on the justice of French state action in these matters and the personal culpability of Louis Renault. Had Renault not died so early, he would no doubt have given the state its fill of litigation and might well have secured a favorable if partial settlement, even in a context of vengeful memories. He was that kind of fighter.
8. Loubet, "Peugeot," in Jean-Louis Jacques Marseille, ed., *Les performances des enterprises françaises,* p. 187.
9. The economic woes of the Depression took some time to cross the Atlantic and settle in for prolonged visit.
10. As with many automakers, Peugeot's extras never disappear altogether. There was just too much fun and too much profit to be had in customizing vehicles for wealthy clients. Even today, one can still order standard Peugeot cars with numerous nonstandard arrangements and features.
11. Alain Jemain, *Les Peugeot: vertiges et secrets d'une dynastie,* p. 100. See especially chap. 13, "Le connétable."
12. The end of World War II and defeat of the Germans found Peugeot in bad shape. Even though Paris had been liberated, the Germans had had time to pillage northeastern France, and the bulk of the company's workforce found itself cut off from production units. Meanwhile, the French

government made a point of reducing damages by half, to account for the dilapidated condition of plant and equipment. And even then, it took a couple of years for the government to remit compensation.

13. Jemain, *Les Peugeot,* p. 100.

14. Ibid., p. 78.

15. On wartime difficulties, see Jean-Paul Caracalla, *L'aventure Peugeot* (Paris: Denoel, 1990), p. 93.

16. Cf. Jean-Louis Loubet, *Histoire de l'automobile française,* (Paris: Le Seuil, 2001), p. 182.

17. On Peugeot postwar, see Jean-Louis Loubet, *Automobiles Peugeot: une réussite industrielle, 1945–1974.*

18. Alain Jemain, historian of the Peugeot auto dynasty, tells us that the note was almost an exact copy of one found in an American kidnap novel.

Chapter Seven: Toyoda

1. When Sakichi's son, Kiichiro, established the automobile branch of the company he chose the name "Toyota" over "Toyoda" for two reasons, both of which reveal a great deal about Japanese customs and business practice. First, he wanted to make a distinction between his family (private life) and his company (public life). Second, in Japan, people count the number of strokes it takes to write characters in the various Japanese scripts (of which there are three: kanji, hiragana, and katakana). In katakana, it takes ten strokes to write "Toyoda" and eight strokes to write "Toyota" (トヨタ). Eight is thought to be a particularly good number, as the kanji used to write eight also has the meaning of "infinity." By using the name "Toyota," he expressed his hope for "unlimited" possibilities for the new company.

2. "The *ie* included all people residing in the household, even those not related by blood, thus providing a model for family-style relations extending beyond the family." From Anne E. Imamura for the Asia Society's *Video Letter from Japan II: A Young Family* (1990), pp. 7–17.

3. Edwin M. Reingold, *Toyota: People, Ideas and the Challenge of the New* (London: Penguin Books, 1999), p. 12. This is an invaluable and reliable survey of the history of the auto firm.

4. At this point both GM and Ford were making passenger cars in Japan, but there were no homegrown Japanese manufacturers. Ed Reingold, "Eiji Toyoda," *Time Asia,* 23–30 August 1999, vol. 154, no. 7/8.

5. Risaburo offers an excellent example of the special Japanese attitude to family reinforcement by adoption. When he married Aiko Toyoda, he was formally adopted into the family, a valuable addition by his intelligence and enterprise.

6. On the role of daughters and sons-in-law, a report on the influential Iwasaki family makes an interesting point. "[The] Iwasaki family also

used marriage extensively to bring talented men into the family. Thus, unusually in a family enterprise, marriageable daughters were valued as highly as sons, if not more highly." See also Randall Morck and Masao Nakamura, "A Frog in a Well Knows Nothing of the Ocean: A History of Corporate Ownership in Japan," in Randall K. Morck, ed., *A History of Corporate Governance Around the World* (Chicago: University of Chicago Press, 2005), pp. 367–465.

7. Seven years later, management asked Kiichiro to return as president. He was reluctant but finally agreed. And then, before he could take the reins, he suffered a stroke and died at age fifty-seven.

8. Michael Schaller, *The American Occupation of Japan* (New York: Oxford University Press, 1985), p. 288.

9. Reingold, *Toyota*, p. 35.

10. Appointed after a labor dispute, Taizo helped reconstruct the company. Several years later he was followed by Nakagawa Fukio. As we see in the cases of Taiichi Ohno and Eiji Toyoda, the titular head of the firm has not always been the driving force in the company, making it difficult for historians to give a clear chronology.

11. Reingold, *Toyota*, p. 41.

12. "The Car Company in Front: Special Report: Toyota," *The Economist*, 2005, 29 January pp. 65–67.

13. Quoted in "Biography of Eiji Toyoda," BookRags Inc., online version, http://www.bookrags.com/biography/eiji-toyoda/.

Part Three: Treasures of the Earth

1. Robert Henriques, *Bearsted: A Biography of Marcus Samuel*, p. 5.

Chapter Eight: The Rockefellers

1. Ron Chernow, *Titan: The Life of John D. Rockefeller, Sr.*, p. 55. I have relied on this as my major source.

2. For a brief time, the firm was known as Clark, Gardner, and Company. The change in name constituted a demotion for John D., for it seemed to announce the hierarchy of the enterprise. Gardner was member of a high-society Cleveland family, bathed in warm repute, and Clark saw him as a living advertisement for the business. John D. swallowed the affront, but it ate at him, especially when Gardner turned out to be something of a playboy. For John D., Gardner's self-indulgence injured the firm's reputation. Gardner's attempts at sociability with the young entrepreneur only reinforced John D.'s frosty sanctimony. In 1862, John D. expelled Gardner from the firm, presumably by buying him out. He felt much better. He went on to buy out Clark three years later.

3. This was the Ohio company that emerged in 1870, when the partnership of Rockefeller, Andrews, and Flagler was converted from private to

public ownership. It was later replicated in a number of other states to get around barriers to interstate operation.

4. On the pipeline issue and story, see David Freeman Hawke, *John D.: The Founding Father of the Rockefellers,* chap. 21.

5. Ibid., pp. 129–31.

6. John D. himself knew about the temptation of fast horses. One of his few indulgences was a rich stable, filled with handsome racers. Anyone who gave signs of matching his equipage on the streets of Cleveland could expect a lesson in fast driving. Now we call it road rage, but then again coaches in those days were far safer than automobiles today.

7. For these and other aspects of the Rockefeller personality, see Chernow, *Titan,* chap. 9, "The New Monarch." For these and other economies, ibid., pp. 124 et seq.

8. This was on the advice of an associate, Paul Babcock, who need not have bothered. No one had to teach John D. how to suck eggs. See Chernow, *Titan,* p. 295.

9. Ferdinard Lundberg, *The Rockefeller Syndrome,* p. 114.

10. Chernow, *Titan,* p. 572. The quotes that follow come from there.

11. On Harper's fears, see Allan Nevins, *John D. Rockefeller: The Heroic Age of American Enterprise,* vol. II, p. 333.

12. Ibid., p. 356, citing a manuscript history by Walter F. Taylor, pp. 127, 170.

13. Nevins, II, 339.

14. Ibid., 523.

15. Ibid.

16. Ibid., p. 524.

17. Quoted in Chernow, *Titan,* p. 498.

18. On Junior as a young man, see especially Mary Ellen Chase, *Abby Aldrich Rockefeller* (New York: Macmillan, 1950), chap. 1. Junior as father was just as parsimonious as his own father had been. He bought his five boys one tricycle to share among them. "They will learn to give to each other," he explained to his mother. William Manchester, *A Rockefeller Family Portrait: From John D. to Nelson,* p. 101. Son Nelson recalled that the children got allowances of twenty-five cents a week: they were required to give 10 percent to charity, to save 10 percent, to account for the rest and balance their books every month, and to work for additional spending money. His wife, of good family, learned to buy linen at the January white sales and to telephone the children at school secretly from the bathroom, because Junior saw these calls as a frivolous and costly surrender to emotions.

19. Chase, *Abby Aldrich Rockefeller,* p. 28.

20. Raymond B. Fosdick, *John D. Rockefeller, Jr.: A Portrait,* p. 334, cited in Chernow, *Titan,* p. 622.

21. The first time young Nelson got a sense of the family's business history was when he interviewed John D. in connection with a college thesis on

the subject. He wanted to defend Standard against its detractors. John D. received him, but offered little.

22. David Rockefeller, *Memoirs*, p. 337.
23. D. Okrent, *Great Fortune: The Epic of Rockefeller Center* (New York: Viking, 2003), caption photos between pp. 272 and 273.
24. Chernow, *Titan*, p. 660.

Chapter Nine: The Guggenheims

1. John H. Davis, *The Guggenheims (1848–1988): An American Epic*, p. 58.
2. Ibid., p. 67.
3. Ibid., p. 106. See also the article "Alaska" in the eleventh edition of the *Encyclopædia Britannica*.
4. Davis, *The Guggenheims*, pp. 102–3.
5. Ibid., p. 427.
6. These may have been people overlooked in the maneuvers for political collaboration. On the court issue, see Larry Rohter, *New York Times*, 27 June 2003, p. A6.
7. Davis, *The Guggenheims*, p. 416. Davis asks what was left of the dynasty and answers, on p. 414: "A fragmented, diminished family, a handful of small companies, and five foundations. . . ."

Chapter Ten: The Schlumberger Saga

1. While the Jansenists were long a faction within the Catholic Church, they shared many core theological ideas—such as predestination—with the Calvinists. The father of Jansenism, Cornelius Jansen (1585–1638), was a Flemish theologian. Like Calvin, he believed in predestination—the idea that a very few people, the "elect," are destined to be saved. Material success was seen as an indication that one was among the elect.
2. John D. Rockefeller would be the strongest individual example whom we have examined in depth, and it bears noting that Weber's book appeared in 1905, contemporaneous with Rockefeller and the other great early industrialists of American capitalism.
3. Among the other notable clans are the Dollfus and Mieg, the Favre and Koechlin, all of whom, through various intermarriages, amassed great fortunes, primarily in textiles.
4. Jean Schlumberger, *Eveils* (Paris: Gallimard, 1950), cited Paulette Teissonnière-Jestin, "Les Schlumberger de 1830 à 1930," in Michel Hau, ed., *Regards sur la société contemporaine: trois familles industrielles d'Alsace: Les Bussière, les Saglio, et les Schlumberger* (Strasbourg: Editions Oberlin, 1989), p. 178. For data on rapid growth by Schlumberger and other Alsatian Calvinist enterprises in the closing years of the French empire (1812–1814), see Paul Leuilliot, *L'Alsace au début du*

XIXe siècle (Paris, SEVPEN, 1959) II, 364–65. For later performance, see Nicolas Stoskopf, *Les patrons du Second Empire: Alsace* (Paris: Picard, 1994); and Michel Hau and Nicolas Stoskopf, *Les dynasties alsaciennes du XVIIe siècle à nos jours* (Paris: Perrin, 2005). I have been much helped in all this by Suzanne Dworsky and Charles Davidson, member of the Schlumberger clan and publisher of the new periodical *The American Interest*. Much thanks.

5. Jean Schlumberger was ennobled by the German emperor William II in 1895. But his children, with their preference for French identity, left this Teutonic social promotion behind.

6. Hau, *Regards sur la société contemporaine: trois familles industrielles d'Alsace,* p. 134.

7. Hau, "Traditions comportementales et capitalisme dynastique," *Entreprises et histoire 9* (September 1995): 48.

8. Anne Gruner Schlumberger, *The Schlumberger Adventure* (New York: Arco, 1982), p. 7.

9. Cf. Hau, "Traditions," pp. 44–45; and Nicolas Stoskopf, "Alsace: vie privée et continuité familiale," *Entreprises et histoire 9* (September 1995): 61–69.

10. "Jean de Menil was a tough-minded capitalist, a bon vivant, and a leftist in the French mold—a man who wanted to right wrongs and change society." Calvin Tomkins, "The Benefactor: Onward and Upward with the Arts," *The New Yorker,* 8 June 1998, p. 54.

11. Georges, the middle child of Dominique and John, is an economist and founding director of the economics research division of the Ecole des Hautes-Etudes en Sciences Sociales in Paris. He is married to a political historian with a Harvard Ph.D. In France he goes by the title of baron. So much for leftist sympathies.

12. On Dominique Schlumberger de Menil, see Tomkins, "The Benefactor," *The New Yorker,* 8 June 1998, pp. 52–67.

13. Schlumberger, *The Schlumberger Adventure,* p. 122.

CHAPTER ELEVEN: THE WENDEL

1. The Seillière family, like so many other successful business dynasties, found it impossible to sustain commitment in the face of wealth. The children found more amusing ways to spend their money. The Banque Seillière closed its doors in 1907. Cf. Nicolas Stoskopf, *Les patrons du Second Empire: banquiers et financiers parisiens* (Paris: Picard, 2002), pp. 328–33.

2. These data come from the new book by Jacques Marseille, *Les Wendel 1704–2004* (Paris: Perrin, 2004), p. 116. Very important. I owe access to this publication to Véronique Goupy, Wendel by descent. *Merci.*

3. The best of this ore, such as it was, was not located until the 1880s, in the Briey basin on the Lorraine border between France and Germany. Reserves amounted to more than three billion tons. The Wendel man-

aged to obtain major concessions in this field, which their biographer Jacques Marseille describes as "a gift from heaven" and an instrument of revenge for defeat by Prussia. *Les Wendel, 1704–2004,* p. 202.

4. For these data, see ibid., pp. 211, 215.

5. Jean-Noel Jeanneney, "La dynastie des Wendel," in Jacques Marseille, ed., *Puissance et faiblesses,* pp. 463–64.

6. On all this, see Henri d'Ainval, *Deux siècles de sidérurgie française,* especially chap. 18.

7. Marseille, *Les Wendel,* p. 338.

8. Cf. Bruno Abescat, "Saga: Les Wendel, une dynastie inoxydable," *L'Express,* 7–13 June 2004, pp. 132–34.

9. I have this from a memorandum prepared for me by Mme Goupy on the role and activities of the ladies de Wendel. Much thanks.

10. Berthilde lives today in a Paris apartment that is a reproduction of the town house residence she once enjoyed. But now it sits atop a new and modern apartment building that constitutes a *mise en valeur* of precious Parisian real estate.

Concluding Thoughts

1. But see also the earlier work by Sargant Florence and the discussion in M. M. Postan, *An Economic History of Western Europe, 1945–1964.* For Chandler, see *Visible Hand.* Also Chandler and Herman Daems, eds., *Managerial Hierarchies.*

2. The limited partnership (*commandite*) combines managing partners with unlimited liability and limited partners with liability typically fixed by share of ownership. These limited liability shares may take the form of sums set out on the books or of tradeable stock (*par actions*).

3. Cf. Adolf Berle and Gardiner Means, *The Modern Corporation and Private Property* (New York: Macmillian, 1932), and R. J. Larner, "The 200 Largest Non-financial Corporations," *American Economic Review.* CVI, no. 4, (September 1956): part 1.

4. I have run into businesspeople who deplore inheritance and sing the virtues and advantages of generational autonomy. By some coincidence, such rebels against human nature have already sold their business to bigger firms.

5. Crouzet, "Editorial," *Entreprises et histoire* 9 (September 1995): 6. An excellent source of information on business forms and numbers thereof is Jacques Marseille, ed., *Créateurs et créations d'entreprises.*

6. Bernadette Angleraud and Catherine Pellissier, *Les dynasties lyonnaises des Morin-Pons aux Mérieux du XIXe siècle à nos jours,* pp. 385f.

7. On the one third of the Standard and Poor 500, and that third usually the best performers, see *BusinessWeek,* 10 November 2003, p. 100ff., which credits earlier research by Ronald C. Anderson and David M. Reeb, published in the June 2003 issue of the *Journal of Finance.*

8. Michael B. Miller, *The Bon Marché* (Princeton: Princeton University Press, 1981). See especially pp. 12–15. Miller describes the Bon Marché as "a firm not only permeated with household relationships, but a firm that relied upon these relationships for its transition into a modern business enterprise." But that is exactly the creative role of successful family enterprises prevented from continuing as such: to lay the foundation of managerial joint-stock companies.

9. Say, *Cours complet d'économie politique pratique,* cited Lucette Le Van-Lemesle, "Les économistes français du XIXe siècle et la création d'entreprises," in J. Marseille, ed., *Créateurs et créations d'entreprises,* p. 37.

10. David Coates and John Hillard, eds., *The Economic Decline of Modern Britain,* p. 231. This, in my opinion, is an important aspect of British anti-American prejudices. On this, see Geoffrey Wheatcroft, "Smiley's (Anti-American) People," *New York Times,* 11 January 2004.

11. Cf. Kevin Phillips, *American Dynasty: Aristocracy, Fortune, and the Politics of Deceit in the House of Bush.*

12. Cf. David Bartal, "The Empire: How the Wallenbergs Built Europe's Most Powerful Family," *The European* (May 1996).

13. Cf. Michel Hau, *La maison de Dietrich de 1684 à nos jours;* and "Le modèle rhénan: la récréation permanente? Le cas de Dietrich," in Marseille, ed., *Créateurs et créations d'entreprises.* The Marseille book is very informative.

14. Nohria, Dyer, and Dalzell, *Changing Fortunes,* p. 106.

15. Cf. Lee Hawkins, Jr., "Reversing 80 Years of History, GM Is Reining In Global Fiefs," *Wall Street Journal,* 6 October 2004, p. A1. And even so, GM's loss of market share has led it to move toward major reductions in personnel and to outsource work to low-cost producers such as China. Managerial companies can be more hardheaded than family enterprises, but also more hard-hearted.

16. And for those who want to complicate their business lives, try moving from one cultural realm to another. For example, see the litigation still under way among the descendants of L. Pathak, died 1997, who was founder of Patak [sic] foods and a migrant from India to Africa to England. (The Brits like Indian cuisine.) His daughters have married, and his male children feel that so doing, they have left the family. Their mother agrees. See Charles Goldsmith, "Two Daughters Fight Hindu Mores for Piece of Chutney Empire," *Wall Street Journal,* 23 February 2004, p. A1.

17. Cf. Jean-Pierre Daviet, *Saint-Gobain, une multinationale à la française, 1665–1989.*

18. Bernard Simon, "Keeping Business in the Family," citing Peter Newman, *New York Times,* 28 February 2003, pp. W1 and 7.

19. Amy Chua, "A World on the Edge," *Wilson Quarterly* (Autumn 2002): 61–77.

20. Ezra N. Suleiman, *Les ressorts cachés de la réussite française,* p. 361. Cf.

Tyler Cowen, "The Fate of Culture," *Wilson Quarterly* (Autumn 2002): 78–84; and Tyler Cowen, *Creative Destruction: How Globalization Is Changing the World's Cultures.*

21. See this argument in Glenn Firebaugh, *The New Geography of Global Income Inequality.*

22. On Arab backwardness and its costs, see the Arab Human Development Report by the United Nations Development Program. Discussed in *The Economist,* 25 October 2003, p. 42.

23. Stanley Chapman, *The Rise of Merchant Banking,* p. 103.

Bibliography

Abels, Jules. 1965. *The Rockefeller Billions: The Story of the World's Most Stupendous Fortune*. New York: Macmillan.

Addis, J. P. 1957. *The Crawshay Dynasty*. Cardiff: University of Wales Press.

Adler, Cyrus. 1928. *Jacob H. Schiff: His Life and Letters*. Vol. I. Freeport, N.Y.: Books for Libraries Press.

Agnelli, Marella. 1998. *The Agnelli Gardens at Villar Perosa: Two Centuries of a Family Retreat*. Nw York: Harry N. Abrams.

Agnelli, Susanna. 1975. *Vestivamo alla marinara*. Milan: Mondadori.

———. 1975. *We Always Wore Sailor Suits*. New York: Viking.

Ainval, Henri d'. 1994. *Deux siècles de sidérurgie française*. Grenoble: Presses Universitaires de Grenoble.

Allaud, Louis A., and Maurice H. Martin. 1977. *Schlumberger: The History of a Technique*. New York, London: John Wiley and Sons.

Allen, Frederick Lewis. 1935. *The Lords of Creation*. New York: Harper and Bros.

———. 1949. *The Great Pierpont Morgan*. New York: Harper and Brothers.

Alvares, Claude. 1980. *Homo Faber: Technology and Culture in India, China and the West from 1500 to the Present Day*. The Hague: Martinus Nijhoff.

Amatori, Franco. 1980. "Entrepreneurial Typology in the History of Industrial Italy 1880–1960: A Review Article," *Business History Review*, 54, 3.

———. 1992. *Impresa e mercato: Lancia 1906–1969*. Milan: Fabbri.

Amin, Samir. 1974. *The Accumulation of Capital on a World Scale*. New York: Monthly Review Press.

Ampalavanar Brown, Rajeswary, ed. 1995. *Chinese Business Enterprise in Asia*. London: Routledge.

Amsden, Alice. 1989. *Asia's Next Giant*. Oxford: Oxford University Press.

Anderson, Verily Bruce. 1980. *Friends and Relations: Three Centuries of Quaker Families*. London: Hodder and Stoughton.

Angleraud, Bernadette, and Catherine Pellissier. 2003. *Les dynasties lyonnaises des Morin-Pons aux Mérieux du XIXe siècle à nos jours.* Paris: Editions Perrin.

Anneser, Jules. 1948. *Vautours sur la Lorraine, dévoilés par leurs archives secrètes.* Metz: Le Lorrain.

Annibaldi, Cesare, and Giuseppe Berta, eds. 1999. *Grande impresa e sviluppo italiano: Studi per i cento anni della Fiat.* 2 vols. Bologna: Il Mulino.

Aoki, Masahiro, and Ronald Dore, eds. 1994/1996. *The Japanese Firm: Sources of Competitive Strength.* Oxford: Clarendon Press.

Archivio Storico Fiat. 1996. *Fiat: Le fasi della crescita: tempi e cifre dello sviluppo aziendale.* Turin: Scriptorium.

Aris, Stephen. 1970. *The Jews in Business.* London: Jonathan Cape.

Arnst, Paul. 1925. *August Thyssen und sein Werk.* Leipzig: G. A. Gloeckner.

Assouline, Pierre. 1999. *Le dernier des Camondo.* Rev. and enl. ed. Paris: Gallimard.

Attali, Jacques. 1986. *A Man of Influence: Sir Siegmund Warburg, 1902–1982.* London: Weidenfeld and Nicolson.

Augustine, Dolores I. 1994. *Patricians and Parvenus: Wealth and High Society in Wilhelmine Germany.* Oxford/Providence: Berg.

Auletta, Ken. 1984. *The Art of Corporate Success: The Story of Schlumberger.* New York: G. P. Putnam's Sons.

Autin, Jean. 1984. *Les Frères Pereire.* Paris: Perrin.

Ayres, Glenn R. 1990. "Rough Justice: Equity in Family Business Succession Planning," *Family Business Review,* III: 3–22.

Baark, Erik, and Andrew Jamison, eds. 1986. *Technological Development in China, India and Japan: Cross-Cultural Perspectives.* New York: St. Martin's Press.

Bairati, Piero. 1983. *Valletta* "La vita sociale della nuova Italia," 32. Turin: UTET.

———. 1986. *Sul filo di lana: cinque generazioni di imprenditori: i Marzotto.* Bologna: Il Mulino.

———. 1988. "Le dinastie imprenditoriali." In Piero Melograni, ed., *La famiglia italiana dall'ottocento ad oggi.* Bari: Laterza, pp. 141–92.

Bak, Richard. 2003. *Henry and Edsel: The Creation of the Ford Empire.* Hoboken, N.J.: Wiley.

Baldwin, Neil. 2001. *Henry Ford and the Jews: The Mass Production of Hate.* New York: Public Affairs.

Balsan, Consuelo Vanderbilt. 1953. *The Glitter and the Gold.* New York: Harper.

Banham, Russ. 2002. *The Ford Century: Ford Motor Company and the Innovations That Shaped the World.* New York: Workman Publishing.

Barbier, Frédéric. 1979. *Trois cents ans de librairie et d'imprimerie: Berger-Levrault, 1676–1830.* Geneva: Droz.

———. 1991. *Finance et politique: la dynastie des Fould XVIIIe–XXe siècle.* Paris: Armand Colin.

———. 1993. "Banque, famille et société en Allemagne au XIXe siècle," *Revue de synthèse,* IVe S.N., no. 1 (January–March): 123–37.

——— et al. 1989. *Le patronat du Nord sous le Second Empire: une approche prosopographique.* Geneva: Droz. EPHE, IVe section, *Hautes études médiévales et modernes* 65.

Bardou, Jean-Pierre, Jean-Jacques Chanaron, Patrick Fridenson, and James M. Laux. 1977. *La révolution automobile.* Paris: Albin Michel.

Barker, Richard J. 1958. *Casimir Perier (1777–1832) and William Ternaux (1763–1833): Two French Capitalists During the Restoration.* Durham, N.C.: Duke University Press.

Barker, Theodore C. 1960. *Pilkington Brothers and the Glass Industry.* London: Allen.

———. 1977. *The Glassmakers: Pilikington: The Rise of an International Company, 1826–1976.* London: Weidenfeld and Nicolson.

———, ed. 1987. *The Economic and Social Effects of the Spread of Motor Vehicles.* Basingstoke: Macmillan.

Barral, Pierre. 1963. *Les Perier dans l'Isère d'après leur correspondance familiale.* Paris: Presses Universitaires de France.

Barton, A., and C. Petit-Castelli. 1991. *La saga des Barton.* Levallois: Manya.

Baudant, A. 1980. *Pont-à-Mousson (1918–1939): stratégies industrielles d'une dynastie lorraine.* Paris: Publications de la Sorbonne.

Baumier, Jean. 1988. *La galaxie Paribas.* Paris: Plon.

Beasley, Norman. 1947. *Knudsen.* New York: McGraw-Hill.

Beaton, Kendall. 1957. *Enterprise in Oil: A History of Shell in the United States.* New York: Appleton-Century-Crofts.

Beaucarnot, J.-L. 1986. *Les Schneider, une dynastie.* Paris: Hachette.

Beck, Ludwig. 1899. *Die Geschichte des Eisens in technischer und kulturgeschichtlicher Beziehung, IV. Das XIX. Jahrhundert von 1801 bis 1860.* Braunschweig: Friedrich Vieweg und Sohn.

Beier, A., David Cannadine, and L. Rosenheim, eds. 1989. *The First Modern Society.* Cambridge: Cambridge University Press.

Beltran, Alain. 1998. *Un siècle d'histoire industrielle en France (1880–1970): industrialisation et société.* Paris: SEDES.

Bender, Marylin. 1975. "The Energy Trauma at General Motors." In her *At the Top.* Garden City, N.Y.: Doubleday.

———. 1975. "Estée Lauder: A Family Affair." In *At the Top,* pp. 167–210.

Bennett, Harry. 1951. *We Never Called Him Henry.* New York: Tom Doherty Assoc.

Berg, Maxine. 1993. "Small Producer Capitalism in Eighteenth-Century England," *Business History* 35.

Bergeron, Louis. 1974. "La fortune des banquiers sous Napoléon," *Souvenir napoléonien* 276.

———. 1978. *Banquiers, négociants et manufacturiers parisiens du Directoire à l'Empire.* Paris: Mouton.

———. 1978. *Les capitalistes en France, 1780–1914.* Paris: Gallimard-Julliard.

———. 1991. *Les Rothschild et les autres: la gloire des banquiers.* Paris: Perrin.

Berghoeffer, Christian W. 1922. *Mayer Amschel Rothschild.* Frankfurt: Englert and Schlosser.

Bergier, Jean-Francois. 1979. "From the Fifteenth in Italy to the Sixteenth Century in Germany: A New Banking Concept?" In Center for Medieval & Renaissance Studies, UCLA, *The Dawn of Modern Banking*, pp. 105–229. New Haven: Yale.

Berle, Adolf and Gardiner Means. 1932. *The Modern Corporation and Private Property.* New York: MacMillan.

Bermant, Chaim. 1971. *The Cousinhood: The Anglo-Jewish Gentry.* London: Eyre and Spottiswoode.

Bevan, Judi. 2001. *The Rise and Fall of Marks and Spencer.* London: Profile Books.

Bianco, Anthony. 1997. *The Reichmanns: Family, Faith, Fortune, and the Empire of Olympia and York.* New York: Random House/Times Books.

Biard, Roger. 1958. *La sidérurgie française: contribution à l'étude d'une grande industrie française.* Paris: Editions Sociales.

Birmingham, Stephen. 1967. *"Our Crowd": The Great Jewish Families of New York.* New York: Harper and Row.

Bonin, Hubert. 1993. "La splendeur des Samazeuilh, banquiers de Boreaux (1810–1913)," *Revue historique* 584 (octobre-décembre): 348–89.

———. 1995. *Les groupes financiers français.* Paris: Presses Universitaires de France; *Que sais-je?*

Bonnafos, Géraldine de, Jean-Jacques Chanaron, Patrick Fridenson, and James M. Laux. 1977. *La révolution automobile.* Paris: Editions La Découverte/Maspero.

———, J.-J, Chanaron, and Laurent de Mautort. 1983. *L'industrie automobile.* Paris: Editions La Découverte.

Born, Karl Erich. 1983. *International Banking in the Nineteenth and Twentieth Centuries.* Stuttgart: Berg Publishers.

Boswell, Johnathan. 1973. *The Rise and Decline of Small Firms.* London: Allen and Unwin.

Bottiglieri, Bruno. 1991. "Strategie di sviluppo: assetti organizzativi e scelte finanzarie nel primo trentennio della Fiat." In Progetto Archivio Storico FIAT, *FIAT 1899–1930: Storia e documenti.* Milan: Fabbri.

Bourset, Madeleine. 1994. *Casimir Perier: Un prince financier au temps du romantisme.* Paris: Publications de la Sorbonne.

Bouvier, Jean. 1970. *Les Rothschild.* Paris: Fayard.

———. 1973. *Un siècle de banque française: les contraintes de l'Etat, et les incertitudes des marchés.* Paris: Hachette littérature.

Bouyer, Christian. 1990. *Les hommes d'argent.* Paris: Editions L'Harmattan.

Boyson, R. 1970. *The Ashworth Cotton Enterprise: The Rise and Fall of a Family Firm, 1818–1880.* Oxford: Oxford University Press.

Bradsher, Keith. 2003. *High and Mighty: The Dangerous Rise of the SUV.* Cambridge, Mass.: Perseus Group.

Bramsen, Bo, and Kathleen Wain. 1979. *The Hambros, 1779–1979.* London: Michael Joseph.

Brands, H. W. 1999. *Masters of Enterprise: Giants of American Business from John Jacob Astor and J. P. Morgan to Bill Gates and Oprah Winfrey*. New York: The Free Press.

Brandt, A. 1951. "Une famille de fabricants mulhousiens au début du XIXe siècle: Jean Koechlin et ses fils," *Annales ESC*, 319–30.

Bremner, Brian, and Chester Dawson. 2003. "Can Anything Stop Toyota?" *BusinessWeek*, 17 November, pp. 114–22.

Breyer, Victor. 1984. *La belle époque à 30 à l'heure*. Paris: Editions France-Empire.

Brézis, Elise S., and Peter Temin, eds. 1999. *Elites, Minorities and Economic Growth*. Amsterdam: Elsevier.

Brinkley, Douglas. 2003. *Wheels for the World: Henry Ford, His Company and a Century of Progress 1903–2003*. New York: Viking.

Broadberry, S. N., and N.F.R. Crafts. 1992. "Britain's Productivity Gap in the 1930s: Some Neglected Factors," *Journal of Economic History* 52, no. 3.

Brooks, John. 1959. *Business Adventures*. New York: Weybright and Talley. See especially chap. 2, "The Fate of the Edsel."

———. 1969. *Once in Golconda: A True Drama of Wall Street, 1920–1938*. New York: W. W. Norton.

Broustail, Joël, and Rodolphe Greggio. 2000. *Citroën: essai sur 80 ans d'anti-stratégie*. Paris: Institut Vital-Roux/Librairie Vuibert.

Brown, J. Crosby. 1909. *A History of Brown Shipley*.

Brown, Jonathan, and Mary B. Rose, eds. 1993. *Entrepreneurship, Networks and Modern Business*. Manchester: Manchester University Press.

Bryant, J. S. 1914. *The Life of the Late George Peabody*. Westminster: Peabody Donation Fund.

Bryce, Robert. 2002. *Pipe Dreams: Greed, Ego, and the Death of Enron*. New York: PublicAffairs.

Buchanan, C. D. 1958. *Mixed Blessing: The Motor in Britain*. London: Hill.

Butel, Paul. 1991. *Les dynasties bordelaises, de Colbert à Chaban*. Paris: Perrin.

Cain, L. P., and Paul J. Uselding, eds. 1973. *British Enterprise and Economic Change*. Kent, Ohio: Kent State University Press.

Calame, Marie-André, et al. 1989. *Familles industrielles d'Alsace*. Strasbourg: Oberlin.

Camplin, J. 1978. *The Rise of the Plutocrats*. London: Constable.

Canfield, Cass. 1974. *The Incredible Pierpont Morgan: Financier and Art Collector*. New York: Hamish Hamilton.

Cannadine, David. 1999. *The Decline and Fall of the British Aristocracy*. New York: Vintage.

Caracalla, Jean-Paul. 1990. *L'aventure Peugeot*. Paris: Editions Denoël.

Cardot, F., ed. 1989. *Des entreprises pour l'électricité*. Paris.

Caron, François, ed. 1983. *Entreprises et entrepreneurs en France aux XIXe et XXe siècles*. Paris.

―――. 1989. *Aux sources de la puissance: sociabilité et parenté*. Rouen.

Carosso, Vincent P. 1970. *Investment Banking in America: A History*. Cambridge, Mass.: Harvard University Press.

―――. 1979. *More Than a Century of Investment Banking: The Kidder, Peabody and Co. Story*. New York: McGraw-Hill.

―――. 1987. *The Morgans: Private International Bankers, 1854–1913*. Cambridge, Mass.: Harvard University Press.

Carr, William H. A. 1965. *The du Ponts of Delaware*. London: Frederick Muller.

Carter, C. F., and B. R. Williams. 1958. *Investment in Innovation*. London: Oxford University Press.

Carter, Miranda. 2001. *Anthony Blunt: His Lives*. New York: Farrar, Straus and Giroux.

Cassis, Youssef. 1984. *Les banquiers de la City à l'époque Edouardienne*. Geneva: Droz.

―――. 1985. "Bankers in English Society in the Late Nineteenth Century," *Economic History Review*, 2d ser., 38: 210–29.

―――. 1985. "The Banking Community of London, 1890–1914," *Journal of Imperial & Commonwealth History* 13, no. 3: 109–26.

―――, Gerald D. Feldman, and Ulf Olsson, eds. 1995. *The Evolution of Financial Institutions and Markets in Twentieth-Century Europe*. Aldershot: Scolar Press for the European Association for Banking History.

―――, and Jakob Tanner, eds. 1993. *Banques et crédit en Suisse / Banken und Kredit in der Schweiz (1850–1930)*. Zurich: Chronos.

Casson, M. 1993. "Entrepreneurship and Business Culture." In Brown and Rose, eds., *Entrepreneurship*.

Castronovo, Valerio. 1971/1977. *Giovanni Agnelli: La Fiat dal 1899 al 1945*. Turin: UTET; reissued Einaudi.

―――. 1999. *Fiat 1899–1999: Un secolo di storia italiana*. Milan: Rizzoli.

Cayez, P. 1980. *Crises et croissance de l'industrie lyonnaise, 1850–1900*. Paris: Editions du CNRS.

Chadeau, Emmanuel. 1988. *L'économie du risque: les entrepreneurs (1850–1980)*. Paris: Orban.

―――. 1993. "The Large Family Firm in Twentieth-Century France," *Business History*. 35, no. 4. Also in Jones and Rose, eds., *Family Capitalism*, pp. 184–205.

Chaline, Jean-Pierre. 1985. "Les industriels normands, un patronat sans dynasties?", *Le mouvement social* 132 (July–September): 43–57.

Chanaron, Jean-Jacques, and E. de Banville, eds. 1991. *Vers un système automobile européen*. Paris: Economica.

Chandler, Alfred D., ed. 1964. *Giant Enterprise: Ford, GM, and the Automobile Industry. Sources and Readings*. New York: Harcourt, Brace, and World.

―――. 1977. *The Visible Hand: The Managerial Revolution in American Business*. Cambridge, Mass.: Harvard University Press/Belknap.

——. 1980. "The Growth of the Transnational Industrial Firm in the U.S. and the U.K.: A Comparative Analysis," *Economic History Review* 33.

——. 1990. *Scale and Scope: The Dynamics of Industrial Capitalism.* Cambridge, Mass.: Harvard University Press.

——, Franco Amatori, and Takashi Hikino, eds. 1997. *Big Business and the Wealth of Nations.* Cambridge: Cambridge University Press.

——, and Hermann Daems, eds. 1980. *Managerial Hierarchies: Comparative Perspectives on the Rise of Modern Industrial Enterprise.* Cambridge, Mass.: Harvard University Press.

——, and Stephen Salsbury. 1971. *Pierre S. Du Pont and the Making of the Modern Corporation.* New York: Beard Books.

——, and Richard Tedlow, eds. 1985. *The Coming of Managerial Capitalism: A Casebook on the History of American Economic Institutions.* Homewood, Ill.: Richard D. Irwin.

Channon, Derek F. 1971. *The Strategy and Structure of British Enterprise.* London: Macmillan.

Chapman, Stanley D. 1967. *The Early Factory Masters: The Transition to the Factory System in the Midlands.* Newton Abbot: David and Charles.

——. 1969. "The Peels in the Early English Cotton Industry," *Business History* 11 (July).

——. 1977. *N. M. Rothschild, 1777–1836.* London: NMR and Sons.

——. 1984. *The Rise of Merchant Banking.* London: Allen and Unwin.

——. 1986. "Aristocracy and Meritocracy in Merchant Banking," *British Journal of Sociology* 37: 180–93.

——. 1992. *Merchant Enterprise in Britain from the Industrial Revolution to World War I.* Cambridge: Cambridge University Press.

——, and S. Chassagne. 1981. *European Textile Printers in the Eighteenth Century: A Study of Peel and Oberkampf.* London and Edinburgh: Old City Publishing.

——, and S. Diaper. 1984. *Kleinwort Benson in the History of Merchant Banking.* Oxford.

Chase, Mary Ellen. 1950. *Abby Aldrich Rockefeller.* New York: Macmillan.

Chassagne, Serge. 1980. *Oberkampf: Un entrepreneur capitaliste au siècle des Lumières.* Paris: Aubier Montaigne.

——. 1991. *Le coton et ses patrons, France, 1760–1840.* Paris: EHESS.

Cheape, Charles W. 1985. *Family Firm to Modern Multinational: Norton Company, a New England Enterprise.* Cambridge, Mass.: Harvard University Press.

Checkland, Sidney G. 1964. 6th ed., 1989. *The Rise of Industrial Society in England, 1815–1885.* London: Longman.

Chernow, Ron. 1990. *The House of Morgan: An American Banking Dynasty and the Rise of Modern Finance.* New York: Simon and Schuster.

——. 1993. *The Warburgs: The Twentieth-Century Odyssey of a Remarkable Jewish Family.* New York: Vintage.

———. 1998/1999. *Titan: The Life of John D. Rockefeller, Sr.* New York: Random House/Vintage.

Chevalier, Jean. 1938. *Trois siècles d'industrie: les forges d'Hayange et de Moyeuvre.* Special number *Plaisir de France,* May.

———. 1946. *Le Creusot.* Paris: Perspectives.

Chilvers, H. A. 1939. *The Story of De Beers.* London: Cassell.

Choulet, Eugène. 1894. *La famille Casimir-Perier, étude généalogique, biographique et historique.* Grenoble: Joseph Baratier.

Church, Roy A. 1969. *Kenricks in Hardware: A Family Business, 1791–1966.* Newton Abbot: David and Charles.

———. 1979. *Herbert Austin.* Introduction by Neil McKendrick. London: Europa.

———. 1990. "The Limitations of the Personal Capitalism Paradigm." In Church et al., "Scale and Scope: A Review Colloquium," *Business History* 64 (Winter): 703–10.

Clark, Rodney. 1979. *The Japanese Company.* New Haven: Yale University Press.

Clarke, Philip. 1972. *Small Businesses: How They Survive and Succeed.* Newton Abbot: David and Charles.

Cleveland, Harold van B., and Thomas Huertas. 1985. *Citibank, 1812–1970.* Cambridge, Mass.: Harvard University Press.

Coates, David, and John Hillard, eds. 1986. *The Economic Decline of Modern Britain.* Hemel Hempstead: Harvester Wheatsheaf.

Cohen, Naomi W. 1999. *Jacob H. Schiff: A Study in American Jewis Leadership.* Hanover, N.H.: University Press of New England; Brandeis University.

Colby, Gerald. 1974. Reprint 1984. *DuPont Dynasty.* Secaucus, N.J.: Lyle Stuart.

Coleman, Donald C. 1969 and 1980. *Courtaulds: An Economic and Social History.* 3 vols. Oxford: Oxford University Press.

———, and Peter Mathias, eds. 1984. *Enterprise and History: Essays in Honour of Charles Wilson.* Cambridge: Cambridge University Press.

Colli, Andrea. n.d. [c. 2001]. "Family Business: Historical and Comparative Perspectives." Typescript.

Collier, Peter, and David Horowitz. 1987. *The Fords: An American Epic.* New York: Summit (Simon and Schuster).

Collins, B., and K. Robbins, eds. 1990. *British Culture and Economic Decline.* New York: St. Martin's Press.

Cooney, John. 1982. *The Annenbergs: The Salvaging of a Tainted Dynasty.* New York: Simon and Schuster.

Corey, Lewis. 1930. *The House of Morgan: A Social Biography of the Masters of Money.* New York: G. Howard Watt.

Corti, Egon Caesar. 1928. *The Rise of the House of Rothschild.* New York: Cosmopolitan Books.

———. 1928. *The Reign of the House of Rothschild.* New York: Cosmopolitan Books.

Cosandey, David. 1997. *Le secret de l'Occident: Du miracle passé au marasme présent.* Paris: Arléa.

Cottrell, Philip L. 1980. *Industrial Finance, 1830–1914: The Finance and Organisation of English Manufacturing Industry.* London: Routledge.

Cowan, C. D., ed. 1964. *The Economic Development of China and Japan: Studies in Economic History and Political Economy.* London: SOAS.

Cowen, Tyler. 2002. "The Fate of Culture," *Wilson Quarterly* (Autumn): 78–84.

————. 2003. *Creative Destruction: How Globalization Is Changing the World's Cultures.* Princeton: Princeton University Press.

Cowles, Virginia. 1973. Revised edition, 1979. *The Rothschilds, a Family of Fortune.* London: Weidenfeld and Nicolson.

Cringely, Robert X. 1992. *Accidental Empires: How the Boys of Silicon Valley Make Their Millions, Battle Foreign Competition, and Still Can't Get a Date.* Reading, Mass.: Addison-Wesley.

Crossen, Cynthia. 2000. *The Rich and How They Got That Way.* London: Nicholas Brealey.

Crouzet, François. 1985. *De la supériorité de l'Angleterre sur la France: l'économique et l'imaginaire, XVIIe–XXe siècle.* Paris: Perrin.

————. 1995. "Les dynasties d'entrepreneurs en France et en Grande Bretagne," *Entreprises et histoire* 9 (septembre): 25–42.

————. 1996. "Encore des dynasties . . .", *Entreprises et histoire* 12 (juin): 5–18.

————, 1996. "Une académie préparatoire au commerce fondée par les Koechlin," *Entreprises et histoire* (juin) 12: 123–26.

————, and Olivier Puydt. 1996. "La question dynastique," *Entreprises et histoire* 12 (juin): 113–22.

Crow, John A. 1985. *Spain: The Root and the Flower.* 3rd ed. Berkeley and Los Angeles: University of California Press.

Cushman, Jennifer. 1991. *Family and State: The Formation of a Sino-Thai Tin-Mining Dynasty, 1797–1932.* Singapore: Oxford University Press.

Cusumano, Michael A. 1985. *The Japanese Automobile Industry: Technology and Management at Nissan and Toyota.* Cambridge, Mass.: Harvard, for the Council on East Asian Studies, Harvard University.

Dahlinger, John Côté, and Frances Spatz Leighton. 1978. *The Secret Life of Henry Ford.* Indianapolis: Bobbs-Merrill.

Dartevelle, Raymond, ed. 1999. *La Banque Seillière-Demachy. Une dynastie familiale au centre du négoce, de la finance et des arts, 1798–1998.* Paris: Perrin and Fondation pour l'Histoire de la Haute Banque. Catalog issued for exposition "La banque Seillière-Demachy, 1798–1998," Hôtel national des Invalides, 27 January–14 February 1999.

Dauliac, Jean-Pierre, Jean Menu, and Pierre Saka. 1982. *Histoire de l'automobile en France.* Paris: Fernand Nathan.

Daumas, Jean-Claude. 1999. *L'amour du drap: Blin et Blin 1827–1975. Histoire d'une entreprise lainière familiale.* Paris: Presses Universitaires Franc-Comtoises.

Daunton, M. J. 1988. "Inheritance and Succession in the City of London in the Nineteenth Century," *Business History*, 30.

———. 1989. " 'Gentlemanly Capitalism' and British Industry 1820–1914," *Past & Present* 122 (February): 119–58.

Davidoff, Leonore. 1973/1986. *The Best Circles: Society, Etiquette and the Season*. London: Cresset Library.

———. 1973. *The Best Circles: Women and Society in Victorian England*. Totowa, N.J.: Rowman and Littlefield.

Davies, Peter N. 1978. *Sir Alfred Jones, Shipping Entrepreneur par Excellence*. London: Europa. Introduction by Neil McKendrick.

Daviet, Jean-Pierre. 1988. "Négoce et industrie textiles dans le rayon de Lille-Roubaix-Tourcoing," *Revue du Nord* (special issue of "Histoire économique"): 64–88.

———. 1988. *Un destin international: la Compagnie de Saint-Gobain de 1830 à 1939*. Paris: Editions des Archives contemporaines.

———. 1989. *Saint-Gobain: une multinationale à la française, 1665–1989*. Paris: Fayard.

Davis, Donald Finlay. 1988. *Conspicuous Production: Automobiles and Elites in Detroit, 1899–1933*. Philadelphia: Temple University Press.

Davis, John H. 1988. *The Guggenheims (1848–1988): An American Epic*. New York: Shapolsky.

Desmond, James. 1964. *Nelson Rockefeller: A Political Biography*. New York: Macmillan.

Deveny, Kathleen. 1989. "Leonard Lauder Is Making His Mom Proud," *BusinessWeek*, 4 September, pp. 68–69.

Dickinson, H. W. 1936. *Matthew Boulton*. Cambridge: Cambridge University Press.

Dion, Jacques, and Pierre Ivorra. 1985. *Sur la piste des grandes fortunes*. Paris: Editions Sociales/Messidor.

Douglas-Home, Charles. 1978. *Evelyn Baring: The Last Proconsul*. London: Collins.

Dower, John W. 1993. *Japan in War and Peace: Selected Essays*. New York: New Press.

Dumont, Pierre. 1976. *Peugeot: Sous le signe du lion*. Paris: Editions Pratiques Automobiles.

Dutton, William S. 1942. *Du Pont, One Hundred and Forty Years*. New York: Charles Scribner's Sons.

Dyer, Davis, and Daniel Gross. 2001. *Generations of Corning: The Life and Times of a Global Corporation*. New York: Oxford University Press.

Edwards, M. M. 1967. *The Growth of the British Cotton Trade, 1780–1815*. Manchester: Manchester University Press.

Elbaum, Bernard, and William Lazonick, eds. 1986. *The Decline of the British Economy*. Oxford: Oxford University Press.

Ellis, Aytoun. 1960. *Heir of Adventure: The Story of Brown, Shipley & Co., Merchant Bankers, 1810–1960*. London: Brown, Shipley.

Elon, Amos. 2002. *The Pity of It All: A History of Jews in Germany, 1743–1933.* New York: Henry Holt.

———. 1996. *Founder: A Portrait of the First Rothschild and His Time.* New York: Viking.

Endlich, Lisa J. 1999/2000. *Goldman Sachs: The Culture of Success.* New York: Knopf; Simon and Schuster; Touchstone Books.

Epstein, R. C. 1928. *The Automobile Industry: Its Economic and Commercial Development.* Chicago: A. W. Shaw.

Espinasse, Francis. 1874/1877. *Lancashire Worthies.* 2 vols. London and Manchester: Simpkin, Marshall.

Evans, C., ed. 1990. *The Letterbook of Richard Crawshay 1788–1797.* Cardiff: South Wales Record Society.

Fallows, James. 1994. *Looking at the Sun.* New York: Pantheon.

Faraut, François. 1987. *Histoire de la Belle Jardinière.* N.p.: Belin.

Farrer, David. 1974. *The Warburgs: The Story of a Family.* New York: Stein and Day.

Fay, Stephen. 1996. *The Collapse of Barings: Panic, Ignorance and Greed.* London: Arrow Business Books.

Feldenkirchen, Wilfried. 1994. *Werner von Siemens Inventor and International Entrepreneur.* Columbus: Ohio State University Press.

Ferguson, Niall. 1998. *The World's Banker: The History of the House of Rothschild.* London: Weidenfeld and Nicolson. 2 vols. in 1.

———. 1999. " 'The Caucasian Royal Family': The Rothschilds in National Contexts." In Michael Brenner, Rainer Liedtke, and David Rechter, eds., *Two Nations: British and German Jews in Comparative Perspective.* Tübingen: Mohr Siebeck.

Ferris, Paul. 1961. *The City.* New York: Random House.

———. 1985. *Gentlemen of Fortune: The World's Merchant and Investment Bankers.* New ed. London: Weidenfeld and Nicolson.

Ferry, John William. 1960. *A History of the Department Store.* New York: Macmillan.

Firebaugh, Glenn. 2003. *The New Geography of Global Income Inequality.* Cambridge, Mass.: Harvard University Press.

Fitton, Robert S. 1989. *The Arkwrights, Spinners of Fortune.* Manchester: Manchester University Press.

———, and A. P. Wadsworth. 1958. *The Strutts and the Arkwrights, 1758–1830: Study of the Early Factory System.* Manchester: Manchester University Press.

Fligstein, N. 1985. "The Spread of the Multidivisional Form Among Large Firms, 1919–79," *American Sociology Review* 50: 377–91.

Flink, J. R. 1970. *America Adopts the Automobile, 1895–1910.* Cambridge, Mass.: MIT Press.

Florence, P. Sargant. 1961. *The Ownership, Control and Success of Large Companies.* London: Sweet and Maxwell, Ltd.

Fohlen, Claude. 1956. *L'industrie textile au temps du Second Empire.* Paris: Plon.

Fontana, Giovanni L. 1986. *Schio e Alessandro Rossi*. Rome: Ed. di Storia e Litteratura.

Forbes, John Douglas. 1974. *Stettinius, Sr.: Portrait of a Morgan Partner*. Charlottesville: University of Virginia Press.

———. 1981. *J. P. Morgan, Jr., 1867–1943*. Charlottesville: University of Virginia Press.

Forden, Sara Gay. 2000. *The House of Gucci: A Sensational Story of Murder, Madness, Glamour, and Greed*. New York: William Morrow.

Fosdick, Raymond B. 1956. *John D. Rockefeller, Jr.: A Portrait*. New York: Harper and Brothers.

Fottorino, Eric. 1996. *Aventures industrielles*. Paris: Stock.

Fox, Stephen. 1999. "I Like to Build Things," *Invention and Technology* 15, no. 1 (Summer): 20–30. Walter Chrysler and the "best-engineered" cars of his day.

Fraser, W. L. 1963. *All to the Good*. Oxford: Heinemann.

Frèrejean, Alain, and Emmanuel Haymann. 1996. *Les maîtres de forges: la saga d'une dynastie lyonnaise, 1736/1886*. Paris: Albin Michel.

Fridenson, Patrick. 1972. "Une industrie nouvelle: l'automobile en France jusqu'en 1914," *Revue d'histoire moderne et contemporaine* 19 (October–December): 557–78.

———. 1972. *Histoire des usines Renault, 1898–1939*. Paris: Seuil.

———, and André Straus, eds. 1987. *Le capitalisme français 19e–20e siècle: blocages et dynamismes d'une croissance*. Paris: Fayard.

Friedman, Alan. 1988. *Agnelli: Fiat and the Network of Italian Power*. New York: New American Library.

Fritsch, P. 1952. *Les Wendel, rois de l'acier*. Paris: Laffont.

Fruin, W. Mark. 1992. *The Japanese Enterprise System: Competitive Strategies and Co-operative Structures*. Oxford: Clarendon Press.

Gadgil, D. R. 1959. *The Origins of the Modern Indian Business Class*. New York: Institute of Pacific Relations.

Galli, Giancarlo. 1997. *Gli Agnelli*. Milan: Arnoldo Mondadori.

Garçon, Anne-Françoise, ed. 1998. *L'automobile: son monde et ses réseaux*. Rennes: Presses Universitaires.

———. n.d. (1999). *Mine et métal 1780–1880: les non-ferreux et l'industrialisation*. Rennes: Presses Universitaires.

Garraty, John A. 1957. *Right-Hand Man: The Life of George W. Perkins*. New York: Harper.

Gash, N. 1961. *Mr Secretary Peel: The Life of Sir Robert Peel to 1830*. London: Longmans, Green and Co.

Gaspari, Danilo, and Walter Panciera. 2000. *I lanifici di Folliha*. Verona: Cierre Edizioni.

Gayot, Gérard. 1979. "Dispersion et concentration de la draperie sédanaise: l'entreprise Poupart de Neuflize," *Revue du Nord* 56, no. 240 (January–March): 127–48.

————. 1986. "Le second empire drapier des Neuflize à Sedan (1800–1830)," *Histoire, économie et société* (1er trimestre): 103–24.

————. 1995. "Le testament économique d'André de Neuflize, failli de haute lignée, 1836," *Entreprises et histoire* 9: 127–31.

————. 1998. *Les draps de Sedan 1646–1870.* Paris: Editions de l'EHESS.

Geisst, Charles R. 1997. *Wall Street: A History.* New York: Oxford University Press.

————. 2001. *The Last Partnerships: Inside the Great Wall Street Money Dynasties.* New York: McGraw-Hill.

Gérard, Max. 1968. *Messieurs Hottinguer, banquiers à Paris.* Paris: Hottinguer.

Gerretson, F. C. 1953–1957. *History of the Royal Dutch.* 4 vols. Leiden: E. J. Brill.

Gibb, G. S. 1950. *The Saco-Lowell Shops: Textile Machinery Building in New England, 1813–1949.* Cambridge, Mass.: Harvard University Press.

Gibbons, Herbert A. 1926. *John Wanamaker.* New York: Harper.

Gille, Bertrand. 1959. *Recherches sur la formation de la grande entreprise capitaliste, 1815–1848.* Paris: SEVPEN.

————. 1963. "Capitaux français et pétroles russes (1884–1894)," *Histoire des entreprises* (novembre) 9–94.

————. 1965–1966. *Histoire de la maison Rothschild.* 2 vols. Geneva: Droz.

————. 1968. *La sidérurgie française au XIXe siècle.* Geneva: Droz.

Girardet, Philippe. 1952. *Ceux que j'ai connus: souvenirs.* Paris: On the Peugeot company.

Glete, J. 1993. "Swedish Managerial Capitalism: Did It Ever Become Ascendant?", *Business History* 35, no. 2 (April).

Gluck, Carol. 1985. *Japan's Modern Myths: Ideology in the Late Meiji Period.* Princeton: Princeton University Press.

Gmeline, P. de. 1995. *Ruinart, la plus ancienne maison de champagne, de 1729 à nos jours.* Paris: Edition Stock.

Graham, John. 2002. "Divided We Stand," *The Tatler,* March, pp.140–47. Fighting in the Thyssen clan.

Graham, Margaret B. W., and Alec T. Shuldiner. 2001. *Corning and the Craft of Innovation.* New York: Oxford University Press.

Grand, Christian. 1991. *Trois siècles de banque: de Neuflize, Schlumberger, Mallet de 1667 à nos jours.* N.p.: Editions E/P/A.

Grandet, Henri. 1909. *Monographie d'un établissement métallurgique sis à la fois en France et en Allemagne.* Chartres: Garnier.

Greenleaf, William. 1964. *From These Beginnings: The Early Philanthropies of Henry and Edsel Ford, 1911–1936.* Detroit, Mich.: Wayne State University Press.

————. 1967. *Monopoly on Wheels: Henry Ford and the Selden Automobile Patent.* Detroit, Mich.: Wayne State University Press.

Grinberg, Ivan, and Florence Hachez-Leroy, eds. 1997. *Industrialisation et sociétés en Europe occidentale de la fin du XIXe siècle à nos jours: l'âge de l'aluminium.* Paris: Armand Colin.

Gros, Patrick. 2002. *Wesserling, une vallée, une famille, une manufacture.* Paris: Editions Familiales.

————, and Jean-Marie Bobenrieth. 2002. *Arbre généalogique des ascendants et descendants de François Gros.* Paris/Wesserling: private.

Grunwald, Kurt. 1930/1981. *Studies in the History of the German Jews in Global Banking.* Jerusalem: University of Jerusalem Press.

Guéna, Yves. 2004. *Les Wendel: Trois siècles d'histoire.* Paris: Perrin.

Guinness, Michele. 1999. *The Guinness Spirit: Brewers and Bankers, Ministers and Missionaries.* London: Hodder and Stoughton.

Hadden, Tom. 1972. *Company Law and Capitalism.* London: Weidenfeld and Nicolson.

Halberstam, David. 1986. *The Reckoning.* New York: William Morrow.

Hammond, John Hays. 1935. *The Autobiography of John Hays Hammond.* New York: Farrar and Rinehart.

Hannah, Leslie, ed. 1976. *Management Strategy and Business Development.* London: Macmillan.

————, ed. 1982. *From Family Firm to Professional Management: Structure and Performance of Business Enterprise.* Budapest.

Harr, John Ensor, and Peter J. Johnson. 1988. *The Rockefeller Century.* New York: Charles Scribner's Sons.

Hau, Michel. 1985. "La longévité des dynasties industrielles alsaciennes," *Le mouvement social* 132 (July–September): 9–25.

————, ed. 1989. *Regards sur la société contemporaine: trois familles d'Alsace: les Bussièrre, les Saglio, et les Schlumberger.* Strasbourg: Editions Oberlin. See P. Teissonnier-Jestin.

————. 1995. "Traditions comportementales et capitalisme dynastique: le cas des 'grandes familles,'" *Entreprises et histoire* 9 (septembre): 43–59.

————. 1998. *La maison de Dietrich de 1684 à nos jours.* Strasbourg: Oberlin.

Hawke, David Freeman. 1980. *John D.: The Founding Father of the Rockefellers.* New York: Harper and Row.

Hayes, Walter. 1990. *Henry: A Life of Henry Ford II.* New York: Grove Weidenfeld.

Headrick, Daniel R. 1988. *The Tentacles of Progress: Technology Transfer in the Age of Imperialism, 1850–1940.* New York and Oxford: Oxford University Press.

Held, David, Anthony McGrew, David Goldblatt, and Jonathan Perraton. 1999. *Global Transformations, Politics, Economics and Culture.* Cambridge: Polity Press.

Hendrickson, Robert. 1979. *The Grand Emporiums: The Illustrated History of America's Great Department Stores.* New York: Stein and Day.

Les Hénokiens: Association d'entreprises familiales et bicentenaires. 1989. Paris.

Henrey, Robert. 1937. *A Century Between.* New York: Longmans, Green. Re. Rothschild.

Henri, Daniel. 1985. "Comptes, mécomptes et redressement d'une gestion industrielle: les Automobiles Peugeot de 1918 à 1930," *Revue d'histoire moderne et contemporaine* (janvier–mars): 30–74.

———. 1985. *La Société Anonyme des Automobiles Peugeot de 1918 à 1930*. Master's thesis. University of Paris I.

———. 1988. "Capitalisme familial et gestion industrielle au XIXe siècle," *Les racines de l'entreprise, Revue française de gestion* 70 (septembre).

———. 1995. "Une famille, une entreprise: les Peugeot au XIXe siècle," *La revue du Musée d'Orsay* 48/14, 1 (septembre).

Henriques, Robert. 1960. *Bearsted: A Biography of Marcus Samuel, First Viscount Bearsted and Founder of "Shell" Transport and Trading Company*. New York: Viking.

Herman, Arthur. 2001. *How the Scots Invented the Modern World: The True Story of How Western Europe's Poorest Nation Created Our World and Everything in It*. New York: Random House.

Herndon, Booton. 1969. *Ford: An Unconventional Biography of the Men and Their Times*. New York: Weybright and Talley.

Heuberger, Georg, ed. 1994. *The Rothschilds: A European Family*. Sigmaringen and Frankfurt: Jan Thorbecke Verlag. Catalog of an exposition at the Jüdisches Museum in Frankfurt.

———, ed. 1994. *The Rothschilds: Essays on the History of a European Family*. Sigmaringen and Frankfurt: Jan Thorbecke Verlag.

Hewins, Ralph. 1961. *J. Paul Getty: The Richest American*. London: Sidgwick and Jackson.

Hibbert, Christopher. 1975. *The House of Medici: Its Rise and Fall*. New York: William Morrow.

Hidy, Muriel Emmie. 1979. *George Peabody, Merchant and Financier, 1829–1854*. New York: Arno Press.

Hidy, Ralph W., G. S. Gibb, and H. M. Larson. 1949, 1956, 1971. *History of Standard Oil Company*. 3 vols. New York: Harper and Brothers.

Hirsch, F. 1977. *Social Limits to Growth*. London: Routledge and Kegan Paul.

Hirst, Paul, and Grahame Thompson. 1999. *Globalization in Question: The International Economy and the Possibilities of Governance*. 2nd ed., rev. Cambridge and Oxford: Polity Press and Blackwell's.

Hofstede, G. 1984. *Culture's Consequences: Comparing Values, Behaviors, Institutions, and Organizations Across Nations*. Newbury Park, Calif.: Sage Publications.

Holmes, C. 1979. *Anti-Semitism in British Society, 1879–1939*. London: Edward Arnold.

Honeyman, Katrina. 1982. *Origins of Enterprise: Business Leadership in the Industrial Revolution*. Manchester: Manchester University Press.

Hopkins, Anthony G., ed. 2002. *Globalization in World History*. London: Pimlico.

Hoppit, J. 1987. *Risk and Failure in English Business, 1700–1800*. Cambridge: Cambridge University Press.

Horn, N., and Jürgen Kocka, eds. 1979. *Recht und Entwicklung der Grossunternehmen im 19. und frühen 20. Jahrhundert*. Göttingen: Vandenhoeck und Ruprecht.

Hovey, Carl. 1912. *The Life Story of J. Pierpont Morgan*. New York: Sturgis and Walton.

Howe, Christopher. 1999. *The Origins of Japanese Trade Supremacy: Development and Technology in Asia from 1540 to the Pacific War*. London: Hurst and Co.

Hower, Ralph M. 1943. *History of Macy's of New York, 1858–1919: Chapters in the Evolution of the Department Store*. Cambridge, Mass.: Harvard University Press.

Hoyt, Edwin P., Jr. 1966. *The House of Morgan*. New York: Dodd, Mead.

———. 1967. *The Guggenheims and the American Dream*. New York: Funk and Wagnalls.

Hudson, Pat. 1986. *The Genesis of Industrial Capital: A Study of the West Riding Wool Textile Industry, c. 1750–1850*. Cambridge: Cambridge University Press.

Hugill, Peter J. 1993. *World Trade since 1431: Geography, Technology, and Capitalism*. Baltimore and London: Johns Hopkins University Press.

Iacocca, Lee, with William Novak. 1984. *Iacocca: An Autobiography*. New York: Bantam.

———, with Sonny Kleinfeld. 1988. *Talking Straight*. New York: Bantam Books.

Innes, Stephen. 1995. *Creating the Commonwealth: The Economic Culture of Puritan New England*. New York: Norton.

Jackson, Stanley. 1968. *The Sassoons*. Oxford: Heinemann.

———. 1983. *J. P. Morgan*. New York: Stein and Day.

Jacquemin, Alexis, and Elizabeth de Ghellinck. 1980. "Familial Control, Size and Performance in the Largest French Firms," *European Economic Review*, 13.

Jeanneney, Jean-Noel. 2004. *François de Wendel en République: L'argent et le pouvoir, 1914–1940*. New ed., rev. Paris: Perrin.

Jemain, Alain. 1987. *Les Peugeot: vertiges et secrets d'une dynastie*. Paris: J.-C. Lattès.

Jobert, P., and M. Moss, eds. 1990. *The Birth and Death of Companies: An Historical Perspective*. Carnforth: Parthenon Publishing Group.

———, eds. 1995. *Naissance et mort des entreprises en Europe, XIXe–XXe siècles*. Dijon: Presses Universitaires de Dijon.

Jones, Charles. 1984. "The Growth and Performance of British Multinational Firms Before 1939: The Case of Dunlop," *Economic History Review* 37, no. 1.

———. 1987. *International Business in the Nineteenth Century: The Rise and Fall of a Cosmopolitan Bourgeoisie*. New York: New York University Press.

———, and Harm G. Schröter. 1994. *The Rise of Multinationals in Continental Europe*. Aldershot: E. Elgar.

Jones, E. L. 1967. "Industrial Capital and Landed Investment: The Arkwrights in Herefordshire, 1809–1843." In E. L. Jones and G. E. Mingay, eds., 1967. *Land, Labour and Population in the Industrial Revolution*. London: Edward Arnold, 48–74.

———. 1987. *A History of GKN*, vol. I: *Innovation and Enterprise, 1759–1918*. London: Macmillan.

Jones, Geoffrey, and Mary B. Rose, eds. 1993. *Family Capitalism*. London: Frank Cass. See also *Business History* 35, no. 4 (October 1993): 1–16.

Josephson, Emanuel M. 1964. *The Truth about Rockefeller, "Public Enemy No. 1": Studies in Criminal Psychopathy*. New York: Chedney Press.

Josephson, Matthew. 1934. *The Robber Barons: The Great American Capitalists, 1861–1901*. New York: Harcourt, Brace.

Kauffman, Reginald Wright. 1973. *Jesse Isidor Strauss, A Biographical Portrait*. New York: private.

Kemp, Tom. 1993. *Historical Patterns of Industrialization*. 2d ed. London and New York: Longmans.

Kennedy, R. D. 1941. *The Automobile Industry*. New York.

Kindleberger, Charles P. 1975. "Commercial Expansion and the Industrial Revolution," in *Journal of European Economic History* 4, no. 3 (Winter): 613–54.

Kirby, M. W. 1984. *Men of Business and Politics: The Rise and Fall of the Quaker Pease Dynasty of North-East England, 1700–1943*. London: Allen and Unwin.

Kirchholtes, H. D. 1969. *Jüdische Privatbanken in Frankfurt-am-Main*. Frankfurt: Kramer.

Klep, P., and E. Van Cauwenberghe, eds. 1994. *Entrepreneurship and the Transformation of the Economy (10th–20th Centuries): Essays in Honour of Herman Van der Wee*. Leuven: Leuven Press.

Kocka, Jürgen. 1978. "Entrepreneurs and Managers in German Industrialisation," *Cambridge Economic History of Europe* VII, no. 1.

Kouwenhoven, John A. 1968. *Partners in Banking: An Historical Portrait of a Great Private Bank: Brown Brothers Harriman & Co. 1818–1968*. Garden City, N.Y.: Doubleday.

Kynaston, David. 1995. *The City of London*: Vol. II. *Golden Years, 1890–1914*. 2002. Vol. IV. *A Club No More 1945–2000*. London: Pimlico.

Lacey, Robert. 1986. *Ford: The Men and the Machine*. Boston: Little, Brown.

Lamard, P. 1988. *Histoire d'un capital familial au XIXe siècle: Le capital Japy (1777–1910)*. Montbéliard.

———. 1994. "Dynasties et stratégies: une même volonté industrielle, deux destins opposés," *Zs. f. Unternehmensgeschichte*, Beiheft 83: 135–52.

———. 1996. *De la forge à la société holding: Vieillard-Migeon et Cie (1796–1996)*. Paris: Polytechnica.

Lambert-Dansette, Jean. 1954. *Quelques familles du patronat textile de Lille-Armentières (1789–1914)*. Lille: Editions L'Harmattan.

———. 1991. *Genèse du patronat, 1780–1880. Histoire de l'entreprise et des chefs d'entreprise en France*. Paris: Hachette.

————. 1992. *La vie des chefs d'entreprise, 1830–1880.* Paris: Hachette.

Lamont, Edward M. 1994. *The Ambassador from Wall Street: The Story of Thomas W. Lamont, J. P. Morgan's Chief Executive.* Lanham, Md.: Madison Books.

Lamoureux, Naomi, Daniel Raff, and Peter Temin, eds. 1998. *Learning by Doing in Markets, Firms, and Countries.* Chicago: Univ. of Chicago Press.

Landes, David S. 1956. "Vieille banque et banque nouvelle: la révolution financière du dix-neuvième siècle," *Revue d'histoire moderne et contemporaine.* 3: 204–22.

————. 1958. *Bankers and Pashas: International Finance and Economic Imperialism in Egypt.* London: Heinemann; Cambridge, Mass.: Harvard University Press.

————. 1960. "The Bleichröder Bank: An Interim Report." In *Yearbook V* of the Leo Baeck Institute (London), pp. 201–20.

————. 1982. "The Spoilers Foiled: The Exclusion of Prussian Finance from the French Liberation Loan of 1871," in C. P. Kindleberger and Guido di Tella, eds., *Economics in the Long View.* 2 vols.; New York: New York University Press, 2: 67–110.

————. 1987. "Piccolo e bello. Ma e bello davvèro?" In Landes, ed., *A che servono i padroni? le alternative storiche dell'industrializzazione.* Torino: Bollati Boringhieri, pp. 162–78.

————. 1991. "Does It Pay to Be Late?" In Colin Holmes and Alan Booth, eds., *Economy and Society: European Industrialisation and Its Social Consequences.* Leicester: University of Leicester Press, pp. 3–23.

————. 1999. "L'automobile e lo sviluppo industriale," in Annibaldi and Berta, eds., *Grande impresa e sviluppo italiano,* pp. 19–66.

————. 2003. "Regard historien sur les entreprises et les entrepreneurs," Postface to Jean-Claude Daumas, ed., *Le capitalisme familial: logiques et trajectoires* (Actes de la journée d'études de Besançon du 17 janvier 2002). Besançon: Presses universitaires franc-comtoises.

Lasky, Victor. 1981. *Never Complain, Never Explain: The Story of Henry Ford II.* New York: Richard Marek.

Lauder, Estée. 1985. *Estée: A Success Story.* New York: Random House.

Laux, James M. 1976. *In First Gear: The French Automobile Industry to 1914.* Liverpool: Liverpool University Press.

————. 1982. *The Automobile Revolution: The Impact of an Industry.* Chapel Hill: University of North Carolina Press.

Lazonick, William. 1991. *Business Organisation and the Myth of the Market Economy.* Cambridge: Cambridge University Press.

Lee, Albert. 1980. *Henry Ford and the Jews.* New York: Stein and Day.

Lee, C. H. 1972. *A Cotton Enterprise, 1795–1840: A History of M'Connel and Kennedy, Fine Cotton Spinners.* Manchester: Manchester University Press.

Lee, Christopher. 2002. *This Sceptered Isle: The Dynasties.* London: BBC Worldwide.

Léger, Catherine. 1996. "Dynasties d'entreprise et dynasties d'entreprendre," *Entreprises et histoire* 12 (juin): 89–100.

Lehideux-Vernimmen, Virginie. 1992. *Du négoce à la banque: les André. Une famille protestante Nîmes-Paris (1600–1800)*. Nîmes: C. Lacour.

Leighton-Boyce, J.A.S.L. 1958. *Smiths the Bankers, 1658–1958*. London: National Provincial Bank.

Lequin, Yves. 1983. *Histoire des Français XIXe–XXe siècles. vol. II: La société*. Paris: A. Colin.

Lévy, Robert. 1912. *Histoire économique de l'industrie cotonnière en Alsace: Etude de sociologie descriptive*. Paris: Alcan.

Lévy-Leboyer, Maurice. 1964. *Les banques européennes et l'industrialisation internationale au XIXe siècle*. Paris: Presses Universitaires de France.

———. 1964. "Quatre générations de maîtres de forges gallois: les Crawshay," *Revue du Nord* 46, no. 180 (janvier–mars): 27–50.

———, ed. 1979. *Le patronat de la seconde industrialisation*. Paris: Editions Ouvrières.

———, and J. C. Casanova, eds. 1991. *Entre l'Etat et le marché: l'économie française des années 1880 à nos jours*. Paris: Gallimard.

Lewchuk, Wayne. 1987. *American Technology and the British Vehicle Industry*. Cambridge: Cambridge University Press.

Lilley, William III, and Laurence J. DeFranco. 1999. *The European Impact of the European Grands Prix*. Brussels: Fédération Internationale de l'Automobile.

Lim, L.Y.C., and L.A.P. Gosling, eds. 1988. *The Chinese in Southeast Asia*. Singapore: Maruzen Asia.

Littlewood, Joan, ed. 1984. *Baron Philippe: The Very Candid Autobiography of Baron Philippe de Rothschild*. New York: Crown.

Livesay, H. C. 1977. "Entrepreneurial Persistence Through the Bureaucratic Age," *Business History Review* 51 (Winter): 415–43.

———. 1989. "Entrepreneurial Dominance in Businesses Large and Small, Past and Present," *Business History Review* 63 (Spring): 1–21.

Lloyd, Humphrey. 1975. *The Quaker Lloyds in the Industrial Revolution*. London: Hutchinson.

Lomüller, G. 1978. *Guillaume Ternaux*. Paris: Editions de la Cabro d'or.

Longhurst, Henry. 1959. *Adventure in Oil: The History of British Petroleum*. London: Sidgwick and Jackson.

Lottman, Herbert R. 1995. *The French Rothschilds: The Great Banking Dynasty Through Two Turbulent Centuries*. New York: Crown.

———. 1998. *Michelin: cent ans d'aventures*. Paris: Flammarion.

———. 2003. *The Michelin Men: Driving an Empire*. London: I. B. Tauris.

Loubet, Jean-Louis. 1990. *Automobiles Peugeot: une réussite industrielle, 1945–1974*. Paris: Economica.

———. 1995. *Citroën, Peugeot, Renault et les autres: soixante ans de stratégies*. Paris: Le Monde Editions.

———. 1995. "Peugeot: de l'entreprise familiale à la multinationale." In

Jacques Marseille, ed., *Les performances des entreprises françaises au XXe siècle*. Paris: Le Monde Editions.

————. 1999. *L'industrie automobile, 1905–1971*. Geneva: Droz; Archives économiques du Crédit Lyonnais.

————. 2001. *Histoire de l'automobile français*. Paris: Seuil.

————. 2002. "Le capitalisme familial: quelles trajectoires?" Journée d'Etudes du 17 janvier 2002, *Bulletin du Centre d'histoire contemporaine de l'Université de Franche-Comté*. In same group of Etudes: "Capitalisme familial et industrie automobile: une autre exception française."

Lowenstein, Roger. 2001. *Buffett: The Making of an American Capitalist*. New York: Broadway Books.

Lundberg, Ferdinand. 1937/1939. *America's 60 Families*. New York: Vanguard Press; Halcyon House.

————. 1968. *The Rich and the Super-rich: A Study in the Power of Money Today*. New York: Lyle Stuart.

————. 1975. *The Rockefeller Syndrome*. Secaucus, N.J.: Lyle Stuart.

Lynch, Patrick, and John Vaizey. 1960. *Guinness Brewery in the Irish Economy 1759–1876*. Cambridge: Cambridge University Press.

MacKie, J.A.C., ed. 1976. *The Chinese in Indonesia*. Honolulu: Hawaii University Press.

Madron, Paolo. 1998. *Date a Cesare . . .* Milan: Longanesi. The life of Cesare Romiti.

Mahoney, Tom, and Leonard Sloane. 1974. *The Great Merchants: America's Foremost Retail Institutions and the People Who Made Them*. New York: Harper and Row.

Mallet Frères. 1943. *250 ans de banque*. Paris.

Malone, Michael. 1985. *The Big Score: The Billion-Dollar Story of Silicon Valley*. Garden City, N.Y.: Doubleday.

Manchester, William. 1959. *A Rockefeller Family Portrait: From John D. to Nelson*. Boston and Toronto: Little, Brown.

Mann, Vivian B., and Richard I. Cohen, eds. 1996. *From Court Jews to the Rothschilds, Art, Patronage, and Power, 1600–1800*. Munich and New York: Prestel.

Mansson, Per-Henrik. 2000. "The Rothschild Dynasty from Frankfurt's Jewish Ghetto to Bordeaux: How the Rothschilds Became the World's Preeminent Family of Wine," *Wine Spectator*, December 15, pp. 40–95. (Title varies.)

Mantle, Jonathan. 1995. *Car Wars: Fifty Years of Backstabbing, Infighting, and Industrial Espionage in the Global Market*. New York: Arcade.

March, Robert M. 1992. *Working for a Japanese Company: Insights into the Multicultural Workplace*. Tokyo: Kodansha.

Marcosson, Isaac. 1949. *The Story of the American Smelting and Refining Company*. New York: Farrar Straus.

Marguerat, Philippe. 1987. *Banque et investissement industriel: Paribas, le pétrole roumain et la politique française, 1919–1939*. Geneva: Neuchatel.

————. 1991. "Patronat et capitaux français face à la seconde industrialisation: l'exemple du pétrole," *Annales ESC,* no. 1 (January–February): 205–18.

Marriner, Sheila, ed. 1980. *Business and Businessmen: Studies in Business, Economic and Accounting History.* Liverpool: Liverpool University Press.

Marseille, Jacques, ed. 1995. *Les performances des enterprises françaises au XXe siècle.* Paris: Le Monde Editions.

————, ed. 1997. *Puissance et faiblesses de le France industrielle.* Paris: Seuil.

————. 2000. *Créateurs et créations d'entreprises de la révolution industrielle à nos jours.* Paris: ADHE.

————. 2004. *Les Wendel, 1704–2004.* Paris: Editions Perrin.

Martin-Fugier, Anne. 1988. *La vie élégante et la formation du "Tout Paris," 1815-1848.* Paris: Fayard.

Mathias, Peter. 1959. *The Brewing Industry in England, 1700–1830.* Cambridge: Cambridge University Press.

Matthews, P. W., and A. W. Tuke. 1926. *History of Barclays Bank, Ltd.*

Maxcy, George. 1981. *The Multinational Automobile Industry.* New York: St. Martin's.

————, and Aubrey Silberston. 1959. *The Motor Industry.* London: Allen and Unwin.

Mayer, Martin. 1997. *The Bankers: The Next Generation.* New York: Truman Talley Books/Plume.

Mayfield, Frank M. 1949. *The Department Store Story.* New York: Fairchild.

McCraw, Thomas K., ed. 1997. *Creating Modern Capitalism: How Entrepreneurs, Companies, and Countries Triumphed in Three Industrial Revolutions.* Cambridge, Mass.: Harvard University Press.

McDonald, John. 2002. *A Ghost's Memoir: The Making of Alfred P. Sloan's My Years with General Motors.* Cambridge, Mass.: MIT Press.

McDonogh, G. W. 1987. *Good Families of Barcelona: A Social History of Power in the Industrial Era.* Princeton: Princeton University Press.

McKnight, Gerald. 1987. *Gucci: A House Divided.* New York: Donald I. Fine; London: Sidgwick and Jackson; Penguin.

McMaster, John. 1966. *Jardines in Japan, 1859–1867.* Groningen: Druk V.R.B.

McVey, Ruth T. 1992. *Southeast Asian Capitalists.* Ithaca: Cornell University Press.

Mension-Rigau, Eric. 1994. *Aristocrates et grands bourgeois.* Paris: Plon.

Meteyard, E. 1871. *A Group of Englishmen (1795–1815), Being Records of the Younger Wedgwoods and Their Friends.* London: Longmans Green.

Michel, Bernard. 1976. *Banques et banquiers en Autriche au début du 20e siècle.* Paris: Presses de la Fondation Nationale des Sciences Politiques.

Milesi, Gabriel. 1990. *Les nouvelles 200 familles françaises.* Paris: Belfond.

Miller, Michael B. 1981. *The Bon Marché: Bourgeois Culture and the Department Store, 1869–1920.* Princeton: Princeton University Press.

Miller, William, ed. 1952/1962. *Men in Business: Essays on the Historical Role of the Entrepreneur.* Cambridge, Mass.: Harvard University Press; New York: Harper and Row.

Minami, Ryoshin. 1994. *The Economic Development of Japan: A Quantitative Study.* 2d ed. London and Hong Kong: Macmillan.

Minchinton, Walter. 1957. "The Merchants in England in the Eighteenth Century." In *The Entrepreneur.* Cambridge, Mass.: Harvard University Press.

Miquel, René. 1962. *Dynastie Michelin.* La Table Ronde.

Miyashita, Kenichi, and David Russell. 1994. *Keiretsu: Inside the Hidden Japanese Conglomerates.* New York: McGraw-Hill.

Moccia, Maria Rosaria, ed. 1998. *Bibliografiat: Saggi, studi, ricerche sulla Fiat (1899–1996).* Turin: Scriptorium.

Moine, J.-M. 1989. *Les barons du fer: Les maîtres de forges en Lorraine du milieu du XIXe siècle aux années trente: histoire sociale d'un patronat sidérurgique.* Nancy.

Mondadori, Arnolda, ed. 1951. *Fiat: A Fifty-Year Record.* Turin.

Morikawa, Hidemasa. 1970. "The Organizational Structure of Mitsubishi and Mitsui Zaibatsu, 1868–1922: A Comparative Study." *Business History Review* 44, no. 1 (Spring): 62–83; reprinted in Rose, ed., *Family Business,* 384–405.

———. 1992. *Zaibatsu: The Rise and Fall of Family Enterprise Groups in Japan.* Tokyo.

———. 1999. "Japan: Increasing Organizational Capabilities of Large Industrial Enterprises, 1880s–1980s." In Chandler, Amatori, and Hikino, eds., *Big Business,* pp. 307–35.

Morin, François. 1974. *La structure financière du capitalisme français.* Paris: Calmann-Lévy.

Morita, Akio, with Edwin M. Reingold and Mitsuko Shimomura. 1986. *Made in Japan: Akio Morita and Sony.* New York: E. P. Dutton.

Moritz, Michael, and Barrett Seaman. 1981. *Going for Broke: The Chrysler Story.* Garden City, N.Y.: Doubleday.

Mosley, Leonard. 1980. *Blood Relations: The Rise and Fall of the du Ponts of Delaware.* New York: Atheneum.

Mosse, Werner E. 1988. "Problems and Limits of Assimilation: Hermann and Paul Wallich, 1833–1938." In Leo Baeck Institute, *Year Book XXXIII.* London: Secker & Warburg; pp. 43–65.

Muhlstein, Anka. 1981. *James de Rothschild. Francfort 1792–Paris 1868: Une métamorphose.* Paris. English translation: *Baron James: The Rise of the French Rothschilds.* London: Collins, n.d. In this version, author's first name is given as Anka.

Müller, Margrit, ed. 1994. *Structure and Strategy of Small- and Medium-Size Enterprises since the Industrial Revolution.* Stuttgart: Zs. f. Unternehmensgeschichte, Beiheft 89.

———. 1996. "Good Luck or Good Management? Multigenerational Family

Control in Two Swiss Enterprises since the Nineteenth Century," *Entreprises et histoire* 12 (June): 19–47.

Nakagawa, K., ed. 1977. *Social Order and the Entrepreneur*. Tokyo.

Nakamura, Takafusa. 1983. *Economic Growth in Prewar Japan*. New Haven: Yale University Press.

Nathan, John. 1999. *SONY: The Private Life*. Boston and New York: Houghton Mifflin.

Needham, Joseph. 1970. *Clerks and Craftsmen in China and the West*. Cambridge: Cambridge University Press.

Neff, Thomas J., and James M. Citrin, with Paul B. Brown. 1999. *Lessons from the Top*. New York: Doubleday.

Neuschwander, Claude, and Gaston Bordet. 1993. *Lip, vingt ans après, 1973–1993, propos sur le chômage*. Paris: Syros.

Nevins, Allan. 1940. *John D. Rockefeller: The Heroic Age of American Enterprise*. 2 vols. New York: Charles Scribner's Sons.

———. 1953. *John D. Rockefeller, Industrialist and Philanthropist*. 2 vols. New York: Charles Scribner's Sons.

———, with collaboration of Frank Ernest Hill. 1954. *Ford: The Times, the Man, the Company*. New York: Charles Scribner's Sons.

———, and Frank Ernest Hill. 1957. *Ford: Expansion and Challenge, 1915–1933*. New York: Charles Scribner's Sons.

———. 1962. *Ford: Decline and Rebirth, 1933–1962*. New York: Charles Scribner's Sons.

Newman, Peter C. 1991. *Merchant Princes*. Toronto: Penguin Books Canada.

Nicholson, T. R. 1982. *The Birth of the British Motor Car*. 3 vols. London: Macmillan.

Nicolay, Pierre-Xavier. 1937 and 1951. *Histoire d'Hayange*. 3 vols. Hayange: Marchal.

Nicolson, B. 1968. *Joseph Wright of Derby*. 2 vols. London.

Nohria, Nitin, Davis Dyer, and Frederick Dalzell. 2002. *Changing Fortunes: Remaking the Industrial Corporation*. New York: John Wiley.

Nossiter, Bernard D. 1987. *The Global Struggle for More: Third World Conflicts with Rich Nations*. New York: Harper and Row.

Nyman, S., and Aubrey Silberston. 1978. "The Ownership and Control of Industry," In *Oxford Economic Papers*, new ser., 30: 90–102.

Ockrent, Christine, and Jean-Paul Séréni, eds. 1998. *Les grands patrons: comment ils voient notre avenir*. Paris: Plon.

O'Connor, Harvey. 1937. *The Guggenheims: The Making of an American Dynasty*. New York: Covici Friede.

O'Connor, Richard. 1971. *The Oil Barons, Men of Greed and Grandeur*. Boston: Little, Brown.

O'Higgins, Patrick. 1971. *Madame: An Intimate Biography of Helena Rubinstein*. New York: Viking.

Okochi, Akio, and Shigeaki Yasuoka, eds. 1984. *Family Business in the Era of*

Industrial Growth: Its Ownership and Management. Tokyo: University of Tokyo Press.

Olofsson, Rune Pär. 2001. *Le roi de la dynamite*. Paris: Gaïa. Trans. from Swedish. Novel re. life Alfred Nobel.

Omoto, Keiko, and Francis Macouin. 1990. *Quand le Japon s'ouvrit au monde*. Paris: Gallimard; Réunion des Musées Nationaux.

Orbell, J. 1985. *Baring Brothers and Co., Limited. A History to 1939*. London: Barings.

Ori, Angiolo Silvio. 1996. *Storia di una dinastia: Gli Agnelli e la Fiat. Cronache "non autorizzate" dei cento anni della più grande industria italiana*. Rome: Editori Riuniti.

Overy, R. J. 1976. *William Morris, Viscount Nuffield*. Introduction by Neil McKendrick. London.

Paganelli, Serge, and Martine Jacquin. 1975. *Peugeot: La dynastie s'accroche*. Paris: Editions Sociales.

Palin, R. 1970. *Rothschild Relish*. London: Cassell.

Pallotta, Gino. 1987. *Gli Agnelli: una dinastia italiana*. Newton Compton.

Palmade, Guy. 1961. *Capitalisme et capitalistes français au XIXe*. Paris.

Pauli, Herta E. 1942. *Alfred Nobel, Dynamite King—Architect of Peace*. New York: L. B. Fischer.

Payne, Peter L. 1961. *Rubber and Railways in the Nineteenth Century*. Liverpool: Liverpool University Press.

———. 1967. "The Emergence of the Large-Scale Company in Great Britain," *Economic History Review*, 2d ser., 20, no. 2.

Penrose, Edith. 1959. *The Theory of the Growth of the Firm*. Oxford: Oxford University Press.

Petzinger, Thomas, Jr. 1987. *Oil and Honor: The Texaco-Pennzoil Wars*. New York: G. P. Putnam's Sons.

Peugeot, Jean-Pierre. 1934/1958. *Le film de l'automobile: Voici la France*. Paris: Arthème Fayard.

Peugeot, Louis. 1935. *Histoire de la famille Peugeot*.

Phillips, Kevin. 2004. *American Dynasty: Aristocracy, Fortune, and the Politics of Deceit in the House of Bush*. New York: Viking Penguin.

Picot, Jacques-Georges. 1993. *Souvenirs d'une longue carrière: de la rue de Rivoli à la Compagnie de Suez, 1920–1971*. Paris: CHEF.

Pietra, Italo. 1985. *I tre Agnelli*. Milan: Garzanti.

Pigott, S. 1949. *Hollins. A Study of Industry, 1784–1949*. Nottingham.

Pinçon, Michel, and Monique Pinçon-Charlot. 1996. *Grandes fortunes: Dynasties familiales et formes de richesse en France*. Paris: Payot.

Plummer, A., and R. E. Early. 1969. *The Blanket Makers, 1669–1969: A History of Charles Early and Marriott (Witney) Ltd*. New York: Routledge.

Pollard, Sidney. 1965. *The Genesis of Modern Management*. London: Arnold.

Pomeranz, Kenneth. 2001. "Is There an East Asian Development Path? Long-Term Comparisons, Constraints, and Continuities," *Journal of Economic and Social History of the Orient* 44, no. 3: 322–62.

———. 2002. "Political Economy and Ecology on the Eve of Industrialization: Europe, China, and the Global Conjuncture," *American Historical Review* 107, no. 2: 425–47.

Postan, M. M. 1967. *An Economic History of Western Europe, 1945–1964.* London: Methuen.

Pressnell, L. S. 1956. *Country Banking in the Industrial Revolution.* Oxford: Clarendon Press.

Preter, René de. 1983. *Les 200 familles les plus riches.* Brussels: Berchem.

Professeurs du Groupe HEC. 1994. *L'Ecole des managers de demain.* Paris: Economica.

Progetto Archivio storico Fiat. 1987. *I primi quindici anni della Fiat: Verbali dei Consigli di amministrazione, 1899–1915.* Milan: Angeli.

———. 1991. *Fiat 1899–1930: Storia e documenti.* 3 vols. Milan: Fabbri.

Pugh, Emerson W. 1995. *Building IBM: Shaping an Industry and Its Technology.* Cambridge, Mass.: MIT Press.

Puissance et faiblesses de la France industrielle XIXe–XXe siècle. Paris: Seuil.

Purcell, Victor. 1980. *The Overseas Chinese in Southeast Asia.* Kuala Lumpur: Oxford University Press.

Rae, John B. 1959. *American Auto Manufacturers: The First Forty Years.* Philadelphia: Chilton.

———. 1965. *The American Automobile: A Brief History.* Chicago: University of Chicago Press.

Raistrick, A. 1953. *Dynasty of Iron Founders. The Darbys and Coalbrookdale.* London: Longmans, Green.

Rapp, D. 1974. "Social Mobility in the Eighteenth Century: The Whitbreads of Bedfordshire, 1720–1815," *Economic History Review* 27, no. 3 (August).

Ratcliffe, B. M., and W. H. Chaloner, eds. 1977. *A French Sociologist Looks at Britain: Gustave d'Eichthal and British Society in 1828.* Manchester: Manchester University Press.

Redding, S. Gordon. 1990. *The Spirit of Chinese Capitalism.* Berlin: de Gruyter.

Redlich, Fritz. 1947; 1951. *The Molding of American Banking: Men and Ideas.* 2 vols. New York: Johnson Reprint Corporation.

Rees, Goronwy. 1969. *St. Michael: A History of Marks & Spencer.* London: Weidenfeld and Nicolson.

Reich, Cary. 1983. *Financier: The Biography of Andre Meyer. A Story of Money, Power, and the Reshaping of American Business.* New York: William Morrow.

Reingold, Edwin M. 1999. *Toyota: People, Ideas and the Challenge of the New.* London: Penguin.

"Report of the [Parliamentary] Committee of Inquiry on Small Firms" [the Bolton Report]. Cmd. 4811. London: HMSO, 1971.

Reynolds, John. 1996. *André Citroën: The Henry Ford of France.* New York: St. Martin's.

Richard, Guy. 1984. *Monographie d'une entreprise alsacienne: De Dietrich (1684–1918).* Paris.

Richardson, Kenneth. 1977. *The British Motor Industry, 1896–1939*. London: Macmillan.

Rimmer, W. G. 1960. *Marshall's of Leeds: Flax Spinners, 1788–1886*. Cambridge: Cambridge University Press.

Robison, Richard, and David S. G. Goodman, eds. 1996. *The New Rich in Asia: Mobile Phones, McDonald's and Middle-Class Revolution*. London: Routledge.

Rock, S. 1991. *Family Firms*. Cambridge: Cambridge University Press.

Rockefeller, David. 2002. *Memoirs*. New York: Random House.

Roland, Joan G. 1968. *Jews in British India: Identity in a Colonial Era*. Hanover, N.H.: University Press of New England.

Rose, Mary B. 1986. *The Gregs of Quarry Bank Mill: The Rise and Decline of a Family Firm, 1750–1914*. Cambridge: Cambridge University Press.

———, ed. 1995. *Family Business*. Aldershot: Elgar.

Rosenbaum, Eduard, and Ari Joshua Sherman. 1979. *M. M. Warburg & Co., 1798–1938: Merchant Bankers of Hamburg*. New York: Holmes and Meier.

Ross, Kristin. 1996. *Fast Cars, Clean Bodies: Decolonization and the Reordering of French Culture*. Cambridge, Mass.: MIT Press.

Roth, Cecil. 1939. *The Magnificent Rothschilds*. A Commentary Classic. London: Robert Hale.

———. 1941. *The Sassoon Dynasty*. London: Robert Hale.

Rothblatt, Sheldon. 1968. *The Revolution of the Dons*. London: Faber and Faber.

Rothschild, Edmund de. 1998. *Edmund de Rothschild, A Gilt-Edged Life. Memoir*. London: John Murray.

Rothschild, Emma. 1973. *Paradise Lost: The Decline of the Auto-Industrial Elite*. New York: Random House.

Rothschild, Philippe de. *Baron Philippe*. See Joan Littlewood.

Rothschild, Victor. 1984. *Random Variables*. London: Collins.

Rubinstein, W. D. 1981. *Men of Property: The Very Wealthy in Britain since the Industrial Revolution*. London: Croom Helm.

———. 1987. *Elites and the Wealthy in Modern British History: Essays in Social and Economic History*. Brighton.

———. 1993. *Capitalism, Culture and Decline in Britain, 1750–1990*. London and New York: Routledge.

Ruiz, José Luis, and Manuel Santos Redondo. 2001. *!Es un motor español! Historia empresarial de barreiros*. Madrid: Editorial Sintesis.

Sagou, M'hamed. 1981. *Paribas: anatomie d'une puissance*. Paris: Fondation Nationale des Sciences Politiques.

Samuel, Y. 1985. *Les milliardaires*. Paris.

Samuels, Richard J. 1994. *"Rich Nation, Strong Army": National Security and the Technological Transformation of Japan*. Ithaca and London: Cornell University Press.

Sanderson, Michael. 1972. *The Universities and British Industry, 1850–1970*. London: Routledge.

Sassoon, David Solomon. 1949. *A History of the Jews in Baghdad.* Letchworth.

Satterlee, Herbert Livingston. 1939. *J. Pierpont Morgan: An Intimate Portrait.* New York: Macmillan.

Saul, S. Berrick. 1962. "The Motor Industry in Britain," *Business History* 5: 1–19.

Saxenian, AnnaLee. 1994. *Regional Advantage: Culture and Competition in Silicon Valley and Route 128.* Cambridge, Mass.: Harvard University Press.

Sayers, R. S. 1957. *Lloyds Bank in the History of English Banking.* Oxford: Clarendon Press.

Schama, Simon. 1987. *The Embarrassment of Riches: Dutch Culture in the Golden Age.* London: Collins.

Schlumberger, Anne Gruner. 1982. *The Schlumberger Adventure.* New York: Arco. Translation of French ed.: 1977. *La boîte magique.* Paris: Arthème Fayard.

Schneider, Dominique, et al., eds. 1995. *Les Schneider, Le Creusot: Une famille, une enterprise, une ville (1836–1960).* Paris: Fayard; Réunion des Musées Nationaux

Schoonhoven, Claudia Bird, and Elaine Romanelli, eds. 2002. *The Entrepreneurship Dynamic: Origins of Entrepreneurship and the Evolution of Industries.* Palo Alto, Calif.: Stanford University Press.

Schück, Henrik, and Ragnar Sohlman. 1929. *The Life of Alfred Nobel.* London: Heinemann.

———. [in reverse order]. 1929. *Nobel: Dynamite and Peace.* New York: Cosmopolitan Books. Both of these are translated from the same German original and yet are very different.

Schweitzer, Sylvie. 1980. *Des engrenages à la chaîne.* Lyon: Presses Universitaires de Lyon.

———. 1992. *André Citroën, 1878–1935: Le risque et le défi.* Paris: Fayard.

Scranton, Philip. 1992. "Large Firms and Industrial Restructuring: The Philadelphia Region, 1900–1980," *Pennsylvania Magazine of History and Biography* 116: 419–65.

———. 1992. "Understanding the Strategies and Dynamics of Long-Lived Family Firms," *Business and Economic History,* 2d ser., 21: 219–27.

Seagrave, Sterling. 1995. *Lords of the Rim: The Invisible Empire of the Overseas Chinese.* New York: G. P. Putnam's Sons.

Sédillot, René. 1958. *La maison de Wendel de mil sept cent quatre à nos jours: deux cent cinquante ans d'industrie en Lorraine.* Paris: Les Petits-Fils de François de Wendel et Cie. Privately printed.

———. 1960. *Peugeot: de la crinoline à la 404.* Paris: Plon.

———. 1988. *Les deux cents familles.* Paris: Perrin; "Vérités et légendes."

Sheahan, John. 1959–1960. "Government Competition and the Performance of the French Automobile Industry," *Journal of Industrial Economics* 8.

Shimokawa, Koichi, ed. 1988. *Toyota: History of the First Fifty Years.* Tokyo: Toyota Motor Company.

Siddiqi, A. 1982. "The Business World of Jamsetjee Jeejeebhoy," *Indian Economic and Social History Review* 19.

Siemens AG. 1997. *150 Years of Siemens: The Company from 1847 to 1997.* Munich: AG Siemens.

Sinclair, Andrew. 1981. *Corsair: The Life of J. Pierpont Morgan.* Boston: Little, Brown.

Slack, Charles. 2002. *Noble Obsession.* New York: Hyperion/Theia. The Goodyear rubber story.

Sloan, Alfred P., Jr. 1964. *My Years with General Motors.* Ed. John McDonald, with Catharine Stevens. Garden City, N.Y.: Doubleday.

Sluyterman, Keetie E., and Hélène J. M. Winkelman. 1993. "The Dutch Family Firm Confronted with Chandler's Dynamics of Industrial Capitalism, 1890–1940," *Business History* 35, no. 4 (October): 152–83.

Sobel, Robert. 2000. *The Entrepreneurs.* New York: Beard Books.

Sorensen, Charles E., with Samuel T. Williamson. 1956. *My Forty Years with Ford.* New York: W. W. Norton.

Sowell, Thomas. 1994. *Race and Culture: A World View.* New York: Basic Books.

———. N.d. *Conquests and Cultures: An International History.* New York: Basic Books.

Spiegelberg, R. 1973. *The City: Power Without Accountability.* Blond & Briggs.

Stansky, Peter. 2003. *Sassoon: The Worlds of Philip and Sybil.* New Haven: Yale University Press.

Stern, Fritz. 1977. *Gold and Iron: Bismarck, Bleichröder, and the Building of the German Empire.* New York. Knopf.

Stone, Lawrence, and J. C. Fawtier Stone. 1984. *An Open Elite? England 1540–1880.* Oxford: Clarendon Press.

Stoskopf, Nicolas. 1995. "Gestion de la vie privée et continuité familiale dans les entreprises alsaciennes du XIXe siècle," *Entreprises et histoire* 9 (septembre): 61–69.

Strouse, Jean. 1999. *Morgan: American Financier.* New York: Random House.

Stucki, Lorenz. 1981. *Das heimliche Imperium: Wie die Schweiz reich wurde.* 7th ed. Frauenfeld: Huber.

Suleiman, Ezra N. 1995. *Les ressorts cachés de la réussite française.* Paris: Seuil. Original edition in English: *France: The Transformation of a Society.*

Supple, Barry E. 1957. "A Business Elite: German-Jewish Financiers in Nineteenth-Century New York," *Business History Review,* 31 no. 2 (Summer): 143–78.

———, ed. 1977. *Essays in British Business History.* Cambridge: Cambridge University Press.

———, ed. 1992. *The Rise of Big Business.* Aldershot: E. Elgar.

Suzuki, Y. 1992. *Japanese Management Structures, 1920–1980.* Tokyo: Macmillan.

Sylla, Richard E. 1975. *The American Capital Market, 1846–1914: A Study of the Effect of Public Policy on Economic Development.* New York: Arno Press.

Szostak, Rick. 1991. *The Role of Transportation in the Industrial Revolution.* Montreal and London: McGill-Queens University Press.

Taylor, Francis H. 1957. *Pierpont Morgan as Collector and Patron, 1837–1913.* New York: Pierpont Morgan Library.

Taylor, Jared. 1983. *Shadows of the Rising Sun: A Critical View of the "Japanese Miracle."* Tokyo: Charles E. Tuttle.

Tedlow, Richard S. 2001. *Giants of Enterprise: Seven Business Innovators and the Empires They Built.* New York: HarperBusiness.

———. 2003. *The Watson Dynasty: The Fiery Reign and Troubled Legacy of IBM's Founding Father and Son.* New York: HarperBusiness.

Teichova, Alice, Maurice Lévy-Leboyer, and Helga Nussbaum, eds. 1986. *Multinational Enterprise in Historical Perspective.* Cambridge: Cambridge University Press; Paris: Editions de la Maison des Sciences de l'Homme.

Teng, Ssu-yü, and John K. Fairbank. 1979. *China's Response to the West: A Documentary Survey, 1839–1923.* Cambridge, Mass.: Harvard University Press.

Tenhover, Gregory R. 1994. *Unlocking the Japanese Business Mind.* Washington, D.C.: Transemantics.

Thane, P., G. Crossick, and R. C. Floud, eds. 1984. *The Power of the Past: Essays for Eric Hobsbaum.* Cambridge: C. W. P.

Thévenet, Jean-Paul. 1985. *Louis Renault: histoire d'une tragédie et d'une nationalisation.* London.

Tibballs, Geoff. 1999. *Business Blunders: Dirty Dealing and Financial Failure in the World of Big Business.* London: Robinson.

Tifft, Susan E., and Alex S. Jones. 1999. *The Trust: The Private and Powerful Family Behind* The New York Times. Boston: Little, Brown.

Tobias, Andrew. 1976. *Fire and Ice: The Story of Charles Revson—the Man Who Built the Revlon Empire.* New York: William Morrow.

Tolf, Robert W. 1976. *The Russian Rockefellers: The Saga of the Nobel Family and the Russian Oil Industry.* Palo Alto, Calif.: Hoover Institution.

Tolliday, S., and Jonathan Zeitlin, eds. 1986. *The International Automobile Industry and Its Workers: Between Fordism and Flexibility.* Cambridge, Mass.: Polity Press. Reissued in 1992 as *Between Fordism and Flexibility: The Automobile Industry and Its Workers.* Providence, R.I.: Berg.

Tomkins, Calvin. 1998. "The Benefactor: Onward and Upward with the Arts," *The New Yorker,* 8 June, pp. 52–67. On Dominique Schlumberger de Menil.

Toussaint, Yvon. 1996. *Les barons Empain.* Paris: Fayard.

Toyoda, Eiji. 1987. *Toyota: Fifty Years in Motion.* Tokyo and New York: Kodansha International.

Traub, Marvin, and Tom Teicholz. 1993. *Like No Other Store . . . The Bloomingdale's Legend and the Revolution in American Marketing.* New York: Random House/Times Books.

Trebilcock, Clive. 1977. *The Vickers Brothers.* London. Introduction by Neil McKendrick.

Treue, Wilhelm, and Helmut Uebbing. 1969. *Die Feuer verlöschen nie: August Thyssen-Hütte, 1926–1966.* Düsseldorf: Econ-Verlag.

Trinder, B. 1974. *The Darbys of Coalbrookdale*. Chichester: Phillimore and Company.

Tsai, Jung-Fang. 1993. *Hong-Kong in Chinese History: Community and Social Unrest in the British Colony, 1842–1913*. New York: Columbia University Press.

Tsuru, Shigeto. 1996. *Japan's Capitalism*. Cambridge: Cambridge University Press.

Tuke, A. W., and R.J.H. Gillman. 1972. *Barclays Bank Limited, 1926–1969*. London: Barclays Bank.

Twyman, Robert W. 1954. *The History of Marshall Field & Co., 1852–1906*. Philadelphia: University of Pennsylvania Press.

Tyack, Geoffrey. 1982. *Clivedon and the Astor Household: Between the Wars*. High Wycombe: Willmot Printers.

Vander Weyer, Martin. 2000. *Falling Eagle: The Decline of Barclays Bank*. London: Weidenfeld and Nicolson.

Verley, Patrick. 1994. *Entreprises et entrepreneurs du XVIIIe siècle au début du XXe siècle*. Paris: Hachette.

———. 1997. *La Révolution industrielle*. Paris: Gallimard.

Vermale, François. 1935. *Le père de Casimir Perier, 1742–1801*. Grenoble: Arthaud.

Vlasic, Bill, and Bradley A. Stertz. 2001. *Taken for a Ride: How Daimler-Benz Drove Off with Chrysler*. New York: HarperBusiness.

Volpato, Giuseppe. 1993. "L'internazionalizzazione dell'industria automobilistica italiana." In *L'industria italiana nel mercato mondiale*, pp. 157–216.

Waller, David. 2001. *Wheels on Fire: The Amazing Inside Story of the Daimler-Chrysler Merger*. London: Hodder and Stoughton.

Wallich, Hermann. 1978. *Aus meinem Leben*. In *Zwei Generationen im deutschen Bankwesen 1833–1914*. Schriftenreihe des Instituts für bankhistorische Forschung e. V., Bd. 2. Frankfurt-am-Main. Publication sponsored by Henry C. Wallich, son of Paul, grandson of Hermann.

Wallich, Hildegard. 1970. *Erinnerungen aus meinem Leben*. Altenkirchen. By the wife and widow of Paul Wallich, née Rehrmann.

Wallich, Paul. 1978. *Lehr- und Wanderjahre eines Bankiers*. In Hermann Wallich collection *Zwei Generationen*, above.

Warren, Lætitia de. 1999. *Les fils de Vulcain: La saga des maîtres de forges*. Paris: Seuil.

Watson, Thomas J., Jr., and Peter Petre. 1990. *Father, Son & Co.: My Life at IBM and Beyond*. New York: Bantam.

Watts, Steven. 2005. *The People Tycoon: Henry Ford and the American Century*. New York: Knopf.

Wechsberg, Joseph. 1966. *The Merchant Bankers*. New York: Little, Brown; Pocket Books.

———. 1999. *Trifles Make Perfection: Selected Essays*. Ed. and introd. David Morowitz. Boston: David Godine.

Wells, F. A. 1968. *Hollins and Viyella: A Study in Business History.* Newton Abbott.

Wendel, Maurice de. 1936. *Etude sur la Maison de Wendel et les attaques dont elle est l'objet.* Hayange: Wormser.

Wessel, Horst A., ed. 1991. *Thyssen & Co. Mülheim a. d. Ruhr: Die Geschichte einer Familie und ihrer Unternehmung.* Stuttgart: Franz Steiner.

Wheatcroft, Geoffrey. 1985. *The Randlords: The Men Who Made South Africa.* London: Weidenfeld & Nicholson.

Wiener, Martin J. 1981. *English Culture and the Decline of the Industrial Spirit, 1850–1980.* Cambridge: Cambridge University Press.

Wilkins, Mira. 1970. *The Emergence of Multinational Enterprise: American Business Abroad from the Colonial Era to 1914.* Cambridge, Mass.: Harvard University Press.

———. 1974. *The Maturing of Multinational Enterprise: American Business Abroad from 1914 to 1970.* Cambridge, Mass.: Harvard University Press.

———. 1986. "The History of European Multinationals: A New Look," *Journal of European Economic History* 15.

———. 1986. "Japanese Multinational Enterprise Before 1914," *Business History Review* 60.

———, ed. 1991. *The Growth of Multinationals.* Aldershot: E. Elgar.

———. 1993. "French Multinationals in the United States: A Historical Perspective," *Entreprises et histoire* 3.

Williamson, Harold, ed. 1975. *Evolution of International Management Structures.* Newark, N.J.

Williamson, Jeffrey. 1996. "Globalization, Convergence, and History," *Journal of Economic History* 56, no. 2: 277–306.

Wilson, Derek. 1988. *Rothschild: The Wealth and Power of a Dynasty.* New York: Charles Scribner's Sons.

Winston, J. E. 1929. "How the Louisiana Purchase Was Financed," *Louisiana Historical Quarterly* XII, no. 2 (April).

Wolff, Jacques. 1993. *Les Perier: la fortune et les pouvoirs.* Paris: Economica.

Wolgensinger, Jacques. 1991. *André Citroën.* Paris: Flammarion.

Womack, James P., Daniel T. Jones, and Daniel Roos. 1990. *The Machine That Changed the World.* New York: Rawson Associates; Macmillan.

Wong, R. Bin. 1997. *China Transformed: Historical Change and the Limits of European Experience.* Ithaca and London: Cornell University Press.

———. 2002. "The Search for European Differences and Domination in the Early Modern World: A View from Asia," *American Historical Review* 107, no. 2: 447–69.

Woronoff, Denis. 1984. *L'industrie sidérurgique en France pendant la Révolution et l'Empire.* Paris: Ecole des Hautes-Etudes.

———. 1994. *Histoire de l'industrie en France du XVIe siècle à nos jours.* Paris: Seuil.

———. 2001. *François de Wendel.* Paris: Presses des Sciences Politiques.

Wyden, Peter. 1987. *The Unknown Iacocca.* New York: William Morrow.

Yew, Lee Kuan. 2000. *From Third World to First: The Singapore Story, 1965–2000, Singapore and the Asian Economic Boom.* New York: Harper-Collins.

Zamagni, Vera. 1990. *Dalla periferia al centro: la seconda rinascita economica dell'Italia (1861–1981).* Bologna: Il Mulino.

———. 1993. *The Economic History of Italy, 1860–1990.* Oxford: Clarendon Press.

Zeitlin, M. 1974. "Corporate Ownership and Control: The Large Corporation and the Capitalist Class," *American Journal of Sociology* 79: 1073–1115.

Ziegler, Philip. 1988. *The Sixth Great Power: A History of One of the Greatest of All Banking Families, the House of Barings, 1762–1929.* New York: Knopf.

Zilkha, Ezra K., with Ken Emerson. 1999. *From Baghdad to Boardrooms: My Family's Odyssey.* Privately printed.

Zorn, Wolfgang. 1957. "Typen und Entwicklungskräfte deutschen Unternehmentums im XIXe Jahrhundert," *Vierteljahrschrift für Sozial- und Wirtschaftgeschichte* 44.

Index

Rockefeller, John D. (*cont.*)
  questioning on restraints of trade, 231–32
  recognition of benefits of pipelines, 224–25
  refining techniques, 230
  refusal to respond to denunciations of Standard Oil, 236, 237
  reluctance to pass responsibility to children, 293
  reputation in later life, 236–38
  retirement of, 231
  Samuel Andrews role in helping, 220, 222
  silence and modesty of, 225–26
  solution to "Lima crude" problem, 230
  South Improvement Company, 229, 232
  stinginess of, 225–27
  takeovers of competitors, 223
  thwarting of pipeline construction, 223–24
  tips by, 221–22
  union unrest at Colorado Fuel and Iron (CFI), 234–35
  view of competitors, 219
  view of credit, 228
  view of labor unions, 234
  view of money, 217
  vision of, 223
  wealth of, 225–27
Rockefeller, John D., III, 240
  manipulation by brother Nelson, 243
  philanthropic pursuits, 244
Rockefeller, John D., Jr., 226
  acquisition of J. P. Morgan's Chinese porcelains, 240
  at Brown University, 238
  children, 240, 242
  courtship and marriage to Abby Aldrich, 239–40
  denial of Ludlow Massacre, 235
  duty to carry on philanthropic work, 241
  in England, 238–39
  failure to groom successive generation for business, 42

  focus on philanthropic pursuits, 240
  justifiable resentment toward Ida Tarbell for attacking father, 237
  self-discipline, 238
  similarities to father, 238
  sinful indulgences, 239
  view of labor unions, 234
Rockefeller, Laurance, 240, 244
Rockefeller, Nelson, 240
  manipulation of brother John, 243
  as politician, 242–43
Rockefeller, William A., 218
Rockefeller, Winthrop, 240, 243–44
Romiti, Cesare, 163–64
Roncoroni, Marie-Hélène (Peugeot), 192
Roosevelt, Franklin D.
  Henry Ford's opinion of, 138
  Jack Morgan's opinion of, 98
Roosevelt, Theodore, 85–86
Rosengart, Louis (Peugeot), 181–82
Rothschild, Alphonse, 69
  arguments for expansion into America, 57
  opinion of August Belmont, 56–57
Rothschild, Anselm, 68
Rothschild, Anthony, 68
Rothschild, Batsheva de, 69
Rothschild, Betty, 52, 66
Rothschild, Carl (Kalman), 51–52
Rothschild, Edmond, 70, 73
Rothschild, Edouard, 69
  attendance at André Citroën's funeral, 177
Rothschild, Elie, 72
Rothschild, Emma, 74
Rothschild, Eric de, 72
Rothschild, Evelyn, 74
Rothschild, Gütel, 43
Rothschild, Guy, 69
Rothschild, Hannah Mayer, 53–54
Rothschild, Henri, 70–71, 81, 177
Rothschild, Jacob, 74
Rothschild, James (Jacob), 48, 53–54
  attendance at André Citroën's funeral, 177
  August Belmont's refusal to follow orders of, 56